STREET FRENCH SLANG
DICTIONARY & THESAURUS

David Burke

John Wiley & Sons, Inc.
New York • Chichester • Weinheim • Brisbane • Singapore • Toronto

Design and Production: David Burke
Copy Editors: Nicolas Caron and Pierre Ferulli
Front Cover Illustration: Ty Semaka
Inside Illustrations: Ty Semaka

ISBN 0-471-16806-8

Printed in the United States of America
10 9 8 7 6 5 4 3 2 1

This book is dedicated to Lee Murphy:
Je t'adore du fond de mon battant!

ACKNOWLEDGMENTS

My special thanks to Ty Semaka for consistently providing illustrations that are distinctive, clever, and downright hilarious.

I consider myself so very fortunate to have been under the wing of so many wonderful people during the creation of this book. A tremendous and warm thanks goes to my pals at John Wiley & Sons: Gerry Helferich, Chris Jackson, Elaine O'Neal, Al Schwartz, and Benjamin Hamilton. They are without a doubt the most friendly, supportive, encouraging, and infinitely talented group of people with whom I've had the pleasure to work.

CONTENTS

STREET FRENCH DICTIONARY

*(Popular French Terms Including Slang, Idioms,
Colloquialisms, Vulgarities, Proverbs, Special
Notes, Synonyms, Antonyms, & Variations)*

POPULAR FRENCH GESTURES

ENGLISH WORDS USED IN FRENCH

STREET FRENCH THESAURUS

(General Slang Synonyms & Expressions)

STREET FRENCH THESAURUS

*(Obscenities, Vulgarities, Insults,
Bodily Functions & Sounds, Sexual Slang,
Offensive Language, etc.)*

INTRODUCTION

Slang, idioms, and colloquialisms are all an active part of the living French language. These nonstandard terms and expressions are used in movies, television and radio shows, news broadcasts, books, newspapers, magazines, business, etc., making it difficult for a nonnative speaker to feel like an "insider."

The **STREET FRENCH SLANG DICTIONARY & THESAURUS** will lead the reader through many of the most popular and colorful terms and expressions rarely, if ever, taught in school.

This unique book is divided into three primary parts:

■ **THE STREET FRENCH DICTIONARY** *(Part 1)*

This section presents the reader with more than 2,000 popular French terms including slang, idioms, colloquialisms, vulgarities, proverbs, special notes, synonyms, antonyms, variations, plus an array of hilarious illustrations. In addition, usage examples are offered throughout this section to give the reader a clear understanding of the weight of a given entry.

■ **POPULAR FRENCH GESTURES** *(Part 2)*

This entertaining section offers the reader a look at some of the most popular gestures used throughout France.

■ **ENGLISH WORDS USED IN FRENCH** *(Part 3)*

Here the reader is presented with a surprising list of the many English words commonly used in the French language.

■ **THE STREET FRENCH THESAURUS** *(Part 4)*

Did you know there are 54 synonyms for *partir* ("to leave"), 59 synonyms for *ivre* ("drunk"), 95 synonyms for *idiot* ("idiot") and 41 synonyms for *manger* ("to eat")? This section offers the reader an extensive list of French slang terms and idioms for a particular English word or expression. Usage examples are offered at the beginning of each category.

■ THE STREET FRENCH THESAURUS (Part 5)

This unique portion of the thesaurus explores some of the most common expletives and obscenities used in France. These pages (marked with a "danger" sign) allow the reader to look up a word in English and find an assortment of colorful, and often shocking, synonyms for each entry.

IMPORTANT: Slang must be used with discretion because it is an extremely casual "language" that certainly should not be practiced with formal dignitaries or employers that you are trying to impress! Most importantly, since a non-native speaker of French may tend to sound forced or artificial using slang, your first goal should be to recognize and understand these types of words. Once you feel that you have a firm grasp on the usage of the slang words and expressions presented in this book, try using some in your conversations for extra color!

Welcome to the expressive and "colorful" world of French slang!

Legend

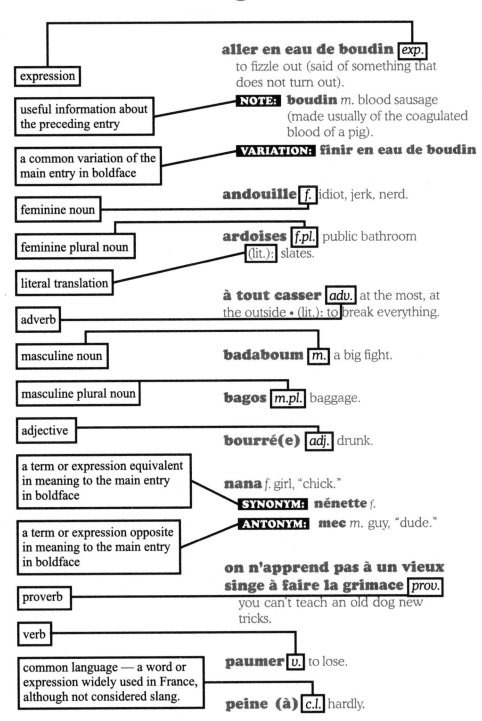

expression

aller en eau de boudin *exp.*
to fizzle out (said of something that does not turn out).

useful information about the preceding entry

NOTE: **boudin** *m.* blood sausage (made usually of the coagulated blood of a pig).

a common variation of the main entry in boldface

VARIATION: **finir en eau de boudin**

feminine noun

andouille *f.* idiot, jerk, nerd.

feminine plural noun

ardoises *f.pl.* public bathroom (lit.): slates.

literal translation

à tout casser *adv.* at the most, at the outside • (lit.): to break everything.

adverb

masculine noun

badaboum *m.* a big fight.

masculine plural noun

bagos *m.pl.* baggage.

adjective

bourré(e) *adj.* drunk.

a term or expression equivalent in meaning to the main entry in boldface

nana *f.* girl, "chick."
SYNONYM: **nénette** *f.*

a term or expression opposite in meaning to the main entry in boldface

ANTONYM: **mec** *m.* guy, "dude."

proverb

on n'apprend pas à un vieux singe à faire la grimace *prov.*
you can't teach an old dog new tricks.

verb

common language — a word or expression widely used in France, although not considered slang.

paumer *v.* to lose.

peine (à) *c.l.* hardly.

STREET FRENCH DICTIONARY

Part 1

(Popular French Terms Including Slang, Idioms, Colloquialisms, Vulgarities, Proverbs, Special Notes, Synonyms, Antonyms, & Variations)

abandonner la partie *exp.* to call it a day • (lit.): to abandon the match.

example: Je suis fatigué. Je vais **abandonner la partie**.

translation: I'm tired. I'm going **to call it a day**.

as spoken: J'suis fatigué. J'vais **abandonner la partie**.

abruti(e) *n.* idiot, jerk, nerd.

example: Quel **abruti**! Jean se promène en shorts alors qu'il pleut dehors!

translation: What a **jerk**! Jean is walking around in shorts and it's raining outside!

as spoken: Quel **abruti**! Jean, y s'promène en shorts alors qu'y pleut dehors!

SYNONYM: SEE: **andouille** - *p. 5.*
NOTE: **abrutir** *v.* to make stupid, to drive crazy.

accrochage *m.* **1.** a fight or quarrel • **2.** a traffic accident.

accrocher (s') *v.* to fight.
NOTE: **accrochage** *m.* a quarrel.

achever à la manivelle (s') *exp.* (of men) to masturbate • (lit.): to reach completion with the hand crank.

à-côtés *m.pl.* perks
• (lit.): on-the-sides.

example: Mon travail a de très bons **à-côtés**.

translation: My work has very good **perks**.

as spoken: Mon travail, il a d'très bons **à-côtés**.

à deux doigts de (être) *exp.* to be on the verge • (lit.): to be two fingers from (doing something).

example: J'étais **à deux doigts de** sortir quand le téléphone a sonné.

translation: I was **on the verge of** leaving when the telephone rang.

as spoken: J'étais **à deux doigts d'**sortir quand l'téléphone a sonné.

à deux on se distrait, à trois on s'ennuie *exp.* two's company, three's a crowd • (lit.): with two it's fun, with three it's bothersome.

example: Pourquoi veux-tu l'inviter à nous rejoindre? **A deux on se distrait, à trois on s'ennuie**!

translation: Why do you want to invite her to join us? **Two's company, three's a crowd**!

as spoken: Pourquoi tu veux l'inviter à nous r'joindre? **A deux on s'distrait, à trois on s'ennuie**!

NOTE: In colloquial French, the inversion form (such as *veux-tu*) is not used. SEE: *Street French 1 — A Closer Look, Inversion and est-ce que forms - p. 37.*

affaires (avoir ses) *exp.* to menstruate • (lit.): to have one's business.

affaires (faire ses) *exp.* to urinate or defecate • (lit.): to do one's business.

agacer le sous-préfet *exp.* (of men) to masturbate • (lit.): to annoy the subprefect.

agiter le poireau (s') *exp.* (of men) to masturbate • (lit.): to agitate the leek.

> **NOTE:** **poireau** *m.* penis, "dick" • (lit.): leek.

agrafer (se faire) *v.* to get arrested • (lit.): to fasten by means of a hook, clasp, or clip, to staple.

example: Le voleur a essayé de s'enfuir, mais il **s'est fait agrafer**.

translation: The thief tried to get away, but he got **nabbed**.

as spoken: Le voleur, il essayait d's'enfuir, mais y **s'est fait agrafer**.

> **NOTE:** **agrafer** *v.* to arrest.

*Le voleur s'est fait **agrafer**!*

(trans.):
*The thief got himself **nabbed**!*

(lit.):
*The thief got himself **stapled**!*

aiguiller *v.* to fornicate, to "dick" someone • (lit.): to give the needle.

> **NOTE:** **aiguille** *f.* penis, dick • (lit.): needle.

air (l'avoir en l') *exp.* to have an erection • (lit.): to have it in the air.

air pour quelqu'un (l'avoir en l') *exp.* (said of a man) to get an erection over someone • (lit.): to have it in the air for someone.

à l'article de la mort (être) *c.I.* to be at death's door • (lit.): to be at the critical point of death.

example: Je ne me sens pas bien. Je suis sûr que je suis **à l'article de la mort**!

translation: I don't feel well. I'm sure I'm at death's door!

as spoken: Je m'sens pas bien. J'suis sûr que j'suis **à l'article d'la mort**!

alfa sur les hauts plateaux (ne plus avoir d') *exp.* to be bald • (lit.): not to have any more alfalfa on the high plateaus.

alléger les bourses (s') *exp.* to have sex, to "get off" • (lit.): to lighten one's purse.

example: Guillaume **s'allège les bourses** avec les prostituées!

translation: William **gets off** with prostitutes!

as spoken: Guillaume, y **s'allège les bourses** avec les prostituées!

> **NOTE:** **bourses** *f.pl.* testicles • (lit.): purses.

aller au renard *exp.* to vomit
• (lit.): to go to the fox.

aller en eau de boudin *exp.* to fizzle out (said of something that does not turn out).

example: Le projet **est allé en eau de boudin**.

translation: The project **fizzled out**.

as spoken: Le projet, il **est allé en eau d'boudin**.

NOTE: **boudin** *m.* blood sausage.

VARIATION: **finir / partir en eau de boudin** *exp.*

aller où le Roi va à pied *exp.* to urinate or defecate • (lit.): to go where the king goes by foot.

allez, va *exp.* come on

example: **Allez, va**! Il fera meilleur la semaine prochaine et tu pourras aller à la plage à ce moment-là.

translation: **Oh, come on**! The weather will be better next week and you'll be able to go to the beach then.

as spoken: **Allez, va**! Y f'ra meilleur la s'maine prochaine et tu pourras aller à la plage à c'moment-là.

allonger la couenne (s') *exp.* (of men) to masturbate • (lit.): to lengthen one's foreskin.

NOTE: **couenne** *f.* skin of ham.

allonger le macaroni (s') *exp.* (of men) to masturbate • (lit.): to lengthen one's macaroni.

NOTE: **macaroni** *m.* penis, "dick" • (lit.): macaroni.

allonger (se l') *exp.* (of men) to masturbate • (lit.): to lengthen it.

à lui le pompon *exp.* he takes the cake • (lit.): to him the pom-pom.

example: Il a mangé tout notre dessert! **A lui le pompom**!

translation: He ate all of our dessert! **He takes the cake**!

as spoken: Il a mangé tout not' dessert! **A lui l'pompom**!

amazone *f.* prostitute
• (lit.): high-class prostitute.

amener le petit au cirque *exp.* to fornicate • (lit.): to take the little one to the circus.

amocher (s') *v.* to beat each other up, to mess each other up physically • (lit.): to make each other look ugly.

NOTE: **moche** *adj.* (very popular) ugly.

amortisseurs *m.pl.* breasts
• (lit.): shock absorbers.

amouracher de quelqu'un (s') *v.* to have a crush on someone, to be infatuated with someone.

NOTE: This comes from the masculine noun *amour* meaning "love."

amuse-gueules *m.pl.* appetizers
• (lit.): mouth amusers.

example: On va dîner dans une heure. Mais si tu as très faim, tu pourras toujours prendre quelques **amuse-gueules** maintenant.

translation: We're going to have dinner in an hour. But if you are really hungry, you can always have some **appetizers** now.

as spoken: On va dîner dans une heure. Mais si t'as très faim, tu pourras toujours prend' quèques **amuse-gueules** maintenant.

NOTE -1: **gueule** f. derogatory for the "mouth" of a human being • (lit.): mouth of an animal.

NOTE -2: In the example above, the verb "*prendre*" was used to mean "to have." This is an extremely popular usage of "*prendre*" when used in connection with food. For example:

example: Je **prends** toujours un croissant et un café pour mon petit déjeuner.

translation: I always **have** a croissant and a coffee for my breakfast.

as spoken: J'**prends** toujours un croissant et un café pour mon p'tit dèj.

amuser tout seul (s') exp.
(of men) to masturbate • (lit.): to have fun alone.

ananas m.pl. breasts • (lit.): pineapples.

andouille f. idiot, jerk, nerd.

example: Quelle **andouille**, ce Patrice! Au restaurant, il a renversé tout un verre de jus de tomate sur Michelle qui portait une nouvelle robe blanche!

translation: What a **nerd** Patrice is. At the restaurant, he spilled an entire glass of tomato juice on Michelle who was wearing a new white dress!

as spoken: Quelle **andouille**, c'Patrice! Au resto, il a renversé tout un verre d'jus d'tomate sur Michelle qui portait une nouvelle robe blanche!

andouille à col roulé f. penis
• (lit.): sausage with a rolled-down collar.

anglais (avoir ses) exp. to have one's period, to be "on the rag"
• (lit.): to have one's English.

Il n'y a pas de doute. Carole ***a ses anglais*** *aujourd'hui.*

(trans.):
*There's no doubt about it. Carole is having **her period** today.*

(lit.):
*There's no doubt about it. Carole is **having her Englishmen** today.*

example: Geneviève ne peut pas nager aujourd'hui parce qu'elle **a ses anglais**.

translation: Geneviève can't go swimming today because she's **on the rag**.

as spoken: Geneviève, è peut pas nager aujourd'hui pasqu'elle **a ses anglais**.

anguille de calecif *f.* penis
• (lit.): underwear eel.
NOTE: calecif *m.* a slang transformation of *caleçon* meaning "underwear."

animal *m.* (applies only to a man)
• (lit.): animal.

à nous deux *exp.* an expression used to signify one's intention to start a fight: "Let's take it outside," "Just you and me" • (lit.): to both of us.

example: Tu oses m'insulter?! **A nous deux**!

translation: How dare you insult me?! **C'm'on! You and me right now**!

as spoken: T'oses m'insulter?! **A nous deux**!

apéro *m.* cocktail, apéritif.

example: Je prends toujours l'**apéro** avant le dîner.

translation: I always have a **cocktail** before dinner.

as spoken: J'prends toujours l'**apéro** avant l'dîner.

appeler un chat un chat *exp.* to call a spade a spade • (lit.): to call a cat a cat.

example: C'est un escroc. J'**appelle un chat un chat**.

translation: He's a crook. I'm **calling a spade a spade**.

as spoken: C't'un escroc. J'**appelle un chat un chat**.

SYNONYM: dire le mot et la chose *exp.* to call it like it is
• (lit.): to say the word and the thing.

appliquer le règlement *exp.* to go by the book • (lit.): to apply the rule.

example: J'ai expliqué au professeur que je n'ai pas pu faire mes devoirs parce que j'avais attrapé la grippe, mais il ne fait pas d'exceptions. Il est connu pour **appliquer le règlement**.

translation: I explained to the teacher that I couldn't do my homework because I caught the flu, but he doesn't make any exceptions. He's known for **going by the book**.

as spoken: J'ai espiqué au prof que j'ai pas pu faire mes d'voirs pasque j'avais attrapé la grippe, mais y fait pas d'exceptions. Il est connu pour **appliquer le règlement**.

à qui le dis-tu *exp.* you're telling me • (lit.): to whom are you speaking?

example: "Paul raconte toujours la même histoire!" "**A qui le dis-tu**!"

translation: "Paul's always telling the same story!" "**You're telling me**!"

as spoken: "Paul, y raconte toujours la même histoire!"
"A qui l'dis-tu?"

araignée dans le plafond (avoir une) *exp.* (applies to either a man or a woman) to have bats in the belfry • (lit.): to have a spider in the ceiling.
NOTE: **plafond** *m.* head • (lit.): ceiling.

ardoises *f.pl.* • public bathroom (lit.): slates.

argagnasses (avoir ses) *f.pl.* to menstruate.

argent foutu [en l'air] *exp.* money down the drain.

example: Tu vas jouer au lotto? Mais c'est de l'**argent foutu [en l'air]**, ça!

translation: Are you going to play the lotto? That's just **money down the drain**!

as spoken: Tu vas jouer au lotto? Mais c'est d'l'**argent foutu [en l'air]**, ça!

arnaquer *v.* to rip off, cheat someone • (lit.): to sting.

example: Je viens d'acheter une nouvelle montre, mais elle ne marche pas! Cette vendeuse, elle m'a **arnaqué**!

translation: I just bought a new watch, but it's not working! That saleswoman **ripped me off**!

as spoken: J'viens d'acheter une nouvelle montre, mais è marche pas! Cette vendeuse, è m'a **arnaqué**!

ALSO: **arnaquer (se faire)** *v.* to get oneself ripped off.

example: Tu as payé combien? Je crois que tu t'es fait **arnaquer** chez le mécanicien.

translation: You paid how much? I think you got **ripped off** at the mechanic's.

as spoken: T'as payé combien? J'crois qu'tu t'es fait **arnaquer** chez l'mécano.

NOTE: In France, the movie entitled *The Hustler,* starring Paul Newman, is known as *L'Arnaqueur* and the popular Newman-Redford comedy, *The Sting,* is called *L'Arnaque.*

SYNONYM: **avoir (se faire)** *exp.*

arpenter le bitume *exp.* (said of a prostitute) to hustle • (lit.): to survey the asphalt.

arquer *v.* to have an erection • (lit.): to bend.

arrêter son char *exp.* to stop one's exaggerating • (lit.): stop your waggon.

example: "Aïe! Je crois que je me suis cassé le bras!"
"Arrête ton char! Tu te l'es foulé un peu. C'est tout!"

translation: "Ow! I think I broke my arm!"
"Stop your exaggerating! You just sprained it a little. That's all!"

as spoken: "Aïe! J'crois qu'je m'suis cassé l'bras!"
"Arrête ton char! Tu t'l'es foulé un peu. C'est tout!"

NOTE: **charrier** *v.* to exaggerate.

arrière-boutique *m.* posterior
- (lit.): back-shop.

arrière-train *m.* posterior
- (lit.): caboose.

arriver à faire quelque chose
c.l. to manage to do something
- (lit.): to arrive at doing something.

example: "Tu peux me soulever cette caisse?"
"Je regrette mais je n'**y arrive** pas. C'est trop lourd."

translation: "Can you lift this case for me?"
"I'm sorry but I can't **seem to manage it**. It's too heavy."

as spoken: "Tu peux m'soul'ver cette caisse?"
"J'regrette mais j'**y arrive** pas. C'est trop lourd."

arriver au ras des fesses *exp.*
to come just up to the cheeks of one's buttocks.

example: Tu as vu la jupe que Mimi a porté aujourd'hui? Elle était super courte. Sa jupe lui **arrivait au ras des fesses**!

translation: Did you see the skirt Mimi wore today? It was super short. Her skirt **came just up to the cheeks of her buttocks**!

as spoken: T'as vu la jupe que Mimi a porté aujourd'hui? Elle était super courte. Sa jupe, è lui **arrivait au ras des fesses**!

arriver dans les délais *exp.* to arrive on time • (lit.): to arrive in the delays.

example: La circulation sur l'autoroute était horrible ce matin. Heureusement, je suis **arrivé à l'aéroport dans les délais**!

translation: The traffic on the freeway was horrible today. Luckily, I **made it to the airport on time**!

as spoken: La circulation sur l'autoroute, elle était horrible c'matin. Heureusement, j'suis **arrivé à l'aéroport dans les délais**!

arriver en trombe *exp.* to storm in • (lit.): to arrive like a tornado.

example: Regarde qui vient d'**arriver en trombe**... Amélie Dupont-Durand. Elle est prétentieuse, elle!

translation: Look who just **stormed in**... Amélie Dupont-Durand. She's so pretentious!

as spoken: [no change]

arriver là (en) *exp.* to come to this
- (lit.): to arrive there from it.

example: Laurent et Jeanne ont divorcé la semaine dernière parce qu'ils ne faisaient que se disputer. C'est dommage que leur marriage **en soit arrivé là**.

translation: Laurent et Jeanne got divorced last week because all they did was argue. It's a shame that their marriage has **come to this**.

as spoken: Laurent et Jeanne, y z'ont divorcé la s'maine dernière pasqu'y n'faisaient que s'disputer. C'est dommage que leur marriage, il **en soit arrivé là**.

arrondir le devant (se faire)
exp. to get pregnant • (lit.): to get one's front end rounded.

arrondir le globe (se faire)
exp. to get pregnant • (lit.): to get one's globe rounded.

arrondir (s') *v.* to be pregnant • (lit.): to make oneself round.

arroser les marguerites *exp.* to urinate • (lit.): to go water the daisies.

arroser une affaire *exp.* to celebrate an event with a drink • (lit.): to water an occasion.

example: Le patron vient de m'augmenter. **Ça s'arrose**!

translation: The boss just gave me a raise. **This calls for a drink**!

as spoken: Le patron, y vient d'm'augmenter. **Ça s'arrose**!

article de la mort (être à l')
c.i. to be at death's door • (lit.): to be at the article of death.

example: Tu devrais lui rendre visite aujourd'hui. Je crois qu'il est **à l'article de la mort**.

translation: You should go pay him a visit today. I think he's **at death's door**.

as spoken: Tu d'vrais lui rend' visite aujourd'hui. J'crois qu'il est **à l'artic' d'la mort**.

asperge *f.* • **1.** penis • **2.** tall and thin person (lit.): asparagus.

asperger le persil *exp.* to fornicate • (lit.): to sprinkle water on the parsley.

NOTE -1: asperge *f.* penis
• (lit.): asparagus.

NOTE -2: persil *m.* vagina, pubic hair • (lit.): parsley.

asperges (aller aux) *exp.* to hustle (said of a prostitute), to go to (find) some penis • (lit.): to go to the asparagus.

NOTE: asperge *f.* penis
• (lit.): asparagus.

assiette au beurre *exp.* cush job • (lit.): plate of butter.

example: J'adore mon travail. J'ai une vraie **assiette au beurre**.

translation: I love my work. I have a real **cush job**.

as spoken: [no change]

assiette (ne pas être dans son) *exp.* to be out of it, not to be with it • (lit.): not to be in one's plate.

example: Je ne suis pas **dans mon assiette** aujourd'hui. J'ai trop d'ennuis.

translation: I'm **out of it** today. I have too many worries.

as spoken: J'suis pas **dans mon assiette** aujourd'hui. J'ai trop d'ennuis.

SYNONYM: sentir tout chose (se) *exp.* • (lit.): to feel all thing.

asticotage *m.* a quarrel • (lit.): a "maggot"-ing.

astiquer la baguette (s') *exp.* (of men) to masturbate • (lit.): to polish one's baguette.

NOTE: baguette *f.* penis, "dick"
• (lit.): baguette, long rounded loaf of bread.

astiquer le bouton (s') *exp.* (of women) to masturbate • (lit.): to polish one's button.

NOTE: bouton *m.* clitoris
• (lit.): button.

astiquer (s') *v.* (of men) to masturbate • (lit.): to polish oneself.

à suivre *exp.* to be continued
• (lit.): to be followed.

example: "...Et le géant a capturé notre héro!" (**à suivre**)

translation: "...And the giant captured our hero!" (**to be continued**)

as spoken: "...Et l'géant, il a capturé notre héro!" (**à suivre**)

à tout casser *adv.* • **1.** at the most, at the outside • **2.** one hell of a
• (lit.): to break everything.

example (1): Sa mère doit avoir trente ans **à tout casser**!

translation: His mother must be thirty years old **at the outside**!

as spoken: Sa mère, è doit avoir trente ans **à tout casser**!

example (2): C'était un film **à tout casser**!

translation: It was **one hell of a** movie!

as spoken: [no change]

attaque (être d') *exp.* to be going strong • (lit.): to be of attack.

example: Ma grand-mère a quatre-vingt ans mais elle est toujours **d'attaque**.

translation: My grandmother is eighty years old but she's still **going strong**.

as spoken: Ma grand-mère, elle a quatre-vingt ans mais elle est toujours **d'attaque**.

attention les dégats! *exp.* Beware of any damage (that I may cause by being out of control!) • (lit.): [same].

example: Essaie cette nouvelle recette de gâteau au chocolat mais alors **attention les dégats** question calories!

translation: Try this new chocolate cake recipe but **you better watch out** for the calories!

as spoken: [no change]
NOTE: In correct academic French, the previous expression should actually be *"Attention aux dégats."* The omission of the preposition *"à"* following *"Attention"* is common in everyday speech.

attraper la crève *exp.* to catch a terrible cold • (lit.): to catch one's death.

example: J'ai **attrapé la crève** en vacances.

translation: I caught a terrible cold on vacation.

as spoken: [no change]
NOTE: crever *v.* to die.

example: Je **crève** de faim!

translation: I'm **dying** of hunger!

as spoken: J'**crève** de faim!

attraper le ballon *exp.* to get pregnant • (lit.): to catch the balloon (in one's stomach).

aussi bête qu'on en a l'air (ne pas être) *exp.* not to be as dumb as one looks • (lit.): not to be as dumb as one looks it.

example: Je sais que tu crois qu'il n'a rien compris. Mais il **n'est pas aussi bête qu'il en a l'air**.

translation: I know you think he didn't understand anything. But he's **not as dumb as he looks**.

as spoken: Je sais qu'tu crois qu'il a rien compris. Mais il **est pas aussi bête qu'il en a l'air**.

avalé le pépin (avoir) *exp.* to get pregnant • (lit.): to have swallowed the seed.

avaler quelque chose *v.* to accept something as truth • (lit.): to swallow something.

example: J'espère que tu n'as pas **avalé** toutes les excuses que Madeleine t'a donné!

translation: I hope you didn't **swallow** all the excuses Madeleine gave you!

as spoken: J'espère que t'as pas **avalé** toutes les excuses qu'è t'a donné, Madeleine!

avantages *m.pl.* breasts • (lit.): advantage.

avant-postes *m.pl.* breasts • (lit.): outposts.

avant-scènes *f.pl.* breasts • (lit.): apron (of stage).

avorton *m.* (applies to a man) runt • (lit.): leftover from an *avortement* meaning "abortion."

example: Georges m'a dit qu'il veut devenir mannequin! Mais il rêve, ce petit **avorton**!

translation: George told me that he wants to become a model! That little **runt** is dreaming!

as spoken: Georges, y m'a dit qu'y veut dev'nir mann'quin! Mais y rêve, ce p'tit **avorton**!

baba *m.* posterior • (lit.): from baba-au-rhum (due to its round shape, like one's buttocks).

badaboum *m.* a big fight.

baderne (vieille) *f.* old lady • (lit.): old horse.

bagarrer (se) *v.* to fight.

example: Arrêtez de vous **bagarrer** tout le temps!

translation: Stop **fighting** all the time!

as spoken: Arrêtez d'vous **bagarrer** tout l'temps!

NOTE: **bagarre** *f.* fight.

example: Tu as entendu la **bagarre** entre Marie et Jean?

translation: Did you hear the **fight** between Marie et Jean?

as spoken: T'as entendu la **bagarre** entre Marie et Jean?

ALSO: **chercher la bagarre** *exp.* to look for a fight.

bagos *m.pl.* (the "s" is pronounced in this term) an abbreviation of *"bagages"* meaning "baggage."

example: J'ai perdu mes **bagos** à l'aéroport!

translation: I lose my **luggage** at the airport!

as spoken: [no change]

baigneur *m.* penis • (lit.): bather

baïonnette *f.* penis • (lit.): bayonet.

baiser *v.* to fornicate • (lit.): to fuck.

NOTE: There is an *enormous* difference between *baiser* the verb and *baiser* the noun. As a noun, *baiser* simply means a "kiss." For example: *Il m'a fait un baiser en rentrant;* He gave me a kiss upon coming home. Mistakenly and dangerously, many Americans use *baiser* as a verb assuming that it means "to kiss" when it actually means "to fuck." Therefore, *Il m'a baisé en rentrant* would be translated as "He fucked me upon coming home."

baiser en levrette *exp.* to make love doggy-style • (lit.): to fuck like a greyhound.

baisette *f.* penis • (lit.): little fucker.

NOTE: This comes from the slang verb *baiser* meaning "to fuck."

baisodrome *m.* (any place where sex takes place such as the bedroom, brothel, etc.) "fuckotorium".

NOTE: This comes from the slang verb *baiser* meaning "to fuck."

baisoir *m.* vagina • (lit.): place where one has sex such as the bedroom, brothel, etc.

NOTE: This comes from the slang verb *baiser* meaning "to fuck."

baisouiller *v.* a slang variation of: *baiser* meaning "to fuck."

baisse (être en) *exp.* to be going downhill • (lit.): to be in a downward motion.

example: Sa santé est **en baisse** depuis des jours.

translation: His / her health has been **slipping** for days.

as spoken: Sa santé, elle est **en baisse** depuis des jours.

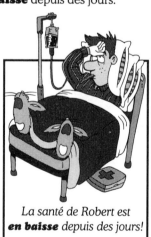

La santé de Robert est ***en baisse** depuis des jours!*

(trans.):
Robert's health has been ***going downhill** for days!*
(lit.):
Robert's health has been ***in decline** for days!*

baisse-froc *m.* scardey-cat
- (lit.): pants lowerer.

> **NOTE:** **froc** *m.* (a pair of) pants.

balader (se) *v.* to stroll.

example: J'aime bien **me balader** le long de la Seine pour regarder le coucher de soleil.

translation: I like **to stroll** along the Seine to watch the sunset.

as spoken: J'aime bien **m'balader** l'long d'la Seine pour regarder l'coucher d'soleil.

> **NOTE -1:** **balade** *f.* stroll.

example: Tu veux faire une **balade** avec moi?

translation: Do you want to take a **stroll** with me?

as spoken: [no change]

> **NOTE -2:** **baladeur** *m.* Walkman.

balancer *v.* • **1.** to throw • **2.** to turn someone in, to put the finger on someone (lit.): to balance.

example (1): Le chien a bousillé ma montre! Quand je le trouverai, je vais le **balancer** dehors!

translation: The dog broke my watch! When I find him, I'm gonna **throw** him outside!

as spoken: Le chien, il a bousillé ma montre! Quand j'le trouv'rai, j'vais l'**balancer** dehors!

example (2): Tu es mon meilleur ami! Comment as-tu pu me **balancer**?!

translation: You're my best friend! How could you **put the finger on me**?!

as spoken: T'es mon meilleur ami! Comment t'as pu m'**balancer**?!

balancer la / sa purée *exp.* to ejaculate • (lit.): to throw the / one's purée.

balancer la sauce *exp.* to ejaculate • (lit.): to throw the sauce.

balancer (s'en) *v.* not to care.

example: Je **m'en balance** de la politique!

translation: I **don't give a hoot** about politics!

as spoken: La politique, j'**m'en balance**!

balayette *f.* penis • (lit.): small broom.

balcon *m.* breasts • (lit.): balcony.

balle *f.* (extremely popular) one franc.

example: J'ai oublié mon portefeuille chez moi. Tu peux me prêter cent **balles**?

translation: I forgot my wallet at home. Can you lend me a hundred **francs**?

as spoken: J'ai oublié mon portefeuille chez moi. Tu peux m'prêter cent **balles**?

> **NOTE:** Of all the slang synonyms for money, this is one of the most popular.

balle dans le canon (avoir une) *exp.* to have an erection
- (lit.): to have a bullet in the cannon.

ballet bleu *m.* orgy involving young boys under legal age • (lit.): blue ballet.

ballet rose *m.* orgy involving young girls under legal age • (lit.): pink ballet.

balloches *f.pl.* testicles • (lit.): balls.

ballon *m.* posterior • (lit.): **1.** balloon • **2.** rubber ball.

ballon (avoir le) *exp.* to be pregnant • (lit.): to have the balloon (in one's stomach).

ballons *m.pl.* large breasts • (lit.): balloons.

ballot *m.* (applies to either a man or a woman) stupid or awkward person • (lit.): bundle.

bandaison (avoir une) *f.* to have an erection • (lit.): to have a boner.

> **SEE:** **bander**, *p. 14.*

bander *v.* (extremely popular) to have an erection • (lit.): to tighten or stretch.

bander pour quelqu'un *exp.* (said of a man) to get an erection over someone • (lit.): to tighten for someone.

bandeuse *f.* a "hot number," sexy woman • (lit.): one who causes men to *bander* meaning "to have an erection."

example: Carole est connue pour être une **bandeuse** et couche avec un gars différent chaque nuit!

translation: Carole is known for being a **nymphomaniac** et goes to bed with a different guy every night!

as spoken: Carole, elle est connue pour êtr'une **bandeuse** et couche avec un gars différent chaque nuit!

bandocher *m.* to have an erection.

> **NOTE:** This is a slang variation of: *bander.*

baraque *f.* (extremely popular) house • (lit.): hut.

example: Michelle habite dans une grande **baraque**.

translation: Michelle lives in a big **house**.

as spoken: Michelle, elle habite dans une grande **baraque**.

baratin *m.* lie, nonsense, "baloney."

example: Ce qu'il te dit, c'est du **baratin**.

translation: What he's telling you is a bunch of **baloney**.

as spoken: C'qu'y te dit, c'est du **baratin**.

> **NOTE:** **baratiner** *v.* to talk nonsense, to B.S.

barbaque *f.* inferior meat.

example: Tu as goûté la **barbaque** que Jacqueline a servi hier soir? C'était horrible!

translation: Did you taste the **shoe leather** that Jacqueline served last night? It was horrible!

as spoken: T'as goûté la **barbaque** qu'elle a servi hier soir, Jacqueline? C't'ait horrible!

barbeau *m.* pimp.

barbu *m.* vagina • (lit.): the bearded one.

barjot • (applies to either a man or a woman) • **1.** *m.* idiot • **2.** *adj.* crazy.
> **NOTE:** This is a verlan transformation of *jobard*. Between the two words, *barjot* is actually the most popular.
> **SEE: jobard**, *p. 107*.

barman *m.* bartender (borrowed from English).
> example: Mon frère est **barman** et bosse toujours la nuit. Il rentre à 4h tous les matins!
> translation: My brother's a **bartender** and always works at night. He comes home at 4:00 every morning!
> as spoken: Mon frère, il est **barman** et bosse toujours la nuit. Y rentre à 4h tous les matins!
> **ANTONYM: bargirl** *n.* woman bartender.
> **NOTE: bosser** is a very popular slang verb meaning "to work hard."

baroud *m.* a big fight.
> **VARIATION -1: barouffe** *m.* (also spelled: *barouf*).
> **VARIATION -2: baroufle** *m.* a quarrel.

barrer (se) *v.* to leave, "to split."
> example: Je suis en retard. Je dois **me barrer**!
> translation: I'm late. I have **to leave**!

as spoken: J'suis en r'tard. J'dois **m'barrer**.
> **NOTE:** The verb *barrer* literally means to strike out or cross out (a word). Therefore, the reflexive form of the verb could be loosely translated as "to strike oneself out."
> **SYNONYMS:** *arracher (s')* • *décambuter* • *décamper* • *donner de l'air (se)* • *évaporer (s')* • *ficher/foutre le camp* • *mettre les adjas* • *mettre les voiles* • *prendre le large* • *tailler (se)*.

bas de laine *m.* savings, money put aside for a rainy day • (lit.): woolen sock (into which money is hidden away).
> example: Elle a un **bas de laine** bien garni.
> translation: She has a nice **nest egg**.
> as spoken: Elle a un **bas d'laine** bien garni.

baston *f.* a big fight.
> **NOTE:** This is from the verb *bâtonner* meaning "to hit with a stick (a *bâton*), to flog, to cane."

bâton (avoir le) *m.* to have an erection • (lit.): to have the club.

battant *m.* heart, "ticker" • (lit.): beater.
> example: Mon grand-père a quatre-vingt-dix (90) ans et pourtant, il a le **battant** très solide.
> translation: My grandfather is ninety years old and yet, he has a very strong **heart**.

as spoken: Mon grand-père, il a quatre-vingt-dix (90) ans et pourtant, il a l'**battant** très solide.

NOTE: This comes from the verb **battre** meaning "to beat."

SYNONYM: **palpitant** *m.*
• (lit.): palpitater.

battre la breloque *exp.* to be off one's rocker; to function badly, to beat the drum.

battre son plein *exp.* to be in full swing • (lit.): to beat one's full.

example: La soirée devrait **battre son plein** d'ici une heure.

translation: The party should **be in full swing** in an hour.

as spoken: La soirée, è d'vrait **batt' son plein** d'ici une heure.

battre une (s'en) *exp.* (of men) to masturbate • (lit.): to beat one.

baveuse *f.* penis • (lit.): drooler.

baveux *m.* vagina • (lit.): drooler.

bazar *m.* penis and testicles • (lit.): bazaar.

beau châssis (avoir un) *exp.* said of a girl with an exceptionally beautiful body • (lit.): to have a handsome chassis.

beau-dab *m.* father-in-law.

example: Le père de ma femme est mon **beau-dab**.

translation: The father of my wife is my **father-in-law**.

as spoken: Le père d'ma femme, c'est mon **beau-dab**.

beauf *m.* brother-in-law.

example: Le frère de mon marie est mon **beauf**.

translation: The brother of my husband is my **brother-in-law**.

as spoken: Le frère d'mon marie, c'est mon **beauf**.

NOTE -1: **beauf** is a shortened version of "*beau-frère.*"

NOTE -1: **beauf** is also used to mean "average, mediocre, narrow-minded guy."

beau milieu (au) *exp.* right in the middle • (lit.): in the handsome middle.

example: J'ai trouvé un portefeuille **au beau milieu** de la rue!

translation: I found a wallet **in the middle** of the street!

as spoken: J'ai trouvé un portefeuille **au beau milieu** d'la rue!

beau (petit) lot *m.* • said of a woman who has a beautiful face and body • (lit.): nice (little) package.

beaux-vieux *m.pl.* parents-in-law.

example: Les parents de mon mari sont mes **beaux-vieux**.

translation: The parents of my husband are my **parents-in-law**.

as spoken: Les parents d'mon mari, ce sont mes **beaux-vieux**.

bec à quelqu'un (faire un) *exp.* to kiss someone • (lit.): to give someone a beak.

NOTE: The masculine noun *bec*, literally meaning "beak of a bird," is commonly used in French slang to mean "mouth."

bécasse *f.* stupid woman or girl.

bêcheuse *f.* a priss, snob.

example: Michelle se croit supérieure parce que son père est Ministre de la Culture. Quelle **bêcheuse**, celle-là!

translation: Michelle thinks she's better than everyone because her father is Minister of Culture. What a **snob**!

as spoken: Michelle, è s'croit supérieure pasque son père, il est Ministre d'la Culture. Quelle **bêcheuse**, celle-là!

bécot à quelqu'un (donner un) *exp.* to kiss someone • (lit.): to give someone a little kiss (generally on the cheek).

bécoter *v.* to kiss, "to neck" • (lit.): to "beak" (since this comes from the masculine noun *bec* meaning "the beak of a bird").

example: J'ai vu Henri et Madeleine **se bécoter** derrière la maison!

translation: I saw Henri and Madeleine **making out** behind the house!

as spoken: J'ai vu Henri et Madeleine **s'bécoter** derrière la maison!

> **NOTE:** **bécot** *m.* a kiss.
> **SYNONYM -1:** **bisou** *m.*
> **SYNONYM -2:** **bise** *f.*

belle / beau *adj.* considerable, "quite a…" • (lit.): pretty / handsome.

example: Tu te feras une **belle** hernie si tu essaies de soulever ça!

translation: You'll give yourself **quite a** hernia if you try to lift that!

as spoken: Tu t'f'ras une **belle** hernie si t'essaies d'soul'ver ça!

belle-doche *f.* mother-in-law.

example: La mère de ma femme est ma **belle-doche**.

translation: The mother of my wife is my **mother-in-law**.

as spoken: La mère d'ma femme, c'est ma **belle-doche**.

belle mécanique *f.* • said of a woman with a beautiful body (lit.): nice mechanics.

bénitier *m.* vagina • (lit.): (holy water) basin.

béquille *f.* penis • (lit.): crutch.

berlingot *m.* clitoris • (lit.): a type of candy made out of burnt sugar.

berloque *f.* penis • (lit.): charm, trinket.

besogner *v.* to fornicate • (lit.): to work hard.

bêta *m.* (applies primarily to a man but may be used in reference to a woman) silly or stupid person.

> **NOTE -1:** This comes from the adjective *bête* meaning "stupid.

> **NOTE -2:** This is usually seen as *gros bêta* and is used by children.

bêtasse *f.* stupid woman or girl.

NOTE: This comes from the adjective *bête* meaning "stupid."

bête à bouffer du foin (être)
exp. (applies to either a man or a woman) to be as stupid as a cow
• (lit.): to be stupid enough to eat hay.

bête comme ses pieds (être)
exp. (applies to either a man or a woman) to be as dumb as an ox
• (lit.): to be as stupid as one's feet.

bibelots *m.pl.* testicles • (lit.): trinkets.

bien balancée (être) *exp.* said of a woman with a beautiful body, to be put together well • (lit.): to be nicely balanced or thrown together.

**bien fait pour sa gueule
(être)** *exp.* to serve someone right
• (lit.): to be well done for one's face / mouth.

example: Elle a échoué à l'examen? Bon. C'est **bien fait pour sa gueule**. Elle est toujours à tricher!

translation: She failed the test? Good. It **serves her right**. She's always cheating!

as spoken: Elle a échoué à l'examen? Bon. C'est **bien fait pour sa gueule**. Elle est toujours à tricher!

NOTE: The feminine noun "*gueule*," literally meaning the "mouth of animal," is commonly used in French slang to signify either "face" or "head" depending on the context.

bien foutu(e) (être) *adj.* to be well built (said of someone's body).

example: Regarde ce bodybuilder! Il est **bien foutu**, lui!

translation: Look at that bodybuilder! He's really **built**!

as spoken: Regarde c'bodybuilder! Il est **bien foutu**, lui!

NOTE: The term *bodybuilder* is an Americanism pronounced *bodi-bildeur*.

bien mis(e) (être) *exp.* to be well-dressed • (lit.): to be well put together.

example: Tu as vu ses vêtements? Elle est toujours **bien mise**.

translation: Have you seen her clothes? She's always so **well-dressed**.

as spoken: T'as vu ses vêtements? Elle est toujours **bien mise**.

bien roulé(e) (être) *adj.* to have a good body • (lit.): to be rolled (together) well.

example: Elle fait de la gymnastique. C'est pour ça qu'elle est **bien roulée**!

translation: She works out. That's why she's got a **great body**!

as spoken: È fait d'la gymnastique. C'est pour ça qu'elle est **bien roulée**!

SYNONYM: **bien balancé(e) (être)** *adj.* • (lit.): to be well-balanced.

bigler *v.* to look from the corner of one's eye.

example: Je crois qu'elle te **bigle**.

translation: I think she's **looking** at you.

as spoken: J'crois qu'è t'**bigle**.

SYNONYM: **zieuter** (or **zyeuter**) *v.* • (lit.): to eye someone.

NOTE: This comes from *les yeux* (pronounced: *les z'yeux* • *z'yeux* = *zyeuter*).

bigorner (se) . to fight.

NOTE: **bigorne** *f.* a big fight.

bijoux de famille *m.pl.* (humorous) penis and testicles • (lit.): family jewels.

bille de billard (avoir une) *exp.* to be bald • (lit.): to have a billiard ball (for a head).

billes *f.pl.* testicles • (lit.): (small) balls.

bique *f.* ugly woman or girl • (lit.): nanny-goat.

bique (vieille) *f.* old lady • (lit.): old nanny-goat.

bisbille *f.* a quarrel.

bise (faire la) *f.* to kiss.

example: N'oublie pas de **faire la bise** à ta maman avant de partir.

translation: Don't forget **to give a kiss** to your mom before leaving.

as spoken: Oublie pas d'**faire la bise** à ta maman avant d'partir.

SYNONYM: **bisou (faire un)** *exp.*

bisenesseuse *f.* a prostitute, "working girl" • (lit.): a "businesswoman."

example: Ce quartier a beaucoup changé. Maintenant, c'est plein de **bisenesseuses**.

translation: This neighborhood has changed a lot. Now it's full of **working girls**.

as spoken: Ce quartier, il a beaucoup changé. Maintenant, c'est plein d'**bisenesseuses**.

bisou à quelqu'un (faire un) *exp.* to kiss someone • (lit.): to give someone a little kiss.

bite *f.* (very popular) penis • (lit.): bitt, bollard (on a ship).

biter *v.* to fornicate, to "dick" someone.

NOTE: **bite** *f.* penis, dick.

bitume (faire le) *m.* to hustle (said of a prostitute) • (lit.): to do the asphalt.

blair (avoir quelqu'un dans le) *exp.* to be unable to stand someone • (lit.): to have someone in the nose.

NOTE: **blair** *m.* nose, "schnoz."

blairer quelqu'un (ne pas pouvoir) *v.* to be unable to stand or tolerate someone.

example: Je ne peux pas le **blairer**!

translation: I can't **stand** him!

as spoken: J'peux pas l'**blairer**!

NOTE -1: **blair** *n.* nose, "schnoz," "honker."

example: Jimmy Durante était connu pour son grand **blair**.

translation: Jimmy Durante was known for his big **honker**.

as spoken: Jimmy Durante il était connu pour son grand **blair**.

NOTE -2: The expression *ne pas pouvoir blairer quelqu'un* could be loosely translated as "to be unable to tolerate someone to the point that even smelling him would be too much to bear."

SYNONYM: **pif** *m.*

blanc *m.* sperm • (lit.): white (stuff).

blanc(he) comme un cachet d'aspirine (être) *exp.* to be as white as a ghost (from shock) • (lit.): to be as white as an aspirin tablet.

example: Quand j'ai appris la nouvelle, j'étais **blanc comme un cachet d'aspirine**!

translation: When I heard the news, I turned **white as a ghost**!

as spoken: [no change]

blaze *m.* name.

example: Quel est son **blaze**?

translation: What's his **name**?

as spoken: Son **blaze**, c'est quoi?

NOTE -1: This is from the masculine noun *blason* meaning "coat of arms."

NOTE -2: The noun *blaze* is considered extremely slangy and is primarily used only by younger people.

boire au succès de quelqu'un
exp. to toast someone's success • (lit.): to drink to someone's success.

example: **Buvons au succès de** Marcel! Félicitations pour ton nouvel emploi!

translation: **Let's drink to** Marcel's success! Congratulations on your new job!

as spoken: **Buvons au succès d'**Marcel! Félicitations pour ton nouvel emploi!

ALSO: **boire à la santé de quelqu'un** *exp.* • (lit.): to drink to someone's health.

boire un pot *exp.* to have a drink • (lit.): to drink a pot.

example: Tu veux aller **boire un pot** après le boulot?

translation: Wanna go **have a drink** after work?

as spoken: Tu veux aller **boire un pot** après l'boulot?

NOTE: **boulot** *n.* (very popular) work, the "grind."

NOTE: **boulonner** *v.* to work.

SYNONYM: **boire un coup** *exp.* • (lit.): to drink a shot.

boîte à ouvrage *f.* vagina • (lit.): work box.

boîte à pâté *f.* anus • (lit.): pâté box.

boîte à puces *f.* bed • (lit.): flea box.

boîtes à lait *f.pl.* breasts • (lit.): milk cans.

bon *adj.* well (used to begin a new thought).

example: **Bon**, je vais rentrer. Je te verrai demain.

translation: **Well**, I'm going home. I'll see you tomorrow.

as spoken: **Bon**, j'vais rentrer. J'te verrai d'main.

NOTE: Ah, bon? *exclam.* Really?

example: "Guy va passer tout l'été à Paris!"
"Ah, bon?"

translation: "Guy is going to spend the entire summer in Paris!"
"Really?"

as spoken: "Guy, y va passer tout l'été à Paris!"
"Ah, bon?"

NOTE: Although the expression *Ah, bon* is literally translated as "Ah, good," it is used to mean "Really" in any context and can, therefore, be used upon hearing bad news as well:

example: "Mon chien est mort ce matin."
"**Ah, bon**? Qu'est-ce qui s'est passé?"

translation: "My dog died this morning."
"**Really**? What happened?"

as spoken: "Mon chien, il est mort c'matin."
"**Ah, bon**? Qu'est-c'qui s'est passé?"

bonbonnière *f.* vagina
• (lit.): sweetmeat box.

bonbons *m.pl.* testicles
• (lit.): goodies.

bon matin (de) *exp.* early in the morning • (lit.): from good morning.

example: Je doit me lever **de bon matin** pour aller à l'école.

translation: I have to get up **early** to go to school.

as spoken: J'dois m'lever **d'bon matin** pour aller à l'école.

SYNONYM: petit jour (au) *exp.* dawn • (lit.): at the little day.

bonne (avoir quelqu'un à la)
exp. to like someone, to have a crush on someone • (lit.): to have someone in good (standing).

bonnet à poils *m.* vagina
• (lit.): hair bonnet.

bonze (vieux) *m.* old man, an "old fart" • (lit.): old Buddhist monk.

bordel • **1.** *interj.* an interjection used in anger or disbelief; "holy shit"
• **2.** *m.* an unruly mess or confusion
• (lit.): brothel.

example (1): Oh, **bordel**! J'ai brûlé le dîner!

translation: Oh, **holy shit**! I burned the dinner!

as spoken: Oh, **bordel**! J'ai brûlé l'dîner!

example (2): Quel **bordel**, ta chambre! Va la ranger tout de suite!

translation: Your bedroom's a **mess**! Go clean it up right now!

as spoken: Quel **bordel**, ta chambre! Va la ranger tout d'suite!

NOTE: foutre le bordel *exp.* to make a mess • (lit.): to put the bordello (*foutre* is a popular slang verb meaning "to put").

bordille *f.* bastard, piece of junk.

borne *f.* turd • (lit.): milestone.

bosse de quelque chose (avoir la) *exp.* to be gifted for something • (lit.): to have the bump of something.

example: Elle a **la bosse du** piano.

translation: She has a **knack** for the piano.

as spoken: [no change]

bosser *v.* to work.

example: Je suis fatigué parce que je **bosse** soixante heures par semaine.

translation: I'm tired because I **work** sixty hours a week.

as spoken: J'suis fatigué pasque j'**bosse** soixante heures par s'maine.

SYNONYM: **boulonner** *v.* to work hard • **boulot** *m.* work, the "grind."

bouboule *n.* (applies to a man) fatso.

example: Ce **bouboule**-là a marché sur mon pied!

translation: That **fatso** stepped on my foot!

as spoken: C'**bouboule**-là, il a marché sur mon pied!

boucher un coin (en) *exp.* to surprise, to flabbergast • (lit.): to stop up a corner of it (with a cork).

example: Elle **m'en bouche un coin** avec ses notes extraordinaires! J'ai toujours pensé qu'elle était un peu lente!

translation: She **really surprises me** with your incredible grades! I always thought she was a little slow!

as spoken: Elle **m'en bouche un coin** avec ses notes extr'ordinaires! J'ai toujours pensé qu'elle était un peu lente!

bouchon *m.* the youngest member of the family • (lit.): stopper, plug, cork (of a bottle).

example: Je suis le **bouchon** de la famille.

translation: I'm the **youngest member** of the family.

as spoken: J'suis l'**bouchon** d'la famille.

boucler son égout *exp.* to shut one's mouth • (lit.): to shut one's sewer.

example: **Boucles ton égout**! Tu racontes des mensonges!

translation: **Shut your trap**! You're telling lies!

as spoken: [no change]

boude *m.* (applies only to a woman) a shortened version of *boudin* meaning "an ugly and fat woman."

SEE: **boudin**, *(next entry).*

boudin *m.* fat woman or girl • blood sausage.

example: C'est la fiancée de Marc? Oh, quel **boudin**!

translation: That's Mark's fiancée? What a **fatso**!

as spoken: C'est la fiancée d'Marc? Oh, quel **boudin**!

ALSO: **boudin** *m.* turd.

boudin blanc *m.* penis • (lit.): white sausage.

bouffe *f.* food, "grub."

example: J'aime la **bouffe** française.

translation: I love French **food**.

as spoken: [no change]

SEE: **bouffer**, *(next entry).*

bouffer *v.* (extremely popular) to eat, "to chow down."

example: Tu veux **bouffer** chez moi ce soir?

translation: Wanna **eat** at my house tonight?

as spoken: Tu veux **bouffer** chez moi c'soir?

SEE: bouffe, *(previous entry)*.

bouffer le nez (se) *exp.* to fight • (lit.): to eat each other's nose.

example: Pourquoi vivent-ils toujours ensemble? Ils **se bouffent le nez** sans arrêt!

translation: Why do they still live together? They **fight** nonstop!

as spoken: Pouquoi y vivent toujours ensemble? Y **s'bouffent le nez** sans arrêt!

NOTE: This humorous expression describes two people yelling at each other so closely that they appear to be eating each other's nose. Any slang synonym for *nez*, meaning "nose," could be used in its place such as: *pif, blair, tarrin, etc.*

bougeotte (avoir la) *exp.* to have the fidgets, to have ants in one's pants.

example: Tu ne peux pas rester tranquille cinq minutes?! Qu'est-ce que tu as la **bougeotte**, toi!

translation: You can't sit still for five minutes?! Are you ever **fidgety**!

as spoken: Tu peux pas rester tranquille cinq minutes?! Qu'est-c'que t'as la **bougeotte**, toi!

NOTE: This expression comes from the verb *bouger* meaning "to move" or "to budge."

bouger d'un poil (ne pas) *exp.* not to budge an inch • (lit.): not to budge a hair.

example: **Ne bouge pas d'un poil**! J'ai une surprise pour toi.

translation: **Don't budge an inch**! I have a surprise for you.

as spoken: **Bouge pas d'un poil**! J'ai une surprise pour toi.

bougre • **1.** *m.* (pejorative) man • **2.** *interj.* darn • (lit.): country man.

NOTE: bougrement *adv.* damned.

boui-boui *m.* bad restaurant, a dive or "greasy spoon."

example: Tu veux manger dans ce **boui-boui**? Berk!

translation: You want to eat at this **dive**? Yuck!

as spoken: Tu veux manger dans c'**boui-boui**? Berk!

*Quel **boui-boui**, ce restaurant!*

(trans.)
This restaurant's a **real dive**!

boule de billard bien cirée (avoir la) *exp.* to be bald
- (lit.): to have the well-waxed billiard.

boules (avoir les) *exp.* to be extremely nervous • (lit.): to have balls (in one's throat).

example: J'ai eu **les boules** quand j'ai fait ma présentation devant les cadres.

translation: I was **extremely nervous** when I did my presentation in front of the executives.

as spoken: J'ai eu **les boules** quand j'ai fait ma présentation d'vant les cadres.

SYNONYM: glandes (avoir les) *exp.* • (lit.): to have glands (that are swollen).

boum *f.* (used by the younger people) big party, "a bash."

example: Demain je vais donner une **boum** chez moi. Je t'invite!

translation: Tomorrow I'm having a **arty** at my house. You're invited!

as spoken: Demain j'vais donner une **boum** chez moi. J't'invite!

bouquin *m.* book.

example: Tu as lu tout ce **bouquin** en une heure?

translation: You read that entire **book** in one hour?

as spoken: T'as lu tout c'**bouquin** en une heure?

NOTE -1: The word **bouquin** used to mean "old book" but has now become a popular slang synonym for "book" in general.

NOTE -2: bouquiner *v.* to read • (lit.): to go through old books.

bourdille *f.* a variation of *bordille* meaning "bastard" or "piece of junk."

bourge *m.* a shortened version of the term "bourgeois(e)," yuppie scum.

example: Laisse-moi tranquille, sale **bourge**!

translation: Leave me alone, you **yuppie scum**!

as spoken: [no change]

NOTE: Since France is rather class conscious, insulting a person's status in society or telling a person that he / she comes from a lower class is considered very offensive.

bourre (aller à la) *exp.* to fornicate • (lit.): to screw.

NOTE: bourre *f.* lay, screw • (*Carole, c'est une bonne bourre!*; Carole is a good lay.)

bourré(e) (être) *adj.* to be very drunk • (lit.): to be stuffed (with alcohol).

example: Tu ne peux pas conduire comme ça. Tu es complètement **bourré**!

translation: You can't drive like that. You're totally **plastered**!

as spoken: Tu peux pas conduire comme ça. T'es complètement **bourré**!

NOTE: bourrer *v.* • (lit.): to stuff, cram, pack tight.

bourrer *v.* (popular) to fornicate
• (lit.): to stuff.

bourrin *m.* prostitute, loose woman
• (lit.): horse or nag.

bourrique *f.* (applies to either a man or a woman) jackass, stubborn individual • (lit.): (jack)ass.

bourriquer *v.* to fornicate, to screw like a donkey.

> **NOTE:** **bourrique** *f.* donkey, she-ass.

bouse *f.* • *bouse de vache;* cow patty.

bousiller *v.* to break or damage.

> example (1): La télévision ne marche plus! Tu l'as **bousillée**!

> translation: The television doesn't work anymore! You **broke** it!

> as spoken: La télé, è marche plus! Tu l'as **bousillée**!

boustifaille *f.* food, "grub."

> example: Hier soir, ma tante nous a préparé de la **boustifaille** que je n'ai pas pu manger! C'tait horrible!

> translation: Last night, my aunt made **food** for us that I couldn't eat! It was horrible!

> as spoken: Hier soir, ma tante è nous a préparé d'la **boustifaille** qu'j'ai pas pu manger! C'était horrible!

> **SYNONYM:** **mangeaille** *f.* (from the verb *manger* meaning "to eat").

> **NOTE:** **boustifailler** *v.* to eat, "to chow down."

bout *m.* penis • (lit.): end.

bout du rouleau (être au)
exp. to be at the end of one's rope
• (lit.): to be at the end of the roller.

> example: Je ne sais plus quoi faire. Je suis **au bout du rouleau**!

> translation: I don't know what else to do. I'm **at the end of my rope**!

> as spoken: Ch'ais pu quoi faire. J'suis **au bout du rouleau**!

bouton d'amour *m.* clitoris
• (lit.): love button.

bouton de rose *m.* clitoris
• (lit.): rose button.

boxon *m.* • **1.** whorehouse • **2.** a complete mess, chaos.

> example (1): Je vois toujours de drôles de mecs et des nanas super sexy entrer chez les voisins d'à côté. Je commence à avoir l'impression que leur maison est un **boxon**!

> translation: I always see strange men and sexy girls go into the neighbor's house next door. I'm starting to get the feeling that their home is a **whorehouse**!

> as spoken: J'vois toujours de drôles d'mecs et des nanas super sexy entrer chez les voisins d'à côté. J'commence à avoir l'impression qu'leur maison, c't'un **boxon**!

> example (2): Va ranger ta chambre tout de suite! Quel **boxon**!

> translation: Go clean up your room right now! What a **pigsty**!

> as spoken: Va ranger ta chamb' tout d'suite! Quel **boxon**!

NOTE: This comes from the masculine noun *box* meaning "cubicle (in a dormitory)."

brancher *v.* • **1.** to talk to someone • **2.** to interest [someone], to be "into" something • (lit.): to plug into.

example (1): Tiens! Voilà mon ami Richard! Je vais le **brancher**.

translation: Hey! There's my friend Richard! I'm going **to talk** with him.

as spoken: Tiens! V'là mon ami Richard! J'vais l'**brancher**.

example (2): La peinture, ça te **branche**?

translation: Are you **into** painting?

as spoken: La peinture, ça t'**branche**?

brancher avec quelqu'un (se) *v.* to get in touch with someone.

example: Après avoir eu les nouvelles du tremblement de terre à Los Angeles, j'ai essayé de **me brancher avec** mon cousin qui habite dans les environs.

translation: After hearing about the earthquake in Los Angeles, I tried **getting in touch with** my cousin who lives in the surrounding area.

as spoken: Après avoir eu les nouvelles du tremblement d'terre à Los Angeles, j'ai essayé d'**me brancher avec** mon cousin qu'habite dans les environs.

brancher quelqu'un sur un sujet *exp.* to get someone started on a subject.

example: Normalement, Etienne est très réservé. Mais tu **le branches** sur le sujet d'art, il peut parler pour des heures!

translation: Normally, Steve is very shy. But it you **get him started** about the subject of art, he can talk for hours!

as spoken: Normalement, Etienne, il est très réservé. Mais tu **l'branches** sur l'sujet d'art, y peut parler pour des heures!

branlée *f.* masturbation • (lit.): shaking.
NOTE: **branler (se)** *v.* to masturbate • (lit.): to shake oneself.

branler (se) *v.* (very popular) to masturbate • (lit.): to shake oneself.

branler (s'en) *v.* (very popular) not to give a damn • (lit.): to shake oneself of it.

example: Je **m'en branle** de ce que tu penses!

translation: I don't **give a damn** what you think!

as spoken: J'**m'en branle** de c'que tu penses!
NOTE: **branler (se)** *v.* to masturbate • (lit.): to shake oneself.

branlette *f.* (popular) masturbation, handjob • (lit.): shaking.
NOTE: **branler (se)** *v.* to masturbate • (lit.): to shake oneself.

branlette maison *f.* masturbation, handjob • (lit.): shaking of the house.
NOTE -1: **branler (se)** *v.* to masturbate • (lit.): to shake oneself.

NOTE -2: This construction, where *maison* is used as an adjective, is commonly seen in restaurants referring to the "house" specialty such as *pâté maison*.

branlure *f.* masturbation, handjob
• (lit.): shaking.
NOTE: **branler (se)** *v.* to masturbate • (lit.): to shake oneself.

braque *m.* (applies to either a man or a woman) harebrained individual
• (lit.): hound.

braquemard *m.* penis • (lit.): the pointer. comes from the verb *braquer* meaning "to point a gun (at something or someone)."
VARIATION: **braquemart** *m.*

breloques *f.pl.* testicles
• (lit.): charms, trinkets.

bréviaire d'amour *m.* vagina
• (lit.): breviary of love.

brioches *f.pl.* posterior
• (lit.): brioches (breads).

brochet *m.* pimp • (lit.): pike.

bronze *m.* turd • (lit.): a bronze (one).

brouille-ménage *m.* humorous for red wine.
example: Tu veux du **brouille-ménage** avec ton repas?
translation: Would you like some **red wine** with your meal?
as spoken: Tu veux du **brouille-ménage** avec ton r'pas?
NOTE: **brouiller** *v.* to mix up, stir up • **ménage** *m.* household. This

literally translates as "something that stirs up the household" since husbands and wives would get into fights after having too much to drink.

brouter la tige *exp.* to perform fellatio • (lit.): to graze the stem.

burettes *f.pl.* testicles • (lit.): oilcans.

burnes *f.pl.* testicles.

buse *f.* (applies to either a man or a woman) extremely stupid person
• (lit.): buzzard.
SEE: **triple buse**, *p. 179.*

business (faire le) *m.* to hustle (said of a prostitute) • (lit.): to do the business.

butte (avoir sa) *exp.* to be pregnant • (lit.): to have one's little hill.

Byzance (être) *adj.* to be bountiful.

example: Tu aurais dû voir le dîner qu'on a mangé chez Madeleine. C'était **Byzance**!

translation: You should have seen the dinner we ate at Madeleine's house. There was **a ton of food**!

as spoken: T'aurais dû voir le dîner qu'on a mangé chez Mad'leine. C'était **Byzance**!

NOTE: This comes from Byzantium, an ancient Greek city known for its abundance and wealth.

cabzingue *m.pl.* short for *cabinet* meaning the "bathroom."

caca *m.* (child language)
- **1.** excrement, "poop" • **2.** gross, filthy • (lit.): caca.

example (1): Attention de ne pas marcher dans le **caca**! Il y a des chiens dans ce quartier.

translation: Be careful not to step in the **poop**! There are dogs in this neighborhood.

as spoken: Attention d'ne pas marcher dans l'**caca**! Y a des chiens dans c'quartier.

example (2): Ne te mets pas ça dans la bouche! C'est du **caca**!

translation: Don't put that in your mouth! It's **filthy**!

as spoken: Te mets pas ça dans la bouche! C'est du **caca**!

NOTE: **caca (faire)** *exp.* (child language) to go poo-poo, *(next entry)*.

caca (faire) *exp.* (child language) to defecate • (lit.): to make caca.

example: Tu as **fait caca** avant d'aller au lit?

translation: Did you **go poo-poo** before going to bed?

as spoken: T'as **fait caca** avant d'aller au lit?

cadran solaire *m.* posterior
- (lit.): sundial.

cafard (avoir le) *exp.* (extremely popular) to be depressed • (lit.): to have the cockroach.

example: J'**ai le cafard** aujourd'hui. Je pense que je vais aller voir un film pour me remonter le moral.

translation: I'm **feeling down** today. I think I'll go see a film to boost my spirits.

as spoken: J'**ai l'cafard** aujourd'hui. J'pense que j'vais aller voir un film pour me remonter l'moral.

Georges semble
avoir le cafard.

(trans.)
*George seems **depressed**.*
(lit.)
George seems to
***have the cockroach**.*

café boullu, café foutu *exp.* "if you boil coffee, it's ruined."

example: Quand tu réchauffes le café, attention de ne pas le faire bouillir. **Café boullu, café foutu**!

translation: When you reheat the coffee, make sure not to boil it. **When you boil coffee, it's ruined**!

as spoken: Quand tu réchauffes le café, attention d'ne pas l'faire bouillir. **Café boullu, café foutu**!

NOTE: The past participle of *bouillir* is actually *bouilli*. However, in this expression, the past participle is humorously transformed in order to rhyme with *foutu*, the past participle of the verb *foutre*," meaning "ruined" (in this case).

caille (avoir quelqu'un à la)

exp. to be unable to stand someone • (lit.): to make someone's blood curdle (since *caille* comes from the verb *cailler* meaning "to curdle").

cailler *v.* to be extremely cold • (lit.): to curdle, clot, congeal.

example: Qu'est-ce qu'il fait froid! Je **caille**!

translation: It's so cold! I'm **freezing**!

as spoken: Qu'est-c'qu'y fait froid! Je **caille**!

ALSO: **se les cailler** *exp.* • (lit.): to freeze them off. In this expression, "*les*" refers to "*les miches*" having the slang meaning "the buttocks" or, more literally, "the loaves."

example: Je **me les caille**!

translation: I'm **freezing them** (my "buns") **off**!

as spoken:

1. Je **m'les caille**!
2. J'**me les caille**!

caillou déplumé (avoir le)

exp. to be bald • (lit.): to have the plucked pebble.

NOTE: **caillou** *m.* head, "noggin" • (lit.): pebble.

Ça la fout mal *exp.* it's a very awkward situation.

example: Louise est arrivée en shorts au bal de la Marquise de Rangnangnan. **Ça la fout mal**!

translation: Louise arrived in shorts to the Marquise of Rangnangnan's ball. **It was really awkward**!

as spoken: Louise, elle est arrivée en shorts au bal d'la Marquise de Rangnangnan. **Ça la fout mal**!

calé(e) en quelque chose (être) *adj.* to be very smart in a particular subject, expert.

example: J'ai toujours une calculatrice dans mon sac. Je ne suis pas du tout **calée** en mathématiques!

translation: I always have a calculator in my purse. I'm not at all **smart** when it comes to math!

as spoken: J'ai toujours une calculatrice dans mon sac. J'suis pas du tout **calée** en maths!

SYNONYM: **fortiche en quelque chose (être)** *exp.* • (lit.): strong, a slang deformation of the adjective *fort(e)* meaning "strong."

caler le bide (se) *exp.* to eat • (lit.): to stabilize one's stomach.

example: J'ai faim. Je dois **me caler le bide**.

translation: I'm hungry. I'm have to **eat something**.

as spoken: J'ai faim. J'dois **m'caler l'bide**.

NOTE: The masculine noun *"bide"* is a shortened version of *"bidon,"* meaning "belly" • (lit.): can or drum.

cambuse *f.* bedroom
• (lit.): storeroom on a ship.

came *f.* sperm • (lit.): cum.

NOTE: **came** *f.* • **1.** sperm • **2.** junk (in general) • **3.** personal belongings, one's "stuff" • **4.** cocaine.

ça ne chie pas *exp.* it doesn't matter a fucking bit.

example: Si tu manques ton avion, **ça ne chie pas**. Tu en prendras un autre demain.

translation: If you miss your plane, **it doesn't matter a fucking bit**. You'll just take another one tomorrow.

as spoken: Si tu manques ton avion, **ça chie pas**. T'en prendras un aut' demain.

"Ça ne tourne pas rond" *exp.* "There's a problem here."

example: J'ai bien suivi les instructions, mais je n'arrive pas à assembler cette bicyclette! **Ça ne tourne pas rond**!

translation: I followed the instructions, but I can't seem to be able to assemble this bicycle! **Something's not right**!

as spoken: J'ai bien suivi les instructions, mais j'arrive pas à assembler c'te bicyclette! **Ça tourne pas rond**!

canne *f.* penis • (lit.): cane.

canne (avoir la) *exp.* to have an erection • (lit.): to have the cane.

capote *f.* condom, "rubber."

example: De nos jours, il faut absolument mettre une **capote** pour avoir des rapports sexuels.

translation: Nowadays, it's absolutely necessary to wear a **rubber** when participating in sexual relations.

as spoken: De nos jours, faut absolument mettre une **capote** pour avoir des rapports sexuels.

SYNONYM: **capote anglaise**
• (lit.): English bonnet.

capote anglaise *f.* condom, "rubber."

SEE: **capote**, *(previous entry)*.

caqueter *v.* (usually in reference to a woman) to blab on and on • (lit.): to cackle.

example: Patricia parle sans arrêt. Elle a **caqueté** pendant toute une heure de la même histoire!

translation: Patricia talks nonstop. She **blabbed on and on** for an entire hour about the same story!

as spoken: Patricia, è parle sans arrêt. Elle a **caqueté** pendant toute une heure d'la même histoire!

carabine *f.* penis • (lit.): rifle.

caramboler *v.* to plow into another car.

example: Regarde la route! Tu as failli **caramboler** la voiture devant toi!

translation: Watch the road! You almost **plowed into** the car in front of you!

as spoken: Regarde la route! T'as failli **caramboler** la voiture d'vant toi!

caramboler (se) *v.* (said of cars) to pile up.

example: Une dizaine de voitures **se sont carambolées** sur l'autoroute ce matin.

translation: About ten cars **piled up** on the highway this morning.

as spoken: Une dizaine de voitures **s'sont carambolées** sur l'autoroute c'matin.

carapater (se) *v.* to leave quickly, "to scram."

example: Voilà le patron! On **se carapate**!

translation: There's the boss! Let's **beat it**!

as spoken: V'là l'patron! On **s'carapate**!

carburer *v.* to be going very well • (lit.): (said of a carburetor) to function well.

example: Salut Jacques! **Ça carbure**?

translation: Hi Jack! **Everything ok**?

as spoken: [no change]

SYNONYMS: *ça boume?* • *ça gaze?* • *ça gazouille?*

cardinales (avoir ses) *f.pl.* to menstruate • (lit.): to have one's cardinals.

carrément *adv.* completely • (lit.): squarely.

example: Je ne peux pas le supporter. Il est **carrément** stupide.

translation: I can't stand him. He's **totally** stupid.

as spoken: J'peux pas l'supporter. Il est **carrément** stupide.

carrossée (être bien) *adj.* to have a beautiful body.

SEE: **carrosserie**, *(next entry)*.

carrosserie *f.* (humorous when applied to a person) body • (lit.): body of a car.

example: Regarde cette fille! Quelle **carrosserie**!

translation: Look at that girl! What a **body**!

as spoken: Regarde c'te fille! Quelle **carross'rie**!

cartonner à un examen *v.* to ace a test.

example: J'ai **cartonné** à l'examen!

translation: I **aced** the test!

as spoken: [no change]

NOTE: The verb **cartonner** literally means " to hit a target." It refers to the cardboard target, or **carton**, that is found in shooting ranges or amusement parks.

Ça saute aux yeux *c.l.* said of something obvious • (lit.): it jumps to the eyes.

example: Quelle maison! **Ça saute aux yeux** qu'il est riche!

translation: What a house! It's **obvious** that he's rich!

as spoken: [no change]

casbah *m.* brothel.

NOTE: This comes from Arabic meaning "the Arab city" or "the house."

case en moins (avoir une) *exp.* to be crazy, not to be cooking on all four burners • (lit.): to be missing a division of the brain.

caser *v.* to put someone up • (lit.): to put or stow (something) away.

example: Si tu veux, je pourrai te **caser** pour la nuit.

translation: If you like, I can **put** you **up** for the night.

as spoken: Si tu veux, j'pourrai t'**caser** pour la nuit.

caser (se) *v.* to get married.

example: Félicitations! J'ai entendu dire que tu vas **te caser** la semaine prochaine!

translation: Congratulations! I heard **you're getting married** next week!

as spoken: Félicitations! J'ai entendu dire qu'tu vas **t'caser** la s'maine prochaine!

casquette en peau de fesses (avoir la) *exp.* to be totally bald • (lit.): to have a cap made out of butt skin.

example: Ça fait dix ans que je n'ai pas vu Guillaume. Il a toujours eu de beaux cheveux, lui. C'est pour ça que j'étais stupéfait de voir qu'il a une **casquette en peau de fesses** maintenant!

translation: It's been ten years since I've seen Guillaume. He's always had such beautiful hair. That's why I was shocked to see that he's **totally bald** now!

as spoken: Ça fait dix ans qu'j'ai pas vu Guillaume. Il a toujours eu d'beaux ch'veux, lui. C'est pour ça qu'j'étais stupéfait d'voir qu'il a une **casquette en peau d'fesses** maintenant!

NOTE: casquette *f.* head, "noggin" • (lit.): helmet.

casse-burnes *m.* (applies to people or things) pain in the ass • (lit.): oil can ("testicles") breaker.

casse-couilles *m.* (applies to people or things) pain in the ass • (lit.): testicles breaker.

example: Quel **casse-couilles**! Il n'arrête pas de m'énerver!

translation: What a **pain in the ass**! He doesn't stop bugging me!

as spoken: Quel **casse-couilles**! Il arrête pas d'm'énerver!

casse-noisettes *m.* (applies to people or things) pain in the ass • (lit.): nutcracker.

casse-pieds *m.* (applies to people or things) pain in the neck
- (lit.): foot-breaker.

example: Quel **casse-pieds**! Il ne me laisse jamais tranquille!

translation: What a **pain in the neck**! He never leaves me alone!

as spoken: Quel **casse-pieds**! Y m'laisse jamais tranquille!

casser la gueule à quelqu'un
exp. to clobber someone • (lit.): to break someone's mouth.

example: Rend-moi ça tout de suite ou je te **casse la gueule**!

translation: Give that back to me right now or I'll **clobber** you!

as spoken: Rend-moi ça tout d'suite ou j'te **casse la gueule**!

NOTE -1: **gueule** *f.* mouth or "mug" • (lit.): mouth of an animal.

casser la gueule (se) *exp.* to break one's "neck" • (lit.): to break one's mouth or "mug."

example: Tu vas faire du ski aujourd'hui? Attention à ne pas **te casser la gueule**!

translation: You're going skiing today? Be careful not **to break your neck**!

as spoken: Tu vas faire du ski aujourd'hui? Attention à n'pas **t'casser la gueule**!

casser la tête (se) *exp.* to strain oneself (figuratively), to rack one's brains over something.

example: "Oh, que je suis distrait! J'ai complètement oublié le nom du restaurant que je voulais recommender!" **"Ne te casse pas la tête**. Tu peux me le donner demain."

translation: "Oh, am I ever absentminded! I completely forgot the name of the restaurant I wanted to recommend!" **"Don't rack your brains over it**. You can give it to me tomorrow."

as spoken: "Oh, que j'suis distrait! J'ai complètement oublié l'nom du resto que j'voulais recommender!" **"Te casse pas la tête**. Tu peux m'le donner d'main."

casser les couilles à quelqu'un *exp.* (vulgar) to annoy someone greatly, to bug the shit out of someone • (lit.): to break someone's testicles or "balls."

example: J'espère que tu n'as pas invité Claude à nous rejoindre. Il **me casse les couilles**, celui-là!

translation: I hope you didn't invite Claude to join us. He **bugs the shit out of me**!

as spoken: J'espère qu't'as pas invité Claude à nous r'joindre. Y **m'casse les couilles**, çui-là!

NOTE -1: This expression can also be softened by replacing *les couilles* with *les: Il me les casse, lui!* • (lit.): He breaks mine!

NOTE -1: See the mild forms of this expression: *casser les oreilles à quelqu'un, (next entry)* and *casser les pieds à quelqu'un, p. 34.*

casser les oreilles à quelqu'un *exp.* to talk someone's ear off • (lit.): to break someone's ears.

example: Voilà Thérèse! Je vais me cacher. Si elle me voit, elle va **me casser les oreilles** comme d'habitude!

translation: There's Theresa! I have to hide. If she sees me, she'll **talk my ear off** as usual!

as spoken: V'là Thérèse! J'vais m'cacher. Si è m'voit, è va **m'casser les oreilles** comme d'habitude!

casser les pieds à quelqu'un *exp.* to annoy someone greatly • (lit.): to break someone's feet.

example: Tu me **casses les pieds** avec toutes tes questions!

translation: You really **annoy** me with all your questions!

as spoken: Tu m'**casses les pieds** avec toutes tes questions!

NOTE -1: This expression is a mild version of the popular expression, *casser les couilles à quelqu'un* meaning "to piss someone off" or literally "to break someone's balls." This expression is also commonly shortened to: *Tu me les casses!* where *"les"* replaces *"couilles."*

NOTE -2: **casse-pieds** *m.* an annoying person • (lit.): foot-breaker.

NOTE: This is a mild version of the popular slang term, *casse-couilles* meaning "a pain-in-the-ass" or literally a "ball-breaker."

SYNONYM: **taper sur le système à quelqu'un** *exp.* to get on someone's nerves • (lit.): to hit on someone's system.

*Il **me casse les pieds, ce type**!*

(trans.)
*This guy **bugs the living daylights out of me**!*
(lit.):
*This guy **breaks my feet**!*

casseur *m.* burglar • (lit.): one who breaks things (such as windows in order to gain entry).

example: Le **casseur** a volé mon manteau neuf et tous mes diamants!

translation: The **burglar** took my new coat and all my diamonds!

as spoken: Le **casseur**, il a pris mon manteau neuf et tous mes diams!

NOTE -1: **casser** *v.* to rob, to break in • (lit.): to break.

NOTE -2: **diams** *m.pl.* a popular abbreviation for *diamants* meaning "diamonds."

catin *f.* prostitute.

ça va chier *exp.* the shit's going to hit the fan.

example: Si le patron découvre que tu étais en retard pour la troisième fois cette semaine, **ça va chier**!

translation: If the boss discovers that you were late for the third time this week, **the shit's gonna hit the fan**!

as spoken: Si l'patron, y découv' que t'étais en r'tard pour la troisième fois cette s'maine, **ça va chier**!

VARIATION -1: **ça va chier dur** *exp.* • (lit.): it's going to shit hard.

VARIATION -2: **ça va chier sec** *exp.* • (lit.): it's going to shit dry.

VARIATION -3: **ça va chier des bulles** *exp.* • (lit.): it's going to shit bubbles.

VARIATION -4: **ça va chier des flammes** *exp.* • (lit.): it's going to shit flames.

cave *m.* (applies only to a man) gullible person, sucker.

cela ne cadre pas avec sa personnalité *exp.* that's out of character (for him, for her, etc.) • (lit.): that doesn't frame with his / her personality.

example: Grégoire m'a réprimandé parce que j'étais en retard de cinq minutes. **Cela ne cadre pas avec sa personnalité**.

translation: Greg reprimanded me because I was five minutes late. **That's out of character for him**.

as spoken: Grégoire, y m'a réprimandé pasque j'étais en r'tard d'cinq minutes. **Cela cadre pas avec sa personnalité**.

VARIATION: **cela ne cadre pas avec son rôle** *exp.* • (lit.): that doesn't frame with his / her role.

ce n'est pas de refus *exp.* don't mind if I do • (lit.): it's not from refusal.

example: "Tu veux une boisson? C'est moi qui te l'offre." **"Ce n'est pas de refus**!"

translation: "Would you like a drink? It's on me." **"Don't mind if I do**!"

as spoken: "Tu veux une boisson? C'est moi qui t'l'offre." **"C'est pas d'refus**!"

ce n'est pas la mer à boire *exp.* it's not such a big deal • (lit.): it's not like drinking the sea.

example: Tu peux apprendre à faire de la planche à voile. **Ce n'est pas la mer à boire**!

translation: You can learn how to windsurf. **It's not such a big deal**!

as spoken: Tu peux apprendre à faire d'la planche à voile. **C'est pas la mer à boire**!

Ce n'est pas tes oignons *exp.* "It's none of your business" • (lit.): "It's none of your onions."

example: "Combien pèses-tu?" **"Ce n'est pas tes oignons**!"

translation: "How much do you weigh?" **"It's none of your business**!"

as spoken: "Combien tu pèses?" "**C'est pas tes oignons**!"

c'est chié *exp.* that's fantastic.

example: Tu as gagné dix mille francs? **C'est chié**, ça!

translation: You won ten thousand francs? **That's fantastic**!

as spoken: T'as gagné dix mille francs? **C'est chié**, ça!

c'est le bouquet *exp.* that's the last straw! • (lit.): that's the bouquet!

example: Il a pris ma voiture sans permission?! **C'est le bouquet**, ça!

translation: He took my car without permission?! **That's the last straw**!

as spoken: Il a pris ma voiture sans permission?! **C'est l'bouquet**, ça!

SYNONYM: **c'est la fin des haricots!** *exp.* • (lit.): that's the end of the beans!

c'est le moins qu'on puisse dire *exp.* that's putting it mildly • (lit.): that's the least one can say.

example: Tu crois qu'il est bizarre? **C'est le moins qu'on puisse dire**!

translation: You think he's strange? **That's putting it mildly**!

as spoken: Tu crois qu'il est bizarre? **C'est l'moins qu'on puisse dire**!

c'est moi qui te le dis *exp.* I'm telling you • (lit.): I'm the one who's telling you.

example: Méfie-toi de lui. **C'est moi qui te le dis**!

translation: Don't trust him! **I'm telling you**!

as spoken: Méfie-toi d'lui. **C'est moi qui t'le dis**!

chabanais *m.* brothel.

chabraque *m.* (applies only to a man) fool.

chagatte *f.* vagina • (lit.): cat, "pussy."
NOTE: This is a javanais transformation of the feminine word *chatte* meaning "cat" or "pussy." Javanais is a formula occasionally applied to slang words where the letters "ag" or "av" are added between syllables. Therefore *chat* becomes *chagatte*.

chambard *m.* a big fight.

chambardement *m.* a big fight.

champ de manœuvres *m.* bed • (lit.): parade ground.

changer de disque *exp.* to change the subject • (lit.): to change the record.

example: Oh, **change de disque**! Tu parles toujours du même sujet!

translation: Oh, **get off it**! You always talk about the same thing!

as spoken: [no change]

chanter *v.* to talk nonsense, to hand someone a line • (lit.): to sing.

example: Marie-Chantal est une princesse? **Qu'est-ce que tu me chantes-là**?!

translation: Marie-Chantal is a princess? **What are you handing me**?!

as spoken: Marie-Chantal, c't'une princesse? **Qu'est-c'que tu m'chantes-là**?!

SYNONYM: **balancer** *v.* • (lit.): to throw.

*Mais qu'est-ce qu'il me **chante**-là!?*

(trans.):
What's he **talking about**?!

(lit.):
What's he **singing about**?!

chapeau • 1. *interj.* "Bravo!" • 2. condom • (lit.): hat.

example: J'ai entendu dire que tu es devenu papa! **Chapeau**!

translation: I heard that you became a father! **Congratulations**!

as spoken: J'ai entendu dire qu't'es dev'nu papa! **Chapeau**!

NOTE: The expression "to hear that..." does not quite translate the same into French. The verb **dire** ("to say") must be added to **entendre** ("to hear"): **entendre dire que** *exp.* • (lit.): to hear say that...

charabia *m.* gibberish, gobbledegook.

example: Ce bébé pleure sans arrêt et je ne sais pas ce qu'il veut! Je n'arrive pas à comprendre son **charabia**!

translation: This baby cries nonstop and I don't know what he wants. I can't seem to understand his **gibberish**!

as spoken: C'bébé, y pleure sans arrêt et j'sais pas c'qu'y veut! J'arrive pas à comprend' son **charabia**!

Charles-le-Chauve *m.* penis • (lit.): Charles the Bald.

charognard *m.* (applies only to a man) bastard • (lit.): carrion feeder, vulture.

charogne *f.* (applies to either a man or a woman) variation of: *charognard* bastard / bitch • (lit.): rotting carcass, carrion.

charrier *v.* to exaggerate.

example: Tu as trouvé dix millions de francs en pleine rue?! Arrête de **charrier**!

translation: You found ten million franc in the middle of the street?! Stop **exaggerating**!

as spoken: T'as trouvé dix millions d'francs en pleine rue?! Arrête de **charrier**!

chasser le mâle *exp.* (said of a prostitute) to hustle • (lit.): to hunt the male (species).

chatouiller le poireau (se) *exp.* (of men) to masturbate • (lit.): to tickle one's leek.

> **NOTE:** **poireau** *m.* penis, "dick" • (lit.): leek.

chatouilles (faire des) *exp.* to fondle, to caress.

> **NOTE:** From the verb *chatouiller* meaning "to tickle."

chatte *f.* (extremely popular) vagina • (lit.): cat, "pussy."

chaud de la pince (être) *exp.* (only applies to men) to be oversexed • (lit.): to have a hot claw.

example: Même à son âge, il est toujours **chaud de la pince**.

translation: Even at his age, he's still **oversexed**.

as spoken: Même à son âge, il est toujours **chaud d'la pince**.

chaude-lance *f.* gonorrhea • (lit.): hot urine.

> **NOTE -1:** **lance** *f.* • 1. water • 2. urine.

> **NOTE -2:** **lancequiner** *v.* • **1.** to rain • **2.** to urinate.

chaude-pince *f.* gonorrhea • (lit.): hot claw.

chaude-pisse *f.* (very popular) gonorrhea • (lit.): hot piss.

> **NOTE:** **pisser** *v.* to urinate, to piss.

chauve comme un genou (être) *exp.* to be as bald as a billiard ball • (lit.): to be as bald as a knee.

chauve souris au plafond (avoir une) *exp.* (applies to either a man or a woman) to be crazy, to have bats in the belfry • (lit.): to have a bat in the ceiling.

cheminée *f.* vagina • (lit.): chimney.

chercher noise à quelqu'un *exp.* to look for a fight.

example: Arrête de me critiquer! Tu essaies de **me chercher noise** ou quoi?

translation: Stop picking on me! Are you trying **to start a fight with me** or what?

as spoken: Arrête d'me critiquer! T'essaies d'**me chercher noise** ou quoi?

cheval sur quelque chose (être à) *exp.* to be a stickler for something.

example: Ma mère est **à cheval** sur l'ordre.

translation: My mother is a **stickler** for cleanliness.

as spoken: Ma mère, elle est **à ch'val** sur l'ordre.

chevaucher *v.* to fornicate
- (lit.): to ride horseback.

chèvre *f.* an ugly woman or girl
- (lit.): goat or nanny-goat.

chialer *v.* to cry (very popular).

example: Ce bébé-là **chiale** sans arrêt!

translation: This baby **cries** nonstop!

as spoken: C'bébé-là, y **chiale** sans arrêt!

chiant(e) (être) *adj.* • **1.** to be annoying as all hell • **2.** to be as boring as shit.

example (1): Oh, il est **chiant**, ce professeur. Il nous donne toujours des devoirs à faire pendant nos vacances.

translation: Oh, this teacher is **annoying as all hell**. He always gives us homework to do over our vacation.

as spoken: Oh, il est **chiant**, c'prof. Y nous donne toujours des d'voirs à faire pendant nos vacances.

example (2): Ce cours de mathématiques est **chiant**!

translation: This math class is **boring as shit**!

as spoken: Ce cours de maths, il est **chiant**!

chiards *m.pl.* (vulgar) bathroom, shithouse.

NOTE: This comes from the verb *chier* meaning "to shit."

chiasse (avoir la) *exp.* • **1.** to have the runs • **2.** to be scared shitless • (lit.): to have the shits.

example (1): Je pense que j'ai mangé quelque chose de malsain. Deux heures après mon déjeuner, j'ai eu **la chiasse**.

translation: I think I ate something bad. Two hours after eating lunch, I **got the shits**.

as spoken: J'pense que j'ai mangé quèque chose de malsain. Deux heures après mon dèj, j'ai eu **la chiasse**.

example (2): J'ai eu **la chiasse** quand l'avion a commencé à ballotter.

translation: I was **scared shitless** when the airplane started pitching back and forth.

as spoken: J'ai eu **la chiasse** quand l'avion, il a commencé à ballotter.

NOTE: This comes from the verb *chier* meaning "to shit."

chiasser *v.* to be scared shitless
- (lit.): to have diarrhea.

example: Quand j'ai vu l'ours, j'ai **chiassé**!

translation: When I saw the bear, I **was scared shitless**!

as spoken: [no change]

chiasseur, euse *n.* scaredy-cat
- (lit.): shitter, one who gets scared shitless.

example: Robert a peur d'entrer dans cette maison parce qu'il pense qu'elle est hantée. Quel **chiasseur**!

translation: Robert is scared to go into that house because he think it's haunted. What a **scaredy-cat**!

as spoken: Robert, il a peur d'entrer dans c'te maison pasqu'y pense qu'elle est hantée. Quel **chiasseur**!

NOTE: **chiasse (avoir la)** *exp.* to have diarrhea.

VARIATION: **chiasseux, euse** *n.*

chiée (une) *f.* a lot, a shitload.

example: J'ai une **chiée** de devoirs à faire ce soir.

translation: I have a **shitload** of homework to do tonight.

as spoken: J'ai une **chiée** de d'voirs à faire c'soir.

chier *v.* to shit, crap.

example: Ah, non! Le chien a **chié** sur le nouveau tapis!

translation: Oh, no! The dog **crapped** on the new rug!

as spoken: Ah, non! Le chien, il a **chié** sur l'nouveau tapis!

chier dans la colle *exp.* to exaggerate, to shit (someone) • (lit.): to shit in the glue.

example: Tu as vu un gars qui faisait trois mètres?! Tu **chies dans la colle**, non?

translation: You saw a guy who was three meters (about ten feet) tall? You're **shitting me**, aren't you?

as spoken: T'as vu un gars qui faisait trois mètres?! Tu **chies dans la colle**, non?

NOTE: **gars** *m.* guy, "dude."

SYNONYM -1: **chier dans la confiture** *exp.* • (lit.): to shit in the jam.

SYNONYM -2: **chier dans le pot** *exp.* • (lit.): to shit in the pot.

chier dans les bottes de quelqu'un *exp.* to play a dirty trick on someone • (lit.): to shit in someone's boots.

example: Je ne parle plus à Christophe. Il a **chié dans mes bottes**!

translation: I'm not speaking to Christopher anymore. He **played a shitty trick on me**!

as spoken: J'parle pu à Christophe. Il a **chié dans mes bottes**!

chier dans son froc *exp.* to be scared shitless • (lit.): to shit in one's pants.

example: En voyant s'approcher la tornade, j'ai **chié dans mon froc**.

translation: When I saw the tornado approaching, I was **scared shitless**.

as spoken: [no change]
NOTE: **froc** *m.* pants.

chier dur *exp.* said of a situation that's going to get worse, the shit's going to hit the fan • (lit.): to shit hard.

example: Quand ta mère verra ce que tu as fait de sa cuisine, ça va **chier dur**.

translation: When your mother sees what you did to her kitchen, the **shit's going to hit the fan**.

as spoken: Quand ta mère verra c'que t'as fait d'sa cuisine, ça va **chier dur**.

chier (être à) *exp.* to be extremely boring.

example: Ce film est **à chier**!

translation: This film is **boring as shit**!

as spoken: Ce film, il est **à chier**!

chier (faire) *v.* to bug the shit out of someone • (lit.): to make someone shit.

example: Je peux supporter Alain pour cinq minutes maximum. Après ça, il commence à **me faire chier**.

translation: I can tolerate Alan for five minutes max. After that, he starts **bugging the shit out of me**.

as spoken: J'peux supporter Alain pour cin' minutes maximum. Après ça, y commence à **m'faire chier**.

chierie *f.* • **1.** (said of a situation or thing) a pain in the ass • **2.** a disorderly mess.

example -1: Mon père m'a demandé de peindre l'extérieur de la maison. Quelle **chierie**!

translation: My father asked me to paint the outside of the house. What a **pain in the ass**!

as spoken: Mon père, y m'a d'mandé d'peind' l'extérieur d'la maison. Quelle **chierie**!

example -2: Quelle **chierie**, cette cuisine!

translation: What a **mess** this kitchen is!

as spoken: Quelle **chi'rie**, c'te cuisine!

chier la honte (ne pas) *exp.* to have nerve • (lit.): not to shit shame.

example: En rencontrant mes amis riches, Louis leur a demandé de lui prêter de l'argent. Il **ne chie pas la honte**, ce type!

translation: Upon meeting my rich friends, Louis asked them to lend him some money. He **has some nerve**, that guy!

as spoken: En rencontrant mes amis riches, Louis, y leur a d'mandé d'lui prêter d'l'argent. Y **chie la honte**, c'type!

NOTE: type *m.* (very popular) guy, "dude" / **typesse** *f.* girl, "chick."

chier pour son matricule *exp.* to be in for it, to be sorry • (lit.): to shit for one's I.D. number.

example: Si tu prends la voiture de ton père sans permission, **ça va chier pour ton matricule**!

translation: If you take your father's car without permission, **you're gonna be sorry**!

as spoken: Si tu prends la voiture d'ton père sans permission, **ça va chier pour ton matricule**!

chier (se faire) *exp.* to be bored shitless • (lit.): to make oneself shit (from boredom).

example: Je **me fais chier** à cette soirée. On s'en va?

translation: I'm **bored shitless** at this party. Wanna get out of here?

as spoken: J'**me fais chier** à c'te soirée. On s'en va?

chieur, euse *n.* an annoying or despicable person • (lit.): shitter.

example: Ce **chieur** de patron vient de baisser mon salaire!

translation: That **asshole** of a boss just lowered my salary!

as spoken: Ce **chieur** d'patron, y vient d'baisser mon salaire!

chieur, euse d'encre *n.* paper pusher, desk jockey • (lit.): shitter of ink.

example: Mon père est vice président de sa société mais il a commencé comme **chieur d'encre**.

translation: My father is vice president of his company but he started out as a **paper pusher**.

as spoken: Mon père, il est vice président d'sa société mais il a commencé comme **chieur d'encre**.

chiottes *f.pl.* (extremely popular) the bathroom, the "shit house."

example: Je dois aller aux **chiottes** avant de partir.

translation: I have to go to the **shit house** before we leave.

as spoken: J'dois aller aux **chiottes** avant d'partir.

NOTE: This comes from the verb *chier* meaning "to shit."

chipé(e) pour quelqu'un (être) *adj.* to be infatuated with someone.

chipie *f.* a shrew, often used in reference to an ill-tempered little girl.

chocottes *f.pl.* teeth.

example: Tu as de très belles **chocottes**, toi. Elle sont très blanches!

translation: You have really pretty **teeth**. They're very white!

as spoken: T'as d'très belles **chocottes**, toi. È sont très blanches!

SYNONYM: **dominos** *m.pl.*

chose curieuse (étonnante, etc.) *c.l.* strangely (surprisingly, etc.) enough • (lit.): strange (interesting, etc.) thing.

example: **Chose curieuse**, il a connu mon nom de famille!

translation: **Oddly enough**, he knew my last name!

as spoken: **Chose curieuse**, il a connu mon nom d'famille!

chouchou(te) *n.* teacher's pet.

example: David est le **chouchou** du professeur. C'est pour ça qu'il reçoit toujours de bonnes notes!

translation: David is the teacher's **pet**. That's why he always gets good grades!

as spoken: David, c'est l'**chouchou** du prof. C'est pour ça qu'y r'çoit toujours de bonnes notes!

NOTE -1: **chouchouter** *v.* to spoil (someone).

NOTE -2: It is common to hear *mon chou* or *mon chouchou* used as a term of endearment. Contrary to what one might think, *mon chou* does not mean "my cabbage," rather "my cream puff" as in the popular French pastry *chou à la crème*.

chouette *interj.* (extremely popular) terrific, neat • (lit.): owl.

> example: Ta maison est super **chouette**!

> translation: Your house is really **cool**!

> as spoken: Elle est super **chouette**, ta maison!

cicatrice *f.* vagina • (lit.): scar.

cigare à moustache *m.* penis • (lit.): cigar with a moustache.

cinglé(e) (être) *adj.* to be crazy, nuts.

> example: J'ai entendu dire que tu comptes sauter en parachute demain! Mais, tu es **cinglé**, non?

> translation: I heard that you're planning on going parachuting tomorrow! Are you **nuts**?

> as spoken: J'ai entendu dire qu'tu comptes sauter en parachute demain! Mais, t'es **cinglé**, non?

> **SYNONYM -1:** **dingue (être)** *adj.*

> **SYNONYM -2:** **déménager** *v.* to go crazy • (lit.): to move (out of one's mind).

cinoche *m.* a slang transformation of "*cinéma*," meaning "movie theater."

> example: Tu veux m'accompagner au **cinoche** ce soir?

> translation: You wanna go to the **movies** with me tonight?

> as spoken: Tu veux m'accompagner au **cinoche** c'soir?

cinq contre un (faire) *exp.* (of men) to masturbate • (lit.): to do five against one.

cirer toujours le même bouton *exp.* to harp on a subject • (lit.): always to wax the same button.

> example: Je ne veux pas **cirer toujours le même bouton**, mais tu ne m'écoutes jamais!

> translation: I don't want **to keep harping all the time**, but you never listen to me!

> as spoken: J'veux pas **cirer toujours le même bouton**, mais tu m'écoutes jamais!

clamser *v.* to die, "to croak."

> example: Qu'il fait chaud! Je vais **clamser**!

> translation: Is it ever hot! I'm gonna **die**!

> as spoken: Qu'y fait chaud! J'vais **clamser**!

> **SYNONYM -1:** **clapser** *v.*

> **SYNONYM -2:** **crever** *v.*

clandé *m.* brothel • (lit.): clandestine.

claque *m.* brothel • (lit.): opera hat.

> **NOTE:** Also spelled: *clac*.

claquer *v.* to spend, to blow one's money.

> example: Tu as **claqué** tout ton fric sur une robe?

translation: You **blew** all your money on a dress?

as spoken: T'as **claqué** tout ton fric sur une robe?

NOTE: **fric** *m.* (extremely popular) money.

claquer la porte *exp.* to quit
• (lit.): to slam the door (behind oneself).

example: Si le patron n'arrête pas de m'embêter, je vais finir par **claquer la porte**!

translation: If the boss doesn't stop bugging me, I'm going to end up **quitting**!

as spoken: Si l'patron, il arrête pas d'm'embêter, j'vais finir par **claquer la porte**!

claquer un muscle (se) *exp.* to pull a muscle • (lit.): to burst a muscle.

example: Quand j'ai essayé de bouger mon réfrigérateur, je **me suis claqué un muscle**.

translation: When I tried to move my refrigerator, I **pulled a muscle**.

as spoken: Quand j'ai essayé d'bouger mon frigo, je **m'suis claqué un muscle**.

clarinette *f.* penis • (lit.): clarinet.

clicli *m.* a slang transformation of: *clitoris*.

client *m.* man, guy • (lit.): client.

cliquette *f.* a slang transformation of: *clitoris*.

clito *m.* (extremely popular) a slang transformation of: *clitoris*.

cliton *m.* a slang transformation of: *clitoris*.

clope *f.* (extremely popular) cigarette.

example: Tu peux me prêter une **clope**?

translation: Can you lend me a **cigarette**?

as spoken: Tu peux m'prêter une **clope**?

cloque (être en) *exp.* to be knocked up • (lit.): to be in blister (to look as if one is wrapped up in a big blister).

example: Tu as entendu les nouvelles? Irène est **en cloque** et elle n'a que seize ans!

translation: Did you hear the news? Irene is **knocked up** and she's only sixteen years old!

as spoken: T'as entendu les nouvelles? Irène, elle est **en cloque** et elle a qu'seize ans!

NOTE -1: **mettre en cloque** *exp.* to knock up.

NOTE -2: **encloquer** *v.* to knock up.

coco *m.* • **1.** communist, "commie," "red" • **2.** darling (as in: *mon coco;* my darling).

coco (drôle de) *m.* a strange guy.

cocotte (faire) *f.* to look whorish.

example: Le décor chez elle **fait cocotte**.

translation: Here home **looks like a whorehouse**.

as spoken: Le décor chez elle, y **fait cocotte**.

cocotter v. to have an overpowering odor.

example: Ça **cocotte** dans cette parfumerie!

translation: It **stinks** in this perfume shop!

as spoken: Ça **cocotte** dans c'te parfum'rie!

SYNONYM: **schlinguer** v.

cocu (être) adj. to be cuckold.

SEE: **cocufier**, (next entry).

cocufier v. to be unfaithful to (one's husband).

SEE: **cocu (être)**, (previous entry).

cogne f. a big fight • (lit.): from the verb cogner meaning "to hit" or "to clobber."

coiffer de quelqu'un (se) exp. (outdated but used in jest) to like someone, to have a crush on someone • (lit.): to style one's hair with someone.

coin m. place in general.

example: Ce **coin**-là est tranquille.

translation: This **place** is very peaceful.

as spoken:

1. C'**coin**-là, il est tranquille.

2. Il est tranquille, c'**coin**-là.

collant(e) (être) adj. to be clingy, said of someone who is hard to get rid of • (lit.): to be sticky.

example: Il me suit partout! Qu'est-ce qu'il es **collant**!

translation: He follows me everywhere! Is he ever **clingy**!

as spoken: Il m'suit partout! Qu'est-c'qu'est **collant**!

colle f. a difficult question to answer, "a sticky question" • (lit.): glue.

example: Elle m'a posé une **colle**!

translation: She asked me a **sticky question**!

as spoken: È m'a posé une **colle**!

ALSO: **coller un étudiant** exp. to flunk a student.

coller une prune à quelqu'un exp. to give someone a traffic citation • (lit.): to stick a plum to someone.

example: Je **me suis fait coller une prune** aujourd'hui pour avoir dépassé la limite de vitesse.

translation: I **got a ticket** today for going over the speed limit.

as spoken: Je **m'suis fait coller une prune** aujourd'hui pour avoir dépassé la limite de vitesse.

NOTE -1: **prune** f. traffic citation • (lit.): plum.

NOTE -2: The term "prune" falls into the category of "faux amis" ("false friends") referring to the many words which resemble English words but have different definitions. For example: prune = plum; pruneau = prune.

colombin *m.* turd • (lit.): pigeon manure.

colonne *f.* penis • (lit.): column.

colporter des cancans *exp.* to spread rumors.

example: Voilà Léon! Excuse-moi de **colporter des cancans,** mais j'ai entendu dire qu'il vient de perdre toute sa fortune à Monte Carle!

translation: There's Léon! I'm sorry **to spread rumors** but I heard that he lost his entire fortune in Monte Carlo!

as spoken: V'là Léon! Excuse-moi d'**colporter des cancans,** mais j'ai entendu dire qu'il a perdu toute sa fortune à Monte Carle!

NOTE: As seen in the previous example, the expression "to hear that" is translated in French as *"entendre dire que"* ("to hear said that").

combine *f.* said of a clever ploy or scheme.

example: Je connais la **combine** pour entrer au cinéma sans payer. Suis-moi!

translation: I know a **ploy** to get us into the movie theater without paying. Follow me!

as spoken: J'connais la **combine** pour entrer au ciné sans payer. Suis-moi!

comme de juste *exp.* as (it) might be expected • (lit.): as of just.

example: Au lieu d'étudier, Fabrice est parti en ville. **Comme de juste**, il a échoué à l'examen.

translation: Instead of studying, Fabrice went into town. **As might be expected**, he flunked the exam.

as spoken: Au lieu d'étudier, Fabrice est parti en ville. **Comme de juste**, il a échoué à l'exam.

comme deux ronds de flan (en rester) *exp.* to be dumbfounded • (lit.): to be motionless like two rounds of custard.

example: Martial n'a que vingt ans? Il fait pourtant beaucoup plus âgé! J'**en reste comme deux ronds de flan**!

translation: Martial is only twenty years old? He looks a lot older! I'm **stunned**!

as spoken: Martial, il a qu'vingt ans? Y fait pourtant beaucoup plus âgé! J'**en reste comme deux ronds d'flan**!

NOTE: In the previous sentence, the verb *"faire"* was used to mean "to look." This is an extremely commonly usage for *"faire."* (*Il fait beaucoup plus âgé!* = He looks a lot older!)

comme on fait son lit, on se couche *prov.* you've made your bed, now lie in it • (lit.): since one makes one's bed, on lies down (in it).

example: Tu es toujours à mentir et maintenant ton problème est que personne ne te croit. **Comme on fait son lit, on se couche**.

translation: You're always lying and now your problem is that no one believes you. **You made your bed, now lie in it**.

as spoken: T'es toujours à mentir et maintenant ton problème, c'est que personne te croit. **Comme on fait son lit, on se couche**.

NOTE: In the previous "as spoken" section, the phrase *"on se couche"* was not reduced to *"on s'couche"* since proverbs generally respect proper rules of pronunciation.

comprenette dure (avoir la)
exp. to be dense, thick skulled.

NOTE: This comes from the verb *comprendre* meaning "to understand."

compter les poils (se) *exp.* (of women) to masturbate • (lit.): to count one's (pubic) hairs.

con • **1.** *adj.* stupid, silly • **2.** *m.* jerk, bastard, asshole • **3.** idiot • **4.** (obsolete) vagina.

example (1): Le film que j'ai vu hier soir était tout à fait **con**.

translation: The movie I saw last night was totally **stupid**.

as spoken: Le film que j'ai vu hier soir, il était tout à fait **con**.

example (2): Ce **con** m'a dénoncé au patron parce que je suis arrivé au boulot avec dix minutes de retard.

translation: That **asshole** reported me to the boss because I arrived ten minutes late.

as spoken: Ce **con**, y m'a dénoncé au patron pasque j'suis arrivé au boulot avec dix minutes de r'tard.

example (3): Guy a échoué à tous ces cours à l'école. Quel **con**!

translation: Guy failed all of his courses at school. What an **idiot**!

as spoken: Guy, il a échoué à tous ces cours à l'école. Quel **con**!

NOTE: espèce de con is a common expression meaning "what a huge idiot," or literally, "species of an idiot."

VARIATION: **conneau** *m.*

con (à la) *adj.* stupid.

example: Comme président, il est abominable. Il a des idées **à la con**.

translation: He's a horrible present. His ideas are **stupid**.

as spoken: [no change]

conard *m.*
SEE: connard, *p. 48.*

conasse *f.*
SEE: connasse, *p. 48.*

con comme la lune (être) *exp.* to be as nutty as a fruitcake • (lit.): to be as crazy as the moon.

example: Mon oncle est **con comme la lune**. Il parle à des personnes imaginaires tout le temps.

translation: My uncle is **as nutty as a fruitcake**. He talks to imaginary people all the time.

as spoken: Mon oncle, il est **con comme la lune**. Y parle à des personnes imaginaires tout l'temps.

NOTE: In this expression, *lune* (meaning "moon") is the root word for the English word "lunatic."

SYNONYM -1: **con comme ses pieds (être)** *exp.* • (lit.): to be as crazy as one's feet.

SYNONYM -2: **con comme un balai (être)** *exp.* • (lit.): to be as crazy as a broom.

SYNONYM -3: **con comme un panier (être)** *exp.* • (lit.): to be as crazy as a basket.

conducteur du dimanche *m.*
Sunday driver • (lit.): same.

example: Oh, ce **conducteur du dimanche** conduit trop lentement!

translation: Oh, this **Sunday driver** is driving too slowly!

as spoken: Oh, c'**conducteur du dimanche**, y conduit trop lent!

NOTE: You may have noticed that in the previous *as spoken* paragraph, *lentement* was changed to *lent*. It is very common in French to change adverbs to adjectives.

con (faire le) *exp.* to act like an idiot.

example: Hier soir, Albert a **fait le con** devant tous mes amis. Il a descendu quatre verres de vin et a fini par danser sur la table!

translation: Last night, Albert **acted like an idiot** in front of all my friends. He downed four glasses of wine and ended up dancing on the table!

as spoken: Hier soir, Albert, il a **fait l'con** d'vant tous mes amis. Il a descendu quat' verres de vin et a fini par danser sur la table!

con fini (un) *m.* a total asshole.

example: Antoine a triché. C'est un **con fini**, lui!

translation: Antoine cheated. He's a **total asshole**!

as spoken: Il a triché, Antoine. C't'un **con fini**, lui!

connard(e) *n.* jerk, idiot.

example: Quel **connard**, Jean. Il a mis du sel dans son café en pensant que c'était du sucre.

translation: What an **idiot** Jean is. He put salt in his coffee thinking it was sugar.

as spoken: Quel **connard**, Jean. Il a mis du sel dans son café en pensant qu'c'était du sucre.

connasse *f.* a very derogatory term for an annoying woman, " fucking bitch."

example: Tu ne vas pas croire ce que cette **connasse** de Marie m'a fait hier soir.

translation: You're not going to believe what that **cunt** Marie did to me last night.

as spoken: Tu vas pas croire c'que c'te **connasse** de Marie m'a fait hier soir.

NOTE: This comes from the masculine noun *con* originally meaning "cunt."

conne *f.* (said of women) • **1.** idiot, jerk • **2.** bitch.

example (1): Josette a oublié de venir me chercher à l'aéroport. Quelle **conne**!

translation: Josette forgot to pick me up at the airport. What an **idiot**!

as spoken: Josette, elle a oublié de v'nir m'chercher à l'aéroport. Quelle **conne**!

example (2): Je ne peux pas supporter cette marchande. C'est une vraie **conne**.

translation: I can't stand that saleswoman. She's a real **bitch**.

as spoken: J'peux pas supporter c'te marchande. C't'une vraie **conne**.

NOTE: The difference between **1.** and **2.** simply depends on the context.

conneau *m.* (applies only to a man) a variation of: *con* meaning "bastard."
SEE: **con**, *p. 47.*

connerie *f.* • **1.** foolishness • **2.** dirty trick.

example (1): Arrête tes **conneries**! Nous sommes en public!

translation: Stop your **foolishness**! We're in public!

as spoken: Arrête tes **conn'ries**! On est en public!

example (2): Je ne parle plus à Marc. La semaine dernière il m'a fait une **connerie** inexcusable.

translation: I'm not speaking to Marc anymore. Last week he played an unforgivable **dirty trick** on me.

as spoken: J'parle pu à Marc. La s'maine dernière y m'a fait une **conn'rie** inexcusable.

constipé de l'entre-jambe (être) *exp.* said of a man who can not "get it up" • (lit.): to be constipated in the "in-between" leg.

example: Quand j'ai eu ma première rencontre, j'étais tellement nerveux que j'étais **constipé de l'entre-jambe**.

translation: When I had my first encounter, I was so nervous that I **couldn't get it up**.

as spoken: Quand j'ai eu ma première rencontre, j'étais tellement nerveux qu'j'étais **constipé d'l'entre-jambe**.

copaille *f.* bitch.

coquelicots (avoir ses) *m.pl.* to menstruate • (lit.): to have one's red poppies.

corbuche *f.* ulcer.

example: J'ai mal au ventre. J'espère que je n'ai pas de **corbuche**!

translation: I have a stomach ache. I hope I don't have an **ulcer**!

as spoken: J'ai mal au ventre. J'espère qu'j'ai pas d'**corbuche**!

cornemuse *f.* penis • (lit.): bagpipe.

corniaud(e) • **1.** *adj.* jerky • **2.** *n.* jerk, fool • (lit.): crossbred dog.

cornichon *m.* (applies only to a man) jerk, fool • (lit.): pickle.

corrida *f.* a big fight.

cossard *m.* a lazy individual, a lazy bum.

example: Tu ne fais rien toute la journée. Quel **cossard**!

translation: You don't do a thing all day. What a **lazy bum**!

as spoken: Tu fais rien toute la journée. Quel **cossard**!

NOTE: **avoir la cosse** *exp.* to be lazy.

example: Ce n'est pas la peine de lui demander de nous aider. Il **a la cosse**, lui.

translation: It's no use asking him to help us. The guy's **totally lazy**.

as spoken: C'est pas la peine d'lui d'mander d'nous aider. Il **a la cosse**, lui.

SYNONYM -1: **flemmard** *m.*

NOTE: **flemme (avoir la)** *exp.* to be lazy.

SYNONYM -2: **poil dans la main (avoir un)** *exp.* to be extremely lazy • (lit.): to have a hair in one's hand.

côté de la plaque (être à) *exp.* to be out of one's mind (lit.): to be next to the plaque.

example: Si tu penses que je vais prêter du fric à Augustin, tu es **à côté de la plaque**! Il ne m'a jamais remboursé la dernière fois.

translation: If you think I'm going to lend money to Augustin, you're **out of your mind**. He never reimbursed me the last time.

as spoken: Si tu penses que j'vais prêter du fric à Augustin, t'es **à côté d'la plaque**! Y m'a jamais remboursé la dernière fois.

NOTE: **fric** *m.* (extremely popular) money.

couche (en avoir une) *exp.* (applies to either a man or a woman) to be stupid • (lit.): to have a coat (of paint, etc.) on it (the brain).

VARIATION: **tenir une couche (en)** *exp.*

coucher avec *exp.* (very popular) to fornicate • (lit.): to sleep with.

couilles *f.pl.* (very popular) testicles.

couillon • (as a noun, it applies only to a man) **1.** *m.* idiot • **2.** *adj.* stupid • **3.** *m.pl.* testicles - SEE: *couillons, p. 51.*

example (1): Le patron ne va pas me permettre de prendre mes vacances la semaine prochaine. Il dit que j'ai trop de travail à faire. Quel **couillon**!

translation: The boss isn't going to let me take my vacation next week. He says I have too much work to do. What an **idiot**!

as spoken: Le patron, y va pas m'permett' de prend' mes vacances la s'maine prochaine. Y dit qu'j'ai trop d'travail à faire. Quel **couillon**!

example (2): Josette est venue me chercher au mauvais aéroport! Elle est **couillon**, celle-là!

translation: Josette came to pick me up at the wrong airport! She's **stupid**!

as spoken: Josette, elle est v'nue m'chercher au mauvais aéroport! Elle est **couillon**, celle-là!

NOTE: This comes from the slang feminine plural noun *couilles* meaning "testicles."

couillonnade *f.pl.* nonsense, "bullshit."

example: Ne crois pas ce qu'il te dit. Tout ce qu'il balance ne sont que des **couillonnades**.

translation: Don't believe anything he tells you. Everything that comes out of his mouth is nothing but **bullshit**.

as spoken: Crois pas c'qu'y t'dit. Tout c'qu'y balance n'est qu'des **couillonnades**.

NOTE -1: **balancer** *v.* to jabber, to chatter on about something • (lit.): to throw.

NOTE -2: The term *couillonnades* comes from the feminine plural noun *couilles* meaning "testicles" or "balls."

couillons *m.pl.* testicles.

NOTE: This is a masculine variation of the feminine plural noun *couilles*.

coulante *f.* gonorrhea • (lit.): dripper (since gonorrhea causes the penis to drip).

couler douce (se la) *exp.* to have it easy • (lit.): to flow it sweetly.

example: Il veut devenir riche pour **se la couler douce** un de ces jours.

translation: He wants to become rich and **have it easy** one of these days.

as spoken: Il veut dev'nir riche pour **s'la couler douce** un d'ces jours.

couler un bronze *exp.* to defecate • (lit.): to flow out a bronze (thing).

coup de fil *exp.* telephone call • (lit.): wire call.

example: Grégoire! Tu as un **coup de fil**!

translation: Gregory! You have a **phone call**!

as spoken: Grégoire! T'as un **coup d'fil**!

NOTE: The previous expression, *"fil"* may be replaced with any number of slang synonyms for the word "telephone" such as: *bigophone, bigorneau, cornichon, escargot, phonard, ronfleur, télémuche, etc.*

coup de foudre *m.* love at first sight • (lit.): thunder clap.

example: Quand j'ai vu ta maman pour la première fois, c'était le **coup de foudre**!

translation: When I saw your mother for the first time, it was **love at first sight**!

as spoken: Quand j'ai vu ta maman pour la première fois, c'était l'**coup d'foudre**!

coup de fusil (être le) *exp.* to be exorbitantly expensive, to be a ripoff • (lit.): be a gunshot.

example: Tu as claqué mille balles pour un déjeuner médiocre?! C'est **le coup de fusil**!

translation: You blew a thousand francs for a mediocre lunch?! That's a **ripoff**!

as spoken: T'as claqué mille balles pour un déjeuner médiocre?! C'est l'**coup d'fusil**!

coup de matraque *exp.*
overcharging, rip-off, fleecing
• (lit.): a blow or hit by a bludgeon.

example: Ça coûte mille balles, ça? Quel **coup de matraque**!

translation: That costs a thousand francs? What a **rip-off**!

as spoken: Ça coûte mille balles, ça? Quel **coup d'matraque**!

coup de pompe (avoir un)
exp. to be exhausted • (lit.): to have the pump strike (meaning that one's energy has been pumped out).

example: J'ai fait du sport pendant trois heures aujourd'hui. J'ai un **coup de pompe**, moi!

translation: I played sports for three hours today. I'm **pooped**!

as spoken: J'ai fait du sport pendant trois heures aujourd'hui. J'ai un **coup d'pompe**, moi!

coup sûr (à) *exp.* for sure • (lit.): at sure blow.

example: Cette fois-ci, je vais gagner le tiercé **à coup sûr**.

translation: This time, I'm going to win at the races **for sure**.

as spoken: Cette fois-ci, j'vais gagner l'tiercé **à coup sûr**.

SYNONYM: **sans faute** *exp.*
• (lit.): without fail.

courante (avoir la) *f.* • (lit.): to have the runs.

cousu(e) d'or (être) *exp.* to be filthy rich • (lit.): to be sewn with gold.

example: Tu lui as prêté de l'argent?! Mais il est **cousu d'or**, lui!

translation: You lent him money?! But he's **filthy rich**!

as spoken: Tu lui as prêté d'l'argent?! Mais il est **cousu d'or**, lui!

coûter la peau des fesses *exp.* to cost an arm and a leg • (lit.): to cost the skin of the buttocks.

example: J'aimerais bien acheter cette robe mais elle **coûte la peau des fesses**.

translation: I'd really like to but this dress but it **costs an arm and a leg**.

as spoken: J'aimerais bien ach'ter c'te robe mais è **coûte la peau des fesses**.

VARIATION: **coûter les yeux de la tête** *exp.* • (lit.): to cost the eyes from the head.

coûter un malheureux *exp.* to cost a measly • (lit.): to cost an unfortunate.

example: Ce tricot **coûte un malheureux** cinquante balles.

translation: This sweater **costs a measly** fifty francs.

as spoken: Ce tricot, y **coûte un malheureux** cinquante balles.

cracher dans le bénitier *exp.* to fornicate • (lit.): to spit in the holy water basin.

NOTE: bénitier *m.* vagina
• (lit.): holy water basin.

cracher le morceau *exp.* to fess
up • (lit.): to spit up the morsel (of
truth).

example: Enfin, le voleur a **craché
le morceau**. C'était lui qui avait
braqué la banque.

translation: Finally, the thief
fessed up. He was the one who
pulled the bank job.

as spoken: Enfin, l'voleur, il a
craché l'morceau. C'était lui qui
avait braqué la banque.

NOTE: braquer *v.* to pull an
armed robbery • (lit.): to aim.

cradingue *adj.* filthy.

example: Je ne sais pas comment
elle arrive à habiter dans cette
maison. C'est **cradingue**!

translation: I don't know how she
manages to live in this house. It's
filthy!

as spoken: J'sais pas comment elle
arrive à habiter dans c'te maison.
C'est **cradingue**!

VARIATION -1: crado *adj.*
VARIATION -2: craspèque *adj.*

crados (être) *adj.* (pronounced:
crados with the "s" articulated) to be
filthy.

example: Enlève tes chaussures
avant d'entrer. Elles sont **crados**!

translation: Take off your shoes
before you come in. They're **filthy**!

as spoken: Enlève tes chaussures
avant d'entrer. È sont **crados**!

craignos (être) *adj.* to be scary
(from the verb *craindre* meaning "to
have fear").

example: Je n'aime pas rendre
visite chez Bernard. Il habite dans
un quartier **craignos**.

translation: I don't like visiting
Bernard at his house. He lives in a
scary neighborhood.

as spoken: J'aime pas rend' visite
chez Bernard. Il habite dans un
quartier **craignos**.

cramer *v.* to burn.

example (1): Je **crame** dans cette
chaleur.

translation: I'm **burning up** in
this heat.

as spoken: J'**crame** dans c'te
chaleur.

example (2): J'ai **cramé** le dîner.

translation: I **burned** the dinner.

as spoken: J'ai **cramé** l'dîner.

crâneur, euse *n.* show-off.

example: Sophie parle toujours de
sa fortune. C'est une vraie
crâneuse, celle-là.

translation: Sophie always talks
about her fortune. That girl's a real
show-off.

as spoken: Sophie, è parle toujours
d'sa fortune. C't'une vraie
crâneuse, celle-là.

NOTE: crâner *v.* to show off.
SYNONYM: frimeur, euse *n.*
NOTE: frimer *v.* to show off.

craquer pour quelqu'un
exp. to like someone.

NOTE: **craquant(e) (être)** *adj.* to be seductive, cute, adorable.

crèche *f.* room or bedroom
• (lit.): manger, crib.

example: Ta **crèche** est petite!

translation: Your **bedroom** is small!

as spoken: Elle est p'tite, ta **crèche**!

NOTE: **crécher** *v.* to live, to stay.

example: Ça fait dix ans que je **crèche** ici.

translation: I've **lived** here for ten years.

as spoken:

1. Ça fait dix ans que j'**crèche** ici.
2. Ça fait dix ans qu'je **crèche** ici.

crêper la tignasse (se) *exp.* said of two women in a physical fight where each woman is pulling the other's hair, to cat fight • (lit.): to crimp each other's hair.

NOTE -1: **tignasse** *f.* hair.

NOTE -2: In this expression, any slang synonyms for the slang word *tignasse,* meaning "hair," could be used in its place such as: **tifs** *m.pl.*, **douilles** *f.pl.*, **chignon** *m.*, **crayons** *m.pl.*, etc.

NOTE -3 **crêpage de tignasse** *m.* a hair-pulling fight • (lit.): a crimping of the hair.

cresson sur la cafetière (ne plus avoir de) *exp.* to be bald
• (lit.): to no longer have watercress on the coffeepot.

NOTE: **cafetière** *f.* head, "noggin"
• (lit.): coffeepot.

cresson sur la fontaine (ne plus avoir de) *exp.* to be bald
• (lit.): to no longer have watercress on the fountain.

NOTE: **fontaine** *f.* head, "noggin"
• (lit.): fountain.

cresson sur la truffe (ne plus avoir de) *exp.* to be bald
• (lit.): to no longer have watercress on the truffle.

NOTE: **truffle** *f.* head, "noggin"
• (lit.): truffle.

cresson sur le caillou (ne plus avoir de) *exp.* to be bald
• (lit.): to no longer have watercress on the stone.

NOTE: **caillou** *m.* head, "noggin"
• (lit.): stone.

crétin *m.* jerk • (lit.): cretin.

example: Ce **crétin** de Robert m'a demandé de sortir avec lui demain soir.

translation: That **jerk** Robert asked me to go out with him tomorrow night.

as spoken: Ce **crétin** d'Robert, y m'a d'mandé d'sortir avec lui d'main soir.

crevasse *f.* vagina • (lit.): crevice.

crever les yeux *exp.* to be obvious
• (lit.): to puncture the eyes.

example: "Pourquoi es-tu si heureuse ce matin?"
"**Ça crève les yeux**! Tu n'as pas remarqué la bague de fiançailles que Xavier m'a donné?!"

translation: "Why are you so happy this morning?"
"It's staring you in the face! Didn't you notice the engagement ring Xavier gave me?!"

as spoken: "Pourquoi t'es si heureuse c'matin?"
"Ça crève les yeux! T'as pas r'marqué la bague de fiançailles que Xavier m'a donné?!"

NOTE: **crever** *v.* to die.

example: Je **crève** de faim!

translation: I'm **dying** of hunger!

as spoken: J'**crève** de faim!

crier à tue-tête *exp.* to scream at the top of one's lungs • (lit.): to scream to the point of killing one's head.

example: J'ai du mal à dormir parce que j'ai des voisins qui **crient à tue-tête** à toute heure de la nuit.

translation: I have trouble sleeping because my neighbors **scream at the top of their lungs** at all hours of the night.

as spoken: J'ai du mal à dormir pasque j'ai des voisins qui **crient à tue-tête** à toute heure d'la nuit.

crier merveille *exp.* to rave about something • (lit.): to scream marvel.

example: Quand Suzanne a acheté sa nouvelle bagnole, elle a **crié merveille**. Mais après avoir dépensé plus de quinze mille balles pour des réparations, elle est prête à la pousser dans un précipice.

translation: When Susan bought her new car, she **raved about it**. But after having spent more than fifteen thousand francs on repairs, she's ready to drive it off a cliff.

as spoken: Quand Suzanne a ach'té sa nouvelle bagnole, elle a **crié merveille**. Mais après avoir dépensé plus d'quinze mille balles pour des réparations, elle est prête à la pousser dans un précipice.

crocheter (se) *v.* to fight • (lit.): to hook into each other.
NOTE: **crochetage** *m.* a big fight.

crocs (avoir les) *m.pl.* to be very hungry.

example: Tu **as les crocs**? Ce n'est pas possible! Tu viens de manger, toi!

translation: You're **hungry**? That's impossible! You just ate!

as spoken: T'**as les crocs**? C'est pas possible! Tu viens d'manger, toi!
NOTE -1: The "cs" in **crocs** is silent.
NOTE -2: **crocs** *m.pl.* slang for "teeth."

croquer pour quelqu'un (en) *exp.* to have a crush on someone • (lit.): to crunch some for someone.

croquer (se faire) *exp.* to perform fellatio • (lit.): to get oneself eaten or munched.

croquignoles *f.pl.* testicles • (lit.): biscuits.

croulant (vieux) *m.* an old
person, an "old fart" • (lit.): old
"fall-apart" from the verb *s'écrouler*
meaning "to collapse."

croupe *f.* posterior • (lit.): rump.

croupion *m.* (also spelled:
croupillon) posterior • (lit.): rump (of
bird).

croûton (vieux) *m.* an old
person, an "old fart" • (lit.): old crust.

cruche *f.* (applies only to a woman) a
real idiot, an awkward fool
• (lit.): pitcher.

cruchon *m.* (applies only to a
woman) a real idiot • (lit.): a small
pitcher.

cuisiner *v.* to interrogate, to pump
or grill someone for information
• (lit.): to cook.

example: Les détectives ont
cuisiné le casseur pendant trois
heures.

translation: The detectives
interrogated the burglar for three
hours.

as spoken: Les détectives, y z'ont
cuisiné l'casseur pendant trois
heures.

cuisse légère (avoir la) *exp.*
said of a loose girl, "to have light
ankles" • (lit.): to have the light thigh.

example: Tous les gars draguent
Véronique parce qu'elle a **la
cuisse légère**.

translation: All the guys flirt with
Veronica because she **has light
ankles**.

as spoken: Tous les gars, y draguent
Véronique pasqu'elle a **la cuisse
légère**.

NOTE: draguer *v.* (extremely
popular) to flirt, to cruise (for sexual
encounters).

cul *m.* (very popular) buttocks
• (lit.): ass.

NOTE: Although the literal
translation of *cul* is "ass," it is
considered very mild and does not
carry the same weight as its English
counterpart.

cul (avoir quelqu'un dans le)
exp. to be unable to stand someone
• (lit.): to have someone in the ass.

cul (mon) *interj.* my ass (in response
to a ridiculous comment) • (lit.): my
ass.

example: "Guy m'a dit qu'il est
millionnaire."
"**Mon cul**! Il travaille nuit et jour
pour faire joindre les deux bouts."

translation: "Guy told me he's a
millionaire."
"**My ass**! He works night and day
to make ends meet."

as spoken: "Guy, y m'a dit qu'il est
millionaire."
"**Mon cul**! Y travaille nuit et jour
pour faire joind' les bouts."

**VARIATION: Et mon cul, c'est
du poulet?** *exp.* • (lit.): and my ass
is made of chicken?

culot (avoir du) *exp.* to have
nerve.

example: J'ai invité Rémy à manger chez moi et il n'a pas arrêté de critiquer le dîner. Qu'est-ce qu'il a **du culot**, lui!

translation: I invited Rémy to eat at my house and he didn't stop criticizing the dinner. Does he ever **have nerve**!

as spoken: J'ai invité Rémy à manger chez moi et il a pas arrêté de critiquer l'dîner. Qu'est-c'qu'il a **du culot**, lui!

cyclope *m.* the "one-eyed monster," penis • (lit.): cyclops.

dalle (avoir la) *exp.* (very mild) to be hungry.

example: J'ai **la dalle**, moi. Tu veux aller prendre à manger?

translation: I'm **hungry**. Do you want to get something to eat?

as spoken: J'ai **la dalle**, moi. Tu veux aller prendr'à manger?

SYNONYM: **fringale (avoir la)** *exp.* (very mild).

dans la merde (être) *exp.* to be up shit creek • (lit.): to be in shit.

example: Si je manque mon avion, je suis **dans la merde**!

translation: If I miss my plane, I'm **up shit creek**!

as spoken: Si j'manque mon avion, j'suis **dans la merde**!

dans la poche (être) *exp.* to be a sure bet • (lit.): to be in the pocket.

example: Je suis certain qu'il va t'engager parce que tu as les meilleures qualifications! Ne t'inquiète pas. C'**est dans la poche**!

translation: I'm sure he's going to hire you because you have the best qualification! Don't worry. It's **a sure bet**!

as spoken: J'suis certain qu'y va t'engager pasque t'as les meilleures qualifications! T'inquiète pas. C'**est dans la poche**!

SYNONYM: **cousu d'avance (être)** *exp.* • (lit.): it's already sewn up.

dans le merdier (être) *exp.* to be up shit creek • (lit.): to be in the craphouse.

example: Si mon père découvre ce que j'ai fait à sa voiture, je serai **dans le merdier**!

translation: If my father finds out what I did to his car, I'm **up shit creek**!

as spoken: Si mon père, y découv' c'que j'ai fait à sa voiture, je s'rai **dans l'**merdier!

dans le sac (être) *exp.* to be a sure thing, to be in the bag • (lit.): to be in the sack.

example: Je suis certain que le patron va t'augmenter. C'est **dans le sac**.

translation: I'm sure the boss will give you a raise. It's **in the bag**.

as spoken: J'suis certain que l'patron, y va t'augmenter. C'est **dans l'sac**.

dans les cordes de quelqu'un (être) *exp.* to be up one's alley • (lit.): to be in one's ropes.

example: Je ne sais pas jouer du piano. Ce n'est pas **dans mes cordes**.

translation: I can't play the piano. It's just not **up my alley**.

as spoken: J'sais pas jouer du piano. C'est pas **dans mes cordes**.

dard *m.* penis • (lit.): prick.

dardillon *m.* penis • (lit.): small prick.

déballer ses salades *exp.* to reel off one's problems • (lit.): to uncrate one's salads.

example: Je regrette d'être en retard, mais je suis tombé sur Marcel Clément qui m'a **déballé ses salades** pendant toute une heure!

translation: I'm sorry to be late, but I ran into Marcel Clément who **went on and on about his problems** for an entire hour!

as spoken: J'regrette d'êtr'en r'tard, mais j'suis tombé sur Marcel Clément qui m'a **déballé ses salades** pendant toute une heure!

NOTE: tomber sur quelqu'un *exp.* to run into someone • (lit.): to fall on someone.

déballonné(e) *n.* scardey-cat, one who loses courage.

NOTE: This noun comes from verb *ballonner* meaning "to be bloated like a balloon due to gas." Therefore, *débalonné(e)* could be loosely translated as "deflated of all gas."

débarquer *v.* to arrive without notice • (lit.): to disembark.

example: Il a **débarqué** chez moi à minuit!

translation: **Without any notice, he arrived** at my house at midnight!

as spoken: Il a **débarqué** chez moi à minuit!

débile (être) *adj.* to be moronic.

débloquer *v.* to defecate • (lit.): to free, to unblock.

déboiser la colline (se faire) *exp.* to get a haircut • (lit.): to deforest or untimber one's hill.

example: Je vois que tu **t'es fait déboiser la colline**! Ça te va très bien!

translation: I see you **got a haircut**! It looks really good on you!

as spoken: J'vois qu'tu **t'es fait déboiser la colline**! Ça t'va très bien!

déboucher son orchestre *exp.* to defecate • (lit.): to uncork one's orchestra (of farting sounds).

débourrer sa pipe *exp.* to defecate • (lit.): to remove the tobacco from one's pipe.

NOTE: This expression may also be shorted simply to: *débourrer*.

décharger *v.* to ejaculate • (lit.): to discharge.

dèche (être dans la) *exp.* to be broke • (lit.): to be in poverty.

example: Ça fait deux mois qu'il est **dans la dèche**.

translation: It's been two months that he's been **on the skids**.

as spoken: Ça fait deux mois qu'il est **dans la dèche**.

déchirer la toile *exp.* to fart
• (lit.): to rip the linen.

déclaration (faire sa) *exp.* to pop the question • (lit.): to make one's declaration (of love).

example: Maman! Jean vient de me **faire sa déclaration**! Admire la superbe bague!

translation: Mom! John just **popped the question**! Take a look at the incredible ring!

as spoken: Maman! Jean, y vient d'me **faire sa déclaration**! Admire la suberbe bagouse!

NOTE: In French, an "engagement ring" is called *"une bague de fiançailles"* whereas a "wedding ring" is referred to as *"un anneau de marriage."*

déconner *v.* • **1.** to goof off • **2.** to talk nonsense, to lose it • **3.** to function erratically (said of a machine).

example (1): Arrête de **déconner**. Nous avons du travail à faire.

translation: Stop **goofing off**. We have work to do.

as spoken: Arrête de **déconner**. On a du travail à faire.

example (2): Oh, mais qu'est-ce que tu racontes? Tu **déconnes**!

translation: Oh, what are you talking about? You're talking absolute **nonsense**!

as spoken: Oh, mais qu'est-c'que tu racontes? Tu **déconnes**!

example (3): Je crois qu'il est temps d'acheter un nouvel ordinateur. Celui-ci **déconne** trop.

translation: I think it's time to buy a new computer. This one **acts goofy** all the time.

as spoken: J'crois qu'il est temps d'ach'ter un nouvel ordinateur. Celui-ci, y **déconne** trop.

décrocher un contrat *exp.* to land a contract • (lit.): to unhook a contract.

example: Je viens de **décrocher un contrat** avec le distributeur du Brésil!

translation: I just **landed a contract** with the distributor from Brazil!

as spoken: J'viens d'**décrocher un contrat** avec le distributeur du Brésil!

SYNONYM: **boucler une affaire** *exp.* to clinch a deal • (lit.): to tie up a deal.

décrotter (se) *v.* to clean oneself
• (lit.): to "uncrap" oneself.

example: On doit quitter la maison d'ici cinq minutes! Va **te décrotter** tout de suite!

translation: We have to leave the house in five minutes! Go **clean yourself up** right now!

as spoken: On doit quitter la maison d'ici cin' minutes! Va **t'décrotter** tout d'suite!

NOTE: crotte *f.* turd, crap.

défendre (se) *v.* to make a living, to hustle (said of a prostitute)
• (lit.): to defend oneself.

défoncer *v.* to fornicate • (lit.): to bash in (a door, a wall, etc.).

défoncer la pastille *exp.* to sodomize • (lit.): to smash through the lozenge.

NOTE: pastille *f.* anus
• (lit.): lozenge.

défoncer (se) *v.* • **1.** to have a great time • **2.** to get high on drugs • **3.** to bust one's butt (in order to get something done) • (lit.): to bash oneself down.

défonceuse *f.* penis
• (lit.): penetrator.

dégager *v.* to pack a wallop • (lit.): to clear out (the nose).

example: De boire de la vodka à sec, ça **dégage**!

translation: Drinking vodka straight up **packs a kick**!

as spoken: De boire d'la vodka à sec, ça **dégage**!

dégaine *f.* look • (lit.): outfit.

example: Mais je ne t'ai presque pas reconnu! Tu as une nouvelle **dégaine**!

translation: I almost didn't recognize you! You have a new **look**!

as spoken: Mais j't'ai presque pas r'connu! T'as une nouvelle **dégaine**!

SYNONYM: look *m.* (borrowed from English).

dégobiller *v.* (very popular).

NOTE: This comes from the verb *gober* meaning "to gobble down (food, etc.)."

dégoiser *v.* to talk a lot, to spout off at the mouth.

example: Il est fatigant, lui! Il a **dégoisé** pendant toute une heure au téléphone!

translation: He's so tiring! He **rattled on an on** for an entire hour on the telephone!

as spoken: Il est fatigant, lui! Il a **dégoisé** pendant toute une heure au téléphone!

SYNONYM: baver *v.* • (lit.): to drool.

dégonflard(e) *n.* scardey-cat
• (lit.): one who is deflated of one's courage.

NOTE: dégonfler (se) *v.* to lose one's courage • (lit.): to deflate.

dégonflé(e) *n.* a variation of *dégonflard(e)* meaning "scardey-cat."

dégonfleur, euse *n.* a variation of: *dégonflard(e)* meaning "scardey-cat."

dégorger *v.* to ejaculate • (lit.): to vomit.

déguerpir *v.* to leave quickly.

example: Nous devons **déguerpir** tout de suite pour arriver chez eux à l'heure.

translation: We have **to leave** right away in order to get to their house on time.

as spoken: On doit **déguerpir** tout d'suite pour arriver chez eux à l'heure.

NOTE: **à l'heure** *exp.* on time • (lit.): at the hour.

dégueuler *v.* (extremely popular) to vomit • (lit.): to "unmouth" oneself.

NOTE: This comes from the feminine noun *gueule* meaning "mouth."

dégueuler ses tripes *exp.* to barf one's guts out • (lit.): to "unmouth" one's guts.

example: Le bateau n'a pas arrêté de balotter de long en large. J'ai **dégueulé mes tripes** pendant tout le voyage.

translation: The boat didn't stop tossing back and forth. I **barfed my guts out** during the entire trip.

as spoken: Le bateau, il a pas arrêté d'balotter d'long en large. J'ai **dégueulé mes tripes** pendant tout l'voyage.

NOTE: **gueule** *f.* derogatory for "mouth" or "face" when applied to a

person since its literal translation is "the mouth of an animal."

déjanter *v.* • **1.** to talk nonsense • **2.** to go crazy.

example (1): Ta grand-mère sait piloter un avion?! Mais, tu **déjantes**, toi!

translation: Your grandmother knows how to fly an airplane?! You're **crazy**!

as spoken: Ta grand-mère, è sait piloter un avion?! Mais, tu **déjantes**, toi!

example (2): Cette dame-là parle toute seule depuis une heure. Je crois qu'elle **déjante**!

translation: That woman over there has been talking to herself for an hour. I think she's **going crazy**.

as spoken: Cette dame-là, è parle toute seule depuis une heure. J'crois qu'è **déjante**!

SYNONYM: **déménager** *v.* • (lit.): to move (out of own's mind).

demain la veille (ne pas être) *exp.* said of something that is not likely to happen in the near future • (lit.): tomorrow is the eve (of something happening).

example: **Ce n'est pas demain la veille** qu'il changera son attitude.

translation: **It's not likely to happen soon** that he's going to change his attitude.

as spoken: **C'est pas d'main la veille** qu'y chang'ra son attitude.

de mal en pis (être) *c.l.* to be getting worse and worse.

example: Ils ont des problèmes chez eux. **Ça va de mal en pis**!

translation: There are problems at their house. **Things are getting worse and worse**!

as spoken: Y z'ont des problèmes chez eux. **Ça va d'mal en pis**!

de malheur *adj.* darned, that which causes unhappiness • (lit.): of unhappiness.

example: Oh, cet ordinateur **de malheur** ne marche plus!

translation: Oh, this **darn** computer isn't working any more!

as spoken: Oh, c't'ordinateur **d'malheur** y marche pu!

*Oh, ces vacances **de malheur**!*

(trans.):
*Oh, what a **lousy** vacation!*
(lit.):
*Oh, these vacations **of misfortune**!*

de mauvais poil (être) *exp.* to be in a bad mood • (lit.): to have one's body hair bristle the wrong way.

example: Tu es **de mauvais poil** aujourd'hui! Qu'est-ce qu'il y a?

translation: You're **in a bad mood** today! What's wrong?

as spoken: T'es **d'mauvais poil** aujourd'hui! Qu'est-c'qu'y a?

ANTONYM: de bon poil (être) *exp.* to be in a good mood.

NOTE: à poil (être) *exp.* to be stark naked.

déménager *v.* to go crazy, to go out of one's mind • (lit.): to move out (of one's senses).

démerdard(e) *n.* a shrewd and crafty individual (who can get out of shit) • (lit.): an "unshitter."

example: Georges est un beau **démerdard**. Il peut se tirer d'une mauvaise situation sans problème.

translation: George is a real **shrewd and crafty guy**. He can get himself out of a bad situation without any problem.

as spoken: Georges, c't'un beau **démerdard**. Y peut s'tirer d'une mauvaise situation sans problème.

NOTE: The adjectives *beau* and *belle* are commonly used in everyday French to mean "a real."

démerder (se) *v.* • **1.** to get out of a fix • (lit.): to pull oneself out of shit • **2.** to get by • **3.** to hurry • (lit.): to get the shit out.

example (1): Quelle situation difficile! Je ne sais pas **me démerder**!

translation: What a difficult situation! I don't know how **to dig myself out**!

as spoken: Quelle situation difficile! J'sais pas **m'démerder**!

example (2): J'ai trop de choses à faire. Je ne peux pas **me démerder** tout seul.

translation: I have too much to do. I can't **get through this** alone.

as spoken: J'ai trop d'choses à faire. J'peux pas **m'démerder** tout seul.

example (3): **Démerde-toi**! Nous sommes en retard!

translation: **Hurry**! We're late!

as spoken: **Démerde-toi**! On est en r'tard!

démerdeur *m.* / **démerdeuse** *f.*
one who always manages to land on his / her feet • (lit.): one who can always get out of (deep) shit.

example: Ne t'inquiète pas pour lui. C'est un sacré **démerdeur**.

translation: Don't worry about him. He's a real **survivor**.

as spoken: T'inquiète pas pour lui. C't'un sacré **démerdeur**.

demi-lunes *f.pl.* posterior • (lit.): half moons.

démon de midi (avoir le) *exp.*
to have a midlife crisis, to be a dirty old(er) man or woman • (lit.): to have the devil strike at high noon (i.e. in the middle of one's life).

example: A l'âge de cinquante ans, M. DuBois sort tous les soirs avec différentes nanas. Je suppose qu'il **a le démon de midi**.

translation: At age fifty, Mr. DuBois goes out every night with all sorts of girls. I guess he **has the midlife hornies**!

as spoken: A l'âge de cinquante ans, M. DuBois, y sort tous les soirs avec différentes nanas. Je suppose qu'il **a l'démon d'midi**!

dénicher *v.* to find or uncover something • (lit.): to pull out of the nest.

example: Je pensais que j'avais perdu mon portefeuille! Où l'as-tu **déniché**?

translation: I thought I'd lost my wallet! Where did you **find** it?

as spoken: J'pensais qu'j'avais perdu mon portefeuille! Où tu l'as **déniché**?

déplafonné(e) (être) *adj.* to be nuts • (lit.): to be "unroofed."

dépuceler *v.* to deflower.
NOTE: **puceau** *m.* / **pucelle** *f.* virgin.

der *m.* posterior • (lit.): abbreviation of *derrière* meaning "backside."

derche *m.* posterior.
NOTE: This is a slang transformation of the masculine noun *derrière* meaning "backside."

derge *m.* posterior.
NOTE: This is a slang transformation of the masculine noun *derrière* meaning "backside."

dernier cri (être le) *exp.* to be the latest style • (lit.): to be the last cry.

example: Ce style est le **dernier cri** à Paris.

translation: This style is the **latest fashion** in Paris.

as spoken: Ce style, c'est l'**dernier cri** à Paris.

NOTE: The expression *"dernier cri"* mail also be used as an adjective:

example: C'est une robe **dernier cri**.

translation: It's a dress of the **latest fashion**.

as spoken: C't'une robe **dernier cri**.

dérouiller à sec *exp.* to dry fuck
• (lit.): to rub the rust off (something dry).

dérouiller la mémoire (se) *exp.* to refresh one's memory.

example: Je ne me souviens pas de lui. Je dois **me dérouiller la mémoire**.

translation: I don't remember her. I need to **refresh my memory**.

as spoken: Je m'souviens pas d'lui. J'dois **m'dérouiller la mémoire**.

dérouiller les jambes (se) *v.* to stretch one's legs • (lit.): to take the rust off one's legs.

example: Après avoir passé huit heures dans cet avion, j'ai hâte de **me dérouiller les jambes**!

translation: After having spent eight hours in this airplane, I'm looking forward to **stretching my legs**!

as spoken: Après avoir passé huit heures dans c't'avion, j'ai hâte de **m'dérouiller les jambes**!

dérouiller son petit frère *exp.* to fornicate • (lit.): to rub the rust off one's little brother.

NOTE: **petit frère** *exp.* penis, dick.
• (lit.): little brother.

dérouiller Totor *exp.* to fornicate
• (lit.): to rub the rust off Totor.
NOTE: **Totor** *m.* penis, dick.

derrière *m.* posterior • (lit.): behind.

derrière la porte [le jour de la distribution] (ne pas être) *exp.* said of a stupid person, not to be in line the day brains were handed out • (lit.): not to be behind the door (the day of distribution).

derrière la tête (avoir quelque chose) *exp.* to have something in the back of one's mind
• (lit.): to have something behind the head.

example: Je ne comprends pas ce qu'il veut, Laurent. On ne sait jamais ce qu'il **a derrière la tête**.

translation: I don't understand what Laurent wants. You never know what's **in the back of his mind**.

as spoken: J'comprends pas c'qu'y veut, Laurent. On sait jamais c'qu'il **a derrière la tête**.

descendre *c.l.* a common way of saying "to stay" or "to stop in on."

example: On va **descendre** chez des amis ce soir.

translation: We're going **to stop in on** some friends.

as spoken: On va **descend'** chez des amis ce soir.

dessus (avoir le) *exp.* to have the upper hand • (lit.): to have the top.

example: Il a joué sa dernière carte. Maintenant, c'est moi qui ai **le dessus**.

translation: He played his last card. Now I'm the one with **the upper hand**.

as spoken: Il a joué sa dernière carte. Maintenant, c'est moi qui ai **l'dessus**.

détacher une pastille *exp.* to fart • (lit.): to detach a lozenge.

SEE: pastille, *p. 131.*

détraqué(e) (être) *adj.* said of anything that is not normal (such as one's health, one's mental state, machinery, etc.) • (lit.): to be off track.

deux doigts (être à) *exp.* on the brink • (lit.): to be at two fingers.

example: Ma mère était **à deux doigts** de hurler!

translation: My mother was **on the edge** of screaming!

as spoken: Ma mère, elle était **à deux doigts** de hurler!

deux frangines *f.pl.* posterior • (lit.): two sisters.

devanture *f.* breasts • (lit.): front (of building, etc.).

déveine (avoir la) *f.* to have bad luck.

example: Encore un pneu crevé! J'ai la **déveine**, moi.

translation: Another flat tire! I have **horrible luck**.

as spoken: [no change]

NOTE -1: **veine (avoir de la)** *f.* to have good luck.

NOTE -2: Note that the "*de*" is dropped in the expression *avoir la déveine* but remains in *avoir **de** la veine*.

SYNONYM -1: **manquer de pot** *exp.* to have bad luck • (lit.): to lack luck • **avoir du pot** *exp.* to have good luck.

SYNONYM -2: **poisse (avoir la)** *exp.*

dingo • 1. *m.* idiot • 2. *adj.* (applies to either a man or a woman) crazy.

NOTE: This is a slang variation of: *dingue, (next entry)*.

dingue (être) *adj.* to be crazy.

example: Tu penses que tu vas apprendre l'italien en deux semaines? Mais, tu es **dingue**, non?

translation: You think you'll be able to learn Italian in two weeks? You **crazy** or what?

as spoken: Tu penses que tu vas apprend' l'italien en deux s'maines? Mais, t'es **dingue**, non?

VARIATION: **dingo (être)** *adj.*

SYNONYMS: *barjot* • *cinglé(e)* • *louftingue* • *marteau* • *siphonné(e)* • *etc.*

dis *exclam.* (used at the end of a sentence) wow • (lit.): say.

example: Je n'ai jamais rien vu de si beau, **dis**!

translation: I've never seen anything so beautiful, **wow**!

as spoken: J'ai jamais rien vu d'si beau, **dis**!

NOTE: The exclamation *"dis"* is used when speaking in the informal, whereas *"dites"* would be applied in the formal.

dissiper les malentendus *exp.* to clear the air • (lit.): to dissipate the misunderstandings.

example: Je crois qu'il est temps de **dissiper les malentendus**.

translation: I think it's time **to clear the air**.

as spoken: J'crois qu'il est temps de **dissiper les malentendus**.

dodo *m.* bed.

NOTE: **dodo (faire)** *exp.* (child language) to go "sleepy-bye."

SEE: **dodo faire**, *(next entry)*.

dodo (faire) *exp.* to go to sleep.

example: Je suis lessivé. Je vais **faire dodo**.

translation: I'm exhausted. I'm going **to sleep**.

as spoken: J'suis lessivé. J'vais **faire dodo**.

NOTE: This expression is actually child language yet is used in jest by adults.

VARIATION: **aller au dodo** *exp.*

doigt du milieu *m.* penis
• (lit.): middle finger.

donné(e) (être) *exp.* to be a bargain • (lit.): to be given away.

example: Cinquante balles pour ce déjeuner? C'est **donné**, ça!

translation: Fifty francs for this lunch? That's a **real bargain**!

as spoken: Cinquante francs pour c'déjeuner? C'est **donné**, ça!

donner *v.* to be productive, to put in a full day • (lit.): to give (it one's all).

example: Enfin, il est temps de rentrer. On a **bien donné** aujourd'hui.

translation: Finally, it's time to go home. We really **put in a full day**.

as spoken: Enfin, il est temps d'rentrer. On a **bien donné** aujourd'hui.

donner à cœur joie (s'en) *exp.* to treat oneself to one's heart's delight • (lit.): to give oneself some of it to joyful heart.

example: Nous **nous en sommes donnés à cœur joie** quand on a visité les caves du Bordelais.

translation: We **consumed to our heart's delight** when we visited the wine cellars in the Bordeaux region.

as spoken: On **s'en est donné à cœur joie** quand on a visité les caves du Bordelais.

donzelle *f.* woman or girl.

dossière *f.* prostitute • (lit.): a woman who lies on her back often.

NOTE: This comes from the masculine noun *dos* meaning "back."

douce (se faire une) *exp.* (of men) to masturbate • (lit.): to do oneself a sweet thing.

douloureuse *f.* bill (in a restaurant) • (lit.): that which causes pain.

example: C'est un bon restaurant, mais ça coute trop cher! As-tu vu la **douloureuse**?!

translation: It's a good restaurant but it's too expensive! Did you see the **bill**?!

as spoken: C't'un bon resto, mais ça coute trop cher! T'as vu la **douloureuse**?!

NOTE: Derived from the feminine noun "*douleur*" meaning "pain."

draguer *v.* to cruise.

example: Tu vois la fille de l'autre côté de la salle? Je crois qu'elle te **drague**.

translation: See that girl at the other side of the room? I think she's **cruising** you.

as spoken: Tu vois la fille d'l'aut' côté d'la salle? J'crois qu'è te **drague**.

drapeau-rouge (avoir son) *m.* to menstruate • (lit.): to have one's red flag.

drôle à chier (être) *exp.* • **1.** to be extremely funny in a sarcastic way • **2.** said of something not funny at all.

example (1): Pierrot a glissé sur une peau de banane et a déchiré son froc. C'était **drôle à chier**!

translation: Pierrot slid on a banana peel and tore his pants. It was **hilarious**!

as spoken: Pierrot, il a glissé sur une peau d'banane et a déchiré son froc. C'était **drôle à chier**!

example (2): L'enterrement était **drôle à chier**.

translation: The burial was **wasn't funny at all**.

as spoken: L'enterrement, il était **drôle à chier**.

drôlement con (être) *exp.* to be really silly and fun.

example: Le film que j'ai vu hier soir était **drôlement con**. Tu devrais aller le voir!

translation: The movie I saw last night was **really silly and fun**. You should go see it!

as spoken: Le film que j'ai vu hier soir, il était **drôlement con**. Tu devrais aller l'voir!

du con *exp.* (used to call someone) "hey, you moron!"

example: Hé, **du con**! Tu as pris mon livre par accident!

translation: Hey, **you moron**! You took my book by mistake!

as spoken: Hé, **du con**! T'as pris mon liv' par accident!

dure (l'avoir) *exp.* to have an erection • (lit.): to have it hard.

écervelé(e) • **1.** *n.* scatterbrain • **2.** *adj.* scatterbrained • (lit.): to be "unbrained."

échanger des politesses *exp.* to fight.

> **NOTE:** This is an ironic expression literally meaning "to exchange polite words."

écliper (s') *v.* to leave quickly, to vanish • (lit.): to eclipse oneself.

> example: Je **me suis éclipsé** avant la conférence.
>
> translation: I **snuck out** before the lecture.
>
> as spoken: Je **m'suis éclipsé** avant la conférence.
>
> **NOTE:** In the sentence above, the term *conférence* was translated as "lecture" not "conference." (In French, *une lecture* is "a reading.") These misinterpretations falls under the heading of *faux amis*; the many terms which appear to be similar in French and English, yet have different definitions.

écoper *v.* to receive something that is unwanted.

> example: C'est toujours moi qui **écope**!
>
> translation: I'm always the one who gets **blamed** for everything!
>
> as spoken: [no change]
>
> **SYNONYM:** **trinquer** *v.*

écrase-merdes *m.pl.* big shoes, shit kickers • (lit.): shit-smashers.

> example: Tu ne peux pas porter des **écrase-merdes** comme ça avec ta nouvelle robe!
>
> translation: You can't wear **shit kickers** like that with your new dress!
>
> as spoken: Tu peux pas porter des **écrase-merdes** comme ça avec ta nouvelle robe!

écraser *v.* to shut up • (lit.): to crush.

> example: **Ecrase**! Tu parles trop, toi!
>
> translation: **Put a sock in it**! You talk too much!
>
> as spoken: [no change]
>
> **NOTE:** This term is not vulgar but it is rather harsh and should be used with caution.

écumer les bars *exp.* to barhop • (lit.): to skim bars.

> example: Il aime passer le vendredi soir à **écumer les bars**.
>
> translation: He likes to spend Friday nights **bar hopping**.
>
> as spoken: Il aime passer l'vendredi soir à **écumer les bars**.

égoutter Popol *exp.* to urinate • (lit.): to drain Popol.

> **NOTE -1:** **Popol** *m.* penis, dick.
> **NOTE -2:** Also spelled: *Popaul*.

égoutter sa sardine *exp.* to urinate • (lit.): to drain one's sardine.

égoutter (se l') *exp.* to urinate • (lit.): to drain it.

égoutter son colosse *exp.* to urinate • (lit.): to drain one's giant.

égoutter son cyclope *exp.* to ejaculate • (lit.): to drain one's cyclops.

> **NOTE:** The masculine noun *cyclope* is a synonym for "penis" or "one-eyed monster."

emballer (s') *v.* to get all worked up • (lit.): to wrap oneself up (in a tight ball due to anxiety).

example: Ne **t'emballe** pas. Il arrivera bientôt.

translation: Don't **get yourself all worked up**. He'll be here soon.

as spoken: **T'emballe** pas. Il arriv'ra bientôt.

emmerdant(e) (être) *adj.* • **1.** to be annoying, to be a pain in the ass • **2.** to be boring.

example (1): Oh, ces nouveaux voisins sont **emmerdants**. Il font du bruit toute la nuit!

translation: Oh, these new neighbors are **pains in the ass**. They make noise all night!

as spoken: Oh, ces nouveaux voisins, y sont **emmerdants**. Y font du bruit toute la nuit!

example (2): Les acteurs n'étaient pas du tout amusants. Quel film **emmerdant**!

translation: The actors weren't funny at all. What a **boring** movie!

as spoken: Les acteurs, y z'étaient pas du tout amusants. Quel film **emmerdant**!

emmerdé(e) (être) *adj.* to be worried and anxious.

example: Mais tu as l'air **emmerdé**. Qu'est-ce qu'y a?

translation: You look really **worried**. What's wrong?

as spoken: Mais t'as l'air **emmerdé**. Qu'est-c'qu'y a?

emmerdements *m.pl.* real problems.

example: Depuis qu'il a quitté son boulot, Jean n'a que des **emmerdements** financiers.

translation: Ever since Jean quit his job, he's had nothing but financial **troubles**.

as spoken: Depuis qu'il a quitté son boulot, Jean, il a qu'des **emmerdements** financiers.

> **NOTE:** **boulot** *m.* (extremely popular) work, job, the "grind."

emmerder *v.* to bug the shit out of someone.

example: Le patron commence à m'**emmerder**. Il me donne trop de responsabilités sans m'augmenter.

translation: The boss is starting to **bug the shit out me**. He's giving too many responsibilities without giving me a raise.

as spoken: Le patron, y commence à m'**emmerder**. Y m'donne trop d'responsabilités sans m'augmenter.

emmerder quelqu'un *v.* • **1.** to annoy someone, to bug the shit out of someone • **2.** to tell someone to fuck off.

example (1): Il **m'emmerde** avec toutes ses questions.

translation: He **bugs the shit out of me** with all of his questions.

as spoken: Y **m'emmerde** avec toutes ses questions.

example (2): Voilà Marguerite! Je **l'emmerde**! Elle a couché avec mon petit ami!

translation: There's Marguerite! She can go **fuck off**! She went to bed with my boyfriend!

as spoken: V'là Marguerite! J'**l'emmerde**! Elle a couché avec mon p'tit ami!

emmerder (s') *v.* to be bored to death, to be bored shitless.

example: Je **m'emmerde** dans cette classe de philosophie!

translation: I'm **bored shitless** in this philosophy class!

as spoken: J'**m'emmerde** dans c'te classe de philo!

emmerdeur, euse *n.* an annoying person, a pain in the ass,

example: Quel **emmerdeur**, ce professeur. Il nous a donné un tas de devoirs à faire ce weekend.

translation: What a **pain in the ass** this professor is. He gave us a pile of homework to do over the weekend.

as spoken: Quel **emmerdeur**, c'prof. Y nous a donné un tas de d'voirs à faire c'weekend.

empaffer *v.* to sodomize.

empaler *v.* to sodomize • (lit.): to impale.

empapaouter *v.* to sodomize.

empétarader *v.* to sodomize • (lit.): to receive something through the back.

NOTE: This is an "antonym" of the verb *pétarader* meaning "to backfire."

encadrer quelqu'un (ne pas pouvoir) *v.* to be unable to stand someone • (lit.): to be unable to frame someone.

encaisser quelqu'un (ne pas pouvoir) *v.* to be unable to stand someone • (lit.): to be unable to cash in someone.

encarrer *v.* to enter.

example: La prochaine fois que tu **encarres** dans ma chambre sans permission, je te casse la gueule!

translation: The next time you **enter** my room without permission, I'll clobber you!

as spoken: La prochaine fois qu't'**encarres** dans ma chamb' sans permission, j'te casse la gueule!

NOTE: As learned in lesson one, the feminine noun *gueule* (literally "the mouth of an animal") means "mug" or "mouth" in slang.

enceinte jusqu'aux dents (être) *exp.* to be pregnant out to here • (lit.): to be pregnant up to one's teeth.

example: Ma mère était **enceinte jusqu'aux dents** mais même le docteur ne savait pas qu'elle allait accoucher de jumeaux!

translation: My mother was
pregnant out to here but even
the doctor didn't know she was
going to have twins!

as spoken: Ma mère, elle était
enceinte jusqu'aux dents mais
même le docteur, y savait pas
qu'elle allait accoucher de jumeaux!

*Marie est **enceinte
jusqu'aux dents**!*

(trans.):
*Marie is **pregnant out to here**!*
(lit.):
*Marie is **pregnant up to her teeth**!*

encloquer *v.* to knock up.

enculé(e) de ta race *exp.*
(extremely vulgar) fucker
• (lit.): fucked of your race.

SEE: **enculer**, *p. 71.*

enculer *v.* to sodomize.

NOTE -1: This comes from the
masculine noun *cul* meaning "ass."

NOTE -2: This verb originally meant
"to sodomize" and is now mainly
used to mean "to fornicate."

enfiler des perles *exp.* to laze
around and do nothing • (lit.): to
string pearls.

example: Je ne suis pas venu pour
enfiler des perles! Au travail!

translation: I didn't come here **to
just sit around**! Let's get to work!

as spoken: J'suis pas v'nu pour
enfiler des perles! Au travail!

enfiler (s') *v.* to consume
something quickly • (lit.): to thread
oneself.

example: Je **me suis enfilé** trois
glaces de suite hier.

translation: I **downed** three ice
cream cones one after the other
yesterday.

as spoken: Je **m'suis enfilé** trois
glaces de suite hier.

NOTE: The verb *"enfiler"* (literally
meaning "to thread a needle, etc.) is
humorously used in French slang to
mean "to stuff something down a
narrow tube (i.e. one's throat)."

SYNONYM -1: **avaler** *v.* • (lit.): to
swallow.

SYNONYM -2: **descendre** *v.*
• (lit.): to down.

ALSO: **enfiler (s')** *v.* to fornicate
• (lit.): to thread oneself.

enflé(e) *m.* fat-head • (lit.): swollen
(one).

enflure *m.* idiot • (lit.): swelling.

enfoirer *v.* to sodomize • (lit.): to
"enter something into one's anus."

NOTE: This is an "antonym" of the verb *foirer* meaning "to have diarrhea."

englander *v.* to sodomize • (lit.): to insert the acorn (which looks like the head of a penis).

NOTE: This comes from the masculine noun *gland* meaning "acorn" and has taken the slang connotation of "penis, dick" due to its shape.

engrossée (être) *adj.* (pejorative) to be pregnant, to be knocked up • (lit.): to be fattened up (used for animals).

NOTE: **engrosser** *v.* to knock up.

engueulade *f.* a quarrel.

NOTE: **engueuler (s')** *v.* to yell and scream and each other.

engueuler *v.* to yell (at someone).

example: Ma mère m'a **engueulé** parce que je suis rentré après minuit.

translation: My mother **yelled** at me because I came home past midnight.

as spoken: Ma mère, è m'a **engueulé** pasque j'suis rentré après minuit.

NOTE: This comes from the slang word **gueule** *f.* which is derogatory for "mouth." Therefore, **engueuler** might be literally translated as "to mouth off at (someone)."

ALSO: **s'engueuler avec quelqu'un** *exp.* to have a verbal fight with someone.

example: Mais qu'est-ce que tu as? Tu **t'es engueulé avec** tout le monde au bureau ce matin!

translation: What's with you? You've **fought with** everyone in the office this morning!

as spoken: Mais qu'est-c'que t'as? Tu **t'es engueulé avec** tout l'monde au bureau c'matin!

enjamber *v.* to fornicate • (lit.): to put in one's "third leg."

NOTE: This comes from the feminine noun *troisième jambe* meaning "third leg" or "penis, dick."

en l'air (foutre quelqu'un)
exp. to kill someone • (lit.): to throw someone up in the air.

example: Elle a **foutu en l'air** son mari quand elle l'a trouvé au lit avec une autre femme.

translation: She **wasted** her husband when she found him in bed with another woman.

as spoken: Elle a **foutu en l'air** son mari quand è l'a trouvé au lit avec une aut' femme.

en moins de deux *exp.* quickly • (lit.): in less than two (seconds).

example: J'arrive **en moins de deux**.

translation: I'll be there **in a flash**.

as spoken: [no change]

entendre comme cul et chemise (s') *exp.* to get along extremely well (with someone) • (lit.): to get along like one's buttocks and shirt.

example: Marius et Rémy étaient ennemis depuis longtemps, mais maintenant ils **s'entendent comme cul et chemise**.

translation: Marius and Rémy were enemies for a long time, but now they **get along famously**.

as spoken: Marius et Rémy, y z'étaient ennemis depuis longtemps, mais maintenant y **s'entendent comme cul et ch'mise**.

enticher de quelqu'un (s') *v.* to have a light crush on someone.

entrée de service *f.* anus
• (lit.): service entrance.

entrer dans le jeu *exp.* to play by the rules, to "play ball" • (lit.): to enter in the game.

example: S'il refuse d'**entrer dans le jeu**, sa vie dans cette société sera très dure.

translation: If he refuses **to play ball**, his life with this company will be very hard.

as spoken: S'y r'fuse d'**entrer dans l'jeu**, sa vie dans cette société, è s'ra très dure.

VARIATION: **jouer le jeu** *exp.*

entuber *v.* • **1.** to sodomize • **2.** to con someone, to rip someone off (*se faire entuber*; to get ripped off) (lit.): to put one's "tube" into something.

envoyer chier quelqu'un *exp.* to tell someone to fuck off • (lit.): to send someone to go shit.

example: Quand il m'a accusé d'avoir menti, je **l'ai envoyé chier**!

translation: When he accused me of lying, I **told him to fuck himself**!

as spoken: Quand y m'a accusé d'avoir menti, j'**l'ai envoyé chier**!

SYNONYM: **envoyer paître** *exp.*
• (lit.): to send out to pasture.

envoyer en l'air (s') *exp.* • **1.** to masturbate • **2.** to fornicate • (lit.): to send oneself into the air.

envoyer quelqu'un se faire foutre *exp.* to tell someone to go fuck off.

example: S'il continue à t'énerver, tu n'as qu'à **l'envoyer se faire foutre**!

translation: If he keeps bugging you, all you have to do is to **tell him to fuck off**!

as spoken: S'y continue à t'énerver, t'as qu'à **l'envoyer s'faire foutre**!

envoyer sa came / la purée / la sauce / la semoule *exp.* to ejaculate • (lit.): to send out one's junk / purée / sauce / cream of wheat.

NOTE: **came** *f.* • **1.** sperm • **2.** junk (in general) • **3.** personal belongings, one's "stuff" • **4.** cocaine.

éponger un retard *exp.* to make up for lost time • (lit.): to sponge up a tardiness.

example: Vite! Il faut **éponger le retard**!

translation: Hurry! We have **to make up for lost time**!

as spoken: Vite! Faut **éponger le r'etard**!

éponges *f.pl.* lungs • (lit.): sponges.

example: Pourquoi est-ce que tu fumes? Ce n'est pas bon pour les **éponges**.

translation: Why do you smoke? It's not good for the **lungs**.

as spoken: Pourquoi tu fumes? C'est pas bon pour les **éponges**.

époques (avoir ses) *exp.* to menstruate • (lit.): to have one's epoch or era.

épouser la forme de *exp.* to cling • (lit.): to marry the form of.

example: Ta chemise est trop serrée, non? Elle **épouse la forme de** ton corps!

translation: Your shirt is too small, don't you think? It's **clinging to** your body!

as spoken: Ta ch'mise, elle est trop serrée, non? Elle **épouse la forme de ton corps!**

épouser la veuve Poignet *exp.* (of men) to masturbate • (lit.): to marry the Widow Wrist.

escagasser *v.* (used in southern France) to fight.

espèce d'ordure *f.* lowlife scum • (lit.): species of trash.

example: **Espèce d'ordure**! Tu as ruiné mon tricot!

translation: **You lowlife scum**! You ruined my sweater!

as spoken: **Espèce d'ordure**! T'as ruiné mon tricot!

essoreuse *f.* a prostitute who squeezes her clients dry of all their money • (lit.): spin dryer.

étau *m.* vagina • (lit.): vise.

étendre (se faire) *exp.* to flunk, to blow a test • (lit.): to get oneself stretched out.

example: Je **me suis fait étendre** à mon examen!

translation: My test went badly. I **totally blew it**!

as spoken: Je **m'suis fait étendre** à mon exam!
SYNONYM: coller (se faire) *v.*

Et merde! *interj.* "What the hell!"

example: **Et merde**! Je vais prendre un dessert.

translation: **What the hell**! I'm going to get a dessert.

as spoken: **Et merde**! J'vais prendr'un dessert.
VARIATION: Et puis merde! *exp.*

étoffe (avoir l') *exp.* to have the makings (of something) • (lit.): to have the fabric.

example: Elle **a l'étoffe** d'un bon médecin.

translation: She **has the makings** of a fine doctor.

as spoken: È **a l'étoffe** d'un bon méd'cin.

étourdi(e) (être) *adj.* to be scatterbrained.

et patati et patata *exp.* and blah, blah, blah.

example: Elle a dégoisé pendant une heure sur ses études, sur ses projets, sur ses amis, **et patati et patata**.

translation: She rattled on for an entire hour about her studies, about her projects, about her friends, **and blah, blah, blah**.

as spoken: Elle a dégoisé pendant une heure sur ses études, sur ses projets, sur ses amis, **et patati et patata**.

étrangler Popaul *exp.* (of men) to masturbate • (lit.): to strangle Popaul.

NOTE -1: Also spelled: *Popol*.

NOTE -2: **Popaul / Popol** *m.* penis, "dick."

étron *m.* turd.

example: C'est dégoutant! Il y a des **étrons** de chiens sur tout le trottoir!

translation: This is disgusting! There are dog **turds** all over the sidewalk!

as spoken: C'est dégoutant! Y a des **étrons** d'chiens sur tout l'trottoir!

évacuer le couloir *exp.* to vomit • (lit.): to evacuate the hall.

évaporé(e) (être) • **1.** *n.* to be an irresponsible and scatterbrained person • **2.** *adj.* to be irresponsible, flighty, scatterbrained • (lit.): to be evaporated.

évidence (à l') *adv.* evidently • (lit.): at the evidence.

example: Marcel a volé mon argent! J'ai toujours pensé que je pouvais me fier à lui, mais je ne peux pas **à l'évidence**!

translation: Marcel stole my money! I always thought I could trust him, but **evidently** I can't!

as spoken: Marcel, il a volé mon argent! J'ai toujours pensé qu'j'pouvais m'fier à lui, mais j'peux pas **à l'évidence**!

exact *adv.* a common abbreviation of *exactement* meaning "exactly."

example: "Tu crois qu'il a volé le moto?" "**Exact**!"

translation: "You think he stole the motorcycle?" "**Exactly**!"

as spoken: "Tu crois qu'il a volé l'moto?" "**Exact**!"

exam *m.* a popular abbreviation of "*examen*" meaning "test."

example: La semaine prochaine, ma mère va passer son **exam** de conduite.

translation: Next week, my mother is going to take her driving **test**.

as spoken: La s'maine prochaine, ma mère, è va passer son **exam** d'conduite.

expliquer (s') *v.* to fight • (lit.): to explain oneself.

VARIATION: **s'expliquer dehors** *exp.* to fight outside, to step outside • (lit.): to explain oneself outside.

exprès (faire quelque chose) *exp.* to do something on purpose.

example: Georgette a cassé mon poste de télévision et l'a **fait exprès**!

translation: Georgette broke my television and did it **on purpose**!

as spoken: Georgette, elle a cassé mon poste télé et l'a **fait exprès**!

fada (être) *adj.* (Southern French — applies to either a man or a woman) to be crazy, cracked.

faillot *m.* brown-noser, one who sucks up • (lit.): bean.

example: Georges est un sacré **faillot**. C'est pour ça que le patron lui donne toujours des augmentations.

translation: George is a real **brown-noser**. That's why the boss always gives him raises.

as spoken: C't'un sacré **faillot**, Georges. C'est pour ça que l'patron, y lui donne toujours des augmentations.

faire chier (ne pas se) *exp.*
• **1.** to have nerve • **2.** to have a good time (lit.): not to make oneself shit.

example (1): Marc s'est invité à mon dîner. Il **ne se fait pas chier**, c'est sûr!

translation: Marc invited himself to my dinner party. He **really has some nerve**, that's for sure.

as spoken: Marc, y s'est invité à mon dîner. Y **s'fait pas chier**, c'est sûr!

example (2): Je **ne me fais pas chier** à cette soirée!

translation: I'm **having a great time** at this party!

as spoken: Je **m'fais pas chier** à c'te soirée!

NOTE: Using a negative to express something positive, as seen in example (2), is extremely popular in French. For example, to signify that something tastes good would commonly be said as: *C'est pas mauvais, ça!* rather then *C'est bon, ça!*

faire dans la dentelle *exp.* to put on kid gloves • (lit.): to do in the lace (suggesting that with lace, as with certain people, one must be very careful).

example: Quand tu lui parles, ne manque pas de **faire dans la dentelle**. Elle est très sensible.

translation: When you speak to her, make sure you **put on kid gloves**. She's very sensitive.

as spoken: Quand tu lui parles, manque pas d'**faire dans la dentelle**. Elle est très sensible.

faire de la bile (se) *exp.* to get all worked up, to worry • (lit.): to make oneself bilious.

example: **Ne te fais pas de bile**. Je suis sûr qu'elle arrivera bientôt!

translation: **Don't worry**. I'm sure she'll be here soon!

as spoken: **Te fais pas d'bile**. J'suis sûr qu'elle arriv'ra bientôt!

faire des mamours à quelqu'un *exp.* to be kissy-kissy with someone, to be all lovey-dovey with someone, to caress someone.

example: Ils **se font des mamours** en public. Ça m'énerve, ça!

translation: They're **all touchy-feely with each other** in public. I can't stand that!

as spoken: Y **s'font des mamours** en public. Ça m'énerve, ça!

SYNONYM -1: **faire des papouilles à quelqu'un** *exp.* to touch someone all over • (lit.): to make sexual touches to someone.

SYNONYM -2: **peloter** *v.* to grope, to neck • (lit.): to ball up together like a ball of wool.

NOTE: **pelotage** *m.* groping, necking.

example: On a fait une partie de **pelotage** pendant trois heures hier soir!

translation: We engaged in a **makeout session** for three hours last night!

as spoken: On a fait une partie d'**pelotage** pendant trois heures hier soir!

faire la bête à deux dos *exp.* to fornicate • (lit.): to make like the beast with two backs (said of two people who are fused together during sex).

faire la gueule *exp.* **1.** to pout, frown • **2.** to give someone the cold shoulder.

example (1): Ma petite sœur **fait la gueule** parce que mes parents lui ont donné une poupée pour son anniversaire, alors qu'elle voulait un vélo.

translation: My little sister is **pouting** because my parents gave her a doll for her birthday, while she wanted a bicycle.

as spoken: Ma p'tite sœur, è **fait la gueule** pasque mes parents, y lui ont donné une poupée pour son anniversaire, alors qu'è voulait un vélo.

example (2): Ça fait deux jours que Thiery me **fait la gueule**.

translation: Thiery's been giving me the **cold shoulder** for two days.

as spoken: Ça fait deux jours que Thiery, y m'**fait la gueule**.

NOTE: The difference between definitions **1.** and **2.** depends on the context.

faire le / la *c.I.* to act like a • (lit.): to make the.

example: Arrête de **faire l'**idiot!

translation: Stop **acting like an** idiot!

as spoken: [no change]

faire le merdeux / la merdeuse *exp.* to have a high opinion of oneself, to think one's shit doesn't stink.

example: Après son augmentation, Cécile **fait la merdeuse**.

translation: After her promotion, Cecily **thinks her shit doesn't stink**.

as spoken: Après son augmentation, Cécile, è **fait la merdeuse**.

faire les infos de vingt heures *exp.* everyone is talking about it • (lit.): it made the eight o'clock news (which is the time of the most popular news broadcast in France).

example: Tu ne sais pas ce qui s'est passé hier soir? **Ça a fait les infos de vingt heures**!

translation: You don't know what happened last night? **Everyone's been talking about it**!

as spoken: Tu sais pas c'qui s'est passé hier soir? **Ça a fait les infos d'vingt heures**!

NOTE: In this expression, the term *"infos"* is a popular abbreviation of *"informations"* meaning "the news." In addition, in France the 24-hour clock is typically used. Therefore, *"vingt heures"* (commonly written "20h") is 8:00pm.

faire pipi *exp.* to urinate • (lit.): to go pee-pee.

faire pleurer le costaud *exp.* to urinate • (lit.): to make the hefty one cry.

faire pleurer le petit Jésus *exp.* to urinate • (lit.): to make little Jesus cry.

faire sa goutte *exp.* to urinate • (lit.): to do one's drop.

faire (se) *exp.* to be getting • (lit.): to make itself.

example: Il **se fait** sombre dehors.

translation: It's **getting** dark outside.

as spoken: Y **s'fait** sombre dehors.

faire une carte *exp.* to have a wet dream • (lit.): to make a map.

faire une partie de balayette *exp.* to fornicate • (lit.): to "play a hand of" small broom.

NOTE: **balayette** *f.* penis, dick • (lit.): small broom.

faire une partie d'écarté *exp.* to fornicate.

NOTE: This is a pun based on the expression *faire une partie de cartes* meaning "to play a hand of cards." However, in this expression, the noun *cartes* has been replaced with the adjective *écarté* meaning "spread apart" as with one's legs during sex.

faire une partie de jambes en l'air *exp.* to fornicate • (lit.): to play a game of "legs in the air."

faire une vidange (se) *exp.* to urinate • (lit.): to do an emptying of oneself.

farcir quelqu'un (se) *v.*
• **1.** to fornicate • **2.** to put up with someone (ex: *Je ne peux pas supporter mon nouveau voisin, mais il faut se le farcir!*; I can't stand my new neighbor but I have to put up with him! • (lit.): to stuff oneself with someone.

farfelu *m.* (applies to either a man or a woman) a total nutcase.

farfouiller *v.* to rummage (without taking much care).

example: J'ai **farfouillé** dans tous les tiroirs pour essayer de dénicher mes clés.

translation: I **rummaged** in all the drawers trying to find my keys.

as spoken: J'ai **farfouillé** dans tous les tiroirs pour essayer d'dénicher mes clés.

fatma *f.* (from Arabic) commonly used to mean "woman" or "wife."

fatmuche *f.* a slang variation of *fatma* meaning "woman" or "girl."

faubourg *m.* posterior
• (lit.): suburb, outlying part (of town).

fauché(e) (être) *adj.* to be broke
• (lit.): to be mowed down.

example: Je ne peux pas t'accompagner au cinéma ce soir. Je suis **fauché**.

translation: I can't go to the movies with you tonight. I'm **broke**.

as spoken: J'peux pas t'accompagner au cinéma c'soir. J'suis **fauché**.

SYNONYM: **à sec (être)** *exp.*
• (lit.): to be all dried up.

NOTE: The verb *faucher* (literally meaning "to mow, cut, or reap") means "to steal" in French slang. For example:

example: C'est un voleur! Il vient de **faucher** mon portefeuille!

translation: He's a thief! He just **stole** my wallet!

as spoken: C't'un voleur! Y vient d'**faucher** mon portefeuille!

fée du logis (être une) *exp.* to be a wiz around the house • (lit.): to be a fairy in the home.

example: J'adore ta maison. Elle n'est jamais en désordre. Tu es une vraie **fée du logis**, toi.

translation: I love your house. It's never messy. You're a real **wiz in the house**.

as spoken: J'adore ta maison. Elle est jamais en désordre. T'es une vraie **fée du logis**, toi.

Nancy est une vraie **fée du logis.**

(trans.):
Nancy is a real **wiz around the house**.

(lit.):
Nancy is a real **house fairy**.

feignasse *f.* a lazy person, a lazy bum.

> example: Tu vas demander à Léon de te donner un coup de main? Bonne chance! C'est une **feignasse** de premier ordre!
>
> translation: You're going to ask Leon to give you a hand? Good luck! He's a big-time **lazy bum**!
>
> as spoken: Tu vas d'mander à Léon de te donner un coup d'main? Bonne chance! C't'une **feignasse** de premier ordre!
>
> **NOTE -1:** This comes from the noun *feignant(e)* meaning "lazy."
>
> **NOTE -2:** Also spelled: *faignasse*.

fêlé(e) (être) *adj.* • (lit.): to be nuts, cracked.

fêlure (avoir une) *f.* to be crazy, nuts • (applies to either a man or a woman) (lit.): to have a crack.

femelle *f.* woman • (lit.): female.

fendue *f.* (very derogatory) woman • (lit.): slit.

fente *f.* vagina • (lit.): crack, crevice, split.

ferme la *interj.* shut up • (lit.): shut it.

> example: Oh, **ferme la**! Tu racontes des bêtises!
>
> translation: Oh, **shut up**! You're talking nonsense!
>
> as spoken: [no change]
>
> **NOTE:** In this interjection, *la* represents *la bouche* meaning "the mouth."
>
> **VARIATION:** **La ferme!** *interj.* Shut up!

> **NOTE:** This is a shortened version of: *Que tu la ferme!* meaning "Would you just shut it!"

fessier *m.* posterior • (lit.): buttock (academic term).

> **NOTE:** This comes from the feminine noun *fesse* meaning the "cheek of the buttock."

feu de paille *exp.* a flash in the pan • (lit.): a straw fire.

> example: Son succès est **un feu de paille**.
>
> translation: His success is **a flash in the pan**.
>
> as spoken: Son succès, c't'**un feu d'paille**.

fiacre *m.* posterior • (lit.): cab.

fiche *v.* (a variation of *ficher*) **1.** to give • **2.** to put • **3.** to do.

> example (1): **Fiche**-moi ça!
>
> translation: **Give** me that!
>
> as spoken: [no change]
>
> example (2): **Fiche**-le sur la table.
>
> translation: Put it on the table.
>
> as spoken: [no change]
>
> example (3): Qu'est-ce que tu **fiches** ici?
>
> translation: What are you **doing** here?
>
> as spoken: Tu **fiches** quoi ici?
>
> **NOTE:** Oddly enough, *fiche* is a verb (although it does not have a traditional ending) and is conjugated as a regular "er" verb: *je fiche, tu fiches, il / elle fiche, nous fichons, vous fichez, ils fichent*. However, its past participle is that of a regular "re" verb: *fichu(e)*.

fiche comme de sa première chaussette (s'en) *exp.* not to care at all about something • (lit.): to care about something as much as about one's first sock.

example: Carole m'a dit que Marcel parle de moi derrière mon dos mais franchement, je **m'en fiche comme de ma première chaussette**.

translation: Carole told me that Marcel is talking about me behind my back but frankly, I **couldn't care less**.

as spoken: Carole, è m'a dit que Marcel, y parle de moi derrière mon dos mais franchement, j'**m'en fiche comme de ma première chaussette**.

VARIATION: **fiche comme de sa première chemise (s'en)** *exp.* • (lit.): to care about something as much as about one's first shirt.

fiche le camp *exp.* to leave, "to beat it" • (lit.): to make the camp.

example: Tu m'énerves! **Fiche le camp**!

translation: You're bugging me! **Beat it**!

as spoken: [no change]

VARIATION: **foutre le camp** *exp.* (a stronger variation of: *fiche le camp*).

fiche quelque chose en l'air *exp.* **1.** to throw something away frivolously • **2.** to kill • (lit.): to throw into the air.

example (1): Il a **fichu** toute sa fortune **en l'air**.

translation: He **blew** his entire fortune.

as spoken: [no change]

example (2): Le voleur a braqué son pistolet sur moi! J'ai failli me faire **fiche en l'air**.

translation: The thief aimed his gun at me. I almost got myself **bumped off**.

as spoken: Le voleur, il a braqué son pistolet sur moi! J'ai failli m'faire **fiche en l'air**.

fiche une rame (ne pas en) *exp.* to do absolutely nothing.

example: Moi, je bosse toute la journée dans cette baraque et lui, il **n'en fiche pas une rame**!

translation: I work all day long in this house and he **doesn't lift a finger**!

as spoken: Moi, j'bosse toute la journée dans c'te baraque et lui, il **en fiche pas une rame**!

NOTE: Oddly enough, *"fiche"* is a verb, although it does not have a traditional ending. *"Fiche"* has replaced the verb *"ficher"* which is a slang version of *"faire,"* meaning "to do / make."

fièvre de cheval (avoir une) *exp.* to have a high fever • (lit.): to have a horse's fever.

example: Je ne peux pas t'accompagner au cinéma ce soir. J'ai une **fièvre de cheval**.

translation: I can't go with you to the movies tonight. I have a **raging fever**.

as spoken: J'peux pas
t'accompagner au ciné c'soir. J'ai
une **fièv' de ch'val**.

fifille *f.* daughter.

example: Tu connais la **fifille** de
Nancy?

translation: Do you know Nancy's
daughter?

as spoken: Tu connais la **fifille**
d'Nancy?

SYNONYM: **fillette** *f.*

figue *f.* vagina • (lit.): fig.

filer *v.* to give, hand over.

example: **File**-moi ça tout de suite!

translation: **Hand** that **over** right
now!

as spoken: **File**-moi ça tout d'suite!

SEE: **refiler**, *p. 154.*

filer le parfait amour *exp.* to
get the perfect relationship • (lit.): to
spin the perfect love.

example: Ça fait longtemps que
Carole essaie de **filer le parfait
amour** mais elle reste toujours
seule.

translation: For a long time now
Carole's been trying to **get the
perfect relationship** but she's
still single.

as spoken: Ça fait longtemps
qu'Carole, elle essaie d'**filer
l'parfait amour** mais è reste
toujours seule.

filer un coup d'arbalète *exp.*
to fornicate • (lit.): to give (someone)
a shot with the crossbow.

NOTE: **arbalète** *f.* penis, dick
• (lit.): crossbow.

filer un coup de brosse *exp.* to
fornicate • (lit.): to give (someone) a
shot of the brush.

filer un coup de sabre *exp.* to
fornicate • (lit.): to give (someone) a
shot with the saber.

NOTE: **sabre** *m.* penis, dick
• (lit.): saber.

filer un mauvais coton *exp.* to
be in a bad way (regarding health or
business), not to be doing well
• (lit.): to spin a bad cotton.

example: Pauvre Louise. Elle **file
un mauvais coton** en ce
moment. Elle n'arrive pas à trouver
d'emploi. Elle ne sait même pas
comment elle va payer son loyer.

*Louise **file un mauvais
coton** depuis des jours!*

(trans.)
*Louise **hasn't been
doing well** for days!*

(lit.):
*Louise **has been spinning
a bad cotton** for days!*

translation: Poor Louise. She's **not doing well** right now. She doesn't seem to be able to find a job. She doesn't even know how she's going to pay her rent.

as spoken: Pauv' Louise. Elle **file un mauvais coton** en c'moment. Elle arrive pas à trouver d'emploi. È sait même pas comment è va payer son loyer.

fille *f.* prostitute • (lit.): girl.

fille de joie *f.* prostitute • (lit.): girl of joy (or "who spreads joy").

fils de pute *m.* son of a bitch • (lit.): son of a whore.

> **VARIATION:** **fille de pute** *f.* bitch • (lit.): daughter of a whore.

fion *m.* posterior, anus • (lit.): end or finish (of an article).

fiston *m.* son.

example: C'est ton **fiston**? Il te ressemble beaucoup.

translation: That's your **son**? He looks a lot like you.

as spoken: C'est ton **fiston**? Y t'ressemble beaucoup.

> **NOTE:** The masculine noun *fiston* is a slang transformation of *"fils."*

flageolet *m.* penis • (lit.): flageolet (which is a type of bean).

flanquer sur la gueule (se)
exp. to hit each other in the face or mouth • (lit.): to throw oneself at each other's face or mouth.

> **NOTE -1:** **flanquer** *v.* to throw, to give.

> **NOTE -2:** **gueule** *f.* derogatory for "mouth" or "face" since its literal translation is "the mouth of an animal."

> **VARIATION:** **flanquer des coups / des gnons (se)** *exp.* to punch each other • (lit.): to throw hits at each other.

flanquer une peignée (se)
exp. said of two women in a physical fight, consequently ruining each other's hairdo • (lit.): to give each other a combing.

> **NOTE -1:** **flanquer** *v.* to throw, to give.

> **VARIATION:** **peigner (se)** *v.* to comb each other's hair.

flasher (faire) *v.* to turn on sexually • (lit.): to startle with a flash of light.

example: Diane n'est pas très belle mais elle **fait flasher** les mecs sans effort.

translation: Diane isn't very pretty but she **turns on** guys without any effort.

as spoken: Diane, elle est pas très belle mais è **fait flasher** les mecs sans effort.

flic *f.* (extremely popular) police officer, "cop."

example: Mais qu'est-ce qui se passe ici? Il y a des **flics** partout!

translation: What's going on here? There are **cops** everywhere!

as spoken: Mais qu'est-c'qui s'passe ici? Y a des **flics** partout!

> **SYNONYM:** **flicard** *m.* • (lit.): [no literal translation].

flicaille *f.* the police (in general).

example: Appelle la **flicaille**! Je crois qu'il y a un cambrioleur chez moi!

translation: Call the **police**! I think there's a burglar in my house!

as spoken: Appelle la **flicaille**! J'crois qu'y a un cambrioleur chez moi!

NOTE: **flic** *m.* (extremely popular) policeman, "cop."

SYNONYM -1: **poulet** *m.* • (lit.): chicken.

SYNONYM -2: **motard** *m.* motorcycle-cop.

flipper *v.* to flip out.

example: Si le patron me donne encore du travail à faire, je vais **flipper**!

translation: If the boss gives me more work to do, I'm going to **flip out**!

as spoken: Si l'patron, y m'donne encore du travail à faire, j'vais **flipper**!

SYNONYM -1: **perdre les pédales** *exp.* • (lit.): to lose the pedals.

SYNONYM -2: **perdre la boule** *exp.* • (lit.): to lose the ball.

NOTE: **boule** *f.* head • (lit.): ball.

flirter *v.* (Americanism) to flirt.

example: Georges a **flirté** avec moi toute la soirée.

translation: George **flirted** with me all night.

as spoken: Georges, il a **flirté** avec moi toute la soirée.

flotter *v.* to rain • (lit.): to float.

example: Il a **flotté** sans arrêt pendant nos vacances.

translation: It **rained** nonstop during our vacation.

as spoken: Il a **flotté** sans arrêt pendant nos vacances.

NOTE: **flotte** *f.* • **1.** water • **2.** rain.

flotteurs *m.pl.* breasts • (lit.): floaters.

flouser *v.* to fart.

flousse *m.* fart.

flûte • **1.** *interj.* darn • **2.** penis • (lit.): flute.

example -1: **Flûte**! J'ai perdu mes clés!

translation: **Darn**! I lost my keys

as spoken: [no change]

foirade (avoir la) *f.* to have diarrhea.

NOTE: This comes from the crude verb *foirer* meaning "to have diarrhea."

VARIATION: **foire (avoir la)** *f.* • (lit.): to have diarrhea.

foireux, euse *n.* scardey-cat, one who is scared shitless • (lit.): shitter (from intense fear).

NOTE: **foire (avoir la)** *exp.* • **foirade (avoir la)** *exp.* • **foirer** *v.* to have diarrhea.

foldingue *adj.* (applies only to a woman) crazy, nuts.

follette *adj.* (applies only to a woman) crazy.

follingue *adj.* (applies only to a woman) crazy, nuts.

fortune en partant de rien (faire) *exp.* to go from rags to riches • (lit.): to make a fortune by starting from nothing.

  example: Elle a démarré sa société avec un malheureux cent dollars. En deux ans, elle a **fait fortune en partant de rien**.

  translation: She started up her company with a measly one hundred dollars. In two years, she **went from rags to riches**.

  as spoken: Elle a démarré sa société avec un malheureux cent dollars. En deux ans, elle a **fait fortune en partant de rien**.

fossile (vieux) *m.* an old person, an "old fart" • (lit.): old fossil.
  NOTE: **fossiliser (se)** *v.* to get old • (lit.): to fossilize.

fouetter *v.* to stink • (lit.): to whip.

fou / folle à lier (être) *exp.* to be crazy enough to commit • (lit.): to be crazy enough to tie up.

fou-fou / fofolle *adj.* a little crazy, eccentric.
  NOTE -1: This comes from the adjectives *fou* and *folle* meaning "crazy."
  NOTE -2: When *fofolle* is applied to a man, its connotation is "effeminate" or "queeny."

fourailler *v.* to fornicate • (lit.): to stuff.

NOTE: This is a variation of the verb *fourrer* meaning "to stuff."

fourrer *v.* to cram, to stick.

  example: Où as-tu **fourré** mes clés? Ça fait une bonne heure que j'essaie de les trouver!

  translation: Where did you **stick** my keys? I've been looking for them for an entire hour!

  as spoken: Où t'as **fourré** mes clés? Ça fait une bonne heure que j'essaie d'les trouver!
  ALSO: **fourrer** *v.* slang for "to fornicate."

fourrer la langue à quelqu'un *exp.* to give someone a "French" kiss • (lit.): to stuff one's tongue to someone.

foutaise *f.* hogwash, bullshit.

  example: C'est de la **foutaise** de prétendre qu'ils sont encore ensemble. Ils sont prêts à divorcer.

  translation: It's **bullshit** to claim that they're still together. They're ready to get divorced.

  as spoken: C'est d'la **foutaise** de prétend' qu'y sont encore ensemble. Y sont prêts à divorcer.
  NOTE: The verb *prétendre* is a common *faux ami* ("false friend") in French. Although it would certainly be reasonable that a native speaker of English would assume that *prétendre* has the same meaning in French, this is not the case: *prétendre* = to claim; *faire semblant* = to pretend.

foutoir *m.* • **1.** a disorderly mess • **2.** whorehouse "fuckodrome" (from the verb *foutoir* originally meaning "to fuck").

example (1): Mais regarde ta chambre! C'est un **foutoir**! Va la ranger tout de suite!

translation: Just look at your bedroom! It's a **disaster area**! Go clean it up right now!

as spoken: Mais r'garde ta chambre! C't'un **foutoir**! Va la ranger tout d'suite!

example (2): Je pense que Louise est une prostituée! Selon Sophie, elle travaille dans un **foutoir**!

translation: I think Louise is a prostitute! According to Sophie, she works in a **whorehouse**!

as spoken: Je pense que Louise est une prostituée! Selon Sophie, elle travaille dans un **foutoir**!

foutre • **1.** *v.* to do • **2.** *v.* to put with force, to throw **3.** *v.* to give • **4.** *m.* sperm • (lit.): to fuck.

example (1): Qu'est-ce que tu **fous** ici?

translation: What are you **doing** here?

as spoken: Tu **fous** quoi ici? [or] Quequ'tu **fous** ici?

example (2): En rentrant, Emile a **foutu** ses clés sur la table.

translation: Upon coming home, Emile **threw** his keys on the table.

as spoken: En rentrant, Emile, il a **foutu** ses clés sur la table.

example (3): Le mauvais temps m'a **foutu** la crève.

translation: The bad weather **gave** me a cold.

as spoken: Le mauvais temps, y m'a **foutu** la crève.

foutre à quelqu'un (pouvoir) *exp.* to be someone's business.

example: Qu'est-ce que ça **peut me foutre**?

translation: What does that **have to do with me**?

as spoken: Qu'est-c'que ça **peut m'**foutre?

foutre comme de l'an quarante (s'en) *exp.* not to give a damn • (lit.): not to give a damn as much as one would about the year forty.

example: Si Marie ne veut pas m'inviter à sa soirée, je **m'en fous comme de l'an quarante**.

translation: If Marie doesn't want to invite me to her party, I **couldn't give a damn**.

as spoken: Si Marie, è veut pas m'inviter à sa soirée, j'**m'en fous comme d'**l'an quarante.

VARIATION -1: **foutre comme de sa première chemise (s'en)** *exp.* • (lit.): not to give a damn as much as one would about one's first shirt.

VARIATION -2: **foutre comme de sa première chaussette (s'en)** *exp.* • (lit.): not to give a damn as much as one would about one's first sock.

foutre dedans (se) *exp.* to blow it, to stick one's foot in it.

example: Le professeur a su que j'ai triché à l'examen. Cette fois-ci, je me suis vraiment **foutu dedans**.

translation: The teacher found out that I cheated on the test. This time, I really **blew it**.

as spoken: Le prof, il a su que j'ai triché à l'exam. Cette fois-ci, je m'suis vraiment **foutu d'dans**.

NOTE: Although the verb *savoir* literally means "to know," when used in the past tense, its connotation becomes "to have found out."

foutre de la gueule de quelqu'un (se) *exp.* to make fun of someone • (lit.): to make fun of someone's face (or "person").

example: Pourquoi est-ce que tu ris? Tu **te fous de ma gueule** ou quoi?

translation: What are you laughing? Are you **making fun of me** or what?

as spoken: Pourquoi tu ris? Tu **t'fous d'ma gueule** ou quoi?

NOTE: gueule *f.* derogatory for "mouth" or "face" when applied to a person, since it's literal translation is "the mouth of an animal."

foutre de quelqu'un (se) *exp.*
• **1.** to make fun of someone • **2.** to rip someone off.

example (1): Tu **te fous de moi**?

translation: Are you **making fun of me**?

as spoken: Tu **t'fous d'moi**?

example (2): Le mec qui t'a vendu cette voiture **s'est foutu de toi**.

translation: The guy who sold you this car **ripped you off**.

as spoken: Le mec qui t'a vendu c'te voiture, y **s'est foutu d'toi**.

NOTE: mec *m.* (very popular) guy, "dude."

foutre en l'air *exp.* • **1.** to ruin • **2.** to kill • **3.** to beat up severely.

example (1): La pluie a **foutu** tous nos projets **en l'air**.

translation: The rain **ruined** all of our plans.

as spoken: La pluie, ça a **foutu** tous nos projets **en l'air**.

example (2): Le marchand s'est fait **foutre en l'air** par le voleur.

translation: The salesman got **killed** by the thief.

as spoken: Le marchand, y s'est fait **foutre en l'air** par l'voleur.

example (3): J'ai un œil au beurre noir parce que je me suis disputé avec mon frère et il a finit par me **foutre en l'air**!

translation: I have a black eye because I had a fight with my brother and he ended up **beating the crap out of me**!

as spoken: J'ai un œil au beurre noir pasque je m'suis disputé avec mon frère et il a finit par m'**foutre en l'air**!

foutre et s'en contre-foutre (s'en) *exp.* not to give a damn whatsoever.

example: Je **m'en fous et m'en contre-fous** de ce qu'il dit.

translation: I **don't give a damn whatsoever** what he says.

as spoken: J'**m'en fous et m'en contre-fous** de c'qu'y dit.

foutre la paix à quelqu'un
exp. to leave someone alone
• (lit.): to give someone peace.

example: Tu m'énerves!
Fous-moi la paix!

translation: You're bugging me!
Beat it!

as spoken: [no change]
SYNONYM: **foutre le camp**,
p. 88.

**foutre la trouille à
quelqu'un** *exp.* to scare the crap
out of someone • (lit.): to give
extreme fear to someone.

example: Ça m'a **foutu la
trouille** quand j'ai fait ma
présentation devant les cadres.

translation: It **scared the crap
out of me** when I did my
presentation in front of the
executives.

as spoken: Ça m'a **foutu la
trouille** quand j'ai fait ma
présentation d'vant les cadres.

foutre le camp *exp.* to beat it.

example: **Fous le camp**!

translation: **Beat it**!

as spoken: **Fous l'camp**!
SYNONYM: **foutre la paix à
quelqu'un**, *p. 88.*

foutrement *adv.* very, totally.

example: Bernard est
foutrement bizarre!

translation: Bernard is **totally**
bizarre!

as spoken: Bernard, il est
foutrement bizarre!

VARIATION -1: **foutument** *adv.*
VARIATION -2: **fichtrement**
adv. a milder variation of: *foutument.*
NOTE: This comes from the verb
foutre originally meaning "to foutre."

foutre (ne rien) *v.* not to do a
damn thing.

example: Tu **ne fous rien** toute
la journée tandis que moi, je me
décarcasse pour nettoyer cette
maison avant que les invités arrivent!

translation: You **don't do a
damn thing** all day whereas I'm
working my butt off to get this house
clean before the guests arrive!

as spoken: Tu **fous rien** toute la
journée tandis que moi, j'me
décarcasse pour nettoyer c'te
maison avant qu'les invités arrivent!

foutre par terre (se) *exp.* • **1.** to
fall flat on one's face • **2.** to
embarrass oneself.

example (1): Je me suis **foutu
par terre** en sortant du
supermarché.

translation: I **fell down** while
leaving the supermarket.

as spoken: Je m'suis **foutu par
terre** en sortant du supermarché.

example (2): Sa présentation à la
classe était mal faite et il s'est **foutu
par terre**.

translation: His presentation to the
class was poorly done and he
totally embarrassed himself.

as spoken: Sa présentation à la
classe, elle était mal faite et y s'est
foutu par terre.

foutre plein la lampe (s'en)

exp. to stuff one's face • (lit.): to fill up one's stomach.

example: Je **m'en suis foutu plein la lampe** à la soirée.

translation: I **stuffed my face** at the party.

as spoken: J'**m'en suis foutu plein la lampe** à la soirée.

NOTE: **lampe** *f.* stomach
• (lit.): lamp.

*David **s'en fout plein la lampe** ce soir!*

(trans.):
David is **eating like a pig** tonight!

(lit.):
David is **stuffing it in his lamp** tonight.

foutre quelque chose en l'air

exp. to fuck something up • (lit.): to fuck something into the air.

example: Je n'ai pas de chance. Le client était à deux doigts de signer le contract mais j'ai tout **foutu en l'air** quand je l'ai insulté par accident.

translation: I don't have any luck. The client was on the verge of signing the contract but I **fucked everything up** when I insulted him by accident.

as spoken: J'ai pas d'chance. Le client, il était à deux doigts d'signer l'contract mais j'ai tout **foutu en l'air** quand j'l'ai insulté par accident.

NOTE -1: **à deux doigts (être)** *exp.* to be on the verge (of doing something) • (lit.): to be two fingers away.

NOTE -2: **foutre quelqu'un en l'air** *exp.* to kill or "waste" someone.

foutre quelqu'un à la porte

exp. to fire someone • (lit.): to throw someone to the door.

example: Le patron m'a dit qu'il va me **foutre à la porte** si je continue à boire.

translation: The boss said he's going **to fire me** if I continue to drink.

as spoken: Le patron, y m'a dit qu'y va m'**foutr'à la porte** si j'continue à boire.

foutre (s'en) *v.* not to give a damn.

example: "Claire est fâchée avec toi."
"**Je m'en fous**! Elle est toujours fâchée avec quelqu'un."

translation: "Claire is angry with you."
"**I don't give a damn**! She is always angry with someone."

as spoken: "Claire, elle est fâchée avec toi."
"**J'm'en fous**! Elle est toujours fâchée avec quelqu'un."

VARIATION -1: **foutre comme de sa première chaussette (s'en)** *exp.* • (lit.): not to give a damn about something as much as one's first sock.

VARIATION -2: **foutre comme de sa première chemise (s'en)** *exp.* • (lit.): not to give a damn about something as much as one's first shirt.

VARIATION -3: **foutre comme de l'an quarante (s'en)** *exp.* • (lit.): not to give a damn about something as much as the year forty.

foutre sur la gueule (se) *exp.* to beat each other up • (lit.): to throw one another on each other's mouth.

example: Hervé et Pierre ont commencé à disputer et ont fini par **se foutre sur la gueule**!

translation: Hervé and Pierre started disputing and ended up **beating each other up**!

as spoken: Hervé et Pierre, y z'ont commencé à disputer et ont fini par **s'fout' sur la gueule**!

foutre un coup *exp.* • **1.** to traumatize, to give someone an emotional jolt • **2.** to give someone a sudden [ ].

example (1): La mort de sa mère lui a **foutu un coup**.

translation: His mother's death **traumatized him**.

as spoken: La mort d'sa mère, ça lui a **foutu un coup**.

example (2): Cela lui a **foutu un coup de** vieux de travailler dans une grande société.

translation: Working in a big company **made him age suddenly**.

as spoken: Cela lui a **foutu un coup d'**vieux d'travailler dans une grande société.

foutre un coup de main *exp.* to give someone a hand.

example: Cette caisse est trop lourde pour moi. Tu peux me **foutre un coup de main**?

translation: This box is too heavy for me. Can you **give me a hand**?

as spoken: C'te caisse, elle est trop lourde pour moi. Tu peux m'**foutr'**un coup d'main?

foutre un coup de pied à quelqu'un *exp.* to kick someone.

example: Quand je me suis accroupi, mon petit frère m'a **foutu un coup de pied**!

translation: When I bent down, my little brother **kicked me**!

as spoken: Quand je m'suis accroupi, mon p'tit frère, y m'a **foutu un coup d'**pied!

foutre un coup (en) *exp.* to work hard.

example: Je suis épuisé. J'**en ai foutu un coup** au boulot aujourd'hui.

translation: I'm exhausted. I **worked my butt off** at work today.

as spoken: J'suis épuisé. J'**en ai foutu un coup** au boulot aujourd'hui.

foutre une baffe à quelqu'un

exp. to give someone a slap in the face • (lit.): to throw a slap at someone.

example: Quand il l'a insultée, elle lui a **foutu une baffe**!

translation: When he insulted her, she **gave him a slap in the face**!

as spoken: Quand il l'a insultée, è lui a **foutu une baffe**!

SYNONYM -1: **foutre un gnon à quelqu'un** *exp.* • (lit.): to throw a hit to someone.

SYNONYM -2: **foutre une prune à quelqu'un** *exp.* to hit someone • (lit.): to throw a plum to someone.

NOTE: The noun *prune* is a common *faux ami* ("false friend") in French. Although it would certainly be reasonable that a native speaker of English would assume that *prune* has the same meaning in French, this is not the case: *prune* = plum; *pruneau* = prune.

foutre une peignée (se) *exp.* a

stronger variation of *flanquer une peignée (se)* meaning "to beat someone up."

SEE: **flanquer une peignée**, *p. 83*.

foutre une rame (ne pas) *exp.*

not to do a fucking thing • (lit.): not

to do an oar's worth of work (in other words, not to pull one's oar while everyone else is rowing).

example: Robert **ne fout pas une rame** au boulot.

translation: Robert **doesn't do a fucking thing** at work.

as spoken: Robert, y **fout pas une rame** au boulot.

NOTE: **boulot** *m.* (extremely popular) work, job, the "grind."

foutu(e) comme l'as de pique (être) *exp.* to be dressed

badly, to be slobbed out.

example: Mais tu ne peux pas aller chez mes parents habillé comme ça. Tu es **foutu comme l'as de pique**, voyons!

translation: You can't go to my parents' house dressed like that. You're **slobbed out**, for crying out loud!

as spoken: Mais tu peux pas aller chez mes parents habillé comme ça. T'es **foutu comme l'as de pique**, voyons!

NOTE: The usage of *voyons* is extremely popular in French. Although its literally meaning is "let's see," it is commonly used to mean "for crying out loud."

foutu(e) de faire quelque chose (être) *exp.* • 1. to be

capable of doing something • 2. to be bound to do something.

example (1): Georges n'est pas **foutu de faire** du ski. Il est trop gros.

translation: George isn't **capable of** skiing. He's too fat.

as spoken: Georges, il est pas **foutu d'faire** du ski. Il est trop gros.

example (2): Mes parents sont **foutus d'**arriver avant que je range la maison!

translation: My parents are **bound to** arrive before I clean up the house!

as spoken: Mes parents, y sont **foutus d'**arriver avant qu'je range la maison!

foutu(e) (être) *adj.* • **1.** to be ruined • **2.** to be done for.

example (1): J'ai fait tomber la télévision. Maintenant, elle est **foutue**.

translation: I dropped the TV. Now it's **wrecked**.

as spoken: J'ai fait tomber la télé. Maintenant, elle est **foutue**.

example (2): Si le patron te voit dans ce bar, tu es **foutu**!

translation: If the boss sees you in this bar, you're **cooked**!

as spoken: Si l'patron, y t'voit dans c'bar, t'es **foutu**!

frais / fraîche émoulu de (être) *exp.* to be fresh out of • (lit.): to be freshly ground (from the verb "*moudre*" meaning "to grind.").

example: Marc est **frais émoulu de** l'université.

translation: Mark is **fresh out of the university**.

as spoken: Marc, il est **frais émoulu d'**l'unif.

framboise *f.* clitoris • (lit.): raspberry.

frangin *m.* brother.

example: Je te présente Henri. C'est le **frangin** de Marcel.

translation: I'd like you to meet Henri. He's Marcel's **brother**.

as spoken: J'te présente Henri. C'est l'**frangin** d'Marcel.

SEE: **frangine**, *(next entry)*.

frangine *f.* sister.

example: Je ne savais pas que tu avais une **frangine**.

translation: I didn't know you had a **sister**.

as spoken: J'savais pas qu't'avais une **frangine**.

frapper le biscuit (se) *exp.* to get oneself all worked up • (lit.): to hit one's head (with both hands from worrying).

example: **Ne te frappe pas le biscuit**. Je suis certain que ton entretien s'est bien passé.

translation: **Don't get yourself all worked up**. I'm sure your interview went well.

as spoken: **Te frappe pas l'biscuit**. J'suis certain qu'ton entretien, y s'est bien passé.

NOTE: **biscuit** *n.* noggin, head • (lit.): cookie.

fréquenter les lits *exp.* to sleep around • (lit.): to frequent beds.

example: Je n'aime pas les mecs qui **fréquentent les lits**.

translation: I don't like guys who **sleep around**.

as spoken: J'aime pas les mecs qui **fréquentent les lits**.

NOTE: **mec** *m.* (extremely popular) guy, dude.

frétillante *f.* penis • (lit.): wagger.

NOTE: This comes from the verb *frétiller* meaning "to wag."

frétillard *m.* penis • (lit.): wagger

NOTE: This comes from the verb *frétiller* meaning "to wag."

fric *m.* (extremely popular) money, "dough."

example: Je ne peux pas t'accompagner au cinéma ce soir. Je n'ai pas assez de **fric**.

translation: I can't go with you to the movies tonight. I don't have enough **money**.

as spoken: J'peux pas t'accompagner au ciné ce soir. J'ai pas assez d'**fric**.

SYNONYMS: *blé (du)* • *galette (de la)* • *grisbi (du)* • *oseille (de l')* • *pèze (du)* • *picaillons (des)* • *pognon (du)* • *ronds (des)* • *sous (des)* • *etc.*

fringué(e) (être mal / bien)

adj. to be poorly / well dressed.

example: Maurice est toujours **mal fringué**. Je crois que je vais lui offrir un joli tricot pour son anniversaire.

translation: Maurice is always so **poorly dressed**. I think I'll give him a pretty sweater for his birthday.

as spoken: Maurice, il est toujours **mal fringué**. J'crois que j'vais lui offrir un joli tricot pour son anniversaire.

NOTE -1: **fringues** *f.pl.* clothes, "threads."

NOTE -2: The verb *offrir*, meaning "to offer," is commonly used in spoken French to mean: **1.** to give (when applied to a gift; and **2.** to treat (*C'est moi qui te l'offre;* It's on me).

SYNONYM: **être mal / bien ficelé(e)** *exp.* • (lit.): to be poorly / well strung (together).

fripe *f.* clothes, "threads"
• (lit.): wrinkles (since fabic tends to wrinkle -- *"friper"* = to wrinkle).

example: Tu ne peux pas être vu avec des **fripes** comme ça à ce restaurant!

translation: You can't be seen with **clothes** like that at this restaurant!

as spoken: Tu peux pas être vu avec des **fripes** comme ça à c'resto!

SYNONYM: **fringues** *f.pl.* clothing.

fripouille *f.* a man without scruples, a shady character, a "snake."

example: Tu vas sortir avec Antoine? Je ne me fierais pas à cette **fripouille** si j'étais à ta place!

translation: You going out with Antoine? I wouldn't trust that **snake** if I were in your shoes!

as spoken: Tu vas sortir avec Antoine? Je m'fi'rais pas à c'te **fripouille** si j'étais à ta place!

NOTE: This term is slightly outdated yet is commonly used in jest or ironically.

frit(e) (être) *adj.* to be done for
• (lit.): to be fried.

example: Si le patron me trouve ici, je suis **frit**!

translation: If the boss finds me here, I'm **done for**!

as spoken: Si l'patron m'trouve ici, j'suis **frit**!

SYNONYM: cuit(e) (être) *adj.* • (lit.): to be cooked.

frotter *v.* to fornicate • (lit.): to rub.

frotter (se) *v.* to fight • (lit.): to rub each other.

froussard(e) *n.* scardey-cat.
NOTE: frousse (avoir la) *exp.* to be scared, to have the creeps.

fumelle *f.* broad.

fumier *m.* a disparaging remark applied to either a man or a woman • (lit.): manure.

example: Il a volé ma voiture, le **fumier**!

translation: That **bastard** stole my car!

as spoken: [no change]

fumiste *m.* (applies to either a man or a woman) lazy individual, one who doesn't want to work • (lit.): one who works with manure.

example: Marcel, tu es un **fumiste**. Tu ne fais jamais rien toute la journée!

translation: Marcel, you're a **lazy bum**. You don't do a thing all day!

as spoken: Marcel, t'es un **fumiste**. Tu fais jamais rien toute la journée!

fusante *f.* • a fart (lit.): that which bursts out (like *une fusée* meaning "a rocket").

fuser *v.* to fart • (lit.): to burst out.
NOTE: fusée *f.* rocket.

gagner gros *exp.* to make big bucks, to win big • (lit.): to win big.

example: Bernard est un cadre dans une grande société. Il **gagne gros**, lui.

translation: Bernie is an executive in a large company. He **makes big bucks**.

as spoken: Bernard, c't'un cadre dans une grande société. Y **gagne gros**, lui.

gagner sa vie *exp.* to make a living • (lit.): to earn life.

example: Comment est-ce qu'elle **gagne sa vie**?

translation: How does she **make a living**?

as spoken: Comment è **gagne sa vie**?

gagneuse *f.* prostitute • (lit.): girl who earns money.

gale *f.* bitch • (lit.): mange.

galère (être la) *f.* to be extremely difficult and unpleasant • (lit.): it's the galleys (as difficult as being a slave in the galleys).

example: Ça fait deux heures que j'essaie de réparer ma bagnole, mais c'est **la galère**!

translation: I've been trying to repair my car for the past two hours, but it's **too difficult**!

as spoken: Ça fait deux heures que j'essaie d'réparer ma bagnole, mais c'est **la galère**!

NOTE: **bagnole** *f.* (extremely popular) car.

galerie *f.* public (in general).

example: Quand elle a commencé à crier, elle m'a embarrassé devant toute la **galerie**!

translation: When she started screaming, she embarrassed me in front of **everyone**!

as spoken: Quand elle a commencé à crier, è m'a embarassé d'vant toute la **gal'rie**!

galoche à quelqu'un (faire une) *exp.* to give someone a "French" kiss • (lit.): to make a boot to someone.

garce *f.* bitch.

example: Tu as rencontré la nouvelle voisine? C'est une vieille **garce**. Elle m'a dénoncé à la police pour avoir joué du piano à huit heures du soir parce que ça l'a dérangé!

translation: Did you meet the new neighbor? She's an old **bitch**. She reported me to the police for playing the piano at eight o'clock at night because it disturbed her!

as spoken: T'as rencontré la nouvelle voisine? C't'une vieille **garce**. È m'a dénoncé à la police pour avoir joué du piano à huit heures du soir pasque ça l'a dérangé!

NOTE: Eight o'clock is commonly seen as *8h* (for morning) and *20h* (for evening). Remember, the French use the 24-hour clock!

garde-à-vous (être au) *exp.* to have an erection • (lit.): (military) to be at attention.

garder froide (la) *exp.* to keep one's cool • (lit.): to keep it cool.

example: Je sais que tu es fâché avec lui, mais essaie de **la garder froide** quand tu lui parleras.

translation: I know you're angry at him, but try and **keep your cool** when you speak to him.

as spoken: Je sais qu't'es fâché avec lui, mais essaie d'**la garder froide** quand tu lui parleras.

gargue *f.* throat.

example: Hier, j'ai crié pendant trois heures au match de football. Aujourd'hui, j'ai mal à la **gargue**.

translation: Yesterday, I yelled for three hours during the soccer game. Today, I have a sore **throat**.

as spoken: Hier, j'ai crié pendant trois heures au match de foot. Aujourd'hui, j'ai mal à la **gargue**.

NOTE: This comes from the verb **se gargariser** meaning "to gargle."

gars *m.* (very popular) guy, "dude."

gâteau (c'est du) *exp.* said of something easy, "a piece of cake" • (lit.): it's cake.

example: Je vais te montrer à faire la cuisine française. **C'est du gâteau**!

translation: I'm going to show you how to prepare French food. **It's a piece of cake**!

as spoken: J'vais t'montrer à faire la cuisine française. **C'est du gâteau**!

gaule *f.* penis or erection • (lit.): (long, thin) pole, stick.

gaule (avoir la) *f.* (popular) to have an erection • (lit.): to have the pole.

gazon sur la platebande (ne plus avoir de) *exp.* to be bald • (lit.): to no longer have lawn on the flowerbed.

NOTE: **platebande** *f.* head, "noggin" • (lit.): flowerbed.

gazon sur la prairie (ne plus avoir de) *exp.* to be bald • (lit.): not to have any more grass on the prairie.

gazon sur la terrasse (ne plus avoir de) *exp.* to be bald • (lit.): not to have any more grass on the terrace.

G.D.B. (avoir la) *exp.* to have a hangover • (lit.): to have the mouth of wood (since G.D.B. is an abbreviation for "*gueule de bois*" • See the following notes).

example: Si tu bois trop ce soir, tu risques d'avoir la **G.D.B.** demain!

translation: If you drink too much tonight, you're asking for a **hangover** tomorrow!

as spoken: Si tu bois trop c'soir, tu risques d'avoir la **G.D.B.** d'main!

NOTE -1: G.D.B. is pronounced *jé, dé, bé* and is an abbreviation for "gueule de bois."

NOTE -2: The feminine noun "*gueule*," literally meaning the "mouth of an animal," is commonly used in French slang to mean "mouth" in general. This expression conjures up an image of someone who is so hungover, that he / she can barely move his / her mouth.

SYNONYM: **mal aux cheveux (avoir)** *exp.* • (lit.): to have a hairache.

gêner pour (ne pas se) *exp.* to make no bones about • (lit.): not to restrain oneself.

example: Elle était fâchée contre moi et **ne s'est pas gênée pour** me le dire!

translation: She was angry with me and **made no bones about** telling me!

as spoken: Elle était fâchée contre moi et **s'est pas gênée pour** me l'dire!

génial(e) (être) *v.* (extremely popular) to be terrific, wonderful.

example: Regarde cette robe! Elle est **géniale**!

translation: Look at this dress! It's **great**!

as spoken: Regarde c'te robe! Elle est **géniale**!

génisse *f.* woman or girl.

gerber *v.* to vomit, to "barf" • (lit.): to sheave (corn, wheat, etc.)

example: Je suis très malade. J'ai **gerbé** toute la matinée.

translation: I'm very sick. I **barfed** all morning.

as spoken: J'suis très malade. J'ai **gerbé** toute la matinée.

*J'ai l'impression que mes parents sont à deux doigts de **gerber**!*

(trans.):
*I have a feeling my parents are on the verge of **barfing**!*

(lit.):
*I have a feeling that my parents are two fingers away from **sheaving**!*

gerber quelqu'un (ne pas pouvoir) *v.* to be unable to stand someone • (lit.): to be unable to vomit someone.

gerbos (être) *adj.* to be gross • (lit.): to be enough to make one vomit.

example: Suzanne est cuisinière horrible. Son dîner d'hier était **gerbos**!

translation: Suzanne is a horrible cook. Her dinner last night was **gross**!

as spoken: Suzanne, elle est cuisinière horrible. Son dîner d'hier, il était **gerbos**!

NOTE: **gerber** *v.* to throw up, to "barf."

gicler *v.* to vomit • (lit.): to spray.

givré(e) (être) *adj.* crazy • (lit.): to be frosted over.

gland *m.* penis • (lit.): acorn.

NOTE: This comes from the masculine noun *gland* meaning "acorn" and has taken the slang connotation of "penis, dick" due to its shape.

glaviot *m.* spit wad, loogie.

glavioter *v.* to hawk a loogie.

glisser un fil *exp.* to urinate • (lit.): to slip (out) a thread (of urine).

globes *m.pl.* breasts • (lit.): globes, spheres.

glouglouter le poireau (se faire) *exp.* (of men) to masturbate • (lit.): to make one's leek gurgle.

NOTE: **poireau** *m.* penis, "dick" • (lit.): leek.

gluau *m.* spit wad, loogie.

gober quelqu'un (ne pas pouvoir) *v.* to be unable to stand someone • (lit.): to be unable to swallow or gulp down someone.

gobeur *m.* (applies to either a man or a woman) gullible person, sucker.

  NOTE: **gober** *v.* to eat, gobble up.

  ALSO: **gobe-tout** *m.* one who believes everything he / she hears, sucker.

godiche (être) *adj.* (applies only to a woman) to be awkward and clumsy.

gogo *m.* (applies to either a man or a woman) a person easily fooled, sucker.

goinfrer (se) *v.* to eat a lot, to "pork out."

  example: J'ai les crocs. Je vais **me goinfrer** ce soir.

  translation: I'm very hungry. I'm going **to pig out** tonight.

  as spoken: J'ai les crocs. J'vais **m'goinfrer** ce soir.

  NOTE: **goinfre** *m.* one who makes a pig of oneself, an "oinker."

gondoler de la devanture *exp.* to be pregnant • (lit.): to warp from the display window.

gonfler son andouille *exp.* (of men) to masturbate • (lit.): to swell one's sausage.

gonze *m.* guy, "dude."

  example: Tu connais ce **gonze**-là? C'est mon nouveau professeur d'anglais.

  translation: Do you know this **guy**? He's my new English teacher.

  as spoken: Tu connais c'**gonze**-là? C'est mon nouveau prof d'anglais.

  NOTE: **gonzesse** *f.* girl, "chick."

  SYNONYM -1: **mec** *m.* (extremely popular).

  SYNONYM -2: **zigue** *m.*

gonzesse *f.* (very popular) girl, "chick."

goupillon *m.* penis • (lit.): sprinkler (for holy water).

gourbi *m.* bedroom • (lit.): (from Arabic) hut.

gourde à poils *f.* penis • (lit.): gourd with hairs.

gourdin *m.* penis • (lit.): club, bludgeon.

gourdin (avoir le) *m.* to have an erection • (lit.): to have the club or bludgeon.

grabuge *m.* a big fight.

graillon *m.* spit wad, loogie.

graillonner *v.* to cough up phlegm.

grain (avoir un) *exp.* (applies to either a man or a woman) to be nuts, touched in the head • (lit.): to have a grain (in the brain).

grande commission (faire sa) *exp.* to defecate • (lit.): to do one's big job.

  SEE: **petite commission (faire sa)**, p. 136.

grands besoins (faire ses) *exp.*
to defecate • (lit.): to do one's big needs.

grand temps (être) *exp.* to be high time • (lit.): to be big time.

example: Je sais que tu es fâché avec le curé mais je crois qu'il est **grand temps** que tu lui pardonnes.

translation: I know you've been angry with the local priest but I think it's **high time** that you forgave him.

as spoken: Je sais qu't'es fâché avec le curé mais j'crois qu'il est **grand temps** qu'tu lui pardonnes.

gratter la tete (se) *exp.* to try and figure out something • (lit.): to scratch one's head (trying to figure out something).

example: Je **me gratte la tête** pour savoir ce qu'elle veut pour son anniversaire.

translation: I **trying to figure out what** she wants for her birthday.

as spoken: J'**me gratte la tête** pour savoir c'qu'è veut pour son anniversaire.

greffier *m.* vagina • (lit.): cat, scratcher, "pussy."
NOTE: This comes from the verb *griffer* meaning "to scratch."

grelotteur, euse *n.* scardey-cat • (lit.): shaker.
NOTE -1: **grelots (avoir les)** *exp.* to have the shakes (due to fear).
NOTE -2: **grelotter** *v.* • (lit.): to shake.

grenouiller *v.* to drink water • (lit.): to do like a frog.

example: J'ai la gargue sèche. Je crois qu'il est temps de **grenouiller**.

translation: I had too much to drink tonight. I think it's time **to stick to only water**.

as spoken: J'ai la gargue sèche. J'crois qu'il est temps d'**grenouiller**.
NOTE: This comes from the feminine noun *grenouille* meaning "frog."

grippette *f.* vagina • (lit.): pouncer.
NOTE: This comes from the verb *gripper* meaning "to seize, pounce upon."

grognasse *f.* an ugly woman or girl • (lit.): a slang variant of the verb *grogner* meaning "to grunt."

gros (faire son) *exp.* to defecate • (lit.): to do one's fat (job).

gros lard (être un) *exp.* (applies to either a man or a woman) to be a fatso • (lit.): to be a big piece of lard.

example: Si tu continues à manger comme ça, tu vas devenir un **gros lard**.

translation: If you keep eating like that, you're going to become a **fat pig**.

as spoken: Si tu continues à manger comme ça, tu vas dev'nir un **gros lard**.
SYNONYM: **gras double (être un)** *exp.* (applies to either a man or a woman) • (lit.): to be a piece of tripe (or "guts").

grosse brioche *f.* fat stomach, paunch, gut • (lit.): fat brioche.

example: Tu veux encore une tranche de tarte? Attention. Tu ne veux pas avoir une **grosse brioche** comme celle de Marcel!

translation: You want another piece of pie? Be careful. You don't want to get a **gut** like Marcel's!

as spoken: Tu veux encore une tranche de tarte? Attention. Tu veux pas avoir une **grosse brioche** comme celle de Marcel!

grosse commission (faire sa) *exp.* to go poo-poo, to go number two • (lit.): to do one's big portion.

example: Attention! Le chien a **fait sa grosse commission** sur le pas de la porte!

translation: Watch out! The dog **pooped** on the doorstep!

as spoken: Attention! Le chien, il a **fait sa grosse commission** sur le pas d'la porte!

SEE: **petite commission (faire sa)**, *p. 136.*

gros sur la patate (en avoir) *exp.* to have a lot on one's mind • (lit.): to have a lot of it on the head.

example: Je ne peux pas me concentrer sur mon travail. J'**en ai gros sur la patate**.

translation: I can't concentrate on my work. I **have a lot on my mind**.

as spoken: J'peux pas m'concentrer sur mon travail. J'**en ai gros sur la patate**.

NOTE: **patate** *f.* head • (lit.): potato.

*J'en ai **gros sur la patate** aujourd'hui.*

(trans.):
I have **a lot on my mind** today.

(lit.):
I have **a lot of it on my potato** today.

grue *f.* prostitute • (lit.): a crane (since cranes are known for standing on one foot much like a prostitute who waits for a client while leaning back against the wall of a building, one foot on the ground with the other against the wall).

grue (faire la) *f.* to hustle (said of a prostitute) • (lit.): to do like a crane (since cranes are known for standing on one foot much like a prostitute who waits for a client while leaning back against the wall of a building, one foot on the ground with the other against the wall).

guenon *f.* an ugly woman or girl
• (lit.): female monkey.

guenuche *f.* an ugly woman or girl •
(lit.) a slang variant of *guenon* meaning "a female monkey."

gueule *f.* (derogatory) mouth or face (depending on the context)
• (lit.): mouth of an animal.

example: Le ski ne m'intéresse pas du tout. Je ne veux pas finir par me casser la **gueule**!

translation: Skiing doesn't interest me at all. I don't want to end up breaking my **neck** (or literally, "mouth" or "face")!

as spoken: Le ski, ça m'intéresse pas du tout. J'veux pas finir par m'casser la **gueule**!

NOTE: **casser la gueule (se)** *exp.* (extremely popular) to break one's neck • (lit.): to break one's mouth or face.

ALSO: **emporter la gueule** *exp.* said of a something strong (alcohol, hot mustard, etc.) that takes the roof off one's mouth, to pack a punch.

gueule à chier dessus (avoir une) *exp.* to be butt-ugly • (lit.): to have a face to shit on.

example: Suzanne veut devenir actrice?! Mais elle **a une gueule à chier dessus**!

translation: Susan wants to become an actress?! But she's **butt ugly**!

as spoken: Suzanne, è veut dev'nir actrice?! Mais elle **a une gueule à chier d'ssus**!

NOTE: **gueule** *f.* (derogatory) •
1. face • **2.** mouth • (lit.): the mouth of an animal.

gueule à coucher dehors (avoir une) *f.* to be ugly
• (lit.): to have a face that should sleep outside.

NOTE: The feminine noun *gueule*, literally meaning the "mouth of an animal," is commonly used in a derogatory fashion to mean "face" or "head."

gueule de raie *f.* ugly person
• (lit.): to have a face like a vagina.

NOTE: **raie** *f.* vagina • (lit.): line.

gueuleton *m.* a huge blow-out of a meal, a huge spread (of food).

example: Nous avons fait un **gueuleton** hier soir!

translation: We **pigged out** last night!

as spoken: On a fait un **gueuleton** hier soir!

NOTE: **gueule** *f.* mouth
• (lit.): mouth of an animal. When used in reference to a person, it becomes derogatory and should be used with discretion.

ALSO: **"Ta gueule!"** *exp.* "Shut up!"

gugusse *m.* idiot.

guibolles *f.pl.* legs.

example: Ça fait six heures que nous dansons sans arrêt! J'ai mal aux **guibolles**, moi!

translation: We've been dancing for six hours! My **legs** hurt!

as spoken: Ça fait six heures qu'on danse sans arrêt! J'ai mal aux **guibolles**, moi!

SYNONYM: cannes *f.pl.*
• (lit.): canes.

guigne *f.* bad luck.

example: J'ai la **guigne**.

translation: I have **bad luck**.

as spoken: [no change]

NOTE: guignard(e) *n.* unlucky individual.

SYNONYM: poisse *f.*

guindal *m.* glass (of water, etc.).

example: Tu veux un **guindal** de flotte?

translation: Do you want a **glass** of water?

as spoken: [no change]

NOTE: flotte *f.* water (from the verb *flotter* meaning "to float").

guitoune *f.* bedroom • (lit.): tent.

gus *m.* (very popular) man, guy.

guss(e) *m.* man, guy.

gym *f.* a common abbreviation of "*gymnase*" meaning "gym" or "gymnasium."

example: Je m'entraîne à la **gym** cinq jours par semaine.

translation: I work out at the **gym** five days a week.

as spoken: J'm'entraîne à la **gym** cin' jours par s'maine.

hareng *m.* pimp • (lit.): herring.

haricot *m.* clitoris • (lit.): bean.

harpie *f.* shrew.

haut(e) comme trois pommes (être) *exp.* to be very short • (lit.): to be as high as three apples.

example: David a beaucoup grandi! L'année dernière, il était **haut comme trois pommes**!

Il est **haut comme trois pommes**, lui!

(trans.):
He's so **short**!

(lit.):
He's **as high as three apples**!

translation: David has really grown! Last year, he was **really short**!

as spoken: David, il a beaucoup grandi! L'année dernière, il était **haut comme trois pommes**!

heu *interj.* (pronounced like the *eu* in *feu*).

example: Au supermarché, je dois acheter du lait, des œufs, et **heu...** du pain.

translation: At the market, I have to buy some mike, some eggs, and **um...** some bread.

as spoken: Au supermarché, j'dois ach'ter du lait, des œufs, et **heu...** du pain.

NOTE: One of the biggest give-aways that a speaker of French is American, is to use the interjection "um" instead of the French *heu*.

heure H (l') *exp.* said of an important moment, "the big moment" • (lit.): "H" hour.

example: Les acteurs! Vous êtes tous à vos places? La pièce va commencer. C'est **l'heure H**!

translation: Actors! Are you all in your places? The play is about to begin. It's **the big moment**!

as spoken: Les acteurs! Vous êtes tous à vos places? La pièce, è va commencer. C'est **l'heure H**!

NOTE: jour J *exp.* D-day.

histoire *v.* ordeal, "adventure" • (lit.): story.

example: J'ai passé deux heures au supermarché parce qu'il y avait un monde fou! Puis ça m'a pris une heure pour rentrer à cause d'un accident en route. Quelle **histoire**!

translation: I spent two hours at the supermarket because there was an enormous crowd! Then it took me an hour to get home because of an accident on the way. What an **ordeal**!

as spoken: J'ai passé deux heures au supermarché pasqu'y avait un monde fou! Puis ça m'a pris une heure pour rentrer à cause d'un accident en route. Quelle **histoire**!

histoires (avoir ses) *exp.* to menstruate • (lit.): to have one's stories.

histoires paillardes *f.pl.* dirty jokes.

SYNONYM -1: **histoires salées** *f.pl.* • (lit.): salted stories.

SYNONYM -2: **histoires de cul** *f.pl.* • (lit.): ass stories.

SYNONYM -3: **gauloiseries** *f.pl.* • (lit.): Gaulish stories.

horizontale *f.* prostitute • (lit.): a horizontal (because of the position she frequently assumes).

ALSO: **grande horizontale** *f.* a very high-class prostitute.

huître *f.* spit wad, loogie • (lit.): oyster.

humecter les amygdales (s') *exp.* (*amygdales* is pronounced with the "g" silent: *amydales*) to drink, "to wet one's whistle" • (lit.): to moisten one's tonsils.

example: Qu'est-ce que j'ai soif! Je vais **m'humecter les amygdales**.

translation: Am I ever thirsty! I'm going **to go wet my whistle**.

as spoken: Qu'est-c'que j'ai soif! J'vais **m'humecter les amygdales**.

hurluberlu *m.* (applies to either a man or a woman) scatterbrain.

il n'y a pas à chier *exp.* there's no two ways about it • (lit.): there's no shitting.

example: **Il n'y a pas à chier**. Elle l'épouse pour son argent.

translation: **There's no two ways about it**. She's marrying him for his money.

as spoken: **Y'a pas à chier**. È l'épouse pour son argent.

il y a de fortes chances que *exp.* chances are that • (lit.): there are strong chances that.

example: **Il y a de fortes chances que** tu vas recevoir ta promotion.

translation: **Chances are that** you're going to get your promotion.

as spoken: **Y a d'fortes chances que** tu vas recevoir ta promotion.

il y a de la merde au bout du bâton *exp.* the shit is going to hit the fan • (lit.): there is shit at the end of the stick.

example: Je ne m'en mêlerais pas si j'étais à ta place. **Il y a de la merde au bout du bâton**.

translation: I wouldn't get involved if I were in your place. **The shit's gonna hit the fan**.

as spoken: J'm'en mêl'rais pas si j'étais à ta place. **Y'a d'la merde au bout du bâton**.

il y a de quoi s'amuser *exp.* said of a woman with large breasts • (lit.): there's a lot to have fun with.

il y a du beau monde *exp.* said of a woman with large breasts • (lit.): there are a lot of people there.

il y a du monde au balcon *exp.* said of a woman with large breasts • (lit.): there are people on the balcony.

Il y a du monde au balcon!

(trans.):
She's stacked!

(lit.):
There are people on the balcony!

imper(méable) à Popol *m.*

condom • (lit.): Popol's raincoat.

NOTE -1: **Popol** *m.* penis.

NOTE -2: Also spelled: *Popaul.*

instrument *m.* penis

• (lit.): instrument.

interêt à faire quelque chose (avoir) *exp.* to be better off doing something • (lit.): to have interest to do something.

example: Tu **as interêt à** partir tout de suite. Sinon, tu risques d'être en retard.

translation: You'd **better** leave right away. Otherwise, you run the risk of being late.

as spoken: T'**as interêt à** partir tout d'suite. Sinon, tu risques d'êtr'en r'tard.

inventé la poudre (ne pas avoir) *exp.* said of an idiot

• (lit.): not to have invented powder.

inventé le fil à couper le beurre (ne pas avoir) *exp.*

(applies to either a man or a woman) said of an idiot • (lit.): not to have invented the wire to cut butter.

itou *adj.* also, same.

example: Moi **itou**, j'aime le chocolat.

translation: I **also** like chocolate.

as spoken: [no change]

jacasser *v.* to talk a lot, to blab.

example: Henri a **jacassé** pendant toute une heure de ses problèmes familiaux.

translation: Henry **went on and on** for an entire hour about his family problems.

as spoken: Henri, il a **jacassé** pendant toute une heure d'ses problèmes familiaux.

*Sophie et Josette passent des heures à **jacasser**!*

(trans.):
*Sophie and Josette spend hours **blabbing**!*

jacter *v.* to speak, chatter, blab.

example: Je ne le comprends pas. Qu'est-ce qu'il **jacte**?

translation: I don't understand him. What's he **blabbing about**?

as spoken: J'le comprends pas. Qu'est-c'qu'y **jacte**?

SYNONYM: **jaspiner** *v.*

jambe du milieu *f.* penis
• (lit.): middle leg.

jambes en parenthèses (avoir les) *exp.* to be bow-legged
• (lit.): to have legs in the shape of parentheses.

example: Regarde comment il a **les jambes en parenthèses**. Il doit monter souvent à cheval.

translation: Look at those **bowed legs**. He must ride horses often.

as spoken: Regarde comment il a **les jambes en parenthèses**. Y doit monter souvent à ch'val.

Je l'emmerde *exp.* To hell with him / her!

example: Je me suis disputé avec Henri pour la dernière fois. **Je l'emmerde**!

translation: I fought with Henry for the last time. **Screw him**!

as spoken: Je m'suis disputé avec Henri pour la dernière fois. **J'l'emmerde**!

je-m'en-foutisme *n.* apathy.

example: Le **je-m'en-foutisme** règne chez les adolescents d'aujourd'hui.

translation: **Apathy** reigns among the adolescents of today.

as spoken: Le **j'm'en- foutisme**, ça règne chez les ados d'aujourd'hui.

NOTE: The preposition *chez* is commonly used in reference to a personality trait and could be translated as "within." Therefore, "*chez lui*" could be translated as either "at his house" or "within him" depending on the context. example: *L'agression est un comportement courant chez les singes;* Agression is a common behavior among monkeys.

je-m'en-foutiste *m.* one who is apathetic and disinterested, one who doesn't give a damn • (lit.): an "I-don't-give-a-damner."

example: Il ne fait jamais bien son travail. C'est un vrai **je-m'en-foutiste**.

translation: He never does good work. He's a real **apathetic person**.

as spoken: Y n'fait jamais bien son travail. C't'un vrai **j'-m'en-foutiste**.

SEE: **je-m'en-foutisme**, *p. 106.*

jeté(e) (être) *adj.* to be crazy, to be "cracked" • (lit.): to be thrown.

example: Ça sent le gaz ici. Oh hé! Mais ne craque pas cette allumette! Tu es **jeté** ou quoi?!

translation: It smells like gas here. Hey! Don't strike that match! What are you, **nuts**?!

as spoken: Ça sent l'gaz ici. Oh hé! Mais craque pas c't'allumette! T'es **sh'té** ou quoi?!

jeter de la lance *exp.* to urinate
• (lit.): to throw out urine.

NOTE: **lance** *f.* • **1.** urine • **2.** water.

SEE: **lancequiner**, *p. 110.*

jeter sa purée / son venin *exp.*
- to ejaculate (lit.): to throw purée / one's venom.

jeter un coup d'œil *exp.* to have a look • (lit.): to throw an eye-stroke.

example: Je vais **jeter un coup d'œil** au bébé.

translation: I'm going **to take a peek** at the baby.

as spoken: J'vais **sh'ter un coup d'œil** au bébé.

jeter un derrière la cravate (s'en) *exp.* to drink • (lit.): to throw one (a drink) behind one's tie.

example: Je crois que le patron **s'en jette un derrière la cravate** au boulot.

translation: I think the boss **drinks** on the job.

as spoken: J'crois que l'patron, y **s'en jette un derrière la cravate** au boulot.

NOTE: **boulot** *m.* (extremely popular) job, work, the "grind."

jeun (à) *c.l.* on an empty stomach • (lit.): after having fasted.

example: Pour ma prise de sang demain matin, je dois arriver chez le médecin **à jeun**.

translation: For my blood test tomorrow morning, I have to go to the doctor's office **on an empty stomach**.

as spoken: Pour ma prise de sang d'main matin, j'dois arriver chez l'médecin **à jeun**.

Je vous ai / t'ai demandé l'heure? *exp.* a contemptuous statement meaning "Was I talking to you?" • (lit.): I asked you the time?

example: **Je t'ai demandé l'heure**? Ta gueule!

translation: **Was I talking to you?** Shut up!

as spoken: **J't'ai d'mandé l'heure**? Ta gueule!

NOTE:: **Ta gueule!** *interj.* Shut up! • (lit.): Your mouth.

SEE: **gueule**, *p. 101.*

jobard *m.* (applies only to a man) idiot, sucker.

jouer *exp.* to play or act a certain way • (lit.): to play at (something).

example: François est très prétentieux. Il **joue** l'important, mais il ne l'est pas du tout.

translation: François is very pretentious. He **acts** important, but he's not at all.

as spoken: François, il est très prétentieux. Y **joue** l'important, mais y l'est pas du tout.

jouer de la mandoline *exp.* (of women) to masturbate • (lit.): to play the mandolin.

NOTE: This is based on a famous painting depicting a naked woman playing the mandolin which covers her genitalia.

jouir *v.* (very popular) to reach orgasm • (lit.): to enjoy.

journal de cul *m.* a dirty magazine • (lit.): a newspaper of butt.

example: Je crois que mon frère cache des **journaux de cul** sous son matelas.

translation: I think my brother hides **dirty magazines** under his mattress.

as spoken: J'crois qu'mon frère, y cache des **journaux d'cul** sous son mat'las.

NOTE: It is important to note that although the term *cul* literally means "ass," it does not carry the same degree of vulgarity as it does in English, and is therefore used much for frequently.

joyeuses *f.pl.* testicles • (lit.): the joyful ones, the ones that cause great joy.

Jules *m.* (very popular) • **1.** pimp • **2.** boyfriend • **3.** dude, guy (ex: *Hé, Jules!*; Hey, my man!) • (lit.): Jules, a man's first name.

Julot *m.* diminutive of: *Jules* meaning "pimp."

NOTE: This is a slang variation of: **Jules**.

jus *m.* sperm • (lit.): juice.

jus de corps *m.* sperm • (lit.): body juice.

jus de cyclope *m.* sperm • (lit.): cyclops juice.

NOTE: **cyclope** *m.* penis, "one-eyed bandit" • (lit.): cyclops.

jus (être au) *exp.* to be up-to-date, current • (lit.): to be in the (electric) juice.

example: Emile a déménagé! Tu **n'est pas au jus**?

translation: Emile moved out of town! You **didn't hear about it**?

as spoken: Emile, il a déménagé! T'**es pas au jus**?

NOTE: The expression *être au jus*, literally meaning "to be in the (electrical) juice," is a humorous play-on-words on the popular expression *être au courant*, literally "to be in the current." In French and English, *courant* ("current") can be used to mean both "up-to-date" as well as "electrical current."

SYNONYM: **hauteur (être à la)** *exp.* • (lit.): to be at the height.

juter *v.* (very popular) to ejaculate • (lit.): to give off juice.

lâcher l'écluse *exp.* to urinate • (lit.): to release the floodgate.

lâcher les gaz *exp.* to fart • (lit.): to release gases.

lâcher les vannes *exp.* to urinate • (lit.): to release the floodgates.

lâcher sa came / une giclée / son jus / sa purée / la semoule / son venin *exp.*
to ejaculate • (lit.): to release one's cum /a squirt / juice / purée / cream of wheat / venom.

> **NOTE:** **came** *f.* • **1.** sperm • **2.** junk (in general) • **3.** personal belongings, one's "stuff" • **4.** cocaine.

lâcher un[e] (en) *exp.* to fart
 • (lit.): to let one go.

lâcher une louise *exp.* to fart
 • (lit.): to release a louise.
 > **SEE:** **louise**, p. 112.

lâcher une perle *exp.* to fart
 • (lit.): to release a pearl.
 > **SEE:** **perle**, p. 134.

lâcher une perlouse *exp.*
 variation of: *lâcher une perle* meaning "to fart."

lâcher un fil *exp.* to urinate
 • (lit.): to release a thread (of urine).

laid(e) à pleurer (être) *exp.* to be extremely ugly • to be ugly enough to cause crying.

 example: Est-ce que tu as vu la chemise que Claude a porté ce soir? Elle était **laide à pleurer**.

 translation: Did you see the shirt that Claude wore tonight? It was **hideously ugly**.

 as spoken: T'as vu la ch'mise qu'il a porté c'soir, Claude? Elle était **laide à pleurer**.

*Elle est **laide à pleurer**, celle-là!*

(trans.)
She's **butt-ugly**!
(lit.)
She's **ugly enough to cry over**!

laissé(e) en carafe (être) *exp.*
 to jilt someone • (lit.): to leave someone like a carafe (after it's been all used up).

 example: C'est vrai ce qu'on m'a raconté? Georges a **laissée Louise en carafe**?

 translation: Is it true what I heard? George **dumped Louise**?

 as spoken: C'est vrai c'qu'on m'a raconté? Georges, il a **laissée Louise en carafe**?

laisser tomber quelqu'un comme une merde *exp.* to drop someone like a bad habit.

 example: Richard et moi, nous étions de bons amis mais récemment, il m'a **laissé tomber comme une merde**.

 translation: Richard and I were good friends but recently he **dropped me like a bad habit**.

as spoken: Richard et moi, on était d'bons amis mais récemment, y m'a **laissé tomber comme une merde**.

VARIATION: laisser tomber quelqu'un comme de la merde *exp.*

la mariée est trop belle *exp.* there's a catch to it • (lit.): the bride is too beautiful.

example: Je ne me fie pas à ce qu'il me dit. **La mariée est trop belle**!

translation: I don't trust what he's telling me. **Something's fishy**!

as spoken: J'me fie pas à c'qu'y m'dit. **La mariée, elle est trop belle**!

SYNONYM: ça ne tourne pas rond *exp.* • (lit.): it doesn't turn round.

lamfé *f.* woman.

NOTE: This is a *largonji* transformation of the feminine noun *femme* meaning "woman."

SEE: *Street French 2 - Largonji - p. 216.*

lancequiner *v.* **1.** to urinate • **2.** to rain.

SEE: jeter de la lance, *p. 106.*

langue dans sa poche (ne pas avoir la) *exp.* to tell it like it is, not to hold back what one is thinking • (lit.): not to have one's tongue in one's pocket.

example: Dès que Marie est entrée chez moi, elle a commencé à critiquer le décor. Elle **n'a pas la langue dans sa poche**, c'est sûr!

translation: As soon as Marie came into my house, she started criticizing the decor. She **really tells it like it is**, that's for sure!

as spoken: Dès que Marie est entrée chez moi, elle a commencé à critiquer l'décor. Elle **a pas la langue dans sa poche**, c'est sûr!

lavabe *m.* public bathroom.

NOTE: This is short for *lavabo* meaning "sink."

La vache! *exclam.* (extremely popular) "Wow!" • (lit.): the cow.

example: Oh, **la vache**! Tu as vu ça?

translation: **Wow**! Did you see that?

as spoken: Oh, **la vache**! T'as vu ça?

NOTE: Used as an exclamation, "*la vache!*" has nothing to do with "cow" although this is the literal translation. It is used in much the same way as the equivalent expression, "Holy cow!"

ALSO -1: vache *adj.* mean, tough.

ALSO -2: vacherie *f.* mean, rotten trick.

lèche-bottes *m.* (applies to either a man or a woman) someone who flatters a boss in order to get in his / her good graces. "ass kisser" • (lit.): boot-licker.

example: Laurent est un vrai **lèche-bottes**. C'est pour ça que le patron l'adore.

translation: Laurent is a real **butt kisser**. That's why the boss loves him.

as spoken: Laurent, c't'un vrai **lèche-bottes**. C'est pour ça qu'le patron, y l'adore.

NOTE -1: **lèche-bottes (faire du)** *exp.* (figurative) to kiss someone's butt.

NOTE -2: The stronger form of *lèche-bottes* is *lèche-cul* meaning "ass-licker."

lèche-cul *m.* (applies to either a man or a woman) kiss-ass • (lit.): ass licker.

example: Le patron adore Jean-Claude parce que c'est un **lèche-cul** fini!

translation: The boss loves Jean-Claude because he's a total **kiss-ass**!

as spoken: Le patron, y adore Jean-Claude pasque c't'un **lèche-cul** fini!

NOTE -1: **fini** *adj.* total, complete • (lit.): finished.

NOTE -2: **lèche-cul (faire du)** *exp.* to kiss up, to kiss someone's ass • (lit.): to do butt-licking.

lécher la gueule (se) *exp.* to kiss, to "suck face" • (lit.): to lick each other's mouth / face.

NOTE: When the feminine noun *gueule,* literally meaning "the mouth of an animal," is used in reference to a person, its connotation is "mouth" or "face," depending on the context.

lécher (se) *v.* to kiss each other deeply, to "suck face," to "French" kiss • (lit.): to lick each other.

lèche-vitrines (faire du) *exp.* to go window-shopping • (lit.): to do window-licking.

example: Ma sœur peut passer des heures en ville à **faire du lèche-vitrine**.

translation: My sister can spend hours in the city **window-shopping**.

as spoken: Ma sœur, è peut passer des heures en ville à **faire du lèche-vitrines**.

les bras m'en tombent *exp.* I'm dumbfounded • (lit.): my arms are falling off me.

example: On a volé ta voiture? **Les bras m'en tombent**!

translation: Your car was stolen? **I'm stunned**!

as spoken: [no change]

SYNONYM: **rester baba (en)** *exp.* to be so stunned that the sound *baba* is all that can be uttered.

lessivé(e) (être) *adj.* to be exhausted • (lit.): to be washed out.

example: Je suis **lessivé**. Je vais me coucher.

translation: I'm **wiped out**. I'm going to bed.

as spoken: J'suis **lessivé**. J'vais m'coucher.

SYNONYM -1: **claqué(e) (être)** *adj.* • (lit.): to be burst.

SYNONYM -2: **crevé(e) (être)** *adj.* • (lit.): to be burst or split.

SYNONYM -3: **esquinté(e) (être)** *adj.* • (lit.): to ruin.

lézarder *v.* to sunbathe, to soak up the rays (like a *lezard* meaning "lizard").

example: Je suis bronzé parce que j'ai **lézardé** toute la journée à la plage.

translation: I'm tan because I **lied in the sun** all day at the beach.

as spoken: J'suis bronzé pasque j'ai **lézardé** toute la journée à la plage.

VARIATION: faire le lézard *exp.* to sunbathe.

lieux *m.pl.* restroom, bathroom • (lit.): the places.

lièvre *m.* woman or girl • (lit.): hare.

limace *f.* bitch • (lit.): slug.

limer *v.* to fornicate • (lit.): to polish.

lolos *m.pl.* breasts • (lit.): little milkers.
NOTE: lolo *m.* child's language for "milk."

louf (être) *adj.* (applies to either a man or a woman) to be nuts.
NOTE: This is a largonji transformation of: *fou* • *SEE: — Street French 2, Largoni - p. 216.*

louise *f.* fart.

loulou(te) *n.* sweetheart, darling.

louper *v.* to miss.

example: J'ai **loupé** mon vol.

translation: I **missed** my flight.

as spoken: [no change]

lourdaud(e) • **1.** *m.* clumsy and awkward person • **2.** *adj.* clumsy, awkward.
NOTE: This is from the adjective *lourd(e)* meaning "heavy."

lourde *f.* door • (lit.): that which is heavy.

example: Quand tu quittes la maison, il faut fermer la **lourde**.

translation: When you leave the house, you have to close the **door**.

as spoken: Quand tu quittes la maison, faut fermer la **lourde**.

loustic *m.* guy, man.

loute *f.* a pretty woman or girl, a foxy woman or girl.

luc *m.* anus, ass.
NOTE: This is a *verlan* transformation of the masculine noun *cul* meaning "ass" — *SEE: Street French 2, Verlan - p. 187.*

lune *f.* posterior • (lit.): moon.

maboul(e) (être) *adj.* (applies to either a man or a woman) crazy, mad.

mac *m.* short for *maquereau* meaning "pimp" • (lit.): mackerel.

example: Tu as vu comment il est habillé, celui-là. Je parie que c'est un **mac**.

translation: Did you see how he's dressed? I bet he's a **pimp**.

as spoken: T'as vu comment il est habillé, çui-là. J'parie que c't'un **mac**.

NOTE: **maquerelle** *f.* Madam (of a brothel).

macadam (faire le) *exp.* (said of a prostitute) to hustle • (lit.): to do the macadam or sidewalk.

machin *m.* penis • (lit.): thing.

Madame Sans Gène *exp.* said of a woman with no manners or shame • (lit.): Madame Without Shame.

example: Louise s'est déshabillée en plein magasin au lieu d'entrer dans une cabine d'essayage. Quelle **Madame Sans Gène**!

translation: Louise took off her clothes in the middle of the store instead of using a dressing room. What a **shameless woman**!

as spoken: Louise, è s'est déshabillée en plein magasin au lieu d'entrer dans une cabine d'essayage. Quelle **Madame Sans Gène**!

NOTE: This expression comes from a character in French history who was known for being rude and shameless.

magner le derche (se) *exp.* to hurry, "to haul one's buns" • (lit.): to activate one's "derrière."

example: **Magne-toi le derche**! Nous sommes en retard!

translation: **Move your butt**! We're late!

as spoken: **Magne-toi l'derche**! On est en r'tard!

NOTE -1: **derche** *m.* a slang transformation of the masculine noun *"derrière"* meaning "buttocks."

NOTE -2: The noun *derche* may certainly be replaced by any other synonym for buttocks such as: **arrière-train** *m.* • **ballon** *m.* • **brioches** *f.pl.* • **dossière** *f.* • **jumelles** *f.pl.* • **popotin** *m.* • **valseur** *m.* • **etc.**

mains baladeuses (avoir les) *exp.* to have roving hands • (lit.): [same].

maison d'abattage *f.* high-volume prostitution house • (lit.): house of slaughter (referring to a business where the pace is fast and mechanical).

maison de passe *f.* an official word for "brothel" • (lit.): house of transaction.

maître / maîtresse de la situation (être) *exp.* to be in control of the situation • (lit.): to be master / mistress of the situation.

example: Après le désastre, je suis resté **maître de la situation**. Je n'ai jamais paniqué.

translation: After the disaster, I remained **in complete control**. I never panicked.

as spoken: Après l'désastre, j'suis resté **maître d'la situation**. J'ai jamais paniqué.

mal baisée *f.* an extremely vulgar insult for a woman implying that she is extremely frigid and sexually undesirable • (lit.): bad fuck.

example: **Mal baisée**! J'en ai ras le bol de vos insultes!

translation: **You pathetic fuck**! I've had it with your insults!

as spoken: **Mal baisée**! J'en ai ras l'bol de vos insultes!

NOTE: **ras le bol (en avoir)** *exp.* (very mild) to have had it, to be fed up • (lit.): to have had it to the brim of the bowl.

mal fichu(e) (être) *adj.* to be sick, under the weather • (lit.): to be badly put together.

example: Qu'est-ce qu'il y a? Tu as l'air **mal fichu** aujourd'hui.

translation: What's wrong? You look **sick** today.

as spoken: Qu'est-c'qu'y a? T'as l'air **mal fichu** aujourd'hui.

NOTE: This is a mild version of *mal foutu(e) (être)*, *(next entry)*.

mal foutu(e) (être) *adj.* to be sick, under the weather.

example: Je ne peux pas aller à l'école ce matin. Je suis **mal foutu** aujourd'hui.

translation: I can't go to school this morning. I'm **really sick** today.

as spoken: J'peux pas aller à l'école c'matin. J'suis **mal foutu** aujourd'hui.

NOTE: This is a strong version of *mal fichu(e) (être)*, *(previous entry)*.

mamelles *exp.* large breasts • (lit.): (anatomy) mammae.

mamours (faire des) *m.pl.* to kiss and fondle.

manche (avoir le) *m.* to have an erection • (lit.): to have the sleeve.

mandrin *m.* penis • (lit.): bandit, ruffian.

manger *v.* to perform fellatio • (lit.): to eat.

manquer que ça (ne plus) *exp.* to be the last thing one needs, to need something like a hole in the head • (lit.): not to miss any more than that.

example: Mes invités arrivent dans une heure et mon four vient de cesser de fonctionner. **Il ne me manquait plus que ça**!

translation: My guests are arriving in an hour and my oven just stopped working. **I need this like a hole in the head**!

as spoken: Mes invités, y z'arrivent dans une heure et mon four, y vient d'cesser d'fonctionner. **Y m' manquait pu qu'ça**!

manquer une case *exp.* (applies to either a man or a woman) to be nuts, crazy • (lit.): to be missing a division in the brain.

SEE: **case en moins (avoir une)**, *p. 32.*

mappemonde *f.* breasts • (lit.): map of the world in two hemispheres.

maquereau *m.* (very popular) pimp • (lit.): mackerel.

marchand de barbaque *m.* pimp, white slaver • (lit.): meat seller.

NOTE: **barbaque** *f.* (low quality) meat.

marchand de bidoche *m.* pimp, white slaver • (lit.): meat seller.

> **NOTE:** **bidoche** *f.* (low quality) meat.

marchand de viande *m.* pimp, white slaver • (lit.): meat seller.

marchandise *f.* penis and testicles • (lit.): merchandise.

marcheuse *f.* a girl who walks the streets, prostitute • (lit.): walker.

marle *m.* an abbreviation of: *marlou* meaning "pimp."

marlou *m.* pimp.

marquer *v.* to menstruate • (lit.): to mark.

marquer midi *exp.* to have an erection • (lit.): to be hitting straight up at noon.

marrant(e) (être) *adj.* (extremely popular) to be funny.

example: Cette comédienne est **marrante**! Personne ne me fait rire comme elle!

translation: That comedienne is so **funny**! No one makes me laugh like her!

as spoken: Elle est **marrante**, c'te comédienne! Personne m'fait rire comme elle!

> **NOTE -1:** The adjective *marrant(e)* is used in the same way as the French word "*drôle*" (and the English word "*funny*") whose meaning is both: **1.** funny and **2.** strange. However, *pas marrant(e)* is used to

describe something which is very unpleasant or "a real drag."

> **NOTE -2:** **se marrer** *v.* **1.** to laugh • **2.** to have a great time.

marre (en avoir) *exp.* to be fed up.

example: J'**en ai marre** de tous ces devoirs.

translation: I'm **fed up** with all this homework.

as spoken: J'**en ai marre** d'tous ces d'voirs.

> **SYNONYM:** **ras le bol (en avoir)** *exp.* (lit.): to have had it up to the rim of the bowl.

marsouin *m.* penis • (lit.): porpoise.

marteau (être) *adj.* (applies to either a man or a woman) to be nuts, cracked • (lit.): to be hammer.

mater *v.* to stare.

example: Il te **mate** sans arrêt, celui-là. Tu le connais?

translation: That guy is **staring** at you nonstop. Do you know him?

as spoken: Y t'**mate** sans arrêt, çui-là. Tu l'connais?

maths *m.pl.* abbreviation of "mathematics."

example: Je suis nul en **maths**.

translation: I'm a big zero when it comes to **math**.

as spoken: J'suis nul en **maths**.

> **NOTE:** In colloquial French, many academic subjects may be abbreviated such as **bio** *f.* biology; **géo** *f.* geography; **gym** *f.* gymnastics;

philo *f.* philosophy, **psycho** *f.* psychology.

mec *m.* (extremely popular) guy, "dude."

example: Tu connais ce **mec**-là? Je crois que c'est notre nouveau professeur d'anglais.

translation: Do you know that **guy**? I think that's our new English teacher.

as spoken: Tu connais c'**mec**-là? J'crois qu'c'est not'nouveau prof d'anglais.

mecqueton *m.* (also spelled: *mecton*) man, guy.

NOTE: This is a slang variation of: **mec**.

mecton *m.* pimp • (lit.): little guy.

médaillon *m.* posterior
• (lit.): medallion.

méga + [**]** *adj.* (used in front of a noun to add emphasis) mega, huge.

example: Je ne peux pas le croire! J'ai eu une **méganote** à mon examen de géo!

translation: I can't believe it! I got a **really high grade** on my geography test!

as spoken: J'peux pas l'croire! J'ai eu une **méganote** à mon exam d'géo!

NOTE: Notice how the preposition *à* follows the noun *méganote* not *sur*, a common mistake made by native English speakers.

mêler (se) *v.* to interfere, to stick one's nose into someone's business
• (lit.): to mix, blend.

example: Ne te **mêle** pas dans mes affaires!

translation: Don't **stick your nose** into my business!

as spoken: Te **mêle** pas dans mes affaires!

melon déplumé (avoir le) *exp.* (humorous) to be completely bald
• (lit.): to have a plucked melon (for a head).

example: Un de ces jours, tu auras **le melon déplumé** comme ton père.

translation: One of these days, you'll be **bald** just like your father.

as spoken: Un d'ces jours, t'auras **l'melon déplumé** comme ton père.

melons *m.pl.* large breasts
• (lit.): melons.

mémé (vieille) *f.* an old lady, an "old fart" • (lit.): old granny.

mener à la baguette *exp.* to boss around • (lit.): to lead with a conductor's baton.

example: Sa sœur le **mène à la baguette**. Franchement, je pense qu'il a peur d'elle!

translation: Her sister **bosses him around**. Frankly, I think he's afraid of her!

as spoken: Sa sœur, è l'**mène à la baguette**. Franchement, j'pense qu'il a peur d'elle!

Merde! *interj.* • **1.** Damn! • **2.** Wow!
• **3.** Good luck! "Break a leg!"
(lit.): Shit!

example (1): **Merde!** J'ai perdu
mon portefeuille!

translation: **Shit!** I lost my wallet!

as spoken: [no change]

example (2): **Merde!** Ta nouvelle
robe est très belle!

translation: **Shit!** Your new dress
is really pretty!

as spoken: **Merde!** Ta nouvelle
robe, elle est très belle!

example (3): Il est temps que tu
montes sur la scène. Ton public
t'attend. Je te dis **merde!**

translation: It's time for you to get
on stage. Your public awaits you.
Break a leg!

as spoken: Il est temps qu'tu
montes sur la scène. Ton public, y
t'attend. J'te dis **merde!**

VARIATION -1: Merde et
contre-merde! *interj.* • (lit.): Shit
and double shit!

VARIATION -2: Et puis merde!
interj.

VARIATION -3: Merde de
merde! *interj.* Holy shit!

VARIATION -4: Mille merdes!
interj. Holy shit!

NOTE: The interjection *merde* is
commonly used in conjunction with
alors to add emphasis: *Merde alors!*
Wow!

**merde dans les yeux (avoir
de la)** *exp.* to be completely
unaware, to be out of it.

example: Tu ne savais pas que
Gisèle est prostituée?! Mais, tu **as
de la merde dans les yeux** ou
quoi?

translation: You didn't know Gisèle
is a prostitute?! What are you,
totally out of it?

as spoken: Tu savais pas qu'Gisèle
est prostituée?! Mais, t'**as d'la
merde dans les yeux** ou quoi?

merde (être de la) *exp.* • **1.** to be
nonsense, bullshit • **2.** junk • (lit.): to
be (a bunch of) shit.

example (1): François t'a dit qu'il
est président d'une grande société?!
C'est de la **merde**, ça!

translation: François told you he's
president of a big company?! That's
a bunch of **bullshit**!

as spoken: François, y t'a dit qu'il
est président d'une grande société?!
C'est d'la **merde**, ça!

example (2): Ne me dis pas que tu
vas acheter ce truc. C'est **de la
merde**, ça!

translation: Don't tell me you're
going to buy that thing. It's **a piece
of shit**!

as spoken: Me dis pas qu'tu vas
ach'ter c'truc. C'est **d'la merde**, ça!

merde (l'avoir à la) *exp.* to be in
a terrible mood • (lit.): to have it
(one's personality) like shit.

example: On dirait que tu **l'as à la
merde**. Qu'est-ce qu'il y a? Ton
interview ne s'est pas bien passé?

translation: You look like you're **in
a shitty mood**. What's wrong?
Your interview didn't go well?

as spoken: On dirait qu'tu **l'as à la merde**. Qu'est-c'qu'il y a? Ton interview, y s'est pas bien passé?

merde (ne pas se prendre pour de la petite) *exp.* to be arrogant, to think one's shit doesn't stink • (lit.): not to take oneself for a little shit.

example: Je ne peux pas supporter cette fille. Elle **se prend pas pour de la petite merde**.

*Richard **ne se prends pas pour de la petite merde**!*

(trans.):
*Richard is **extremely arrogant**!*
(lit.):
*Richard **doesn't take himself for a little shit**!*

translation: I can't stand that girl. She **thinks her shit doesn't stink**.

as spoken: J'peux pas supporter c'te fille. È **s'prend pas pour d'la p'tite merde**.

NOTE: This is a stronger version of the expression *ne pas se prendre pour de la petite bière,* literally "not to take oneself for a little beer."

VARIATION: prendre pour de la merde (ne pas se) *exp.*
• (lit.): not to take oneself for shit.

merder *v.* to fail miserably.

example: J'ai complètement **merdé à** l'examen.

translation: I totally **blew** the test.

as spoken: J'ai complètement **merdé à** l'exam.

merder (se) *v.* to fail or botch something.

example: Je me suis **merdé** à l'examen!

translation: I **botched** the test!

as spoken: Je m'suis **merdé** à l'exam!

merdeux, euse *n.* a despicable person, a little "shit" • (lit.): shitty person.

example: Comment est-ce que tu arrives à supporter ce petit **merdeux** de François? Il est carrément méchant.

translation: How do you manage to tolerate that little **shit** François? He's plain mean.

as spoken: Comment t'arrives à supporter c'p'tit **merdeux** d'François? Il est carrément méchant.

merdier *m.* a predicament, a "shitload" of trouble.

example: Je suis dans un sacré **merdier**. J'ai emprunté la voiture de mon père et je l'ai démolie dans un accident!

translation: I'm in a real **fix**. I borrowed my father's car and I wrecked it in an accident!

as spoken: J'suis dans un sacré **merdier**. J'ai emprunté la voiture d'mon père et j'l'ai démolie dans un accident!

merdique (être) *adj.* • **1.** to be difficult, to be a real bitch (said of a situation or problem) • **2.** to be for the birds, for shit.

example (1): Je n'arrive pas à résoudre ce problème. C'est complètement **merdique**.

translation: I can't seem to solve this problem. It's a real **bitch**.

as spoken: J'arrive pas à résoud' ce problème. C'est complètement **merdique**.

example (2): Cette pièce de théâtre est complètement **merdique**.

translation: This play is really **shitty**.

as spoken: C'te pièce de théâtre, elle est complètement **merdique**.

merdouille *f.* a little nothing of a knickknack.

example: J'ai un cadeau pour toi. C'est une petite **merdouille** que j'ai acheté en vacances.

translation: I have a gift for you. It's a little **knickknack** I bought on vacation.

as spoken: J'ai un cadeau pour toi. C't'une petite **merdouille** qu'j'ai ach'té en vacances.

merdouiller *v.* to flounder.

example: Ça ne m'étonnerait pas si Georges trouvait un nouveau boulot. Il ne fait que **merdouiller** ici.

translation: It wouldn't surprise me if George found a new job. He does nothing but **flounder** here.

as spoken: Ça m'étonn'rait pas si Georges trouvait un nouveau boulot. Y fait que **merdouiller** ici.

NOTE: **boulot** *m.* (extremely popular) work, job, the "grind."

merlan *m.* • **1.** barber • **2.** pimp • (lit.): whiting (fish).

example (1): Je vais aller chez le **merlan** me faire couper les cheveux.

translation: I'm going to go to the **barber** to get my hair cut.

as spoken: J'vais aller chez l'**merlan** m'faire couper les ch'veux.

mettre au clou *exp.* to hock • (lit.): to hang on the nail.

example: Si tu as besoin de fric, **met** ta guitare **au clou**.

translation: If you need some money, **hock** your guitar.

as spoken: Si t'as b'soin d'fric, **met** ta guitare **au clou**.

mettre la main à la pâte *exp.*
(used in the culinary world) to get in
there with one's hands, (of men) to
masturbate • (lit.): to put the hand to
the dough.

mettre (le) *exp.* to fornicate
• (lit.): to put it (in).

mettre les bouts *exp.* to leave
• (lit.): to put the ends (together).

example: Pascale a **mis les bouts**
sans me dire au revoir!

translation: Pascale **took off**
without saying good-bye to me!

as spoken: Pascale, il a **mis les
bouts** sans m'dire au revoir!

SYNONYM: **prendre la
tangeante** *exp.* • (lit.): to take the
tangent.

mettre les choses au point
exp. to set the record straight
• (lit.): to put things to the point.

example: Michel m'a demandé de
sortir avec lui ce soir. Alors, j'ai **mis
les choses au point** et lui ai dit
que j'étais mariée.

translation: Michel asked me to go
out with his tonight. So, I **set the
record straight** and told him I
was married.

as spoken: Michel, y m'a d'mandé
d'sortir avec lui c'soir. Alors, j'ai
mis les choses au point et lui ai
dit qu'j'étais mariée.

**mettre les doigts de pieds en
éventail** *exp.* to reach orgasm
• (lit.): to spread one's toes apart.
NOTE: This expression also means
"to relax."

mettre les voiles *exp.* to leave, to
hit the road.

example: Il est déjà midi?! Je dois
mettre les voiles!

translation: It's already noon?!
I have **to leave**!

as spoken: Il est déjà midi?! J'dois
mett'les voiles!

mettre quelqu'un en boîte
exp. to make fun of someone
• (lit.): to put someone in a box.

example: Je ne peux pas sortir avec
cette nouvelle coupe de cheveux.
C'est affreux! Tout le monde va **me
mettre en boîte**!

translation: I can't go out with this
new haircut. It's horrible! Everyone's going to **make fun of me**!

as spoken: J'peux pas sortir avec
c'te nouvelle coupe de ch'veux.
C't'affreux! Tout l'monde va
m'mettre en boîte!

mettre sa main au feu (en)
exp. to be absolutely sure of
something • (lit.): to put one's hand
in fire over it.

example: Je te dis qu'elle ment.
J'**en mettrais ma main au feu**.

translation: I'm telling you she's
lying. I **would swear to it**.

as spoken: J'te dis qu'è ment. J'**en
mettrais ma main au feu**.

mettre son véto (y) *exp.* to draw
the line, to put one's foot down
• (lit.): to put one's veto there.

example: Vous ne pouvez pas jouer
au ballon dans la maison. Là, j'**y
mets mon véto**.

translation: You can't play ball in the house. I'm **drawing the line** there.

as spoken: Vous pouvez pas jouer au ballon dans la maison. Là, j'**y mets mon véto**.

meuf *f.* (very popular) woman or wife.

NOTE: This is a *verlan* transformation of the feminine noun *femme* meaning "woman" or "wife."

SEE: *Street French 2 - Verlan - p. 187.*

meules *f.pl.* **1.** posterior • **2.** breasts • (lit.): stacks, piles (of hay, etc.).

NOTE: The difference between definitions **1.** and **2.** simply depends on the context.

M.I. *m.* an abbreviation of *meuble inutile* meaning "someone who is useless" • (lit.): useless furniture.

example: Jeannette travaille soixante heures par semaine tandis que son mari ne fait rien toute la journée! C'est un vrai **M.I.**, lui!

translation: Jeannette works sixty hours a week whereas her husband doesn't do anything all day long! He's totally **useless**!

as spoken: Jeannette, è travaille soixante heures par semaine tandis que son mari, y fait rien toute la journée! C't'un vrai **M.I.**, lui!

SYNONYM: **bon à rien** *m.* • (lit.): good-for-nothing.

miches *f.pl.* breasts • (lit.): loaves of bread.

micheton *m.* prostitute's client, "john."

example: Afin de combattre le problème de la prostitution dans le quartier, la police a commencé à arrêter tous les **michés**.

translation: In order to fight the prostitution problem in this neighborhood, the police have started to arrest all the **johns**.

as spoken: Afin d'combatt' le problème d'la prostitution dans l'quartier, la police, elle a commencé à arrêter tous les **michés**.

mille-feuilles *m.pl.* vagina • (lit.): Napoleon pastry.

Mince! *interj.* (a common euphemism for *merde* meaning "shit") Wow!

example: **Mince** alors! Je n'ai jamais rien vu de pareil!

translation: **Wow**! I've never seen anything like it!

as spoken: **Mince** alors! J'ai jamais rien vu d'pareil!

minet *m.* vagina • (lit.): kitty, "pussy."

minou *m.* vagina • (lit.): kitty, "pussy."

mistonne *f.* bitch.

mitrailleuse *f.* a very talkative woman, blabbermouth • (lit.): machine gun.

example: Evelyne parle sans arrêt. Quelle **mitrailleuse**, cella-là!

translation: Evelyn talks nonstop. What a friggin' **blabbermouth**!

as spoken: Evelyne, è parle sans arrêt. Quelle **mitrailleuse**, cella-là!

mochard *m.* one who is *moche* ("ugly").

moche *adj.* • 1. ugly • 2. mean, nasty.

example (1): Hélène était très **moche** quand elle était petite. Maintenant, elle est devenue une très belle fille.

translation: Helen was very **ugly** when she was little. Now she's become a beautiful girl.

as spoken: Hélène, elle était très **moche** quand elle était p'tite. Maintenant, elle est d'venue une très belle fille.

example (2): C'est **moche** ce que tu m'as fait!

translation: What you did to me was **mean**!

as spoken: C'est **moche** c'que tu m'as fait!

moche à caler des roues de corbillard (être) *exp.* (humorous) to be extremely ugly • (lit.): to be ugly enough to stop the wheels of a hearse.

example: Il est **moche à caler des roues de corbillard**, lui!

translation: He has **a face that could stop a clock**!

as spoken: Il est **moche à caler des roues d'corbillard**, lui!

SYNONYM: **laid(e) à faire peur (être)** *exp.* • (lit.): to be ugly enough to cause fear.

mocheté *f.* an ugly woman or girl • (lit.): ugliness (from the slang noun *moche* meaning "ugly").

mochetingue *m.* a slang variant of *mocheté* meaning "ugliness."

mocheton *m.* a slang variant of *mocheté* meaning "ugliness."

molard *m.* spit wad, loogie.

molarder *v.* to spit, to hock "loogies."

example: Il est interdit de **molarder** dans le métro.

translation: It's forbidden to **spit** in the subway.

as spoken: Il est interdit d'**molarder** dans l'métro.

mollo *exp.* carefully and slowly • (lit.): [no literal translation].

example: Tu vas jouer au football? Vas-y **mollo**, hein? Tu as été malade pendant une semaine.

translation: You're going to play soccer? Take it **easy**, huh? You've been sick for a week.

as spoken: Tu vas jouer au foot? Vas-y **mollo**, hein? T'as été malade pendant une s'maine.

monté (être bien) *adj.* to be well hung • (lit.): to be well mounted.

morceau *m.* penis • (lit.): morsel, piece.

mordre la poussière *exp.* to bite the dust • (lit.): [no change].

example: En descendant de la montagne, j'ai **mordu la poussière** quand j'ai glissé sur un caillou.

translation: Coming down the mountain, I **bit the dust** when I slipped on a stone.

as spoken: En descendant d'la montagne, j'ai **mordu la poussière** quand j'ai glissé sur un caillou.

mordre les doigts (s'en) *exp.* to regret something • (lit.): to bite one's fingers over something.

example: Marie est toujours impolie. Si elle ne change pas sa conduite, un de ces jours elle va **s'en mordre les doigts**.

translation: Marie is always so rude. If she doesn't change her behavior, one of these days she's going **to regret it**.

as spoken: Marie, elle est toujours impolie. Si è change pas sa conduite, un d'ces jours è va **s'en mord' les doigts**.

mordu(e) de quelqu'un (être) *adj.* to have a crush on someone • (lit.): to be bitten by someone.

example: Tu as vu la nouvelle étudiante dans notre cours de biologie? Je suis **mordu d'elle**!

translation: Did you see the new student in our biology class? I have such a **crush on her**!

as spoken: T'as vu la nouvelle étudiante dans not' cours de bio? J'suis **mordu d'elle**!

NOTE: **mordu(e)** *n.* fanatic (*un mordu de tennis:* a tennis buff).

morfaler (se) *v.* to pig out.

example: Je me sens malade. Je **me suis morfalé** trop de desserts.

translation: I feel sick. I **pigged out** on too many desserts.

as spoken: Je m'sens malade. Je **m'suis morfalé** trop d'desserts.

motte *f.* vagina • (lit.): mound.

motus et bouche cousue *exp.* don't say a word to anyone • (lit.): ("*motus*" has no literal translation) and sewn up mouth.

example: C'est un secret. **Motus et bouche cousue**!

translation: It's a secret. **Mum's the word**!

as spoken: C't'un secret. **Motus et bouche cousue**!

mouche à merde *f.* housefly • (lit.): shit-fly.

example: Il y a trop de **mouches à merde** chez ma tante!

translation: There are too many **houseflies** at my aunt's house!

as spoken: Il a trop d'**mouches à merde** chez ma tante!

mouchodrome (avoir un) *exp.* to be bald • (lit.): to have a fly landing pad.

moufflet dans le tiroir (avoir un) *exp.* to be pregnant • (lit.): to have a kid in the drawer.

mouiller le goupillon *exp.* to fornicate • (lit.): to wet one's sprinkler.

NOTE: **goupillon** *m.* penis, dick • (lit.): sprinkler (for holy water).

mouiller le mur *exp.* to urinate • (lit.): to wet the wall.

mouiller une ardoise *exp.* to urinate • (lit.): to wet a slate.

moukère *f.* (from Arabic) woman.

moule *f.* (extremely popular) vagina • (lit.): mussel.

mouler un bronze *exp.* to defecate • (lit.): to mold a bronze (thing).

moulin à paroles *m.* blabber-mouth • (lit.): a windmill of speech.

example: Il parle sans arrêt! Quel **moulin à paroles**!

translation: He talks nonstop! What a **blabbermouth**!

as spoken: Y parle sans arrêt! Quel **moulin à paroles**!

SYNONYM -1: **jacteur** *m.* (from the verb *jacter* meaning "to blab").

SYNONYM -2: **jacasseur** *m.* (from the verb *jacasser* meaning "to blab").

mourir de sa belle mort *exp.* to die of old age • (lit.): to die of one's pretty death.

example: Elle n'a jamais été malade. Elle est **morte de sa belle mort**.

translation: She's never been sick. She **died of old age**.

as spoken: Elle a jamais été malade. Elle est **morte de sa belle mort**.

mousser le créateur (se faire) *exp.* (of men) to masturbate • (lit.): to make one's creator foam.

moutards *m.pl.* kids.

example: Ma frangine travaille dans une école primaire. Heureusement qu'elle adore les **moutards**!

translation: My sister works in a primary school. It's a good thing she loves **kids**!

as spoken: Ma frangine, è travaille dans une école primaire. Heureusement qu'elle adore les **moutards**!

SYNONYM -1: **mômes** *m.pl. & f.pl.*

SYNONYM -2: **mioches** *m.pl. & f.pl.*

nage (être en) *exp.* to be soaking wet from perspiration • (lit.): to be wet as if one had been swimming.

example: Quand j'ai finit mon footing ce matin, j'étais **en nage**!

translation: When I finished jogging this morning, I was **soaked in sweat**!

as spoken: Quand j'ai finit mon footing c'matin, j'étais **en nage**!

VARIATION: **tout en nage (être)** *exp.* to be completely soaking wet from perspiration.

nana *f.* (extremely popular) girl, "chick."

example: Elle s'appelle comment, cette **nana**?

translation: What's that **girl**'s name?

as spoken: È s'appelle comment, c'te **nana**?

SYNONYM: **nénette** *f.*

ANTONYM: **mec** *m.* guy, "dude."

navet *m.* a bomb (said of a bad movie) • (lit.): turnip.

example: Quel **navet**, ce film!

translation: This film is a real **bomb**!

as spoken: Quel **navet**, c'film!

nénés *m.pl.* breasts

nénesse *f.* woman or girl.

nénette *f.* woman or girl.

nez (avoir quelqu'un dans le) *exp.* to be unable to stand someone • (lit.): to have someone in the nose.

nibards *m.pl.* breasts

nib de tifs (avoir) *exp.* to be bald • (lit.): not to have any hair.

NOTE -1: **nib de** *adj.* no more, none • Also seen as: *nib de nib:* nothing at all, zilch.

NOTE -2: **tifs** *m.pl.* hair.

nichons *m.pl.* (very popular) breasts.

nickel *adj.* very clean, "spotless."

example: La maison de Gisèle est toujours **nickel**.

translation: Gisèle's house is always **spotless**.

as spoken: La maison d'Gisèle, elle est toujours **nickel**.

nid *m.* bed • (lit.): nest.

niquer *v.* (from Arabic) to fornicate • (lit.): to fuck.

nique ta mère *exp.* (extremely vulgar) disparaging remark about someone's mother • (lit.): fuck your mother.

NOTE: This is also the name of a popular rap group in France.

nœud *m.* penis • (lit.): knot.

noisette • **1.** *f.* clitoris • **2.** *f.pl.* testicles (lit.): hazelnut.

noix *f.pl.* testicles • (lit.): nuts.

noix (vieille) *f.* an old person, an "old fart" • (lit.): old (wal)nut.

nom de deux *interj.* my gosh.

example: **Nom de deux**! Je ne sais pas comment il a pu faire ça!

Nom de deux! *Il y a un cambrioleur dans la maison!*

(trans.):
Holy cow!
There's a burglar in the house!

(lit.):
Name of two!
There's a burglar in the house!

translation: **My gosh**! I don't know how he did managed to do that!

as spoken: **Nom de deux**! J'sais pas comment il a pu faire ça!

NOTE: This is a euphemism for *nom de Dieu* meaning "my God" or literally, "(in the) name of God."

nouille *f.* (applies to either a man or a woman) nerd • (lit.): noodle.

nouveau (de) *c.l.* again • (lit.): of new.

example: Demain, je vais faire du ski **de nouveau**.

translation: Tomorrow, I'm going skiing **again**.

as spoken: Demain, j'vais faire du ski **d'nouveau**.

NOTE: *de nouveau* = again • *à nouveau* = in a new and different way (*Je vais le faire à nouveau*; I'm going to go about it differently).

numéro *m.* man, guy • (lit.): number.

œil (mon) *interj.* my foot (in response to a ridiculous comment) • (lit.): my eye.

NOTE: This is a mild version of: *mon cul!*

SEE: **cul (mon)**, *p. 56.*

œil à quelqu'un (faire de l')
exp. to give someone the eye
• (lit.): to make the eye to someone.

example: Il te **fait de l'œil**! Va lui parler!

translation: He's **giving you the eye**! Go talk to him!

as spoken: Y t'**fait d'l'œil**! Va lui parler!

œil de bronze *m.* anus
• (lit.): bronze eye.

œillet *m.* (extremely popular) anus
• (lit.): carnation.

œil qui dit merde à l'autre (avoir un) *exp.* to be cross-eyed
• (lit.): to have an eye that says shit to the other.

example: Je crois qu'il a besoin de porter des lunettes. Il **a un œil qui dit merde à l'autre**.

translation: I think he needs glasses. He's **cross-eyed**.

as spoken: J'crois qu'il a b'soin d'porter des lunettes. Il **a un œil qui dit merde à l'autre**.

œil qui dit zut à l'autre (avoir un) *exp.* (humorous) said of someone who is cross-eyed
• (lit.): to have an eye (which is completely independent of the other) which says "Darn!" to the other.

example: J'ai mal aux yeux parce que ça fait quatre heures que je lis ce livre. J'ai l'impression que je commence à **avoir un œil qui dit zut à l'autre**!

translation: My eyes are hurting me because I've been reading this book for four hours. I feel like I'm going **cross-eyed**!

as spoken: J'ai mal aux yeux pasque ça fait quatre heures que j'lis c'livre. J'ai l'impression que j'commence à **avoir un œil qui dit zut à l'autre**!

SYNONYM: **œil qui joue au billard et l'autre qui compte les points (avoir un)** *exp.*
• (lit.): to have one eye that's playing billiards while the other is off counting the points.

NOTE: This is a mild version of: *œil qui dit merde à l'autre, (previous entry).*

oh, là, là *exclam.* wow (used to signify surprise or disbelief).

example: **Oh, là, là!** Qu'est-ce qu'il est bizarre, lui!

translation: **Wow!** Is he ever bizarre!

as spoken: **Oh, là, là!** Qu'est-c'qu'il est bizarre, lui!

NOTE -1: Many Americans mistakenly pronounce this exclamation as *"Oooooo, là, là!"*

NOTE -2: In the previous example, *"qu'est-ce que"* was used before the phrase *"il est bizarre, lui."* This is an extremely common formula used to add emphasis to a statement. For example: ***Qu'est-ce qu'****elle est grande!*; Is she ever tall! • ***Qu'est-ce qu'****il pleut aujourd'hui!*; Is it ever raining today!

oiseau *m.* man, guy • (lit.): bird.

olives *f.pl.* testicles • (lit.): olives.

ombre de soi-meme (n'être que l') *exp.* to be but a shadow of one's (former) self • (lit.): [no change].

example: Est-ce que tu as été malade? Tu **n'es que l'ombre de toi-même**!

translation: Have you been sick? You're nothing but **a shadow of your former self**!

as spoken: T'as été malade? T'**es que l'ombre de toi-même**!

On dirait que… *exp.* "It looks like…" • (lit.): "One would say that…"

example: **On dirait qu'**il va pleuvoir.

translation: **It looks like** it's going to rain.

as spoken: **On dirait qu'**y va pleuvoir.

onduler de la toiture *exp.* (applies to either a man or a woman) humorous for "to have a screw loose" • (lit.): to have a buckling roof.

on n'apprend pas à un vieux singe à faire la grimace *prov.* you can't teach an old dog new tricks • (lit.): you can't teach an old male monkey to make faces.

example: A mon âge, tu veux m'apprendre à conduire? **On n'apprend pas à un vieux singe à faire la grimace**.

translation: At my age, you want to teach me to drive? **You can't teach an old dog new tricks**.

as spoken: A mon âge, tu veux m'apprendre à conduire? **On apprend pas à un vieux singe à faire la grimace**.

On n'apprend pas à un vieux singe à faire la grimace.

(trans.):
You can't teach an old dog new tricks.

(lit.):
You can't teach an old monkey to smile.

ouatères *m.pl.* (from British-English) a shorten version of *water-closet* meaning "bathroom."

oui ou merde *exp.* yes or no
• (lit.): yes or shit.

example: Tu vas me rendre mon argent? Oui ou **merde**.

translation: Are you going to give me back my money? Yes or **no**.

as spoken: Tu vas m'rend' mon argent? Oui ou **merde**.

ours (avoir ses) *m.pl.* to menstruate • (lit.): to have one's bears.

outil *m.* penis • (lit.): tool.

ouvrir les écluses *exp.* to urinate
• (lit.): to open the floodgates.

ordure *f.* a disparaging remark applied to either a man or a woman
• (lit.): trash.

orphelin *m.* turd • (lit.): orphan.

os à moelle *m.* penis • (lit.): marrow bone.

os (avoir l') *m.* to have an erection
• (lit.): to have the bone.

paddock *m.* bed • (lit.): a paddock (a place where horses are kept), horse's stall.

NOTE: paddocker (se) *v.* to go to bed, to hit the hay.

pageot *m.* bed.

example: Ton **pageot** est trop mou. C'est pour ça que tu as mal au dos.

translation: Your **bed** is too soft. That's why your back is sore.

as spoken: Ton **pageot**, il est trop mou. C'est pour ça qu't'as mal au dos.

NOTE -1: **pageoter (se)** *v.* to go to bed.

NOTE -2: **dépageoter (se)** *v.* to get out of bed.

SYNONYM -1: **plumard** *m.* • (lit.): that which is made of feathers or *"plumes."*

SYNONYM -2: **pieu** *m.* • (lit.): stake or post.

paillasse *f.* woman or girl • (lit.): straw mattress.

paillasson *m.* an easy lay • (lit.): a doormat.

example: Tu es sorti avec Margot? On dit que c'est un **paillasson**, celle-là!

translation: You went out with Margot? They say she's a real **easy lay**!

as spoken: T'es sorti avec Margot? On dit qu'c't'un **paillasson**, celle-là!

SYNONYM: **cuisse légère (avoir la)** *exp.* said of someone who is an easy lay • (lit.): to have a light thigh (since they're always up in the air).

palmées (les avoir) *exp.* to be extremely lazy • (lit.): to have them (hands) webbed (and therefore unable to do any work).

example: Elle ne m'aide jamais. Ce qu'elle **les a palmées**!

translation: She never helps me. Is she ever **lazy**!

as spoken: È m'aide jamais. C'qu'è **les a palmées**!

NOTE -1: **l'envers (les avoir à)** *exp.* • (lit.): to have them (hands) inside out.

NOTE -2: As seen in the previous example, *ce que* is often added to a statement to add emphasis: *Il est bizarre!* (He's strange!); *Ce qu'il est bizarre!* (Is he ever strange!).

paluche *f.* masturbation, handjob • (lit.): slang for "hand."

palucher (se) *v.* (of men) to masturbate • (lit.): to give oneself a hand job.

NOTE: **paluche** *f.* hand.

panier *m.* vagina • (lit.): basket.

panier à crottes *m.* posterior • (lit.): turd basket.

panier d'amour *m.* vagina • (lit.): love basket.

papouilles (faire des) *f.pl.* to fondle sexually.

paquet *m.* • **1.** a lot, "a pile" • **2.** penis and testicles • (lit.): a package.

example: J'ai un **paquet** de soucis aujourd'hui!

translation: I have a **pile** of worries today!

as spoken: J'ai un **paquet** d'soucis aujourd'hui!

ALSO: **mettre le paquet** *exp.* to do something with abandon, to let out all the stops.

example: J'ai fait la cuisine toute la journée parce que ma famille vient dîner chez moi ce soir. Ça va être un dîner à douze plats! J'ai vraiment **mis le paquet**!

translation: I cooked all day long because my family is coming over for dinner tonight. We going to have a twelve-course meal! I really **let out all the stops**.

as spoken: J'ai fait la cuisine toute la journée pasque ma famille, è vient dîner chez moi c'soir. Ça va êtr'un dîner à douze plats! J'ai vraiment **mis l'paquet**!

pare-chocs *m.pl.* breasts
• (lit.): bumpers.

parier son dernier sou *exp.* to bet one's bottom dollar • (lit.): to bet one's last cent.

example: Je **parie mon dernier sou** qu'il vont finir par divorcer.

translation: I'll **bet my bottom dollar** that they end up getting divorced.

as spoken: J'**parie mon dernier sou** qu'y vont finir par divorcer.

partouse *f.* orgy.

partouse à la bague *f.* daisy chain • (lit.): anus game.
NOTE: **partouse** *f.* a slang variant of *partie* meaning "game."

partouse carrée *f.* wife swapping • (lit.): square game or four-person game.
NOTE: **partouse** *f.* a slang variant of: *partie* meaning "game."

partouser *v.* to participate in orgies.

partouzard(e) *n.* one who likes orgies.

pas jojo *adj.* not very pretty (from *joli(e)* meaning "pretty)."

example: Sa maison n'est pas **jojo**.

translation: His house isn't very **pretty**.

as spoken: Sa maison, elle est pas **jojo**.

pas mal *exp.* quite a bit • (lit.): not [a] bad [number of].

example: Je n'aime pas ce parc. Il y a **pas mal** de moustiques ici!

translation: I don't like this park. There are **quite a few** mosquitos here!

as spoken: J'aime pas c'parc. Y a **pas mal** d'moustiques ici!

passer l'arme à gauche *exp.* to die, to kick the bucket • (lit.): to pass the firearm to the left.

example: Que j'étais malade hier soir. Je pensais que j'allais **passer l'arme à gauche**.

translation: Was I ever sick last night. I thought I was gonna **kick the bucket**.

as spoken: Que j'étais malade hier soir. J'pensais qu'j'allais **passer l'arme à gauche**.

SYNONYM: **avaler son extrait de naissance** *exp.* • (lit.): to swallow one's birth certificate.

passer l'éponge [là-dessus]
  exp. to reconcile, to let bygones be
  bygones • (lit.): to pass the sponge
  (that "soaks up" our differences).

  example: Oublions notre querelle
  et **passons l'éponge
  [là-dessus]**.

  translation: Let's forget about our
  quarrel and **let bygones be
  bygones**.

  as spoken: Oublions not' querelle
  et **passons l'éponge [là-d'ssus]**.

passer quelqu'un à tabac *exp.*
  to beat someone up, to give
  someone a thrashing • (lit.): to pass
  someone like tobacco.

  example: Le voleur s'est fait
  prendre, et la foule l'a **passé à
  tabac**.

  translation: The thief got himself
  nabbed, and the crowd
  pulverized him.

  as spoken: Le voleur y s'est fait
  prendre, et la foule, è l'a **passé à
  tabac**.

  SYNONYM: **battre comme
  plâtre** *exp.* to beat to a pulp
  • (lit.): to beat up like plaster.

passer sur le billard *exp.* to
  undergo surgery • (lit.): to go onto
  the billiard table.

  example: Demain tu **passes sur
  le billard**? Mais qu'est-ce que
  tu as?

  translation: Tomorrow you're
  going in for surgery? What's
  wrong with you?

  as spoken: Demain, tu **passes
  su'l'billard**? Mais qu'est-c'que
  t'as?

pas si con *exp.* not such a bad idea
  • (lit.): not so stupid.

  example: "Tu veux aller faire un
  pique-nique aujourd'hui?"
  "Pas si con. Il fait très beau
  dehors."

  translation: "Do you want to go on
  a picnic today?"
  "That's not such a bad idea.
  The weather is beautiful outside."

  as spoken: "Tu veux aller faire un
  pique-nique aujourd'hui?"
  "Pas si con. Y fait très beau
  dehors."

pastille *f.* • **1.** fart • **2.** anus
  • (lit.): lozenge.
  SEE: **détacher une pastille**,
  p. 65.

patapouf *m.* (applies to either a man
  or a woman) fatso, tub of lard.

  example: Je dois me mettre au
  régime après mes vacances. Sinon,
  je vais devenir un gros **patapouf**.

  translation: I have to put myself on
  a diet after my vacation. Otherwise,
  I'm going to become a **tub of lard**.

  as spoken: J'dois m'mettr'au
  régime après mes vacances. Sinon,
  j'vais dev'nir un gros **patapouf**.

patate *f.* (applies to either a man or a
  woman) • **1.** idiot • **2.** big nose,
  "honker" (lit.): potato.

patouilles (faire des) *f.pl.* to
  fondle.

NOTE: From the feminine plural noun "pattes" (literally meaning "paws") used to mean "hands" in French slang.

pattes d'araignée (faire des)

f.pl. to do light touching with the tips of the fingers • (lit.): to make spider feet.

paumer *v.* to lose.

example (1): J'ai **paumé** mon chapeau.

translation: I **lost** my hat.

as spoken: [no change]

example (2): Je suis **paumé**!

translation: I'm **lost**!

as spoken: J'suis **paumé**! Où suis-je?

NOTE: **un paumé** *m.* a loser.

pauvre con *m.* poor or pathetic guy.

example: Oh, le **pauvre con**. Il a été mis à la porte deux jours avant Noël.

translation: Oh, the **poor guy**. He was fired two days before Christmas.

as spoken: Oh, l'**pauv'** con. Il a été mis à la porte deux jours avant Noël.

pavé dans la cour (avoir du)

exp. to have teeth • (lit.): to have flagstones in the courtyard.

example: Mon grand-père **n'a pas de pavé dans la cour.**

translation: My grandfather **doesn't have a tooth in his head**.

as spoken: Mon grand-père, il **a pas d'pavé dans la cour**.

pavé (faire le) *m.* (said of a prostitute) to hustle • (lit.): to do the pavement.

paye (faire une) *exp.* to be a long time • (lit.): to be a pay period (a period of time, usually a month, between pay checks).

example: Salut Robert! Ça **fait une paye** qu'on ne s'est pas vu!

translation: Hi Robert! It's **been a long time** since we've see each other!

as spoken: Salut Robert! Ça **fait une paye** qu'on s'est pas vu!

SYNONYM: **bail (faire un)** *exp.* • (lit.): to be a rent period (a period of time between when one's rent is due).

payer une tranche (s'en) *exp.* to have a great time • (lit.): to treat oneself to a slice of it ("it" signifying "fun").

example: Nous **nous en sommes payé une tranche** à la plage!

translation: What a **great time** we had at the beach!

as spoken: On **s'en est payé une tranche** à la plage!

NOTE: **payer (se)** *v.* to treat oneself.

payer un petit coup (s'en)

exp. to fornicate • (lit.): to treat oneself to a little bit.

peau (avoir quelqu'un dans la) *exp.* to be in love with someone • (lit.): to have someone in the skin.

peau de vache *f.*
a disparaging remark applied primarily to a woman but may also be used in reference to a man • (lit.): cow skin.

peau neuve (faire) *exp.* to turn over a new leaf • (lit.): to make new skin.

example: J'ai décidé de **faire peau neuve**. A partir de demain, je vais renoncer à fumer.

translation: I decided to **turn over a new leaf**. Starting tomorrow, I'm going to give up smoking.

as spoken: J'ai décidé d'**faire peau neuve**. A partir de d'main, j'vais renoncer à fumer.

pébroc *m.* umbrella.

example: N'oublie pas ton **pébroc**. Je pense qu'il va pleuvoir.

translation: Don't forget your **umbrella**. I think it's going to rain.

as spoken: Oublie pas ton **pébroc**. J'pense qu'y va pleuvoir.

SYNONYM -1: **chamberlain** *m.*
SYNONYM -2: **pépin** *m.*

pêche *f.* turd • (lit.): peach.

peine (à) *c.l.* hardly • (lit.): to difficulty.

example: Je le connais **à peine**.

translation: I **hardly** know him.

as spoken: J'le connais **à peine**.

peinturlurer *v.* to wear gobs off makeup, to wear "war paint" • (lit.): to paint (a building, etc. using all of the color of the rainbow).

example: Tu as vu la nouvelle employée? Ce n'est pas possible comme elle se **peinturlure**, cette fille!

translation: Did you see the new employee? It's unreal how that girl **paints** up her face!

as spoken: T'as vu la nouvelle employée? C'est pas possible comme è s'**peinturlure**, c'te fille!

SYNONYM: **badigeonner** *v.* • (lit.): to color-wash (a wall, etc.).

ALSO: **badigeon** *m.* makeup, "war paint" • (lit.): color-wash.

pelotage *m.* heavy petting.

peloter *v.* to pet (someone) heavily, to fondle.

pelotes *f.pl.* breasts • (lit.): balls (of wool, string, etc.).

pendeloques *f.pl.* testicles • (lit.): pendants.

pendentifs *m.pl.* testicles • (lit.): pendentives, "hangers."

pépée *f.* woman or girl.

pépé (vieux) *m.* an old person, an "old fart" • (lit.): old grandpa.

pépin pour quelqu'un (avoir un / le) *exp.* to have a crush on someone • (lit.): to have a / the apple pip for someone (from the expression *être le pépin de ses yeux* meaning "to be the apple [pip] of one's eye").

perdre la boule *exp.* to lose one's mind, "to lose it" • (lit.): to lose the ball.

example: Tu ne sais pas ce que tu as fait de tes clés? C'est la troisième fois en deux jours que ça t'arrive! Je crois que tu commences à **perdre la boule**.

translation: You don't know what you did with your keys? That's the third time in two days that's happened to you! I think you're starting **to lose it**.

as spoken: Tu sais pas c'que t'as fait d'tes clés? C'est la troisième fois en deux jours qu'ça t'arrive! J'crois qu'tu commences à **perd' la boule**.

perdre la boussole *exp.* (applies to either a man or a woman) to lose one's mind • (lit.): to lose the compass.

perdre le nord (ne pas) *exp.* (applies to either a man or a woman) to be rational, to know where one is going • (lit.): not to lose the north (point on the compass).

NOTE: This expression is usually used in the negative:

example: Tu **ne perds pas le nord**, toi!

translation: You've **got that right**!

as spoken: Tu **perds pas l'nord**, toi!

perdre les pédales *exp.* to lose it (one's sanity and patience) • (lit.): to lose the pedals.

example: S'il n'arrête pas de jouer cette musique de hardrock, je vais **perdre les pédales**!

translation: If he doesn't stop playing that hardrock music, I'm gonna **lose it**!

as spoken: S'il arrête pas d'jouer c'te musique de hardrock, j'vais **perd' les pédales**!

perle *f.* fart • (lit.): pearl.

perlouse *f.* a slang transformation of: *perle* meaning "fart."

perruque en peau de fesses (avoir une) *exp.* to be bald • (lit.): to have a wig that looks like one's rear end.

perte de vue (à) *c.l.* as far as the eye can see • to the loss of the view.

example: Quelle belle forêt! Il y a des arbres **à perte de vue**!

translation: What a beautiful forest! There are trees **as far as the eye can see**!

as spoken: Quelle belle forêt! Y a des arbres **à perte de vue**!

pétasse *f.* a disparaging remark applied only to a woman • (lit.): fart.
NOTE: This comes from the verb *péter* meaning "to fart."

péter la forme *exp.* to be in tip-top shape • (lit.): to burst with good shape.

example: J'ai été malade pendant une semaine, mais maintenant je **pète la forme**!

translation: I was sick for a week, but now I'm **in tip-top shape**!

as spoken: J'ai été malade pendant une s'maine, mais maintenant j'**pète la forme**!

péter la rondelle *exp.* to sodomize • (lit.): to explode the ring.

NOTE: **rondelle** *f.* anus • (lit.): ring, small round disc.

pèter le feu *exp.* • **1.** to be hyperactive, to have tons of energy • **2.** to be in great health (lit.): to fart fire.

example (1): Il **pète le feu**, cet enfant. C'est épuisant!

translation: This child **is so hyper**. It's exhausting!

as spoken: Y **pète le feu**, c't'enfant. C'est épuisant!

example (2): Mon grandpère vient d'avoir 90 ans et il continue à **péter le feu**!

translation: My grandfather is 90 years old and he still continues to be **bursting with vitality**!

as spoken: Mon grandpère, y vient d'avoir 90 ans et y continue à **péter l'feu**!

péter les plombs *exp.* to freak out • (lit.): to blow fuses.

example: Si ces enfants n'arrêtent pas de crier, je vais **péter les plombs**!

translation: If these children don't stop screaming, I'm **going to lose it**!

as spoken: Si ces enfants, y z'arrêtent pas d'crier, j'vais **péter les plombs**!

péteur *m.* one who farts a lot • (lit.): farter (from the verb *péter* meaning "to fart").

example: Si tu ne manges rien qu'des fibres, tu vas devenir un **péteur** de premier ordre!

translation: If you eat nothing but fiber, you're doing to turn into one heck of a **farter**!

as spoken: Si tu manges rien que des fibres, tu vas dev'nir un **péteur** de premier ordre!

péteux, euse *n.* scardey-cat • (lit.): farter.

NOTE: This comes from the verb *péter* meaning "to fart." Therefore, *péteux, euse* could be translated as "one who farts" (due to intense fear causing a loss of control).

petit *m.* anus • (lit.): the little (area).

petit à côté *exp.* a sexual fling • (lit.): a little on the side.

example: Le patron n'est jamais dans son bureau à midi. Tu crois qu'il a un **petit à côté** quelque part?

translation: The boss is never in his office at noon. You think he's having a **little fling** somewhere?

as spoken: Le patron, il est jamais dans son bureau à midi. Tu crois qu'il a un **p'tit à côté** quèque part?

ALSO: **jeter un vite fait (s'en)** *exp.* to have a quickie • (lit.): to throw oneself a quickly-done.

petit à petit *c.l.* little by little • (lit.): little to little.

example: J'ai été malade pendant deux semaines, mais **petit à petit** je vais mieux.

translation: I've been sick for two weeks, but **little by little** I'm doing better.

as spoken: J'ai été malade pendant deux s'maines, mais **p'tit à p'tit** j'vais mieux.

petit coin *m.* (child language) bathroom • (lit.): the little corner.

petit con *m.* (commonly pronounced: *ti-con*) small-minded idiot, little geek • (lit.): little idiot.

example: Ah, le **petit con**. Ça fait trois fois qu'il a versé un verre de jus de tomate sur la robe de sa femme.

translation: Oh, the **little geek**. He's spilled a glass of tomato juice on his wife's dress three times already.

as spoken: Ah, l'**tit con**. Ça fait trois fois qu'il a versé un verre d'jus d'tomate sur la robe d'sa femme.

petite commission (faire sa) *exp.* to go pee-pee, to go number one • (lit.): to do one's little portion.

example: N'oublie pas de **faire ta petite commission** avant de quitter la maison.

translation: Don't forget to **go number one** before you leave the house.

as spoken: Oublie pas d'**faire ta p'tite commission** avant d'quitter la maison.

SEE: **grosse commission (faire sa)**, *p. 100.*

petit merdeux *m.* / **petite merdeuse** *f.* a little twerp • (lit.): a little shit.

example: Ce **petit merdeux** me suit partout!

translation: That **little shit** follows me everywhere!

as spoken: Ce **p'tit merdeux**, y m'suit partout!

petit oiseau *m.* (child language) penis, "pee-pee" • (lit.): little bird.

example: Le bébé passe des heures à tripoter son **petit oiseau**.

translation: The baby spends hours playing with his **pee-pee**.

as spoken: Le bébé, y passe des heures à tripoter son **p'tit oiseau**.

SYNONYM -1: **sifflet** *m.* • (lit.): whistle.

SYNONYM -2: **zizi** *m.*

petit polichinelle dans le tiroir (avoir un) *exp.* to be pregnant • (lit.): to have a little joker in the drawer.

NOTE: A *polichinelle* is the little clown figure often seen in a group of marionettes.

petits oignons *m.pl.* testicles • (lit.): little onions.

petits papiers de quelqu'un (être dans les) *exp.* to be on someone's good side • (lit.): to be in someone's little papers.

example: J'ai complètement oublié l'anniversaire de mon père. Pour le moment, je **ne suis pas dans ses petits papiers**.

translation: I completely forgot my father's birthday. At the moment, I'm **not on his good side**.

as spoken: J'ai complètement oublié l'anniversaire d'mon père. Pour l'moment, j'**suis pas dans ses p'tits papiers**.

pétochard(e) *n.* scardey-cat
• (lit.): farter.
NOTE: This is a variation of: *péteux, euse.*

pétroleuse *f.* prostitute • (lit.): a woman who heats up a man (since *pétrole* means "petroleum").

phénomène *m.* a strange person
• (lit.): a phenomenon.

example: Roger, c'est un vrai **phénomène**. Il ne porte que du noir tous les jours.

translation: Roger is a **strange guy**. He dresses in black every day.

as spoken: Roger, c't'un vrai **phénomène**. Y porte que du noir tous les jours.

piaf *m.* • **1.** bird • **2.** small man, a "shrimp" • (lit.): Parisian sparrow.

example (1): Elle donne à manger aux **piafs**.

translation: She's feeding the **birds**.

as spoken: È donne à manger aux **piafs**.

example (2): Marcel, c'est un **piaf** mais attention! Il se connait en karate!

translation: Marcel is a **little squirt** but watch out! He knows karate!

as spoken: Marcel, c't'un **piaf** mais attention! Y s'connait en karate!

piaule *f.* bedroom, room.

picoler *v.* to drink alcohol.

example: Je viens d'apprendre que le patron **picole** chaque matin avant d'arriver au boulot.

translation: I just learned that the boss **drinks** every morning before coming to work.

as spoken: J'viens d'apprend' que l'patron, y **picole** chaque matin avant d'arriver au boulot.

NOTE -1: **pictance** *f.* alcohol.
NOTE -3: **boulot** *m.* (extremely popular) work, the "grind."

pied (faire du) *exp.* to play footsie
• (lit.): to make (with the) foot.

example: Le dîner d'affaires était horrible! Quand nous étions tous à table, le client a commencé a me **faire du pied**!

translation: The business dinner was horrible! When we were all at the table, the client started **playing footsie** with me!

as spoken: Le dîner d'affaires, il était horrible! Quand on était tous à table, le client, il a commencé a m'**faire du pied**!

pieu *m.* (most popular) bed
• (lit.): spike.
NOTE: **pieuter (se)** *v.* to go to bed, to hit the hay.

pif *m.* nose, "honker."

example: Ce gamin a un grand **pif** comme celui de son vieux.

translation: That kid has a big **honker** like his father's.

as spoken: C'gamin, il a un grand **pif** comme celui d'son vieux.

SYNONYM: **blair** *m.*

piffrer quelqu'un (ne pas pouvoir) *exp.* to be unable to stand someone • (lit.): to be unable to smell someone (from the masculine slang word *pif* meaning "nose" or "schnoz").

example: Tu as invité Marie à la soirée? Mais je **ne peux pas la piffrer**, celle-là!

translation: You invited Marie to the party? But I **can't stand her**!

as spoken: T'as invité Marie à la soirée? Mais j'**peux pas la piffrer**, celle-là!

SYNONYM: **blairer quelqu'un (ne pas pouvoir)** *exp.* (from the slang word *blair* also meaning "nose" or "schnoz").

pige *f.* year.

example: Le trois novembre, j'aurai trente **piges**.

translation: On November third, I'll be thirty **years** old.

as spoken: [no change]

pigeon *m.* (applies to either a man or a woman) gullible person, sucker • (lit.): pigeon

pinarium *m.* brothel.

NOTE: This comes from the feminine noun *pine* meaning "penis."

pince *f.* • **1.** hand • **2.** vagina • (lit.): holder, gripper, pincher (from the verb *pincer* meaning "to pinch").

example: Tu peux me donner un coup de **pince**?

translation: Can you give me a **hand**?

as spoken: Tu peux m'donner un coup d'**pince**?

SYNONYM: **paluche** *f.*

pincer pour quelqu'un (en) *exp.* to have a crush on someone.

example: Cette fille-là te regarde. Je crois qu'elle **en pince pour toi**!

translation: That girl over there is looking at you. I think she has a **crush on you**!

as spoken: C'te fille-là, è t'regarde. J'crois qu'elle **en pince pour toi**!

*Pierre **en pince pour** Michelle.*

(trans.):
*Pierre **has a crush on** Michelle.*

(lit.):
*Pierre **pinches some for** Michelle.*

pine *f.* (extremely popular) penis.

piner *v.* to fornicate • (lit.): to "dick" (someone).

NOTE: This comes from the feminine noun *pine* meaning "penis, dick."

pioncer *v.* to sleep.

example: Je vais camper ce weekend. Ça me plaît énormément de **pioncer** à la belle étoile.

translation: I'm going to the desert this weekend. I love **sleeping** under the stars.

as spoken: J'vais camper c'weekend. Ça m'plaît énormément d'**pioncer** à la belle étoile.

NOTE: **à la belle étoile** *c.l.* outside • (lit.): under the pretty star.

SYNONYM -1: **roupiller** *v.* • **roupillonner** *v.*

SYNONYM -2: **faire un roupillon** *exp.* to take a nap.

pipe *f.* blow job • (lit.): pipe.

example: Marcel m'a dit que Lucienne lui a fait une **pipe** dans la voiture!

translation: Marcel told me that Lucienne gave him a **blow job** in the car!

as spoken: Marcel, y m'a dit qu'Lucienne, è lui a fait une **pipe** dans la voiture!

NOTE: **faire une pipe** *exp.* to give a blow job.

pipe (faire une) *exp.* (extremely popular) to perform fellatio • (lit.): to do a pipe.

pipi (faire) *exp.* to go pee-pee.

example: Le chat a **fait pipi** sur le tapis.

translation: The cat **went pee-pee** on the carpet.

as spoken: Le chat, il a **fait pipi** sur l'tapis.

ALSO: **pipi de chat** *m.* poor quality wine or beer • (lit.): cat pee-pee.

pipi-room *m.* (Americanism) bathroom.

piqué(e) (être) *adj.* to be nuts, cracked, touched in the head • (lit.): to be stung.

piquer *v.* to steal, "swipe" • (lit.): to prick or sting.

example: Arrêtez-le! Il a **piqué** mon vélo!

translation: Stop him! He **stole** my bike!

as spoken: [no change]

SYNONYM: **barboter** *v.* • (lit.): to paddle in the mud or water.

piquer une crise *exp.* to have (to throw) a fit, to flip out • (lit.): to take a crisis.

example: J'ai **piqué une crise** quand j'ai appris que mon frère a emprunté ma voiture sans permission.

translation: I **flipped out** when I found out my brother borrowed my car without permission.

as spoken: J'ai **piqué une crise** quand j'ai appris qu'mon frère, il a emprunté ma voiture sans permission.

NOTE: The verb *piquer*, literally meaning "to prick or sting," is used in slang to mean "to take or steal."

piquer une ronflette *exp.* to take a nap • (lit.): to take a little snore.

example: Je suis fatigué. Je crois que je vais **piquer une ronflette** pendant une heure.

translation: I'm tired. I think I'll **take a little snooze** for an hour.

as spoken: J'suis fatigué. J'crois que j'vais **piquer une ronflette** pendant une heure.

NOTE -1: The verb *"piquer"* has a slang meaning of "to take" or "to swipe." For example: *Qui a piqué mon stylo?*; Who took my pen?

NOTE -2: The feminine noun *"ronflette"* comes from the verb *"ronfler,"* meaning "to snore."

pisse *f.* urine • (lit.): piss.

example: Tu as un chat? Ça sent la **pisse** dans le salon.

translation: Do you have a cat? It smells like **piss** in the living room.

as spoken: T'as un chat? Ça sent la **pisse** dans l'salon.

SEE: pisser, *(next entry)*.

pisser *v.* to urinate • (lit.): to piss.

example: Quand j'ai soulevé le bébé, il a commencé à **pisser**.

translation: When I lifted the baby, he started **pissing**.

as spoken: Quand j'ai soul'vé l'bébé, il a commencé à **pisser**.

SEE: pisse, *(previous entry)*.

pisser son coup *exp.* to urinate • (lit.): to piss one's shot.

pissoir *m.* bathroom.

NOTE: This comes from the verb *pisser* meaning "to piss."

pissotière *f.* bathroom.

NOTE -1: This comes from the verb *pisser* meaning "to piss."

NOTE -2: Although the *pissotières* no longer exist (due to their horrible smell), the term is still used in jest.

placard *m.* jail • (lit.): closet.

example: Le flic a mis le voleur dans le **placard**.

translation: The cop put the thief in **jail**.

as spoken: Le flic, il a mis l'voleur dans l'**placard**.

placer une (en) *exp.* to get a word in edgewise • (lit.): to place one.

example: Il parle tellement que je ne peux même pas **en placer une**.

translation: He talks so much that I can't even **get a word in edgewise**.

as spoken: Y parle tellement qu'j'peux même pas **en placer une**.

NOTE: In this expression, *"une"* represents *"une parole"* meaning "speech" or a "word."

VARIATION: placer un mot *exp.* • (lit.): to place a word.

planquer *v.* to hide.

example: Je dois **planquer** ce cadeau. C'est une surprise pour ma femme.

translation: I have **to hide** this present. It's a surprise for my wife.

as spoken: J'dois **planquer** c'cadeau. C't'une surprise pour ma femme.

NOTE: **planque** *f*. hiding place.

planter une borne *exp*. to defecate • (lit.): to plant a milestone.

plaquer *v*. to jilt, to dump • (lit.): [none].

example: Après onze ans de mariage, Laurent a **plaqué** sa femme.

translation: After eleven years of marriage, Laurent **dumped** his wife.

as spoken: Après onze ans d'mariage, Laurent, il a **plaqué** sa femme.

VARIATION: **plaquouser** *v*.
SYNONYM: **laisser choir** *exp*. • (lit.): to let (someone) drop.

plaquer quelqu'un *v*. to jilt someone.

example: Henri a **plaqué** sa femme après avoir été marié quinze ans.

translation: Henry **dumped** his wife after having been married fifteen years.

as spoken: Henri, il a **plaqué** sa femme après avoir été marié quinze ans.

plat de nouilles *m*. (applies to either a man or a woman) airhead, noodle brain • (lit.): plate of noodles.

pleurer le cyclope (faire) *exp*. to masturbate • (lit.): to make the cyclops cry.

NOTE: The masculine noun *cyclope* is a popular synonym for "penis" or "one-eyed monster."

pleurer son colosse (faire) *exp*. to urinate, to take a leak • (lit.): to make one's colossal one cry.

example: Après tous les verres d'eau que j'ai descendu, je dois **faire pleurer mon colosse**.

translation: After all the glasses of water I downed, I need to **take a leak**.

as spoken: Après tous les verres d'eau qu'j'ai descendu, j'dois **faire pleurer mon colosse**.

plier bagages *exp*. to leave, to scram • (lit.): to fold (up) suitcases.

example: Je m'ennuie à cette soirée. On **plie bagages**?

translation: I'm bored at this party. Should we **beat it**?

as spoken: J'm'ennuie à c'te soirée. On **plie bagages**?

plomb dans la cervelle / tête (ne pas avoir de) *exp*. (applies to either a man or a woman) to be scatterbrained, not to be cooking on all four burners • (lit.): not to have any lead in the brain.

plombe *f*. hour.

example: Il est trois **plombes**.

translation: It's three **o'clock**.

as spoken: Il est trois **plombes**.

NOTE: This comes from the feminine noun *plombe* meaning "lead." The word *plombe* conjures up a picture of an old lead chime being struck every hour.

plomber du goulot *exp.* to have bad breath • (lit.): to fall like lead from the bottleneck.

plumard *m.* bed • (lit.): that which has feathers (from the feminine noun *"plume"* meaning "feather").

example: Mon **plumard** est trop mou!

translation: My **bed** is too soft!

as spoken: Mon **plumard**, il est trop mou!

NOTE: **plumarder (se)** *v.* to go to bed.

SYNONYM: **pieu** *m.*

plume *m.* bed • (lit.): feather.

NOTE: **plumer (se)** *v.* to go to bed, to hit the hay.

plus on est de fous, plus on rit *prov.* the more the merrier • (lit.): the more goofy people there are, the more we'll laugh.

example: Venez nous rejoindre! **Plus on est de fous, plus on rit**!

translation: Come join us! **The more the merrier**!

as spoken: V'nez nous rejoindre! **Plus on est d'fous, plus on rit**!

plus profond de la nuit (au) *c.l.* in the dead of night • (lit.): at the deepest of the night.

example: **Au plus profond de la nuit**, j'ai entendu un bruit sourd au salon! C'était le chien qui avait renversé un fauteuil.

translation: **In the dead of night**, I heard a thud in the living room! It was the dog who had turned over an armchair.

as spoken: **Au plus profond d'la nuit**, j'ai entendu un bruit sourd au salon! C'était l'chien qui avait renversé un fauteuil.

plus total(e) (le / la) *exp.* totally, "big time" • (lit.): the most total.

example: Après son divorce, Michelle est dans la dépression **la plus totale**.

translation: After her divorce, Michelle has been in a **big time** depression.

as spoken: Après son divorce, Michelle, elle est dans la dépression **la plus totale**.

SYNONYM: **le plus complet / la plus complète** *exp.* • (lit.): the most complete.

pocher un œil au beurre noir à quelqu'un *exp.* to give someone a black eye • (lit.): to poach someone an eye of black butter.

example: Quand je l'ai insulté, il m'a **poché un œil au beurre noir**.

translation: When I insulted him, he **gave me a black eye**.

as spoken: Quand j'l'ai insulté, y m'a **poché un œil au beurre noir**.

ALSO: **coquelicot** *n.* black eye • (lit.): poppy.

pognon *m.* money, "loot," "dough."

example: Tu as du **pognon** sur toi?

translation: Do you have any **money** on you?

as spoken: T'as du **pognon** sur toi?

SYNONYMS: *blé (du)* • *fric (du)* • *galette (de la)* • *grisbi (du)* • *oseille (de l')* • *pèze du* • *picaillons (des)* • *pognon (du)* • *ronds (des)* • *sous (des)* • *etc.*

poil (être à) *exp.* to be butt naked • (lit.): to be to [the] hair.

example: Dans les colonies de nudistes, tout le monde est complètement **à poil**.

translation: In nudist camps, everyone is completely **naked**.

as spoken: Dans les colonies d'nudistes, tout l'monde est complètement **à poil**.

poil sur le caillou (ne pas avoir un) *exp.* to be bald • (lit.): not to have a hair on the pebble.
NOTE: **caillou** *m.* head • (lit.): pebble.

pointe *f.* penis • (lit.): point.

pointer (se) *v.* to arrive, to show up • (lit.): to sprout up.

example: Georges **s'est pointé** au boulot deux heures en retard! C'est la deuxième fois cette semaine!

translation: George **showed up** to work two hours late! It's the second time this week!

as spoken: Georges, y **s'est pointé** au boulot deux heures en r'tard! C'est la deuxième fois cette s'maine!

SYNONYM: **radiner (se)** *v.*

poireau *m.* penis • (lit.): leek.

poireauter *v.* to wait, "to take root."

example: Ça fait une heure que tu me fais **poireauter** ici!

translation: You've been keeping me **waiting** here an hour!

as spoken: Ça fait une heure qu'tu m'fais **poireauter** ici!

NOTE: This comes from the masculine noun *poireau* meaning "leek." Therefore, *poireauter* might be translated as "to stand erect and motionless like a leek."

VARIATION: **poireau (faire le)** *exp.*

SYNONYM: **pied de grue (faire le)** *exp.* • (lit.): to stand like a crane (since the crane, or *grue,* is often seen standing motionless on one foot).

poivrot *m.* drunkard.

example: Il t'apprend à conduire? Mais c'est un **poivrot**! Tu n'as pas remarqué?

translation: He's teaching you how to drive? But he's a **drunk**! You didn't notice?

as spoken: Y t'apprend à conduire? Mais c't'un **poivrot**! T'as pas r'marqué?

SYNONYM: **soûlard** (also spelled: *saoûlard*).

pomper *v.* (very popular) to perform fellatio • (lit.): to pump.

pompette (être) *f.* to be tipsy.

pompier (faire un) *exp.* to
perform fellatio • (lit.): to do (like) a
fireman and pump (water).

pomplard (faire un) *exp.* to
perform fellatio • (lit.): to do (like) a
fireman.

> **NOTE -1:** This is a variation of: *faire
un pompier.*

> **NOTE -2:** The masculine noun
pomplard is a slang synonym for
pompier meaning "fireman."

pont arrière *m.* posterior
• (lit.): rear axle.

Popaul *m.* penis.

> **VARIATION:** **Popol** *m.*

popo *m.* excrement • (lit.): caca.

example: Le chien n'est pas permis
d'entrer dans la maison. La dernière
fois, il a fait **popo** dans le salon.

translation: The dog isn't allowed to
come into the house. The last time,
he **pooped** in the living room.

as spoken: Le chien, il est pas
permis d'entrer dans la maison. La
dernière fois, il a fait **popo** dans
l'salon.

popotin *m.* (extremely popular)
posterior • (lit.): [no literal
translation].

portail *m.* vagina • (lit.): portal.

porté(e) sur la bagatelle
(être) *exp.* to be oversexed, to
have sex on the brain • (lit.): to be
carried on the frivolity.

example: Grégoire sort avec une
différente nana chaque soir. Il est
vraiment **porté sur la bagatelle**,
celui-là.

translation: Gregory goes out with a
different girl every night. He's really
got sex on the brain.

as spoken: Grégoire, y sort avec
une différente nana chaque soir. Il
est vraiment **porté sur la
bagatelle**, çui-là.

porté(e) sur la chose (être)
exp. to have a one-track mind
• (lit.): to be carried on the thing.

porté(e) sur quelque chose
(être) *exp.* to be driven by
something • (lit.): to be carried by
something.

example: Il est **porté sur** la bouffe.

translation: He's **driven by** food.

as spoken: Il est **porté sur** la
bouffe.

> **NOTE:** **bouffe** *f.* (very popular)
food, grub • **bouffer** *v.* (very
popular) to eat.

> **SYNONYM:** **raffoler de
quelque chose** *exp.* to be wild for
something.

example: Je **raffole du** chocolat!

translation: I'm **crazy for**
chocolate!

as spoken: J'**raffole du** chocolat!

**porte-manteau dans le
pantalon (avoir un)** *exp.* to
have an erection • (lit.): to have a
coat rack in the pants.

portrait tout craché de quelqu'un (être le) *exp.* to be the spitting image of someone
• (lit.): to be the portrait all spit of someone.

example: Tu es le **portrait tout craché** de ton père.

translation: He's the **spit and image** of his father.

as spoken: T'es l'**portrait tout craché** d'ton père.

poser un lapin à quelqu'un
exp. to stand someone up (on a date or meeting) • (lit.): to pose a rabbit to someone.

example: Ça fait une heure que je l'attends. Il m'a **posé un lapin** pour la dernière fois!

translation: I've been waiting for him for an hour. He's **stood me up** for the last time!

as spoken: Ça fait une heure qu'j'l'attends. Y m'a **posé un lapin** pour la dernière fois!

postère *m.* an abbreviation of: *postérieur* meaning "posterior, buttocks."

postérieur *m.* posterior
• (lit.): [same].

postillon *m.* spit, spittle.

NOTE: **postillonner** *v.* to spit while one speaks.

potache *m.* student.

example: Quand j'étais **potache**, je n'avais jamais le temps de me marrer.

translation: When I was a **student**, I never had time to have any fun.

as spoken: Quand j'étais **potache**, j'avais jamais l'temps de m'marrer.

NOTE: **marrer (se)** *v.* (extremely popular) • **1.** to have a good time • **2.** to laugh.

*Il m'a **posé un lapin**, le crétin!*

(trans.):
*That jerk **stood me up**!*

(lit.):
*That jerk **posed me a rabbit**!*

*Il aime lire, ce **potache**!*

(trans.)
*That **student** likes to read!*

potasser *v.* to study hard, to bone up on (a subject).

example: Je dois **potasser** mon français ce soir.

translation: I have **to bone up on** my French tonight.

as spoken: J'dois **potasser** mon français c'soir.

pot d'échappement *m.* anus
• (lit.): exhaust pipe.
NOTE: This can also be shorten to: *pot.*

pouffiasse *f.* (derogatory) a fat woman or girl, whore.

example: Si tu continues à manger comme ça, tu vas devenir **pouffiasse**.

translation: If you keep eating like that, you're going to turn into a **fatso**.

as spoken: Si tu continues à manger comme ça, tu vas dev'nir **pouffiasse**.

poule *f.* • **1.** girl, prostitute • **2.** darling (*ma [petite] poule;* my sweetheart) (lit.): hen.

poule mouillée *f.* scardey-cat
• (lit.): wet hen.

poulette *f.* sweetheart • (lit.): a young hen.

pouliche *f.* woman, "chick"
• (lit.): filly.

example: Tu connais cette **pouliche**-là? Je la trouve super jolie!

translation: Do you know that **chick**? I think she's really beautiful!

as spoken: Tu connais c'te **pouliche**-là? J'la trouve super jolie!

poupée *f.* woman or girl • (lit.): a doll.

pour autant que *c.l.* as far as
• (lit.): for as much as that.

example: **Pour autant que** je sache, il va arriver à midi.

translation: **As far as** I know, he is going to arrive at noon.

as spoken: **Pour autant que** j'sache, y va arriver à midi.
SYNONYM: **jusqu'à** *exp.*
• (lit.): up to.
NOTE: As seen above, the expression *autant que* (as well as *jusqu'à*) are followed by the subjunctive tense).

pour comble de malheur *c.l.* to top it all • (lit.): for an overflowing of misfortune.

example: J'ai eu une crevaison en pleine autoroute. Et **pour comble de malheur**, il a commencé à pleuvoir.

translation: I got a flat tire on the highway. And **to top it all off**, it started to rain.

as spoken: J'ai eu une crevaison en pleine autoroute. Et **pour comble d'malheur**, il a commencé à pleuvoir.

pourlécher les babines (s'en) *exp.* to lick one's lips over something • (lit.): to lick one's chops over something.

example: Demain, ma mère va préparer du coq au vin. Je **m'en pourlèche les babines** d'avance!

translation: Tomorrow, my mother is going to make chicken in red wine. **My mouth is** already **watering**!

as spoken: Demain, ma mère, è va préparer du coq au vin. J'**m'en pourlèche les babines** d'avance!

pourriture *f.* a disparaging remark applied primarily to a man but can also be used in reference to a woman • (lit.): rotting trash.

pousser sa pointe *exp.* to fornicate • (lit.): to push (in) one's point.

> **NOTE:** **pointe** *f.* penis, dick • (lit.): point.

pouvoir (ne plus en) *c.l.* to be unable to stand it any longer • (lit.): to be no longer capable of it.

example: Il m'énerve sans arrêt. Je **n'en peux plus**!

translation: He bothers me nonstop. I **can't take it any more**!

as spoken: Y m'énerve sans arrêt. J'**en peux plus**!

pouvoir voir quelqu'un en peinture (ne pas) *exp.* to be unable to stand someone • (lit.): to be unable to see a painting of someone (since just the mere sight of him / her would be too much to bear).

example: Voilà Bernard! Je **ne peux pas le voir en peinture**!

translation: There's Bernard! I **can't stand him**!

as spoken: V'là Bernard! J'**peux pas l'voir en peinture**!

> **SYNONYM:** **pouvoir blairer quelqu'un (ne pas)** *exp.* • (lit.): not to be able to smell someone.
> **NOTE:** The verb *blairer* comes from the masculine noun *blair* meaning "nose" or "schnoz."

praline *f.* clitoris • (lit.): praline.

précieuses *f.pl.* testicles, "family jewels" • (lit.): precious ones.

première (de) *adj.* excellent, first-rate.

example: Cette soirée est **de première**!

translation: This party's **top drawer**!

as spoken: Cette soirée, elle est **d'première**!

> **NOTE:** This is a common shortened version of *de première classe* meaning "of first class quality."

prendre au berceau (les) *exp.* to rob the cradle • (lit.): to take them from the cradle.

example: Hier soir j'ai vu Jean-Claude avec une très jeune fille. Evidemment il aime **les prendre au berceau**!

translation: Last night I saw Jean-Claude with a very young girl. Evidently he likes **to rob the cradle**!

as spoken: Hier soir j'ai vu Jean-Claude avec une très jeune fille. Evidemment il aime **les prendr'au berceau**!

prendre la tangente *exp.* to slip away without being seen • (lit.): to take the tangent.

example: Je m'ennuie ici. Je vais **prendre la tangente**.

translation: I'm bored here. I'm going **to sneak out**.

as spoken: J'm'ennuie ici. J'vais **prend' la tangente**.

prendre pour de la petite bière (ne pas se) *exp.* said of someone who is conceited • (lit.): not to take oneself for a small beer.

example: Cette vedette-là **ne se prend pas pour de la petite bière**.

translation: That movie star **is very conceited**.

as spoken: Cette vedette-là, è **s'prend pas pour d'la p'tite bière**.

ANTONYM: **terre à terre (être)** *exp.* to be down to earth • (lit.): to be earth to earth.

prendre pour de la petite merde (ne pas se) *exp.* to think highly of oneself, to think one's shit doesn't stink • (lit.): not to take oneself for a little shit.

example: Cécile est très arrogante. Elle **ne se prend pas pour de la petite merde**.

translation: Cecily is very arrogant. She **thinks her shit doesn't stink**.

as spoken: Cécile est très arrogante. È **s'prend pas pour d'la p'tite merde**.

NOTE: The mild form of this expression is: *prendre pour de la petite bière (ne pas se)* literally meaning "not to take oneself for a little beer."

prendre ses cliques et ses claques *exp.* to take one's personal belongings • (lit.): to take one's "this and that."

example: **Prends tes cliques et tes claques** et déguérpis!

translation: **Take your things** and get out of here!

as spoken: [no change]

NOTE: **déguérpir** *v.* to leave, to scram.

prendre son panard / son pied *exp.* (extremely popular) to reach orgasm • (lit.): to take one's foot / one's foot.

près de ses sous (être) *exp.* to be stingy, • (lit.): to be close to one's coins.

example: Chaque fois que je sors dîner avec Antoine, c'est moi qui paie. Il est très **près de ses sous, lui**!

translation: Every time I go out to have dinner with Antoine, I'm the one who pays. He's such a **tightwad**!

as spoken: Chaque fois qu'je sors dîner avec Antoine, c'est moi qui paie. Il est très **près d'ses sous, lui**!

pris(e) au dépourvu (être)

exp. to be taken off guard • (lit.): to be taken short (as in destitute).

example: Quand il a donné sa démission, j'ai été **pris au dépourvu**.

translation: When he gave his resignation, I was **taken off guard**.

as spoken: Quand il a donné sa démission, j'ai été **pris au dépourvu**.

prise de bec *f.* a quarrel
• (lit.): taking of the beak.

NOTE: **bec** *m.* mouth • (lit.): beak (of a bird).

prise de gueule *f.* a quarrel
• (lit.): taking of the mouth.

NOTE: **gueule** *f.* derogatory for "mouth" or "face" since its literal translation is "the mouth of an animal."

prix coûtant (au) *exp.* at cost
• (lit.): at costing price.

example: Léon est un bon ami. Il m'a vendu sa voiture **au prix coûtant**!

translation: Leon's a great friend. He sold me his car **at cost**!

as spoken: Léon, c't'un bon ami. Y m'a vendu sa voiture **au prix coûtant**!

Prix de Diane *m.* a beautiful woman or girl.

NOTE: The *Prix de Diane* is a famous horse race in Paris.

probable *adv.* a common abbreviation of *probablement* meaning "probably."

example: "Je me demande pourquoi elle est partie si vite!" "**Probable** qu'elle était en retard pour un meeting."

translation: "I wonder why she left so quickly!" "**Probably** because she was late for a meeting."

as spoken: "J'me d'mande pourquoi elle est partie si vite!" "**Probab'** qu'elle était en r'tard pour un meeting."

prof *m. & f.* teacher, professor.

example: Tu as vu la nouvelle **prof** d'anglais? Elle est très jeune, elle!

translation: Did you see the new English **teacher**? She's so young!

as spoken: T'as vu la nouvelle **prof** d'anglais? Elle est très jeune, elle!

NOTE: The word *professeur* is a masculine noun. However, its abbreviated form, *prof* is both masculine *and* feminine.

propre-sur-soi (être) *exp.* to be squeaky-clean (said of a person)
• (lit.): to be clean on oneself.

example: Je vois que tu as pris une douche. Voilà ce qui s'appelle **propre-sur-soi**!

translation: I see you took a shower. Now that's what I call **squeaky-clean**!

as spoken: J'vois qu't'as pris une douche. V'là c'qui s'appelle **propre-sur-soi**!

proprio *m.* an abbreviation of *propriétaire* meaning "owner" or "proprietor."

example: Je suis **proprio** d'un nouveau restaurant à Paris.

translation: I'm the **owner** of a new restaurant in Paris.

as spoken: J'suis **proprio** d'un nouveau resto à Paris.

proxémac *m.*

NOTE: This is a slang transformation of the masculine noun *proxénète* meaning "white slaver."

proxo *m.* an abbreviation of: *proxénète*.

prune *f.* traffic ticket • (lit.): plum.

example: Je me suis fait coller une **prune** pour avoir dépasser la limite de vitesse.

translation: I got a **ticket** for passing the speed limit.

as spoken: Je m'suis fait coller une **prune** pour avoir dépasser la limite de vitesse.

ALSO: **pour des prunes** *exp.* for nothing, for peanuts.

example: Pourquoi est-que que tu n'essaies pas de trouver un autre emploi. Ton patron devient de plus en plus riche et toi, tu travailles **pour des prunes**!

translation: Why don't you try finding another job. Your boss is getting richer and richer and you're working **for peanuts**!

as spoken: Pourquoi t'essaies pas d'trouver un autr'emploi. Ton patron, il d'vient d'plus en plus riche et toi, tu travailles **pour des prunes**!

NOTE: The noun *prune* is a common *faux ami* ("false friend") in French. Although it would certainly be reasonable that a native speaker of English would assume that *prune* has the same meaning in French, this is not the case: *prune* = plum; *pruneau* = prune.

puceau / pucelle *c.l.* virgin.

example: A l'âge de trente ans, Jeanne est toujours **pucelle**.

translation: At thirty years of age, Jeanne is still a **virgin**.

as spoken: A l'âge de trente ans, Jeanne, elle est toujours **pucelle**.

puer du bec *exp.* to have bad breath • (lit.): to stink from the mouth.

NOTE: **bec** *m.* mouth • (lit.): beak of a bird.

puer la merde *exp.* • **1.** to stink to high heaven • **2.** to smell fishy (said of something dishonest or shady) (lit.): to stink like shit.

example (1): Nous sommes près des égouts? Ça **pue la merde** ici.

translation: Are we near a sewer? It **stinks like shit** here.

as spoken: On est près des -gouts? Ça **pue la merde** ici.

example (2): Cette voiture t'a coûté un malheureux mille francs?! Ça **pue la merde**. Ça peut être une voiture volée, ça!

translation: That car cost you a measly one thousand francs?! That **smells fishy**. It could be a stolen car!

as spoken: C'te voiture, è t'a coûté un malheureux mille francs?! Ça **pue la merde**. Ça peut êtr'une voiture volée, ca!

purée *f.* sperm • (lit.): purée.

putain • **1.** *interj.* used to denote surprise or anger • **2.** *f.* whore.

example (1): Oh, **putain**! Elle est jolie, cette nana!

translation: Oh, **holy shit**! That girl is beautiful!

as spoken: Oh, **putain**! Elle est jolie, c'te nana!

example (2): Je n'arrive pas à le croire. Georgette gagne sa vie comme **putain**?

translation: I can't believe it. Georgette earns a living as a **hooker**?

as spoken: J'arrive pas à l'croire. Georgette, è gagne sa vie comme **putain**?

NOTE: nana *f.* (extremely popular) girl, "chick."

pute *f.* prostitute, whore.

example: Edouard a une nouvelle petite amie et tout le monde sait qu'elle est **pute** sauf lui!

translation: Edward has a new girlfriend and everyone knows she's a **prostitute** except for him!

as spoken: Edouard, il a une nouvelle p'tite amie et tout l'monde sait qu'elle est **pute** sauf lui!

SYNONYM: putain *f.*

quand les poules auront des dents *exp.* (humorous) never, "when pigs fly" • (lit.): when hens have teeth.

example: Je l'inviterai à dîner **quand les poules auront des dents**! Je ne peux pas le tolérer!

translation: I'll invite him to dinner **when pigs fly**! I can't stand him!

as spoken: J'l'invit'rai à dîner **quand les poules auront des dents**! J'peux pas l'tolérer!

quart (faire le) *m.* (said of a prostitute) to hustle • (lit.): to keep watch.

que je ne te raconte pas *exp.* I won't even go into it.

example: Je ne me suis pas du tout amusé en vacances. Elles étaient horribles, **que je ne te raconte pas**!

translation: I didn't have a good time at all on vacation. It was horrible! I **won't even go into it**!??

as spoken: Je m'suis pas du tout amusé en vacances. È z'étaient horribles, **que j'te raconte pas**!

quelle mouche te / le / la / les pique? *exp.* what's gotten into you / him / her / them? • (lit.): what fly biting you / him / her / them?

example: **Quelle mouche te pique**, Charles? Tu as l'air énervé!

translation: **What's eating you**, Charles? You look upset!

as spoken: **Quelle mouche te pique**, Charles? T'as l'air énervé!

François est en mauvaise humeur!
*Mais **quelle mouche le pique**?!*

───────

(trans.):
Frank's in a bad mood!
***What's eating him**?!*

(lit.):
Frank's in a bad mood!
***What fly's eating him**?!*

quéquette *f.* (child language) penis.

Qu'est-ce que ça peut me foutre? *exp.* What's it got to do with me?

example: "Je dois te parler de ce qui est arrivé hier."
"**Qu'est-ce que ça peut me foutre**?"

translation: "I have to talk to you about what happened yesterday."
"**What's it got to do with me**?"

as spoken: "J'dois t'parler d'c'qui est arrivé hier."
"**Qu'est-c'que ça peut m'foutre**?"

SYNONYM: Qu'est-ce que j'en ai à foutre? *exp.* • (lit.): What do I have to do with that?

queue *f.* penis • (lit.): tail.

queuter *v.* to fornicate • (lit.): to "dick" (someone).

NOTE: This comes from the feminine noun *queue* which literally means "tail" but has taken the slang connotation of "penis, dick" particularly in Belgium.

quiquette *f.* penis.

quiqui *m.* (child language) penis.

quoi de neuf? *exp.* what's new? • (lit.): what of new?

example: Salut Etienne! **Quoi de neuf?**

translation: Hi Steve! **What's new?**

as spoken: Salut Etienne! **Quoi d'neuf?**

SYNONYM: qu'est-ce qu'il y a de nouveau? *exp.* • (lit.): what is there of new?

rab (en) *exp.* (borrowed from Arabic) to spare • (lit.): more.

example: Si tu as toujours faim, il y a du poulet **en rab**.

translation: If you're still hungry, there's **more** chicken.

as spoken: Si t'as toujours faim, y a du poulet **en rab**.

ALSO: **rab (du)** *exp.* more, seconds.

example: Si tu as toujours faim, il y a **du rab**.

translation: If you're still hungry, there are **seconds**.

as spoken: Si t'as toujours faim, y a **du rab**.

raccroc (faire le) *m.* (said of a prostitute) to hustle.

SEE: **raccrocher**, *(next entry)*.

raccrocher *v.* (said of a prostitute) to hustle • (lit.): to accost (men).

SEE: **raccroc (faire le)**, *(previous entry)*.

raccrocheuse *f.* prostitute • (lit.): woman who accosts men.

raclure *f.* a disparaging remark applied to a man • (lit.): scrapings.

ALSO: **raclure de bidet** *f.* • (lit.): bidet scrapings.

racoleuse *f.* prostitute • (lit.): woman who recruits or solicits men.

radiner *v.* to show up, to arrive.

example: Mon père était supposé **radiner** il y a une heure. Il est toujours en retard.

translation: My father was supposed **to arrive** an hour ago. He's always late.

as spoken: Mon père, il était supposé **radiner** y a une heure. Il est toujours en r'tard.

NOTE: Although the verb *arriver* is conjugated with *être*, its slang synonym **radiner** is conjugated with *avoir*: *Je suis arrivé* = **J'ai radiné**.

raffoler de quelqu'un *v.* to be crazy about someone.

NOTE: This comes from the adjective *fou / folle* meaning "crazy."

raide (l'avoir) *exp.* to have an erection • (lit.): to have it stiff.

ramasser la chtouille *exp.* to catch a venereal disease, to catch the "clap."

example: La première fois que j'ai eu des rapports sexuels, j'ai **ramassé la chtouille**.

translation: The first time I had sex, I **got the clap**.

as spoken: La première fois qu'j'ai eu des rapports sexuels, j'ai **ramassé la chtouille**.

ramiaous (avoir ses) *m.pl.* to menstruate.

ramoner *v.* (humorous) to fornicate
- (lit.): to sweep (a chimney).

NOTE: **cheminée** *f.* vagina
- (lit.): chimney.

ras le cul (en avoir) *exp.* a harsh expression meaning "to be fed up"
- (lit.): to have had it up to one's ass.

example: Maurice, il a encore menti? Oh, j'**en ai ras le cul**!

translation: Maurice lied again? Oh, I've **had it**!

as spoken: Maurice, il a encore menti? Oh, j'**en ai ras l'cul**!

rasoir (être) *adj.* to be boring
- (lit.): to be razor.

example: Mon nouveau professeur de biologie est tout à fait **rasoir**. J'ai du mal à rester éveillé dans sa classe.

translation: My new biology teacher is really **boring**. I have trouble staying awake in his class.

as spoken: Mon nouveau prof de bio, il est tout à fait **rasoir**. J'ai du mal à rester éveillé dans sa classe.

recevoir quelqu'un comme un chien dans un jeu de quilles *exp.* to be cold toward someone • (lit.): to receive someone like a dog in a lawn bowling game.

example: J'ai l'impression que Margot et ses amis ne m'aiment pas. Quand je me suis arrêté pour leur dire bonjour, elles **m'ont reçu comme un chien dans un jeu de quilles**.

translation: I don't think Margot and her friends like me. When I stopped to say hi to them, they **were really cold toward me**.

as spoken: J'ai l'impression qu'Margot et ses amies, elles m'aiment pas. Quand je m'suis arrêté pour leur dire bonjour, elles **m'ont r'çu comme un chien dans un jeu d'quilles**.

recharger les accus *exp.* to set 'em up (the glasses for another round of drinks) • (lit.): to recharge the batteries.

example: Et maintenant, buvons à la santé de Louise! **Rechargeons les accus**!

translation: And now, let's drink to Louise! **Stack 'em up again**!

as spoken: Et maintenant, buvons à la santé d'Louise! **Rechargeons les accus**!

reculer d'une semelle (ne pas) *exp.* not to give an inch
- (lit.): not to back up from a [shoe's] sole.

example: J'ai essayé de discuter le problème avec lui, mais il **ne recule pas d'une semelle**.

translation: I tried to discuss the problem with him, but he **wouldn't give an inch**.

as spoken: J'ai essayé d'discuter l'problème avec lui, mais y **r'cule pas d'une s'melle**.

refiler *v.* to unload something on someone, to give someone something that is no longer wanted.

example: Mon frère m'a **refilé** son vieux manteau.

translation: My brother **unloaded** his old coat on me.

as spoken: Mon frère, y m'a **r'filé** son vieux manteau.

régaler *v.* to treat • (lit.): to entertain, to regale.

example: C'est moi qui **régale**!

translation: It's **on me**!

as spoken: [no change]

régulière *f.* wife • (lit.): legitimate one.

example: Ma **régulière** est présidente d'une grande société à Paris.

translation: My **wife** is the president of a big company in Paris.

as spoken: Ma **régulière**, elle est présidente d'une grande société à Paris.

relever de (se) *exp.* to be getter over (a sickness) • (lit.): to get back up (from something).

example: Mon père est très fatigué parce qu'il **se relève d'**une grippe.

translation: My father is very tired because he's **getting over** the flu.

as spoken: Mon père, il est très fatigué pasqu'y **s'relève d'**une grippe.

remarquer *v.* to take notice, to consider something, to listen.

example: **Remarque**. Les gens dépassent la limite de vitesse tout le temps sans attraper de contraventions.

translation: **Think about it**. People break the speed limit all the time without getting a ticket for it.

as spoken: **Remarque**. Les gens, y dépassent la limite de vitesse tout l'temps sans attraper de contraventions.

remède d'amour *m.* said of someone ugly • (lit.): a remedy for love.

remonter à *c.l.* to date back to • (lit.): to go back (in time) to.

example: Cette peinture **remonte au** dix-septième siècle!

translation: This painting **dates back to** the seventeenth century!

as spoken: Cette peinture, è **r'monte au** dix-septième siècle!

remplir la bedaine (se) *exp.* to eat • (lit.): to fill one's gut.

example: Le dîner était excellent. Je **me suis bien rempli la bedaine** ce soir!

translation: The dinner was excellent. I **really ate well** tonight!

as spoken: Le dîner, il était excellent. Je **m'suis bien rempli la bedaine** c'soir!

rencart *m.* (from *rendez-vous*) date.

example: Je dois me dépêcher. J'ai un **rencart** avec Maurice ce soir!

translation: I have to hurry. I have a **date** with Maurice tonight!

as spoken: J'dois m'dépêcher. J'ai un **rencart** avec Maurice ce soir!

NOTE -1: Also spelled: *rencard*.

NOTE -2: **rencarter** *v.* to have a date with someone.

rendre *v.* a polite form of "vomir" meaning "to vomit" • (lit.): to give back.

rendre son quatre heures *exp.* to vomit • (lit.): to give back one's cookies and milk (that which one eats at *quatre heures* meaning "four o'clock").

rengaine *f.* repetitious story.

example: C'est toujours la même **rengaine**. Je l'invite chez moi et il me dit qu'il est trop occupé.

translation: It's always the same **old story**. I invite him to my house and he tells me that he's too busy.

as spoken: C'est toujours la même **rengaine**. J'l'invite chez moi et y m'dit qu'il est trop occupé.

renifler quelqu'un (ne pas pouvoir) *v.* to be unable to stand someone • (lit.): to be unable to sniff someone (since the mere smell of the person would be too much to bear).

example: Je ne vais pas inviter Suzanne à ma soirée. Je **ne peux pas la renifler**.

translation: I'm not going to invite Suzanne to my party. I **can't stand her**.

as spoken: J'vais pas inviter Suzanne à ma soirée. J'**peux pas la renifler**.

rentrer au bercail *exp.* to return to one's own home • (lit.): to return to the crib.

example: Après trois semaines de vacances, je suis prêt à **rentrer au bercail**.

translation: After three weeks of vacation, I'm ready to **get back home**.

as spoken: Après trois s'maines de vacances, j'suis prêt à **rentrer au bercail**.

rentrer la bite sous le bras *exp.* to come home without having scored a date • (lit.): to come home with the "dick" under one's arm.

NOTE: bite *f.* penis • (lit.): bitt or bollard (on a ship).

renvois (donner / faire des) *exp.* to burp.

NOTE: This comes from the verb *renvoyer* meaning "to send back" or in this case "to send back up."

repeindre sa grille en rouge *exp.* to menstruate • (lit.): to repaint one's grill red.

repousser du goulot *exp.* to have bad breath • (lit.): to repel from the bottleneck.

NOTE: goulot *m.* neck • (lit.): bottleneck.

reprendre le collier *exp.* to get back to work or school, "to get back to the grind" • (lit.): to get back under the harness.

example: J'ai passé de bonnes vacances mais demain je dois **reprendre le collier**.

translation: I had a great vacation but tomorrow I have **to get back to the grind**.

as spoken: J'ai passé d'bonnes vacances mais d'main j'dois **r'prend' le collier**.

requinquiner (se) *v.* to perk up after being sick.

example: J'ai été malade pendant une semaine. Aujourd'hui, je me sens **requinquiné**.

translation: I was sick for a week. Today, I feel **perked up**.

as spoken: J'ai été malade pendant une s'maine. Aujourd'hui, je m'sens **requinquiné**.

rester baba (en) *exp.* to be so stunned with amazement or surprise.

example: Richard est ton frère?! J'**en reste baba**! Je ne l'aurais jamais su si tu ne me l'avais pas dit. Vous ne vous ressemblez même pas!

translation: Richard is your brother?! I'm **stunned**! I would never have known if you hadn't told me. You don't even look alike!

as spoken: Richard, c'est ton frère?! J'**en reste baba**! J'l'aurais jamais su si tu m'l'avais pas dit. Vous vous ressemblez même pas!

resto *m.* abbreviation of "restaurant."

example: Ce **resto** coûte cher!

translation: This **restaurant** is expensive!

as spoken: C'**resto**, y coûte cher!

NOTE: This abbreviation got its name from Coluche, the late, popular comedian who launched a chain of low-priced eateries for the destitute. These restaurants were called *les restos du cœur* ("restaurants from the heart").

Retournez dans votre banlieue de merde! *exp.* an insulting meaning "Get the fuck out of here!" • (lit.): Go back to your suburb of shit.

example: Arrêtez de gueuler et **retournez dans votre banlieue de merde**!

translation: Stop screaming and **get the fuck out of here**!

as spoken: Arrêtez d'gueuler et **retournez dans vot' banlieue d'merde**!

retrouver ses forces *exp.* to get back to one's old self again (after an illness) • (lit.): to find one's forces again.

example: Petit à petit, je **retrouve mes forces** après l'opération.

translation: Little by little, I'm **getting back to my old self** after the operation.

as spoken: P'tit à p'tit, je **r'trouve mes forces** après l'opération.

réveil pénible *c.l.* rude awakening • (lit.): painful awakening.

example: Un de ces jours, il va avoir un **réveil pénible**.

translation: One of these days, he's going to have a **rude awakening**.

as spoken: Un d'ces jours, y va avoir un **réveil pénible**.

revenir (ne pas en) *exp.* to disbelieve.

example: On a volé la voiture de Jean? Je **n'en reviens pas**.

translation: Jean's car was stolen? I **can't believe it**.

as spoken: On a volé la voiture d'Jean? J'**en r'viens pas**.

"Revenons à nos mouton"

exp. "Let's get back to what we were talking about" • (lit.): "Let's get back to watching over our sheep."

example: Nous nous sommes trop écartés de notre sujet. **Revenons à nos moutons**.

translation: We just got way off the subject. **Let's get back to what we were talking about**.

as spoken: Nous nous sommes trop écartés d'not'sujet. **Revenons à nos moutons**.

rien à chiquer *exp.* nothing doing, no way • (lit.): nothing to chew.

example: Tu veux que je te prête mille balles? **Rien à chiquer**! Tu me dois toujours mille francs de la semaine dernière!

translation: You want me to lend you a thousand francs? **No way**! You still owe me a thousand francs from last week!

as spoken: Tu veux qu'j'te prête mille balles? **Rien à chiquer**! Tu m'dois toujours mille francs d'la s'maine dernière!

NOTE: The verb *chiquer* literally means "to chew tobacco."

rien à faire *exp.* no way • (lit.): nothing doing.

example: Tu veux que j'invite Louise à ma soirée?! **Rien à faire**! La dernière fois que je l'ai invitée chez moi, elle m'a humilié devant mes tous amis!

translation: You want me to invite Louise to my party?! **No way**! The last time I invited her to my house, she humiliated me in front of all my friends!

as spoken: Tu veux qu'j'invite Louise à ma soirée?! **Rien à faire**! La dernière fois qu'j'l'ai invitée chez moi, è m'a humilié devant mes tous amis!

rien à foutre *exp.* no way, nothing doing • (lit.): nothing to fuck.

example: Tu veux que j'aille chercher Christophe à l'aéroport?! **Rien à foutre**! La dernière fois, ça m'a mis deux heures avec les embouteillages et en plus, il ne m'a même pas remercié!

translation: You want me to go pick up Christopher at the airport?! **No fuckin' way**! The last time, it took me two hours with all the traffic and not only that, he didn't even thank me!

as spoken: Tu veux qu'j'aille chercher Christophe à l'aéroport?! **Rien à foutre**! La dernière fois, ça m'a mis deux heures avec les embouteillages et en plus, y m'a même pas r'mercié!

rien de temps (en un) *exp.* in no time flat • (lit.): in a nothing of time.

example: Si tout va bien, je pourrai réparer ta voiture **en un rien de temps**.

translation: If everything goes well, I'll be able to repair your car **in no time flat**.

as spoken: Si tout va bien, J'pourrai réparer ta voiture **en un rien d'temps**.

rien ne lui échappe *c.l.*

• (lit.): nothing escapes him / her.

example: Le professeur sait que tu as triché à l'examen. **Rien ne lui échappe**.

translation: The teacher knows you cheated on the test. **Nothing gets by him**.

as spoken: Le prof, y sait qu't'as triché à l'exam'. **Rien lui échappe**.

riffer (se) *v.* to quarrel.

NOTE-1: **rif** *m.* a big fight.

NOTE-2: **rififi** *m.* a big fight.

rincer le sifflet (se) *exp.* to wet one's whistle • (lit.): to rinse one's whistle.

example: J'ai soif. Je vais **me rincer le sifflet**.

translation: I'm thirsty. I'm going **to wet my whistle**.

as spoken: J'ai soif. J'vais **m'rincer l'sifflet**.

roberts *m.pl.* breasts

rognons *m.pl.* testicles • (lit.): kidneys.

roi des cons (le) *exp.* a complete idiot or jerk • (lit.): the king of the idiots / jerks.

example: C'est la cinquième fois cette semaine que Michel a enfermé ses clés dans la voiture. Je te jure, c'est **le roi des cons**.

translation: This is the fifth time this week that Michel locked his keys in the car. I swear to you, he's the **biggest idiot**.

as spoken: C'est la cinquième fois cette s'maine que Michel, il a enfermé ses clés dans la voiture. J'te jure, c'est **l'roi des cons**.

*Comme chauffeur, Jean est **le roi des cons**!*

(trans.):
*As a driver, John is **the biggest jerk**!*

(lit.):
*As a driver, John is **the king of jerks**!*

rombière *f.* bitch, old hag, overbearing woman.

rond(e) comme une bille (être) *exp.* to be roaring drunk • (lit.): to be as round as a marble.

example: Mais tu ne peux pas conduire comme ça! Tu es **rond comme une bille**!

translation: You can't drive like that! You're **bombed out of your skull**!

as spoken: Mais tu peux pas conduire comme ça! T'es **rond comme une bille**!

NOTE: This expression is a play on words since the adjective "*rond(e)*" (meaning "round") is commonly used to mean drunk. Therefore, "*être rond(e) comme une bille*" simply emphasizes the subject's intoxicated condition.

*Henri est **rond comme une bille**!*

(trans.):
*Henry is **as drunk as a skunk**!*

(lit.):
*Henry is **as round as a marble**!*

rond(e) comme une queue de billard (être) *exp.* to be roaring drunk • (lit.): to be round like a billiard cue.

example: Tu ne peux pas conduire! Tu es **rond comme une queue de billard**!

translation: You can't drive! You're **wasted**!

as spoken: Tu peux pas conduire! T'es **rond comme une queue d'billard**!

NOTE: This expression is a play on words since the adjective "*rond(e)*" (meaning "round") is commonly used to mean drunk. Therefore, "*être rond(e) comme une bille*" simply emphasizes the subject's intoxicated condition.

VARIATION: **rond(e) comme une manche de pelle (être)** *exp.* • (lit.): to be round like a shovel handle.

rondelle *f.* (popular) anus • (lit.): washer.

rondin *m.* turd • (lit.): log.

ronger son frein *c.l.* to keep one's self-control, to chomp at the bit • (lit.): to chew one's bit.

example: Je **ronge mon frein** en attendant que mon argent arrive!

translation: I'm **chomping at the bit** waiting for my money to arrive!

as spoken: J'**ronge mon frein** en attendant qu'mon argent arrive!

rosette *f.* (popular) anus • (lit.): that which is pink.

rot (faire un) *exp.* to burp • (lit.): to make a burp.

roublard(e) (être) *adj.* to be devious or cunning.

example: Je ne me fie pas du tout à Antoine. Il est très **roublard**, celui-là.

translation: I don't trust Antoine at all. He's very **devious**.

as spoken: Je m'fie pas du tout à Antoine. Il est très **roublard**, c'ui-là.

rougnotter *v.* to stink.

rouleaux *m.pl.* testicles • (lit.): rollers.

rouler des biscottos *exp.* to flex one's biceps • (lit.): to roll one's biceps.

example: Regarde cet athlète-là. Il **roule des biscottos**.

translation: Look at that athlete. He's **flexing his biceps**.

as spoken: Regarde c't'athlète-là. Y **roule des biscottos**.

NOTE: biscotto *m.* bicep.

rouler des saucisses *exp.* (said of two people kissing) to "French" kiss • (lit.): to roll sausages (referring to the look of the tongue).

rouler une escalope *exp.* to "French" kiss • (lit.): to roll a thin slice of meat.

rouler une galoche *exp.* to "French" kiss • (lit.): to roll a shoe.

rouler une pelle *exp.* to deep-kiss with the tongue, to "French" kiss • (lit.): to roll a shovel.

example: Quand il m'a fait un baiser, il m'a **roulé une pelle**!

translation: When he kissed me, he **slipped me his tongue**!

as spoken: Quand y m'a fait un baiser, y m'a **roulé une pelle**!

SYNONYM: **rouler une escalope** *exp.* • (lit.): to roll a thin slice of meat.

rouler un paleau *exp.* to "French" kiss.

rouler un patin *exp.* to "French" kiss • (lit.): to roll a skate.

roustons *m.pl.* (extremely popular) testicles.

rue barrée (avoir sa) *f.* to menstruate • (lit.): to have one's street closed • *Rue barrée;* No thoroughfare.

sabre *m.* penis • (lit.): saber.

sacristi *interj.* (a common interjection used in comic books) Holy cow!

example: **Sacristi**! Le loup nous poursuit!

translation: **Holy cow**! The wolf is after us!

as spoken: **Sacristi**! Le loup, y nous poursuit!

SYNONYM -1: **saperlipopette** *interj.*

SYNONYM -2: **saperlotte** *interj.*

SYNONYM -3: **sapristi** *interj.*

sado (être) *n. & adj.* a common abbreviation of *sadique* meaning "sadist" or "sadistic."

example: Je n'aime pas aller chez mon dentiste. Je crois qu'il est **sado**!

translation: I don't like going to my dentist. I think he's a **sadist**!

as spoken: J'aime pas allez chez mon dentiste. J'crois qu'il est **sado**!

salaud *m.* (extremely popular; applies only to a man) bastard.

example: Ce **salaud** de Pierre! Il m'a menti!

translation: Pierre, that **bastard**! He lied to me!

as spoken: Ce **salaud** d'Pierre! Y m'a menti!

SEE: salope, *p. 162.*

salé(e) (être) *adj.* to be expensive • (lit.): to be salted.

example: Tu as claqué mille balles pour cette liquette? C'est **salé**!

translation: You blew a thousand francs on this shirt? That's **expensive**!

as spoken: T'as claqué mille balles pour c'te liquette? C'est **salé**!

NOTE: liquette *f.* shirt.

sale gueule (avoir une) *f.* to be ugly • (lit.): to have a dirty face.

sale histoire (une) *exp.* a sordid story.

example: "Mais qu'est-ce qui s'est passé avec ton œil? C'est tout gonflé!"
"Je me suis disputé avec mon boucher. Oh, c'est **une sale histoire**."

translation: "What happened to your eye? It's all swollen!"
"I got into a fight with my butcher. Oh, it's a **sordid story**."

as spoken: "Mais qu'est-c'qui s'est passé avec ton œil? C'est tout gonflé!"
"Je m'suis disputé avec mon boucher. Oh, c't'**une sale histoire**."

saligaud *m.* a variation of *salaud* meaning "bastard."

salopard *m.* variation of *salaud* meaning "bastard."

saloparde *v.* variation of *salope* meaning "bitch."

salope *f.* (extremely popular) bitch.

example: Cette **salope** de Marie. Elle a volé mon petit ami!

translation: Marie, that **bitch**. She stole my boyfriend!

as spoken: C'te **salope** de Marie. Elle a volé mon p'tit ami!

SEE: salaud, *p. 162.*

NOTE: The term *salope* also has the connotation of "a sexually promiscuous woman."

saloperie *f.* • **1.** said of something nasty done to someone • **2.** piece of junk.

example (1): Je ne parle plus à Richard. Il m'a fait une **saloperie**.

translation: I'm not speaking to Richard anymore. He did **something really nasty** to me.

as spoken: J'parle pu à Richard. Y m'a fait une **salop'rie**.

example (2): Tu as vu la robe qu'elle porte, Nancy? Elle a payé deux cent dollars cette **saloperie**!

translation: Did you see the dress Nancy's wearing? She paid two hundred dollars for that **piece of junk**!

as spoken: T'as vu la robe qu'è porte, Nancy? Elle a payé deux cent dollars c'te **salop'rie**!

salut *interj.* hi.

example: **Salut**, Carole! Ça va?

translation: **Hi** Carole! How's everything going?

as spoken: [no change]

NOTE: The interjection *salut* is used to mean both "hi" and "good-bye" depending on the context.

sans histoire(s) *exp.* without a problem • (lit.): without a story.

example: La construction de la maison s'est passée **sans histoires**.

translation: The construction of the house went without **a hitch**.

as spoken: La construction d'la maison, è s'est passée **sans histoires**.

sans rigoler *exp.* no kidding • (lit.): without laughing.

example: Tu as trouvé mille francs? **Sans rigoler**?

translation: You found a thousand francs? **No kidding**?

as spoken: T'as trouvé mille francs? **Sans rigoler**?

SYNONYM -1: **sans blague** *exp.* • (lit.): without joke.

SYNONYM -2:: **sans rire** *exp.* • (lit.): without laughing.

sauce *f.* sperm • (lit.): sauce.

saucée *f.* • **1.** downpour • **2.** scolding, thrashing.

*Quelle **saucée**! Notre pique-nique est ruiné!*

(trans.):
What a **downpour**! Our picnic is ruined!

(lit.):
What a **saucing**! Our picnic is ruined!

example (1): J'ai peur de conduire dans cette **saucée**.

translation: I'm scared to drive in this **downpour**.

as spoken: J'ai peur d'conduire dans c'te **saucée**.

example (2): Elle lui a donné une vraie **saucée**.

translation: She gave him a real **thrashing**.

as spoken: È lui a donné une vraie **saucée**.

SYNONYM -1: **raclée** *f.* scolding, thrashing.

SYNONYM -2: **trempe** *f.* scolding, thrashing.

sauce-tomate (avoir sa) *f.* to menstruate • (lit.): to have one's tomato sauce.

saucisson *m.* an ugly (or fat) person • (lit.): (large dry) sausage.

sauter *v.* (very popular) to fornicate • (lit.): to jump (one's bones).

sauterelle *f.* prostitute • (lit.): grasshopper.

NOTE: This is actually a play on words since the verb *sauter* (literally meaning "to jump") has the slang meaning of "to jump sexually."

sauter (faire) *exp.* to blow up • (lit.): to make jump.

example: Pendant la manifestation, les étudiants ont **fait sauter** la voiture du directeur.

translation: During the demonstration, the students **blew up** the principal's car.

as spoken: Pendant la manif, les étudiants, y z'ont **fait sauter** la voiture du dirlo.

savoir sur quel pied danser (ne pas) *exp.* not to know where you stand with someone • (lit.): not to know which foot to dance on.

example: Des fois, elle est gentille. Des fois, elle est méchante. On **ne sait jamais sur quel pied danser** avec elle.

translation: Sometimes she's nice. Sometimes she's mean. You **never know where you stand** with her.

as spoken: Des fois, elle est gentille. Des fois, elle est méchante. On **sait jamais sur quel pied danser** avec elle.

savon *m.* a quarrel • (lit.): soap.

NOTE: **passer un savon (se faire)** *exp.* to get yelled at.

scaphandre de poche *m.* condom • (lit.): pocket-size diving suit.

schlinguer *v.* to stink.

example: Je n'aime pas ce fromage parce que ça **schlingue**!

translation: I don't like this cheese because it **stinks**!

as spoken: J'aime pas c'fromage pasque ça **schlingue**!

NOTE: Also spelled *chlinguer*.

VARIATION: **schlingoter** *v.*

schnock *m.* (applies only to a man) imbecile, jerk

VARIATION: **duchenock** *m.*

NOTE: **vieux schnock** *m.* an old a senile man.

schtouille *f.* (also spelled: *chtouille*) gonorrhea.

sécher *v.* to cut class.

example: J'ai **séché** mon cours de biologie aujourd'hui pour aller au cinéma.

translation: I **skipped** my biology class today in order to go to the movies.

as spoken: J'ai **séché** mon cours de bio aujourd'hui pour aller au ciné.

secouer la poêle à marrons *exp.* • (lit.): to shake the roasted chestnut pan.

NOTE: **marron** *m.* blackeye • (lit.): chestnut.

secouer le bonhomme (se) *exp.* (of men) to masturbate • (lit.): to shake one's good-natured man.

sellette (mettre sur la) *exp.* to call on the carpet, to rake over the coals • (lit.): to put on the saddle.

example: Etienne! Le patron veut te voir dans son bureau. J'espère pour toi qu'il ne compte pas te **mettre sur la sellette** comme la semaine dernière!

translation: Steve! The boss wants to see you in his office. I hope for your sake that he's not planning on **raking you over the coals** like last week!

as spoken: Etienne! Le patron, y veut t'voir dans son bureau. J'espère pour toi qu'y compte pas t'**mett' sur la sellette** comme la s'maine dernière!

semer quelqu'un *v.* to ditch or shake someone • (lit.): to sow someone.

example: Il me suit partout! Je n'arrive pas à le **semer**!

translation: He follows me everywhere! I can't **ditch** him!

as spoken: Y m'suit partout! J'arrive pas à l'**semer**!

sensass *adj.* a common abbreviation of *sensationel(le)* meaning "sensational."

example: Ta robe est **sensass**!

translation: Your dress is **sensational**!

as spoken: Ta robe, elle est **sensass**!

sentir la merde *exp.* • **1.** to stink to high heaven • **2.** to smell fishy • (lit.): to smell of shit.

example (1): Ça **sent la merde** dans cette poissonnerie!

translation: It **stinks to high heaven** in this fish market!

as spoken: Ça **sent la merde** dans c'te poissonnerie!

example (2): Depuis que nous avons engagé Cécile, la caisse est toujours à court d'argent. Ça **sent la merde**!

translation: Ever since we hired Cecilia, the cash register is always short of money. That **smells fishy**!

as spoken: Depuis qu'on a engagé Cécile, la caisse, elle est toujours à court d'argent. Ça **sent la merde**!

sentir le fauve *exp.* to stink • (lit.): to smell like wild animal.

sentir quelqu'un (ne pas pouvoir) *v.* to be unable to stand someone • (lit.): to be unable to smell someone (since the mere smell of the person would be too much to bear).

serrer les fesses *exp.* to hang in there, to be courageous • (lit.): to squeeze the cheeks of one's buttocks.

example: Ma cousine reste chez moi pour encore une semaine et elle me rend fou! Je dois **serrer les fesses**!

translation: My cousin is staying at my house for another week and she's driving me crazy! I have to **hang in there**!

as spoken: Ma cousine, è reste chez moi pour encore une s'maine et è m'rend fou! J'dois **serrer les fesses**!

SYNONYM: **tenir bon** *exp.* to hold tight, to stick to your guns • (lit.): to hold good.

SIDA *m.* an abbreviation for *Syndrome Immuno-Déficitaire Acquis* meaning "AIDS (Acquired Immune Deficiency Syndrome)."

example: Le **SIDA** est une maladie qui attaque le système immunitaire.

translation: **AIDS** is a disease that attacks the immune system.

as spoken: Le **SIDA**, c't'une maladie qui attaque le système immunitaire.

sidérant(e) (être) *adj.* to be astonishing, incredible.

example: Je viens d'apprendre que mon neveu est devenu président de la plus grande société à Paris. C'est **sidérant**! Il n'a que vingt-huit ans!

translation: I just found out that my nephew became president of the biggest company in Paris. It's **incredible**! He's only twenty-eight years old!

as spoken: J'viens d'apprend' que mon neveu, il est dev'nu président d'la plus grande société à Paris. C'est **sidérant**! Il a qu'vingt-huit ans!

signer un bail *v.* to get married • (lit.): to sign a lease.

example: Ralph et Jacqueline vont **signer un bail** dans deux jours!

translation: Ralph and Jacqueline are going **to get hitched** in two days!

as spoken: Ralph et Jacqueline, y vont **signer un bail** dans deux jours!

siphonné(e) (être) *adj.* to be nuts, crazy • (lit.): siphoned (of all intelligence).

soixante-neuf (faire le) *exp.* to sixty-nine (involving two partners who have positioned their bodies to be able to engage in mutual oral sex).

son compte est bon! *exp.* he's/she's a dead duck! • (lit.): his/her account is good!

example: Elle m'a trompé! **Son compte est bon**!

translation: She tricked me! **She's dead meat**!

as spoken: È m'a trompé! **Son compte est bon**!

sonné(e) (être) *adj.* to be nuts, a "ding-a-ling" • (lit.): to be rung.

son pain cuit (avoir) *exp.* to have it made, to be on easy street • (lit.): to have one's bread cooked.

example: David a hérité d'un million de dollars! Il **a son pain cuit**, lui.

translation: David inherited a million dollars! He **has it made**.

as spoken: David, il a hérité d'un million d'dollars! Il **a son pain cuit**, lui.

sortir de ses gonds *exp.* to fly off the handle • (lit.): to exit one's hinges.

example: Si ton père voit ce que tu as fait de sa voiture, il va **sortir de ses gonds**!

translation: If your father sees what you did to his car, he's gonna **fly off the handle**!

as spoken: Si ton père, y voit c'que t'as fait d'sa voiture, y va **sortir d'ses gonds**!

NOTE: As seen above, in spoken French, it is much more common to use the progressive future (*va sortir*) than the simple future (*sortira*).

SYNONYM: **mettre en boule (se)** *exp.* • (lit.): to put oneself in a ball (since every muscle is cramping from anger).

souche *f.* (applies to either a man or a woman) silly person, dumbbell • (lit.): stump (of a tree).

souffler dans la canne *exp.* to perform fellatio • (lit.): to blow in the cane.

souffler dans le mirliton *exp.* to perform fellatio • (lit.): to blow in the toy flute.

soulager (se) *v.* **1.** to masturbate • **2.** to go to the bathroom • (lit.): to relieve oneself.

soupé (en avoir) *exp.* to have had it, to be fed up • (lit.): to have souped from it.

example: Le professeur nous a donné encore des devoirs pour le weekend. J'**en ai soupé**, moi!

translation: The teacher gave us homework over the weekend again. I'm **fed up**!

as spoken: Le prof, y nous a donné encore des d'voirs pour le weekend. J'**en ai soupé**, moi!

NOTE: The noun *"professeur"* is always masculine even when referring to a woman. However, in its popular abbreviated form *"prof,"* it can be either masculine or feminine: *"le prof," "la prof."*

SYNONYM: **ras le bol (en avoir)** *exp.* • (lit.): to have had it to the brim of the bowl.

souris *f.* woman or girl • (lit.): mouse.

succès fou (avoir un) *exp.* to go over with big bang • (lit.): to have a crazy success.

example: Notre pièce de théâtre **a eu un succès fou**!

translation: Our theater play **went over with a big bang**!

as spoken: Not' pièce de théâtre, elle **a eu un succès fou**!

sucer *v.* (very popular) to perform fellatio • (lit.): to suck.

sucer la poire (se) *exp.* to kiss, to "suck face" • (lit.): to suck each other's pear.

> **NOTE:** **poire** *f.* face • (lit.): pear.

sur la même longueur d'ondes (être) *exp.* to be on the same wave length • (lit.): same.

example: Je ne suis pas du tout d'accord avec toi. Normalement, nous sommes **sur la même longeur d'ondes** mais pas cette fois-ci.

translation: I don't agree with you at all. Usually, we're **on the same wave length** but not this time.

as spoken: J'suis pas du tout d'accord avec toi. Normalement, on est **sur la même longeur d'ondes** mais pas cette fois-ci.

sur la paille (être) *exp.* to be down and out, broke • (lit.): to be on the straw.

example: C'est difficile à croire que l'année dernière Silvie était riche et maintenant elle **est sur la paille**. Elle a perdu tout son argent aux courses.

translation: It's hard to believe that last year Silvia was rich and now she's **totally broke**. She lost all her money at the horse races.

as spoken: C'est difficile à croire que l'année dernière Silvie, elle était riche et maint'nant è **est sur la paille**. Elle a perdu tout son argent aux courses.

sur mesure (faire) *exp.* to be custom-made • (lit.): to make on measurement.

example: Je suis tellement grand que tous mes complets doivent être **faits sur mesure**.

translation: I'm so tall that all of my suits have to be **custom-made**.

as spoken: J'suis tellement grand qu'tous mes complets, y doivent êt' **faits sur mesure**.

survolté(e) (être) *exp.* to be all worked up • (lit.): to be boosted up (in regards to electrical current).

example: Ne lui parle pas! Il est **survolté** aujourd'hui!

translation: Don't speak to him! He's **all worked up** today!

as spoken: Lui parle pas! Il est **survolté** aujourd'hui!

syph *f.* an abbreviation for: *syphilis*.

syphlotte *f.* a slang transformation of: *syphilis*.

système D *m.* (an abbreviation of: *système démerde*) operation "get out of deep shit."

example: Quel problème! Il est temps d'employer le **système D**.

translation: What a problem! It's time to implement **operation get out of shit**.

as spoken: Quel problème! Il est temps d'employer l'**système démerde**.

tabac *m.* a quarrel • (lit.): tobacco.

tabasser *v.* to beat up.

example: La foule a **tabassé** le voleur.

translation: The crowd **beat up** the thief.

as spoken: La foule, elle a **tabassé** l'voleur.

ta grand-mère fait du vélo sans selle *exp.* disparaging remark about someone's grandmother • (lit.): your grandmother rides a bike without a seat (and therefore rides on the end of the rod).

ta gueule *interj.* shut up • (lit.): your mouth.

example: **Ta gueule**! Arrête de parler de David comme ça!

translation: **Shut up**! Stop talking about David like that!

as spoken: [no change]

NOTE: When the feminine noun *gueule*, literally meaning "the mouth of an animal," is used in reference to a person, its connotation becomes

derogatory for "mouth" or "face," depending on the context.

tailler une pipe *exp.* to perform fellatio • (lit.): (very popular) • (lit.): to trim a pipe.

tailler une plume *exp.* to perform fellatio • (lit.): to trim a pen.

ta mère a le dos chaud *exp.* disparaging remark about someone's mother • (lit.): your mother has a hot back.

tapage *m.* a loud quarrel • (lit.): loud noise.

ALSO: **tapage nocturne** *m.* late-night noise, noise in the middle of the night.

tapé(e) (être) *adj.* to be crazy, nuts • (lit.): to be touched (in the head).

taper *v.* to stink • (lit.): to hit.

taper du saladier *exp.* to have bad breath • (lit.): to knock from the salad bowl.

NOTE: **saladier** *m.* head • (lit.): salad bowl.

taper la cloche (se) *exp.* to eat well.

example: Nous **nous sommes bien tapés la cloche** chez tes vieux ce soir.

translation: We really **ate up a storm** at your parents house tonight.

as spoken: On **s'est bien tapé la cloche** chez tes vieux ce soir.

NOTE: In the previous sentence, the term *vieux* was used which is an extremely popular slang synonym for parents:

vieille *f.* mother • (lit.): old woman.

vieux *m.* father • (lit.): old man.

vieux (or **vioques**) *m.pl.* parents • (lit.): "oldies."

taper (se) *v.* to treat oneself to (something) • (lit.): to hit back.

example: Je **me suis tapé** un bon dîner hier soir.

translation: I **treated myself** to a good dinner last night.

as spoken: Je **m'suis tapé** un bon dîner hier soir.

taper sur les nerfs à quelqu'un *exp.* to get on someone's nerves • (lit.): to tap or hit on someone's nerves.

example: Arrête! Tu **me tapes sur les nerfs**, toi!

translation: Stop it! You're really **getting on my nerves**!

as spoken: Arrête! Tu **m'tapes sur les nerfs**, toi!

SYNONYMS: **taper / courir sur le haricot à quelqu'un** *exp.* • (lit.): to tap or hit / to run on someone's bean.

taper sur le système à quelqu'un *exp.* to bug someone, to get on someone's nerves • (lit.): to hit on someone's system.

example: Je ne veux pas l'inviter à ma soirée. Elle me **tape sur le système**.

translation: I don't want to invite her to my party. She **gets on my nerves**.

as spoken: J'veux pas l'inviter à ma soirée. È m'**tape sur l'système**.

SYNONYM ·1: **taper sur les nerfs à quelqu'un** *exp.* • (lit.): to hit on someone's nerves.

SYNONYM ·2: **casser les pieds à quelqu'un** *exp.* • (lit.): to break someone's feet.

tapiner *v.* (said of a prostitute) to hustle.

SEE: **tapin (faire le)**, *(previous entry)*.

tapineuse *f.* prostitute.

tapin (faire le) *exp.* (said of a prostitute) to work the streets, to hustle.

example: La pauvre. Elle **fait le tapin** pour gagner sa vie.

translation: The poor thing. She **works the streets** to earn her living.

as spoken: La pauvre. È **fait l'tapin** pour gagner sa vie.

NOTE: **tapineuse** *f.* hooker, prostitute.

tarderie *f.* an ugly person.

tardingue *f.* a slang transformation of *tarderie* meaning "an ugly person."

tartempion *m.* also used to mean "so-and-so" or "what's-his-name."

tartine *f.* • **1.** endless speech • **2.** big fuss • (lit.): a slice of bread with a spread on top (such as butter, jam, etc.).

example (1): Elle m'a raconté toute une **tartine**.

translation: She told me a
long-winded story.

as spoken: È m'a raconté toute une
tartine.

example (2): Elle en a fait toute une
tartine.

translation: She made a **big fuss**
about it.

as spoken: Elle en a fait toute une
tartine.
NOTE -1: The connotation of
tartine becomes clear when it is
thought of as something "spread
out" over a long period of time.
NOTE -2: **tartiner** *v.* to make a
long-winded speech, to make a big
deal out of nothing • (lit.): to spread
(out).

tas (faire le) *m.* (said of a
prostitute) to hustle • (lit.): to do
(a lot of) work.
NOTE: **tas** *m.* work • (lit.): heap,
stack.

tatie *f.* aunt.

example: La sœur de ma mère est
ma **tatie**.

translation: My mother's sister is my
aunt.

as spoken: La sœur d'ma mère,
c'est ma **tatie**.
SYNONYM: **tantine** *f.*

taupe (vieille) *f.* an old person, an
"old fart," someone who can't see
• (lit.): old mole.

téléphone *m.* bathroom, restroom.
NOTE: This come from the fact that
many public outhouses found on the
street resemble telephone booths.

téloche *f.* television.

example: J'ai vu une bonne
émission à la **téloche** ce soir.

translation: I saw a good show on
TV tonight.

as spoken: J'ai vu une bonne
émission à la **téloche** c'soir.

temps de chien *exp.* bad weather
• (lit.): a dog's weather.

example: Il flotte depuis quatre
jours! Quel **temps de chien**!

translation: It's been raining for
four days! What **lousy weather**!

as spoken: Y flotte depuis quat'
jours! Quel **temps d'chien**!

tendre et cher / chère *exp.* an
affectionate term for one's husband
or wife • (lit.): tender and dear.

example: Je te présente mon
tendre et cher. Ça fait quinze ans
que nous sommes mariés.

translation: I'd like you to meet my
husband. We've been married for
fifteen years.

as spoken: J'te présente mon
tendre et cher. Ça fait quinze ans
qu'on est mariés.
SYNONYM -1: **son cinquante
pour cent** *exp.* • (lit.): one's fifty
percent.
SYNONYM -2: **sa douce moitié**
exp. • (lit.): one's sweet half.

tendre pour *exp.* to have an
erection for someone • (lit.): to
tighten for (someone).

tenir l'âne par la queue *exp.* to urinate • (lit.): to hold the donkey by the tail.

tenir pour quelqu'un (en) *exp.* to have a crush on someone • (lit.): to have some of it (affection) for someone.

tenir une dose (en) *exp.* (applies to either a man or a woman) to be hopelessly dumb • (lit.): to hold a dose of it (stupidity).

tête de linotte *f.* (applies only to a woman) scatterbrain • (lit.): birdhead.

tête de nœud *f.* (applies to either a man or a woman) scatterbrain • (lit.): head of knots.

tête dure (avoir la) *exp.* (applies to either a man or a woman) to be thick-skulled, dense, stubborn • (lit.): to have a hard head.

tête en compote (avoir la) *exp.* to have a horrible headache • (lit.): to feel like one's head has been turned to compote.

example: Je ne peux pas me lever du lit. J'ai **la tête en compote**!

translation: I can't get out of bed. I have a **monster headache**!

as spoken: J'peux pas m'lever du lit. J'ai **la tête en compote**!

tête nickelée (avoir la) *exp.* to be bald • (lit.): to have a nickel-plated head.

tétés *m.pl.* breasts.

NOTE: This comes from the verb *téter* meaning "to suck (a mother's breast)."

tétons *m.pl.* tits.

NOTE: This comes from the verb *téter* meaning "to suck (a mother's breast)."

thune *f.* (also spelled: *tune*) a five-franc coin.

example: Je n'en donnerais pas deux **thunes**!

translation: I wouldn't give two cents (**10 francs**) for that!

as spoken: J'en donn'rais pas deux **thunes**!

tifs *m.pl.* hair.

example: Ma frangine a des **tifs** très longs. Ils descendent jusqu'à ses genoux!

translation: My sister has very long **hair**. It goes down to her knees!

as spoken: Ma frangine, elle a des **tifs** très longs. Y descendent jusqu'à ses genoux!

tignasse *f.* a mop of hair.

example: Elle n'a pas hônte de sortir avec une telle **tignasse**? On dirait qu'elle ne se coiffe jamais!

translation: Isn't she ashamed to go out with that **hair**? It looks like she's never brushed it!

as spoken: Elle a pas hônte de sortir avec une telle **tignasse**? On dirait qu'è s'coiffe jamais!

SYNONYM: **tifs** *m.pl.*

timbré(e) (être) *adj.* to be crazy, cracked • (lit.): to be rung.

example: Il conduit dans le mauvais sens! Il doit être **timbré**, celui-là!

translation: He's driving in the wrong direction! He must be **nuts**!

as spoken: Y conduit dans l'mauvais sens! Y doit êt' **timbré**, c'ui-là!

SYNONYM -1: **cinglé(e) (être)** *adj.*

SYNONYM -2: **fêlé(e) (être)** *adj.* (from the verb *fêler* meaning "to crack").

timbre fêlé *m.* crackpot, idiot
• (lit.): cracked bell.

tiré(e) par les cheveux (être) *exp.* to be farfetched • (lit.): to be pulled by the hair.

example: Son excuse était **tirée par les cheveux**.

translation: His excuse was **farfetched**.

as spoken: Son excuse, elle était **tirée par les ch'veux**.

tire-lire *f.* vagina • (lit.): piggy bank.

tirer à bon compte (s'en) *exp.* to get off easy (cheap) • (lit.): to pull oneself out of it at good accounting.

example: Il a démoli la bagnole, mais lui **s'en est tiré à bon compte**.

translation: He totaled the car, but he **got out unscathed**.

as spoken: Il a démoli la bagnole, mais lui, y **s'en est tiré à bon compte**.

SYNONYM: **quitte à bon compte (en être)** *exp.* • (lit.): to be even at good accounting.

tirer haut la main (s'en) *exp.* to come through with flying colors • (lit.): to pull oneself out of it with the hand high.

example: L'examen était difficile, mais je **m'en suis tiré haut la main**.

translation: The exam was difficult, but I **came through with flying colors**.

as spoken: L'examen, il était difficile, mais j'**m'en suis tiré haut la main**.

tirer les ficelles *exp.* to run the show • (lit.): to pull the strings (of a theater curtain).

example: C'est moi qui **tire les ficelles** ici! Pas vous!

translation: I'm the one **running the show** here! Not you!

as spoken: [no change]

SYNONYM: **commandes (être aux)** *exp.* to call the shots • (lit.): to be at the commands.

tirer (se) *v.* to leave.

example: Je dois **me tirer** tout de suite. Je suis en retard!

translation: I have **to leave** right away. I'm late!

as spoken: J'dois **m'tirer** tout d'suite. J'suis en r'tard!

SYNONYMS: *barrer (se)* • *débarasser le plancher* • *éclipser (s')* • *mettre les bouts* • *mettre les voiles* • *plier bagages* • *prendre la tangeante* • *tailler (se)* • *virer (se)* • *etc.*

tirer une giclée *exp.* to ejaculate • (lit.): to pull a squirt.

tissu de mensonges *exp.* pack of
lies • (lit.): cloth of lies.

example: Quand je lui ai demandé
pourquoi elle ne m'a pas téléphoné,
elle m'a raconté un **tissu de
mensonges**.

translation: When I asked her why
she didn't telephone me, she
handed me a **pack of lies**.

as spoken: Quand j'ui ai d'mandé
pourquoi è m'a pas téléphoné, è
m'a raconté un **tissu
d'mensonges**.

tomates (avoir ses) *f.pl.* to
menstruate • (lit.): to have one's
tomatoes.

tombé(e) sur le crâne (être)
exp. to be crazy • (lit.): to have fallen
on one's skull.

tomber dans les pommes *exp.*
to faint, to pass out • (lit.): to fall in
the apples.

example: Quand Nancy a vu le
spectre, elle est **tombée dans les
pommes**!

translation: When Nancy saw the
ghost, she **passed out**!

as spoken: Quand Nancy, elle a vu
l'spectre, elle est **tombée dans les
pommes**!

tomber des cordes *exp.* to rain
heavily • (lit.): to fall cords (of rain).

example: Je comptais faire des
courses aujourd'hui mais il **tombe
des cordes** dehors.

translation: I was planning on going
shopping today but it's **pouring**
outside.

as spoken: J'comptais faire des
courses aujourd'hui mais y **tombe
des cordes** dehors.

**tomber sur le nez de
quelqu'un** *exp.* to come
suddenly to someone (said of good /
bad news) • (lit.): to fall on the nose
of someone.

example: Quand les nouvelles de sa
banqueroute **me sont tombées
sur le nez**, j'en étais stupéfait!

translation: When the news of his
bankruptcy **came to me**, I was
shocked!

as spoken: [no change]

tombeur *m.* a womanizer, seducer,
"Don Juan" • (lit.): a faller (i.e. girls
fall before him or under his charm).

example: Eric va se marier?! Mais
c'est un sacré **tombeur**, celui-là! Il
ne sera jamais content avec une
seule fille dans sa vie.

translation: Eric is getting married?!
But the guy's a real **womanizer**!
He'll never be happy with just one
girl in his life.

as spoken: Eric, y va s'marier?!
Mais c't'un sacré **tombeur**, çui-là!
Y s'ra jamais content avec une seule
fille dans sa vie.

SYNONYM: dragueur *m.*
NOTE: draguer *v.* to cruise (for
guys or girls), to flirt.

tonton *m.* uncle.

example: Le frère de mon père est
mon **tonton**.

translation: My father's brother is
my **uncle**.

as spoken: Le frère d'mon père, c'est mon **tonton**.

toquade pour quelqu'un (avoir une) *exp.* to have a strong crush on someone.

toqué(e) de quelqu'un (être) *exp.* a variation of *toquade pour quelqu'un (avoir une)* meaning "to have a crush on someone."

toqué(e) (être) *adj.* to be crazy, cracked.

ALSO: **toqué(e) de quelqu'un (être)** *exp.* to have a crush on someone.

torche-cul *m.* toilet paper, "ass-wipe" • (lit.): wipe-ass.

example: La dernière fois que je suis allé faire du camping, j'avais complètement oublié d'apporter le **torche-cul**.

translation: The last time I went camping, I totally forgot to bring **toilet paper**.

as spoken: La dernière fois qu'j'suis allé faire du camping, j'avais complètement oublié d'apporter l'**torche-cul**.

SYNONYM: **pécul** *m.* an abbreviation of *papier-cul* meaning "toilet paper" or literally, "ass paper."

torchée *f.* a quarrel • (lit.): a wiping.

ALSO: **flanquer une torchée (se faire)** *exp.* to get beaten up.

torcher (se) *v.* to quarrel • (lit.): to wipe each other (out).

ALSO: **torcher le cul à quelqu'un** *exp.* to beat someone

up • (lit.): to wipe someone's ass • *Je vais te torcher le cul!;* I gonna pulverize you!

NOTE: **torchée** *f.* a large fight or quarrel.

torchon et serviette (être comme) *exp.* said of two people who are completely opposite in personality • (lit.): to be like rag and napkin.

example: Guillaume et Charlotte se sont mariés? Mais pourtant ils sont **comme torchon et serviette**!

translation: Guillaume and Charlotte got married? But they're **about as opposite as two people could be**!

as spoken: Guillaume et Charlotte, y s'sont mariés? Mais pourtant y sont **comme torchon et serviette**!

tord-boyaux *m.* very strong alcohol, "rot-gut" • (lit.): gut-twister.

example: Mais comment tu arrives à descendre ce **tord-boyaux**?!

translation: How can you down that **rot-gut**?!

as spoken: Mais comment t'arrives à descend' ce **tord-boyaux**?!

tordu(e) (être) *adj.* to be crazy, cracked, bizarre • (lit.): to be twisted.

torpiller *v.* to fornicate • (lit.): to torpedo (someone).

touche à quelqu'un (faire une) *exp.* to seduce someone, to make a good impression on someone • (lit.): to make a touch (to someone).

175

toucher (se) *v.* (of men) to masturbate • (lit.): to touch oneself.

NOTE: This applies to both male and female and is often used as a polite way to report that a child has started masturbating.

toucher un gros héritage *exp.* to get a large inheritance • (lit.): to touch a big inheritance.

example: Comme j'ai **touché un gros héritage**, je pourrai passer tout mon temps à voyager.

translation: Since I **got a big inheritance**, I'll be able to spend all my time traveling.

as spoken: Comme j'ai **touché un gros héritage**, j'pourrai passer tout mon temps à voyager.

toujours est-il que *exp.* the fact remains that • (lit.): always is it that.

example: Je sais que c'est ton frère, mais **toujours est-il qu'**il m'énerve!

translation: I know he's your brother, but **the fact remains that** he's bothering me!

as spoken: Je sais qu'c'est ton frère, mais **toujours est-il qu'**y m'énerve!

toupie (vieille) *f.* an old person, an "old fart" • (lit.): old (spinning) top.

tour du cadran (faire le) *exp.* to sleep the day away • (lit.): to do the tour of the clock's face.

example: Quand je suis malade, je reste au lit et je **fais le tour du cadran**.

translation: When I'm sick, I sleep around the clock.

as spoken: Quand j'suis malade, je reste au lit et j'**fais l'tour du cadran**.

tournée *f.* round (of drinks) • (lit.): a tour.

example: Je paie la première **tournée**, moi si tu paies la seconde. D'accord?

translation: I'll pay for the first **round** if you pay for the second. Okay?

as spoken: J'paie la première **tournée**, moi si tu paies la z'gonde. D'acc?

NOTE: **paier / offrir une tournée** is a popular expression meaning "to treat to a round of drinks."

tourner en rond *exp.* • **1.** to have nothing to do • **2.** to go around in circles.

example (1): Depuis que Marc a quitté son travail, il **tourne en rond**.

translation: Ever since Marc quit his job, he **has nothing to do**.

as spoken: Depuis qu'Marc, il a quitté son travail, y **tourne en rond**.

example (2): Je ne comprends pas ce problème de mathématiques. Je **tourne en rond**.

translation: I don't understand this math problem. I'm **going around in circles** (trying to figure it out).

as spoken: J'comprends pas c'problème de maths. J'**tourne en rond**.

NOTE: **maths** *m.pl.* a popular abbreviation for *"mathématiques"* meaning "mathematics."

tout début (au) *exp.* at the very beginning • (lit.): at the complete beginning.

example: **Au tout début** de l'année scolaire, le professeur était sympatique, mais maintenant il est carrément ennuyant.

translation: **At the very beginning** of the school year, the teach was very nice, but now he's downright annoying.

as spoken: **Au tout début** d'l'année scolaire, le prof, il était sympa, mais maintenant il est carrément ennuyant.

toute une salade (en faire) *exp.* to make a big deal about something • (lit.): to make a big sald over something.

example: Je n'ai pas mis ma chambre en ordre et ma mère **en a fait toute une salade**!

translation: I didn't clean up my bedroom and my mother **made a big stink about it**!

as spoken: J'ai pas mis ma chambre en ordre et ma mère, elle **en a fait toute une salade**!

tout feu tout flame (être) *exp.* to be enthusiastic, gung-ho • (lit.): to be all fire all flame.

example: Quand Antoine a commencé à lui faire la cour, il était **tout feu tout flame**. Mais maintenant qu'ils sont mariés, il ne fait que lire son journal.

translation: When Antoine started courting her, he was **all gung-ho**. But now that they're married, he just reads his paper.

as spoken: Quand Antoine il a commencé à lui faire la cour, il était **tout feu tout flame**. Mais maintenant qu'y sont mariés, y fait qu'lire son journal.

tout propos (à) *exp.* at every turn, opportunity • (lit.): at every subject.

example: Etienne est extrêmement ennuyant! Il m'interrompt **à tout propos**!

translation: Steve is extremely annoying. He interrupts me **at every turn**!

as spoken: Etienne, il est extrêmement ennuyant! Y m'interrompt **à tout propos**!

tracassin *m.* penis • (lit.): worrier (since the penis has a tendency to get wet when excited, like a person's forehead when worried).

train *m.* posterior • (lit.): train.
ALSO: **arrière-train** *m.* • (lit.): caboose.

traînée *f.* slut prostitute • (lit.): one who loiters (on the sidewalk, etc.).
NOTE: This comes from the verb *traîner* meaning "to dawdle, to loiter."

traîner quelqu'un dans la merde *exp.* • **1.** to drag someone through a lot of shit • **2.** to slander someone's reputation.

example (1): Mon patron m'a **traîné dans la merde** pendant deux ans. J'en ai assez!

translation: My boss **dragged me through a lot of shit** for two years. I've had it!

as spoken: Mon patron, y m'a **traîné dans la merde** pendant deux ans. J'en ai assez!

example (2): Nous avons parlé à Cécile des problèmes de caisse, sur quoi elle s'est mise en colère et nous a accusés de la **traîner dans la merde**! Tu te rends comptes?

translation: We spoke to Cecily about the cash register problems, at which point she got mad and accused us of **slandering her**! Can you believe it?

as spoken: On a parlé à Cécile des problèmes de caisse, sur quoi è s'est mise en colère et nous a accusés d'la **traîner dans la merde**! Tu te rends comptes?

tranche (en avoir une) *exp.*
(applies to either a man or a woman) to be crazy, nuts • (lit.): to have a slice of it (craziness).

tranche-lard *m.* (humorous) surgeon • (lit.): fat-slicer.

example: Ma mère est **tranche-lard**.

translation: My mother's a **surgeon**.

as spoken: Ma mère, c't'un **tranche-lard**.

NOTE: Although it may look somewhat strange to see the masculine article "un" used in reference to "Ma mère," this is indeed correct since *tranche-lard* is an invariable noun being built on a verb.

tranche (s'en payer une) *exp.*
to have a great time • (lit.): to treat oneself to a slice (of fun).

example: Nous **nous en sommes payés une tranche** à la fête du village.

translation: We **had a blast** at the village festival.

as spoken: On **s'en est payé une tranche** à la fête du village.

NOTE: payer (se) *v.* to treat oneself • (lit.): to pay oneself (something).

example: Je **me suis payé** une glace.

translation: I **treated myself to** an ice cream.

as spoken: Je **m'suis payé** une glace.

travailler de la casquette *exp.*
(applies to either a man or a woman) to be crazy • (lit.): to ferment from the cap.

NOTE -1: In this expression, the verb *travailler* (literally meaning "to work") is used to mean "to ferment" as in wine.

NOTE -2: casquette *f.* head • (lit.): cap • *Quand je bois trop, j'ai mal à la casquette*; When I drink too much, I get a headache.

travailler du chapeau *exp.*
(applies to either a man or a woman) to be crazy • (lit.): to work from the hat.

NOTE -1: In this expression, the verb *travailler* is used to mean "to ferment" as in wine.

travailler du chou *exp.* (applies to either a man or a woman) to be crazy • (lit.): to work from the cabbage.
> **NOTE -1:** In this expression, the verb *travailler* is used to mean "to ferment" as in wine.
> **NOTE -2:** **chou** *m.* head • (lit.): cabbage.

travailleuse *f.* prostitute
• (lit.): working girl.

tremper (la) *exp.* to fornicate
• (lit.): to dip it in.
> example: Tu as entendu les nouvelles? Albert **la trempe** avec une nana deux fois plus âgée que lui.
> translation: Did you hear the news? Albert **is having sex** with a woman twice as old as he is.
> as spoken: T'as entendu les nouvelles? Albert, y **la trempe** avec une nana deux fois plus âgée qu'lui.
> **NOTE:** In this expression, *la* represents *la pine* meaning "penis."

tremper son baigneur *exp.* to fornicate • (lit.): to dip one's bather.
> **NOTE:** **baigneur** *m.* penis, dick • (lit.): bather.

tremper son biscuit *exp.* to fornicate • (lit.): to dip one's biscuit.

triple buse *f.* (applies to either a man or a woman) an extremely stupid person • (lit.): triple idiot.
> **NOTE:** **buse** *m.* buzzard.

triste à chier (être) *exp.* to be extremely sad and tragic.
> example: La mère de Robert est sénile. C'est **triste à chier**.
> translation: Robert's mother is senile. It's **so sad**.
> as spoken: La mère de Robert, elle est sénile. C'est **triste à chier**.

troisième jambe *f.* penis • (lit.): third leg.

tronche *f.* head; face • (lit.): log.
> example: Avec une telle **tronche**, elle ne pourras jamais devenir actrice!
> translation: With such a **face**, she'll never be able to be an actress!
> as spoken: Avec une telle **tronche**, è pourras jamais dev'nir actrice!
> **SYNONYM -1:** **poire** *f.* • (lit.): pear.
> **SYNONYM -2:** **pêche** *f.* • (lit.): peach.

troncher *v.* • **1.** to sodomize • **2.** to fornicate.
> **NOTE:** This comes from the feminine noun *tronche* meaning "log."

trottoir (faire le) *exp.* (very popular) to hustle (said of a prostitute) • (lit.): to do the sidewalk.

trou *m.* • **1.** place in general, "joint" • **2.** (very vulgar) vagina • (lit.): hole.
> example: Je refuse d'entrer dans ce **trou**. C'est plein de fumeurs!
> translation: I refuse to go into that **joint**. It's full of smokers!
> as spoken: Je r'fuse d'entrer dans c'**trou**. C'est plein d'fumeurs!

trou de balle *m.* anus
- (lit.): gunshot hole.

trouduc *m.* an abbreviation of *trou du cul* meaning "asshole."

trou du cul *m.* asshole • (lit.): hole of the ass.

troufignard *m.* a variation of *trou du cul* meaning "asshole."

troufignon *m.* a variation of *trou du cul* meaning "asshole."

troufion *m.* anus • (lit.): asshole (since *fion* means "anus" in French slang).

trouillard(e) *n.* (*very popular*) scardey-cat.

> **NOTE:** **trouille (avoir la)** *exp.* to have intense fear.

trouille (avoir la) *exp.* to be scared to death.

*J'ai eu **la trouille** pendant tout le film!*

(*trans.*):
*I was **scared to death** during the entire movie!*

example: J'ai eu **la trouille** pendant le tremblement de terre!

translation: I was **scared to death** during the earthquake!

as spoken: J'ai eu **la trouille** pendant l'tremblement de terre!

> **SYNONYM:** **les jetons (avoir les)** *exp.* to be scared, to have the jitters • (lit.): to have tokens.

trucs (avoir ses) *m.pl.* to menstruate • (lit.): to have one's things.

truie *f.* old bitch • (lit.): sow.

tuer les mouches à quinze pas *exp.* said of someone who has bad breath • (lit.): to kill flies fifteen feet away.

example: Oh, ce chien! Il **tue les mouches à quinze pas**, lui!

translation: Oh, this dog! He has **horrible breath**!

as spoken: Oh, c'chien! Y **tue les mouches à quinze pas**, lui!

"Tu parles" *exp.* **1.** "You said it!"
- **2.** "You've gotta be kidding!"

example (1): "Léon est bizarre, lui!" **"Tu parles!"**

translation: "Léon is really strange!" **"You said it!"**

as spoken: "Léon, il est bizarre, lui!" **"Tu parles!"**

example (2): "Julie est ta meilleure amie, n'est-ce pas?" **"Tu parles!** Je ne peux pas la supporter!"

translation: "Julie's your best friend, right?"
"**You've gotta be kidding**! I can't stand her!"

as spoken: "Julie, c'est ta meilleure amie, n'est-c'pas?"
"**Tu parles**! J'peux pas la supporter!"

VARIATION: "**Tu parles, Charles!**"

turbine à chocolat *f.* anus • (lit.): chocolate turbine.

turbiner *v.* (said of a prostitute) to hustle.
SEE: **turbin (faire le)**, *(previous entry)*.

turbin (faire le) *exp.* (said of a prostitute) to hustle • (lit.): to do hard work
NOTE: **turbin** *m.* work, grind.

turf (aller au) *exp.* (said of a prostitute) to hustle • (lit.): to go to the turf.
SEE: **turf (faire le)**, *(next entry)*.

turfer *v.* (said of a prostitute) to hustle.
SEE: **turf (faire le)**, *(previous entry)*.

turf (faire le) *exp.* (said of a prostitute) to hustle • (lit.): to do the turf.

"Tu rigoles" *exp.* "You're kidding!"
example: "Ce matin j'ai trouvé un diamant sur le trottoir!"
"**Tu rigoles!**"

translation: "This morning I found a diamond on the sidewalk!"
"**You're kidding**!"

as spoken: "C'matin j'ai trouvé un diam su'l'trottoir!"
"**Tu rigoles**!"

turne *f.* room.
NOTE: **co-turne** *n.* roommate.

tuyau à gaz *m.* anus • (lit.): gas pipe.

type *m.* guy, "dude" • (lit.): type.
example: Il est beau, ce **type**-là!
translation: That **guy**'s handsome!
as spoken: Il est beau, c'**type**-là!
SYNONYM: **mec** *m.*
NOTE: In the feminine form, *typesse*, this term becomes derogatory for "girl" or "chick."

typesse *f.* woman or girl.
NOTE: **type** *m.* guy, "dude."

un de ces quatre *exp.* one of these days • (lit.): one of these four.
example: **Un de ces quatre**, je vais m'installer à Tahiti.
translation: **One of these days**, I'm going to move to Tahiti.
as spoken: **Un d'ces quat'**, j'vais m'installer à Tahiti.

NOTE: This is a shortened version of the expression *"un de ces quatre matins"* (pronounced: *un d'ces quat' matins)* meaning "one of these four mornings."

usiner *v.* (said of a prostitute) to hustle • (lit.): to work hard (as one would in a *usine* or "factory").

vache • **1.** *adj.* (extremely popular) mean, nasty • **2.** *f.* a disparaging remark applied primarily to a woman but may be used in reference to a man • (lit.): cow.

example (1): Daniel était de mauvaise humeur aujourd'hui. Il a été **vache** envers moi pour aucune raison!

translation: Daniel was in a bad mood today. He was **nasty** to me for no reason!

as spoken: Daniel, il était d'mauvaise humeur aujourd'hui. Il a été **vache** envers moi pour aucune raison!

example (2): Quelle **vache**, ce professeur! Il nous a donné un tas de devoirs à faire pendant nos vacances!

translation: This teacher's a real **prick**! He gave us a pile of homework to do during our vacation!

as spoken: Quelle **vache**, ce prof! Y nous a donné un tas de d'voirs à faire pendant nos vacances!

NOTE: **Oh, la vache!** *exclam.* Wow!

example: **Oh, la vache!** Tu as vu les prix dans ce restaurant? Ils sont astronomiques!

translation: **Wow!** Did you see the prices at this restaurant? They're sky-high!

as spoken: **Oh, la vache!** T'as vu les prix dans c'resto? Y sont astronomiques!

vacherie à quelqu'un (faire une) *exp.* to do a dirty trick on someone.

example: Je ne parle plus à Joseph. La semaine dernière, il m'a fait une **vacherie**.

translation: I don't speak to Joseph any more. Last week, he played a real **dirty trick** on me.

as spoken: J'parle pu à Joseph. La s'maine dernière, y m'a fait une **vach'rie**.

SYNONYM -1: **cochonnerie à quelqu'un (faire une)** *exp.*

SYNONYM -2: **saloperie à quelqu'un (faire une)** *exp.*

valoir le coup *exp.* to be worth it • (lit.): to be worth the exploit.

example: Ça **ne vaut pas le coup** d'aller à Paris pour juste deux jours!

translation: Its **not worth it** to go to Paris for just two days!

as spoken: Ça **vaut pas l'coup** d'aller à Paris pour juste deux jours!

valoir un pet de lapin (ne pas) *exp.* not to be worth a red cent • (lit.): not to be worth a rabbit's fart.

example: Tu as vu le collier que Nicole a porté à la soirée? Elle se vantait que son mari l'a payé une fortune mais ça sautait aux yeux que ça **ne valait pas un pet de lapin**!

translation: Did you the see that necklace Nicole wore to the party? She was bragging that her husband paid a fortune for it but it was obvious that it wasn't **worth shit**!

as spoken: T'as vu l'collier qu'Nicole, elle a porté à la soirée? È s'vantait qu'son mari, y l'a payé une fortune mais ça sautait aux yeux qu'ça **valait pas un pet d'lapin**!

NOTE: *sauter aux yeux exp.* to be obvious • (lit.): to jump to the eyes.

valseuses *f.pl.* testicles • (lit.): waltzers.

va te faire foutre *exp.* fuck off.

example: Laisse-moi tranquille! **Va te faire foutre**!

translation: Leave me alone! **Fuck off**!

as spoken: Laisse-moi tranquille! **Va t'faire foutre**!

veau *m.* a big, slow car • (lit.): veal.

vécé *m.* (extremely popular) bathroom, restroom.

NOTE: This is a doubly shortened version of the masculine noun *water-closet* meaning "bathroom."

Water-closet is commonly shortened to *W.C.* and further shortened to *V.C.* (pronounced: *vécé*).

veine (avoir de la) *exp.* to be lucky.

example: Tu as gagné au loto? Mais tu as de la **veine**, toi!

translation: You won the lottery? Do you ever have **luck**!

as spoken: T'as gagné au loto? Mais t'as d'la **veine**, toi!

ANTONYM: **déveine (avoir la)** *exp.* to be unlucky.

NOTE: Note that in the expression *"avoir la déveine"* that the article *"de"* is dropped, whereas *"avoir de la veine"* keeps the article *"de."*

vélodrome à mouches (avoir un) *exp.* to be bald • (lit.): to have a velodrome (which is very smooth-looking) for flies.

venir aux mains (en) *exp.* to come to blows • (lit.): to come to hands.

example: Albert et Antoine disputent de nouveau. J'espère qu'ils **n'en viennent pas aux mains** comme la dernière fois!

translation: Albert and Anthony are disputing again. I hope they **don't come to blows** like last time!

as spoken: Albert et Antoine, y disputent de nouveau. J'espère qu'ils **en viennent pas aux mains** comme la dernière fois!

verge *f.* (medical term) penis • (lit.): rod, wand, cane.

verger *v.* to fornicate • (lit.): to "dick" (someone).

NOTE: This comes from the feminine noun *verge*, which literally means "rod, wand, cane," but has taken the slang connotation of "penis, dick."

vérole *f.* gonorrhea • (lit.): the old-fashioned word for "pox."

vesse *f.* silent fart, S.B.D. (silent but deadly).

vesser *v.* to fart silently.

vestige (vieux) *m.* an old person, an "old fart" • (lit.): old ruin.

veuve Poignet *m.* masturbation, handjob • (lit.): Widow Wrist.

vider les burettes (se) *exp.* to masturbate • (lit.): to empty one's testicles.

NOTE: **burettes** *f.pl.* testicles, balls • (lit.): oilcans.

vie en rose (la) *exp.* said of a wonderful life, life through rose-colored glasses • life like a rose.

example: J'ai été pauvre toute ma vie. Mais après avoir gagné au lotto, c'est **la vie en rose**.

translation: I've been poor all my life. But after having won in the lottery, **life is wonderful**.

as spoken: J'ai été pauv' toute ma vie. Mais après avoir gagné au lotto, c'est **la vie en rose**.

vieille *f.* (disrespectful) mother • (lit.): old lady.

example: C'est aujourd'hui l'anniversaire de ma **vieille**.

translation: Today's my **mother**'s birthday.

as spoken: C'est aujourd'hui l'anniversaire d'ma **vieille**.

SYNONYM: **vioque / vioc** *f.*

vieille branche *exp.* old pal, chum, buddy • (lit.): old branch.

example: Salut ma **vieille branche**! Comment vas-tu?

translation: Hi my **old chum**! How are you?

as spoken: Salut ma **vieille branche**! Comment tu vas?

vieille peau *f.* bitch, old hag • (lit.): old skin.

vieux • **1.** *m.* (disrespectful) father • **2.** *m.pl.* (disrespectful) parents, old folks • (lit.): **1.** old man • **2.** old people.

example (1): C'est ça ton **vieux**?

translation: Is that your **father**?

as spoken: [no change]

SYNONYM: **vioque / vioc** *m.*

example (2): Mes **vieux** sont partis pour le Méxique pour un mois.

translation: My **old folks** left for Mexico for a month.

as spoken: Mes **vieux**, y sont partis pour l'Méxique pour un mois.

SYNONYM -1: **vioques / viocs** *m.pl.*

SYNONYM -2: **dabs** *m.pl.*

vieux bonze *m.* old man, an "old fart" • (lit.): old buddhist monk.

example: Carole est très jeune et très jolie. Je ne sais pas pourquoi elle sort avec un **vieux bonze** comme celui-là.

translation: Carole is very young and very pretty. I don't know why she goes out with an **old fart** like him.

as spoken: Carole, elle est très jeune et très jolie. C'hais pas pourquoi è sort avec un **vieux bonze** comme ç'ui-là.

vieux (mon) *m.* • **1.** my pal, my ol' buddy • **2.** mon father, my old man • (lit.): my old (person).

example (1): Salut, **mon vieux**! Ça va?

translation: Hi, **pal**! How's everything going?

as spoken: [no change]

example (2): Je vais demander à **mon vieux** s'il peut me prêter sa bagnole.

translation: I'll ask **my old man** if he'll lend me his car.

as spoken: J'vais d'mander à **mon vieux** s'y peut m'prêter sa bagnole.
NOTE: **bagnole** *f.* (extremely popular) car.

vioc *m.* (also spelled: *vioque*) an old person, an "old fart" (also spelled: *vioque*).
NOTE: **vioquer** *v.* to get old.

visiter la veuve et les cinq orphelines *exp.* (of men) to masturbate • (lit.): to visit the widow and five orphans.

vite dans le casque (en avoir) *exp.* to go quickly to one's head (said of alcohol) • (lit.): to have it quickly in the helmet.

example: Quand je bois du vin, j'**en ai vite dans le casque**.

translation: When I drink wine, it **goes right to my head**.

as spoken: Quand j'bois du vin, j'**en ai vite dans l'casque**.
NOTE: **casque** *f.* head • (lit.): helmet.

v'là *interj.* a commonly heard reduction of "*voilà.*"

example: **V'là** le patron! Cours!

translation: **There's** the boss! Run!

as spoken: **V'là** l'patron! Cours!

voilà qui s'appelle... *exp.* that's what I call... • (lit.): that's what's called...

example: **Voilà qui s'appelle** bizarre!

translation: **That's what I call** strange!

as spoken: [no change]

voir la feuille à l'envers *exp.* to have sex under a tree • (lit.): to see the leaf (or leaves) from underneath.

voir les anges *exp.* to reach orgasm • (lit.): to see angels.

voir quelqu'un en peinture (ne pas pouvoir) *exp.* to be unable to stand someone • (lit.): to be unable to see someone in a painting (since ever the mere sight of the person would be too much to bear).

volière *f.* brothel • (lit.): henhouse (since *poule*, literally meaning "hen," is used in French slang to mean "prostitute").

vouloir à (en) *exp.* to have a grudge against • (lit.): to want someone from it.

example: Je **lui en veux** parce qu'il me ment sans arrêt.

translation: I **have a grudge against him** because he lies to me nonstop.

as spoken: J'**ui en veux** pasqu'y m'ment sans arrêt.

voyons *exp.* for crying out load • (lit.): let's see.

example: "Ça, c'est ton mari?" "Mais, non **voyons**! C'est mon fils!"

translation: "That's your husband, isn't it?" "Of course not, **for crying out loud**! That's my son!"

as spoken: [no change]

yeux en face des trous (ne pas avoir les) *exp.* to be unaware, out of it • (lit.): not to have eyes in front of their holes (or sockets).

example: Tu n'as pas vu Georges à la soirée? Mais il était droite devant toi pendant une demi-heure! Tu **n'avais pas les yeux en face des trous** hier soir!

translation: You didn't see George at the party? He was right in front of you for a half hour! You were **really out of it** last night!

as spoken: T'as pas vu Georges à la soirée? Mais il était droite devant toi pendant une demi-heure! T'**avais pas les yeux en face des trous** hier soir!

zeb *m.* penis.

zèbre *m.* guy, "dude."

ALSO: **drôle de zèbre** *m.* weirdo.

zieuter *v.* to look • (lit.): to eye.

*Mais **zieute** un peu ses cheveux!*

(trans.):
Get a load of her hair!

(lit.):
Eye a little her hair!

example: Tu as **zieuté** l'arc-en-ciel? C'était incroyable!

translation: Did you **get a load of the** rainbow? It was unbelievable!

as spoken: T'as **zieuté** l'arc-en-ciel? C'était incroyable!

NOTE -1: The verb **zieuter** comes from *"les yeux (z'yeux)"* meaning "the eyes."

NOTE -2: Also spelled: *zyeuter*.

zig *m.* (also spelled: *zigue*) guy, "dude."

zigomar(d) *m.* guy, man, "dude."
NOTE: This is a slang variation of: zig.

zigoteau *m.* guy, man, "dude."
NOTE: This is a slang variation of: zig.

zigoto *m.* man, guy, "dude."
NOTE: This is a slang variation of: zig.

zinc *m.* airplane • (lit.): zinc.

example: Ce vol est trop long! J'en ai marre d'être collé dans ce **zinc**!

translation: This flight is too long! I'm tired of being stuck in this **airplane**!

as spoken: Il est trop long, c'vol! J'en ai marre d'êt' collé dans ce **zinc**!

zinzin (être) *adj.* (applies to either a man or a woman) to be nuts.

zizi *m.* (child language) penis.

zob *m.* (extremely popular) penis.

zobi *m.* penis.

zouave *m.* guy, man, "dude" • (lit.): a type of soldier (known for being very tough) in the Napoleonic army.

Zut alors! *interj.* Darn!

example: **Zut alors**! J'ai laissé mes clés au restaurant!

translation: **Darn**! I left my keys at the restaurant!

as spoken: **Zut alors**! J'ai laissé mes clés au resto!

NOTE: *Zut* may also be used all by itself. However, *alors* is commonly used for extra emphasis.

POPULAR FRENCH GESTURES

GESTURES

Part 2

A CLOSER LOOK:
Surely You Gesture!

Most people think of the Italians as cornering the market on gestures and all the dramatics that go along with them. The French certainly hold their own in expression themselves nonverbally and seem to include a great deal of slang in many of their gestures:

A. "That person's drunk!"

As learned in lesson four, the adjective *rond(e)*, whose meaning is literally "round," is commonly used in slang to mean "drunk." As well known as this slang adjective is the gesture which conveys this condition:

- Make a fist.

- Hold it up against the tip of your nose with your little finger farthest away from you.

- Now twist your fist as if you were tightening the tip of your nose.

B. "That's crazy!"

The expression *ça ne tourne pas rond* is also used to refer to one's brain in which the "wheels" aren't turning. The gesture for this is similar to the American gesture of "crazy" in which the index finger is held a few inches away from the ear then circles the outline of the ear several times. In French, it's a little more subtle:

- Holding your index finger straight, place the very tip of your finger against your temple.

- Make sure the pad of your finger is facing slightly forward.

- Now twist the pad of your finger down and slightly back.

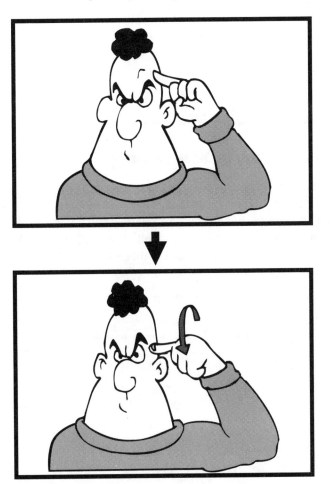

C. "My eye!"

In English, when someone tries to pull the wool over our eyes by recounting something ludicrous, we may respond with the expression "My foot!" However, the French decided to go in the opposite direction...up to the "eye." *Mon œil* is extremely popular in France as is its gesture:

- Put your index finger just underneath your lower eyelid.

- Now pull down slightly.

D. "What are you talking about?!"

This gesture may be used in place of the gesture for *Mon œil*; however, it is much more subtle. The gesture for *Mon œil* is used to let the other person know that what he/she has just said is absolutely and undeniably hogwash, whereas the gesture for "What are you talking about?" lets him know that if he doesn't clear up what he's talking about, he will be on the verge of getting a *Mon œil!*:

- Simply cock your head to the left or right with an expression of "Oh, brother!" on your face.

E. "Beats me!"

A gesture which is constantly encountered in France, especially when asking for directions, is the one for "I dunno" or "Beats me!" It's a lovely little number that can be accessorized beautifully:

The basic gesture

- Protrude your lower lip slightly past your upper lip to form a tight pout.
- Make sure to hold the lips tightly together as you force out a quick "*ppp*" sound.

Add one or all of the following as you do the "ppp" sound:
- Lift your eye brows.
- Push your head slightly forward.
- Lift your shoulders.

Now...go for broke!

Doing all of the above at the same time is *extremely* common, which will probably be proven by the first person who can't give you directions once in Paris. However, occasionally you will encounter the *pièce de résistance* in which all of the above ingredients will be mixed together along with one another:

- Hold the palms of your hands facing upward and level to the outside of your shoulders.
- Now, as you make the "*ppp*" sound, lift your eyebrows, push your head slightly forward, and lift your shoulders and simply push the palms of your hands upward slightly.

F. "Nothing!"

The next one is a common insulting gesture in Italy. However, in French this gesture simply means "Absolutely nothing!" For example, if someone asks you what you got for your birthday and your reply is "Zip! Zero! Not a thing!" this gesture would come in quite handy:

- Make a fist holding your thumb on the side of your index finger.

- Place the nail of your thumb behind your front teeth.

- Now quickly force the thumb forward making a clicking sound.

G. **Count with your fingers like the French**

"Holding up two fingers to indicate that I want two of a certain item couldn't be easier. Then why do I keep getting *three*?" Simply…your thumb is being counted as well! In France and almost all of Europe, the thumb starts off the countdown and the little finger ends it:

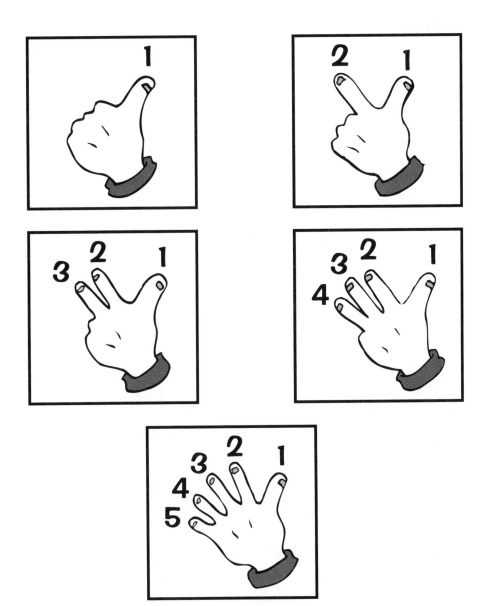

ENGLISH WORDS USED IN FRENCH

Part 3

Often as you speak French, you may find yourself having to stop midstream because you've suddenly run into a word that you don't know how to say. It is quite possible that the English word is the same in French (yet still pronounced with a French accent).

The following words should be pronounced the same as you would if they *were* French words. The noted exceptions are in quotes and should also be articulated following the rules of French pronunciation.

baby-sitting *m.* (pronounced: *bébi-sitting*).

bacon *m.* (pronounced: *béconne*).

bank-note *f.*

bar *m.*

barmaid *f.* (pronounced: *bar-maide*).

barman *m.* (pronounced: *bar-mane*).

base-ball *m.* (pronounced: *bèz-bol*).

basket-ball *m.* (pronounced: *baskette-bol*).

> **NOTE:** This may also be shortened to: *basket*.

bestseller *m.* (pronounced: *best-selleur*).

betting *m.*

bikini *m.*

black-out *m.* (pronounced: *blak-aoute*).

blazer *m.* (pronounced: *blazère*).

blue-jean *blou-djine.* (pronounced: *blues*).

blues *m.* (pronounced: *blouze*).

bluff *m.* (pronounced: *blœ*).

> **NOTE:** **bluffer** *v.* to bluff.

bookmaker *m.* bookie • (pronounced: *boukmékeur*).

boss *m.*

bowling *m.* (pronounced: *boling*).

box-window *m.*

brain-trust *m.* (pronounced: *brène-trœst*).

breakfast *m.* (pronounced: *brèkfast*).

building *m.* (pronounced: *bilding*).

bulldozer *m.* (pronounced: *bul-dozeur*).

cake *m.* (pronounced: *kèk*).

call-girl *f.* (pronounced: *kal-gœrl*).

caméraman *m.* (pronounced: *caméra-mane*).

camping *m.*

campus *m.* (pronounced: *cam-pusse*).

caravane *f.*

cash *m.* (used in the phrase: *payer cash* meaning "to pay cash").

chewing-gum *m.* (pronounced: *shwing-gome*).

chips *m.* (pronounced: *shipse*).

clergyman *m.* (pronounced: *clergy-mane*).

clown *m.* (pronounced: *cloune*).

cocker *m.* (pronounced: *cockère*).

cocktail *m.* (pronounced: *cock-tèl*).

cold-cream *m.* (pronounced: *kold-krime*).

cool *adj.*

copyright *m.* (pronounced: *kopi-raït*).

corned-beef *m.* (pronounced: *korn-bif*).

cover-girl *f.* (pronounced: *koveur-gœrl*).

cow-boy *m.* (pronounced: *kau-boï*).

crash *m.*

crawl *m.* (swimming) • (pronounced: *kraule*).

curry *m.*

dog *m.*

drugstore *m.* (pronounced: *drœg-store*).

dry *adj.* (pronounced: *draï*) • *champagne dry*; dry champagne.

fair-play *adj.* (pronounced: *fèrplè*) to play fair • *Il n'est pas fair-play*; He doesn't play fair.

far-west *m.*

ferry-boat *m.* (pronounced: *fèri-bot*).

flash *m.*

football *m.* (pronounced: *foot-baule*) soccer.

> **NOTE:** This may also be shortened to: *foot.*

footing *m.* jogging

freezer *m.* (pronounced: *frizeur*).

gadget *m.* (pronounced: *gadjette*).

gag *m.*

gang *m.* (pronounced: *gangue*).

gangster *m.* (pronounced: *gangue-staire*).

gin *m.* (pronounced: *dgine*).

glass *m.* glass or drink.

groggy *adj.* (pronounced: *grogui*).

hand-ball *m.* (pronounced: *ande-bale*).

NOTE: This may also be shortened to: *hand.*

hold-up *m.* (pronounced: *olde-op*).

home *m.* (pronounced: *aume*).

hard rock *m.* (pronounced: *arde-roque*).

NOTE: This may also be shortened to: *hard.*

iceberg *m.* (pronounced: *aïcebœrg* or *isebèrgue*).

interview *m.*

jeep *m.* (pronounced: *djip*).

jersey *m.* (pronounced: *jèrsè*).

jet *m.* (pronounced: *djette*).

job *m.* (pronounced: *djob*).

jockey *m.* (pronounced: *djokè*).

joint *m.* (as in marijuana).

joker *m.* (pronounced: *djokeur*).

kleenex *m.* (pronounced: *klinex*).

leader *m.* (pronounced: *lideur*).

lob *m.* (in tennis).

NOTE -1: **lober** *v.* to lob.

NOTE -2: **balle lobée** *f.* a lobbed ball.

lunch *m.* (pronounced: *lœnch*).

meeting *m.* (pronounced: *miting*).

melting-pot *m.* (pronounced: *melting-pote*).

music-hall *m.* (pronounced: *musique-ol*).

no man's land *m.* (pronounced: *no-mann'z-lande*).

offset *m.* (pronounced: *of-sette*).

okay *interj.* (pronounced: *oké* or *oque*).

parking *m.*

pickles *m.pl.* (pronounced: *picœlz*).

pickpocket *m.* (pronounced: *peek-pokette*).

pin-up *f.* (pronounced: *pinope*).

pipe-line *m.* (pronounced: *pipline*).

playback *m.* (pronounced: *plaibak*).

play-boy *m.* (pronounced: *plaiboï*).

pop-corn *m.*

pudding *m.* (pronounced: *pouding*).

pullover *m.* (pronounced: *pule-au-veur* or *pule-auvair*).

NOTE: This may also be shortened to: *pull*.

punch *m.* (the drink) • (pronounced: *ponch*).

puzzle *m.* (pronounced: *pœzl*).

racket *m.* a dishonest scheme • (pronounced: *raquette*).

remake *m.* (pronounced: *rimèk*).

rock n'roll *m.* (pronounced: *roque-'n-rol*).

NOTE: This may also be shortened to: *roque*.

rocking-chair *m.* (pronounced: *roking-tchair*).

rodeo *m.* (pronounced: *rode-yo*).

round *m.* (in boxing) • (pronounced: *raounde*).

rush *m.* (pronounced: *rœsh*) • *C'est le grand rush vers la plage*; It's the big rush to the beach.

scooter *m.* (pronounced: *sku-teur* or *sku-taire*).

score *m.*

script *m.*

script-girl *f.* (pronounced: *skript-gœrl*).

self-made-man *m.* (pronounced: *self-mèd-mane*).

self-service *m.*

set *m.* (in tennis, ping-pong, volleyball, etc.) • (pronounced: *sète*).

sex-appeal *m.* (pronounced: *sex-apile*).

shaker *m.* (used in making alcoholic drinks) • (pronounced: *shèkeur*).

shampooing *m.* (pronounced: *shampoin*).

shocking *m.* (pronounced: *shoking*).

shoot *m.* (of basketball) • (pronounced: *shoute*).

NOTE: **shooter** *v.* to shoot the ball.

short *m.* shorts • *J'ai acheté un nouveau short pour l'éte;* I bought some new shorts for the summer.

shopping *m.*

show *m.* (pronounced: *shau*).

sitting *m.* a sit-down strike • *faire un sitting;* to execute a sit-down strike.

skate-board *m.* (pronounced: *skaite-borde*).

sketch *m.*

slang *m.* (pronounced: *slangue*).

slow *m.* slow dance • (pronounced: *slau*).

smart *adj.* chick • (pronounced: *smarte*).

NOTE: Interestingly enough, the French use the English word "smart," whereas in the English language, the French word *chic* is used!

smash *m.* (of tennis).

smoking *m.* tuxedo.

snack-bar *m.*

snob *m.*

snow-boot *m.* (pronounced: *snau-boute*).

soda *m.*

sofa *m.*

speaker *m.* a male public speaker (pronounced: *spikeur*).

NOTE: **speakerine** *f.* a female public speaker.

spot *m.* spotlight.

sprint *m.* (pronounced: *sprinnte*) • *Elle a gagné au sprint;* She won the sprint race.

sprinter *m.* (pronounced: *sprine-teur*).

NOTE: **sprinter** *v.* (pronounced: *sprine-té*) to sprint.

standing *m.* status.

star *m.* movie-star.

starter *m.* (pronounced: *startaire*) • **1.** one who gives the signal to start a race • **2.** chock (of car).

starting-block *m.* (sports).

starting-gate *m.* (pronounced: *starting-gète).*

steak *m.* (pronounced: *stèk).*

steward *m.* (pronounced: *stuwar).*

stick *m.* riding whip.

stock *m.*

stone *adj.* "stoned," high on drugs.

stop *m.* stop sign.

stress *m.*

strict *adj.*

strip-tease *m.* (pronounced: *stripe-tiz).*

surf *m.*

suspense *m.* (pronounced: *suspèns).*

sweater *m.* (pronounced: *swèteur).*

sweat-shirt *m.* (pronounced: *swète-shœrt).*

sweepstake *m.* (pronounced: *swip-stèk).*

swing *m.* (in music) • *Cet orchestre a du swing!;* This orchestra really swings!

traveler chèque *m.* (pronounced: *trav'leur chèque).*

> **NOTE:** Interestingly enough, the French *do not* say *chèque de voyageur* as one might think.

trench-coat *m.* (pronounced: *trènch-kaute).*

trust *m.* (as in cartel) • (pronounced: *trœst).*

t-shirt *m.* (pronounced: *ti-shœrt).*

tub *m.* (pronounced: *tœb).*

water-polo *m.* (pronounced: *wataire-polo).*

weekend *m.* (pronounced: *wikènde).*

western *m.*

whisky *m.*

tank *m.*

taxi *m.*

tempo *m.*

toast *m.* (pronounced: *tauste)*
> • **1.** toast (grilled bread) • **2.** a toast (as in "to make a toast").

traffic *m.*

yacht *m.* (pronounced the same as in English).).

yachting *m.* (pronounced: *yating).*

zigzag *m.*

> **NOTE:** **zigzaguer** *v.* to zigzag.

STREET FRENCH THESAURUS

Part 4

(General Slang Synonyms & Expressions)

A LOT

beaucoup

example: Prends encore du gâteau! Il y en a **bésef**!

translation: Take more cake! There's **plenty**!

as spoken: Prends encore du gâteau! Il y en a **bésef**!

---

bésef *adv.*

example: Regarde toutes ces fleurs à cette cérémonie de mariage! Il y en a **bésef**!

translation: Look at all those flowers at this wedding ceremony! There's **so many**!

as spoken: Regarde toutes ces fleurs à cette cérémonie d'mariage! Y en a **bésef**!

VARIATION: bézef *adv.*

flopée *f.* a bunch.

example: Suzanne possède une **flopée** de robes.

translation: Suzanne owns a **bunch** of dresses.

as spoken: Suzanne, elle possède une **flopée** d'robes.

gogo (à) *adv.* a bunch.

example: Tu ne savais pas que Carole a des enfants **à gogo**?

translation: You didn't know that Carole has **a bunch** of children?

as spoken: Tu savais pas que Carole, elle a des enfants **à gogo**?

ribambelle *f.* a bunch.

example: J'ai une **ribambelle** de devoirs à faire ce soir.

translation: I have **a bunch** of homework to do tonight.

as spoken: J'ai une **ribambelle** de d'voirs à faire c'soir.

tire-larigot (à) *adv.* a great amount.

example: Il boit **à tire-larigot**.

translation: He drinks **a great deal**.

as spoken: Y boit **à tire-larigot**.

tripotée *f.* a bunch.

example: Robert a une **tripotée** d'amis à Paris.

translation: Robert has a **bunch** of friends in Paris.

as spoken: Robert, il a **tripotée** d'amis à Paris.

AFRAID (TO BE)

peur (avoir)

example: J'ai eu **les chocottes** pendant le tremblement de terre!

translation: I was **scared to death** during the earthquake!

as spoken: J'ai eu **les chocottes** pendant l'tremblement de terre!

---

chair de poule (avoir la) *exp.*
- (lit.): to have chicken skin or "goose bumps."

chocottes (avoir les) *f.pl.* to have the jitters, shakes.

> **NOTE:** **chocottes** *f.pl.* slang for "teeth" • *avoir les chocottes* might be loosely translated as "to have teeth (that are chattering from fear)."

colique (avoir la) *f.* to have intense fear • (lit.): to have diarrhea and cramps.

dans le ventre (ne rien avoir) *exp.* to have not guts • (lit.): to have nothing in the stomach.

déglonfer (se) *v.* to lose one's courage, to lose one's nerve • (lit.): to deflate.

> **NOTE:** **dégonflard(e)** • **dégonflé(e)** • **dégonfleur, euse** *n.* scaredy cat.

frousse (avoir la) *f.* to have the creeps.

grelots (avoir les) *m.pl.* to have the jitters • (lit.): to have the shakes.

> **NOTE:** **grelotter** *v.* to shake or tremble (from fear, cold, etc.).

grolles (avoir les) *f.pl.* to have the jitters, shakes.

> **NOTE:** **grolle** *f.* shoe • *avoir les grolles* might be loosely translated as "to have shoes that shake (from fear)" or "to shake in one's boots."

jetons (avoir les) *m.pl.* (pronounced: avoir les sh'ton) to have the jitters, shakes.

> **NOTE:** **jeton** *m.* small token that is used for public telephones • *avoir les jetons* might be loosely translated as "to have tokens (that are jingling because the possessor is shaking from fear)."

nerfs en pelote (avoir les) *exp.* said of someone whose nerves are shot • (lit.): to have one's nerves in a ball.

pétoches (avoir les) *m.pl.* to have great feat • (lit.): to have farts (out of intense fear).

> **NOTE:** The masculine noun *pet*, meaning "fart," comes from its infinitive *péter*. It is often the case in French slang that special slang suffixes are added to adjectives and nouns either to create a slang word or to make an already slang word even more colorful. Some of the slang suffixes include: *-asse, -aille, -ouche, -ouille, -ouse, -ace, etc.*

pétouille (avoir la) *f.* slang variant of: *avoir la pétoche*.

trac (avoir le) *f.* to have stage fright.

traquette (avoir la) *f.* to have the jitters.

> **NOTE:** **traquer** *v.* to hunt or track down • *la traquette* might be loosely translated as "the jittery and unsettling feeling that one might have if being pursued."

traquouse (avoir la) *f.* slang variant of: *avoir la traquette*.

> **NOTE:** The common suffix *-ette* has been changed to the slang suffix *-ouse* to give this variant a heavier slang feeling.

tremblotte (avoir la) *f.* to have the jitters, shakes • (lit.): to have the trembles.

trouille (avoir la) *f.* (very popular) to have intense fear.

> **NOTE:** **trouillard(e)** *n.* one who is terribly scared, scaredy cat.

venette (avoir la) *f.* to have the jitters.

ALCOHOL

alcool

example: Si je bois trop de **pictance**, ça me donne mal à la tête.

translation: If I drink too much **alcohol**, I get a headache.

as spoken: Si j'bois trop d'**pictance**, ça m'donne mal à la tête.

---

bibine *f.* any alcoholic drink.

brouille-ménage *m.* red wine.

> **NOTE:** **brouiller** *v.* to mix up, to stir up • **ménage** *m.* household • This literally translates as "something that stirs up the household" since husbands and wives often get into fights after having too much to drink.

brutal *m.* ordinary wine • (lit.): brutal.

casse-gueule *m.* very strong liquor • (lit.): mouth-breaker.

> **NOTE:** **gueule** *f.* derogatory for "mouth" • (lit.): mouth of an animal.

casse-pattes *m.* very strong liquor • (lit.): paw-breaker.

> **NOTE:** **patte** *f.* limb • (lit.): paw.

casse-poitrine *m.* very strong liquor • (lit.): chest-breaker.

gniole *f.* brandy or alcohol in general.

gros rouge qui tache *m.* ordinary red wine • (lit.): the fat red that stains.

gros rouge *m.* ordinary red wine • (lit.): fat red.

moussante *f.* beer.

> **NOTE:** This comes from the feminine noun *mousse* literally meaning "foam."

pétrole *m.* brandy • (lit.): petrol.

pictance *f.* alcohol in general.

> **NOTE:** **picter** *v.* to drink alcohol.

pousse-au-crime *m.* ordinary red wine • (lit.): push-to-crime.

rouquin *m.* ordinary red wine.

> **NOTE:** **rouquin(e)** *n.* red, redhead.

schnaps *m.* (borrowed from German) alcohol in general.

tord-boyaux *m.* very strong or poor quality brandy, rot gut • (lit.): gut-twister.

vitriol *m.* low quality liquor • (lit.): vitriol.

ANGRY (TO BE)

colère (être en)

example: Ma mère était **furibarde** quand elle a su que j'ai cassé son nouveau vase!

translation: My mother was really **ticked** off when she found out that I broke her new vase!

as spoken: Ma mère, elle était **furibarde** quand elle a su qu'j'ai cassé son nouveau vase!

à prendre avec des pincettes (ne pas être) *exp.* • (lit.): to be unable to be picked up with tweezers (because the person is so hot with rage).

baver (en) *v.* to foam at the mouth • (lit.): to drool about something.

bisquer *v.* to be very angry.

boule (se mettre en) *exp.* to be furious over something • (lit.): to get oneself into a ball (because the muscles are so tight due to anger).

caille (l'avoir à la) *f.* to be furious • (lit.): to have it (one's blood) to the point of curdling.

cran (être à) *adj.* to be ready to explode with anger • (lit.): to be one notch away (from getting angry).
> **NOTE:** **cran** *m.* • (lit.): notch.

crin (être comme un) *exp.* to be ready to explode with anger • (lit.): to be like a horsehair.

emporter (se laisser) *v.* to flare up with anger, to lose one's temper • (lit.): to carry oneself away.

example: Calme-toi! Tu **te laisses emporter**!

translation: Relax! You're **letting yourself get all worked up**!

as spoken: Calme-toi! Tu **t'laisses emporter**!

rogne (être en) *adj.* to be furious.

fâcher tout(e) rouge (se) *exp.* to be furious • (lit.): to get red with anger.

fou / folle de rage (être) *exp.* • (lit.): to be crazy with rage.

fumer *v.* to burn with anger • (lit.): to smoke (with anger).

furibard(e) être) *adj.* a slang variation of the adjective *furieux, ieuse* meaning "furious."

furibond(e) être) *adj.* a slang variation of the adjective *furieux, ieuse* meaning "furious."

mal vissé(e) (être) *adj.* to be in a bad mood • (lit.): to be badly screwed (together).

monter l'échelle *exp.* to hit the ceiling • (lit.): to go up the ladder.
> **VARIATION:** **grimper l'échelle** *exp.* • (lit.): to climb the ladder.

pester *v.* to be furious • (lit.): to storm (with anger).

rager *v.* to be furious • (lit.): to rage.

râler *v.* to be furious • (lit.): to rile.

sauter *v.* to become suddenly angry • (lit.): to jump.

tempêter *v.* • (lit.): to storm (with anger).

tête près du bonnet (avoir la) *exp.* to be in a bad mood • (lit.): to have the head close to the bonnet.

voir rouge *exp.* to be furious • (lit.): to see red.

ANNOY (TO)

ennuyer

example: Charles me suit partout. Il m'**assome** sans arrêt!

translation: Charles follows me everywhere. He **bugs** me all the time!

as spoken: Charles, y m'suit partout. Y m'**assome** sans arrêt!

---

assommer *v.* to annoy greatly • (lit.): to knock senseless.

barber *v.* to annoy greatly.

bassiner *v.* to annoy to the point of anger • (lit.): to bathe (wound, etc.) with water of in this case with annoyance.

canuler *v.* to annoy little by little until it becomes too much to bear • (lit.): to inject with a syringe.

casser les oreilles à quelqu'un *exp.* to annoy and tire someone out by talking nonstop • (lit.): to break one's ear.

casser les pieds à quelqu'un *exp.* to annoy greatly • (lit.): to break someone's feet.

NOTE: casse-pieds *m.* annoying person • (lit.): foot-breaker.

courir *v.* to pester constantly • (lit.): to run.

cramponner *v.* to annoy by hanging around too much, to cramp one's style • (lit.): to cramp.

embêter *v.* to annoy greatly • (lit.): to cause to go crazy.

enquiquiner *v.* to annoy to the point of suffocation.

NOTE: This comes from the masculine noun *quiqui* meaning the "neck."

faire suer *v.* to annoy greatly • (lit.): to make sweat.

raser *v.* to annoy by boredom or dullness • (lit.): to shave.

NOTE: rasoir *m.* a boring, dull person • (lit.): razor.

taper sur les nerfs à quelqu'un *exp.* to get one someone's nerves • (lit.): to tap on one's nerves.

tarabuster *v.* to pester.

tracasser *v.* to plague.

example: Cette idée me **tracasse**.

translation: This idea is **plaguing** me.

as spoken: Cette idée, è m'**tracasse**.

ARREST (TO)

arrêter

example: Dominique s'est fait **agrafer** par la police!

translation: Dominique got **arrested** by the police!

as spoken: Dominique, y s'est fait **agrafer** par la police!

SEE: JAIL - *p. 255.*

---

agrafer *v.* • (lit.): to staple.

ballonner *v.* • (lit.): to put into the *balloon* (literally "jail" or "slammer").

bon (être) *adj.* to be caught, to be done for • (lit.): to be good.

choper au tournant *exp.* • (lit.): to catch at the bend of the road.

NOTE: choper *v.* to catch.

coffrer *v.* to put into prison • (lit.): to put in the trunk.

NOTE: coffre *m.* • (lit.): trunk.

cravater *v.* • (lit.): to grab someone by tie (or neck).

NOTE: cravate *f.* • (lit.): tie.

cueillir *v.* • (lit.): to pick, gather, pluck.

cuit(e) être) *adj.* • (lit.): to be cooked (as in "one's goose").

emballer *v.* • (lit.): to wrap up.

épingler *v.* • (lit.): to pin.

NOTE: **épingle** *f.* • (lit.): pin.

fabriquer *v.* • (lit.): to fabricate.

fait(e) (être) *adj.* • (lit.): to be done for.

fiche dedans *v.* • (lit.): to throw inside (the slammer).

NOTE: **fiche** *v.* to throw.

flanquer dedans *v.* same as: *fiche dedans.*

NOTE: **flanquer** *v.* to throw, chuck.

grouper *v.* • (lit.): to group or gather.

harponner *v.* • (lit.): to harpoon.

jeter dedans *v.* • (lit.): to throw inside (the slammer).

mettre à la boîte *exp.* • (lit.): to put in the box.

NOTE: **boîte** *f.* prison • (lit.): box.

mettre sous les verrous *exp.* • (lit.): to put under the locks.

pincer *v.* • (lit.): to pinch.

piper *v.* • (lit.): to lure, decoy.

NOTE: **pipé(e) sur le tas (être)** *exp.* to be caught red-handed.

piquer *v.* • (lit.): to catch.

poisser *v.* • (lit.): to coat with a stick wax.

prendre *v.* • (lit.): to take.

ramasser *v.* • (lit.): to gather.

sucrer *v.* • (lit.): to sweeten.

ARRIVE (TO)

arriver

example:　Le train va **se pointer** dans trois minutes.

translation:　The train is going **to arrive** in three minutes.

as spoken:　Le train, y va **s'pointer** dans trois minutes.

amener (s') *v.* • (lit.): to bring oneself along.

amener comme une fleur (s') *exp.* to drop in quietly, to breeze in • (lit.): to bring oneself along like a flower.

amener sa graisse *exp.* • (lit.): to bring along one's fat.

example:　**Amène ta graisse!**

translation:　**Get your butt over here!**

as spoken:　[no change]

amener sa viande *exp.* • (lit.): to bring along one's meat.

NOTE: The slang word for "meat" (*bidoche*) is commonly used in place of *viande* in this expression.

arriver comme une flèche *exp.* to drop in quietly, to breeze in • (lit.): to arrive like an arrow.

débarquer *v.* to arrive without notice • (lit.): to disembark.

pointer (se) *v.* to show up • (lit.): to point oneself.

radiner (se) *v.* to show up.

ralléger *v.* to come, to arrive.

rappliquer *v.* to arrive, to turn up, to come back.

BAD LUCK (to have)

malchance (avoir de la)

example: Quelle **déveine**! J'ai raté mon bus!

translation: What **lousy luck**! I missed my bus!

as spoken: [no change]

SEE: **LUCKY (TO BE)** - *p. 268.*

---

déveine (avoir la) *f.*
   NOTE: **avoir la déveine** = to be unlucky • **avoir de la veine** = to be lucky.

guignard(e) *n.* unlucky individual.

guigne (avoir la) *f.* to have bad luck.

main malheureuse (avoir la) *f.* • (lit.): to have a sad hand.

mal loti (être) *adj.* • (lit.): to be poorly provided for.

manque de bol *m.* • (lit.): lack of luck.
   NOTE: **bol** *m.* luck • *avoir du bol;* to be lucky.

manque de pot *m.* • (lit.): lack of luck.
   NOTE: **pot** *m.* luck • *avoir du pot;* to be lucky.

pas verni *adj.* • (lit.): badly varnished (with luck).

poissard(e) *n.* unlucky individual.

poisse (avoir la) *f.* to have bad luck.

série noire *f.* run of bad luck
   • (lit.): black series.

tuile *f.* unexpected bad luck
   • (lit.): tile.

   NOTE: The feminine noun *tuile* has taken on this slang connotation because "unexpected bad luck" can fall on a person as unexpectedly as a tile off a roof.

BALD HEAD

chauve

example: Ce bébé n'a pas de cheveux. Je n'ai jamais vu un **melon déplumé** pareil!

translation: That baby doesn't have any hair. I've never seen such a **bald head**!

as spoken: Ce bébé, il a pas d'ch'veux. J'ai jamais vu un **melon déplumé** pareil!

---

billard *m.* • (lit.): billiard.

boule de billard *f.* • (lit.): billiard ball.

caillou *m.* • (lit.): pebble.

genou *m.* • (lit.): knee.

melon déplumé (avoir le) *m.*
   • (lit.): to have a featherless melon.

tête de veau *f.* • (lit.): head of veal.

BARBER

coiffeur

example: J'ai les cheveux qui commencent à être trop longs. Je crois qu'il est temps d'aller voir le **merlan**.

translation: My hair is starting to get too long. I think it's time to go see the **barber**.

as spoken: J'ai les ch'veux qui commencent à êt' trop longs. J'crois qu'il est temps d'aller voir le **merlan**.

---

figardo *m.*

> **NOTE:** This is from Beaumarchais' *Barber of Seville*.

merlan *m.* • (lit.): whiting (fish).

pommadin *m.* • (lit.): the one who puts *pomade* (or "ointment") in someone's hair.

tiffier *m.* • (lit.): the one who works with the *tifs*.

> **NOTE:** **tifs** *m.pl.* hair.

BAWL SOMEONE OUT (TO)

réprimander

example: Mon père **m'a engueulé** parce que j'ai pris sa voiture sans permission.

translation: My father **chewed me out** for taking his car without permission.

as spoken: Mon père, il **m'a engueulé** pasque j'ai pris sa voiture sans permission.

> **SEE -1:** **FIGHT (TO)** - *p. 236.*
> **SEE -2:** **THRASHING** - *p. 291.*

---

attraper *v.* • (lit.): to catch.

dire ses quatre vérités à quelqu'un *exp.* to give someone what for • (lit.): to tell someone his / her four truths.

example: J'en ai assez de Marie! Un de ces jours, je vais **lui dire ses quatre vérités**!

translation: I've had it with Marie! One of these days, I'm going to tell **her just what I think of her**!

as spoken: J'en ai assez d'Marie! Un d'ces jours, j'vais **lui dire ses quat' vérités**!

dire son fait à quelqu'un *exp.* same as: *dire ses quatre vérités à quelqu'un* • (lit.): to tell someone his / her fact.

engueuler *v.* to yell at someone.

> **NOTE:** This comes from the feminine noun *gueule* which is derogatory for a person's "mouth" since it is literally the "mouth of an animal" • This verb might be loosely translated as "to mouth off at someone."

> **ALSO:** **engueuler (s')** *v.*

example: Je **me suis engueulé** avec la marchande.

translation: I **had a fight** with the sales woman.

as spoken: Je **m'suis engueulé** avec la marchande.

enguirlander *v.* to chew someone out.

laver la tête à quelqu'un *exp.*
• (lit.): to wash someone's head.

lessiver la tête à quelqu'un
exp. • (lit.): to soap up someone's head.

mettre les pieds dans le plat
exp. to give someone a piece of one's mind • (lit.): to put the feet in the platter.

example: J'en ai marre! Je vais **mettre les pieds dans le plat** tout de suite!

translation: I've had it! I'm going **to give him / her a piece of my mind** right now!

as spoken: J'en ai marre! J'vais **mett' les pieds dans l'plat** tout d'suite!

passer un savon à quelqu'un
exp. to give someone a bawling out • (lit.): to give a soaping to someone.

rembarrer *v.* to chew someone out royally.

example: Il s'est fait vertement **rembarrer**!

translation: He got himself royally **bawled out**!

as spoken: Y s'est fait vertement **rembarrer**!

remettre quelqu'un à sa place *exp.* • (lit.): to put someone in his / her place.

savon *m.* a scolding • (lit.): a soap(ing).

savonnage *v.* same as: *savon*.

savonner la tête à quelqu'un
exp. • (lit.): to soap up someone's head.

BED
lit

example: Je suis fatigué. Je crois qu'il est temps d'aller au **plumard**.

translation: I'm tired. I think it's time to go to **bed**.

as spoken: J'suis fatigué. J'crois qu'il est temps d'aller au **plumard**.

SEE: **BED (TO GO TO)** - *p. 214.*

---

paddock *m.* • (lit.): paddock.

page *m.*

pageot / pajot *m.*

pieu *m.* • (lit.): stake, post.

plumard *m.*

plume *f.* • (lit.): feather.

pucier *m.* • (lit.): flea-bag.

BED (TO GO TO)
coucher (se)

example: Comme tu vas te lever de bonne heure, tu ferais mieux d'aller **faire dodo** tout de suite.

translation: Since you're getting up early, you'd be smart **to go to bed** right away.

as spoken: Comme tu vas t'lever d'bonne heure, tu f'rais mieux d'aller **faire dodo** tout d'suite.

SEE: **SLEEP (TO GO TO)** - *p. 284.*

aller au schloff *v.* (borrowed from German).

bâcher (se) *v.* • (lit.): to sheet something over, to cover with a *bâche f.* (cover).

dodo (faire) *exp.*

NOTE: This is common child language, yet usually commonly in jest by adults.

mettre au page (se) *exp.*
• (lit.): to put oneself into the *page* meaning "bed."

paddocker (se) *v.*

ANTONYM: **dépaddocker (se)** *v.* to get out of bed.

pageoter (se) *v.*

ANTONYM: **dépageoter (se)** *v.* to get out of bed.

pager (se) *v.*

ANTONYM: **dépager (se)** *v.* to get out of bed.

pagnoter (se) *v.*

ANTONYM: **dépagnoter (se)** *v.* to get out of bed.

pieuter (se) *v.*

ANTONYM: **dépieuter (se)** *v.* to get out of bed.

plumer (se) *v.*

ANTONYM: **déplumer (se)** *v.* to get out of bed.

BEDROOM

chambre

example: Va ranger ta **piaule** tout de suite! Quel désordre!

translation: Go clean up your **bedroom** right now! What a mess!

as spoken: Va ranger ta **piaule** tout d'suite! Quel désordre!

---

cambuse *f.* • (lit.): storeroom, poorly kept room.

carrée *f.* • (lit.): square.

piaule *f.*

turne *f.*

NOTE: **co-turn** *m.*

BIG WHEEL

personnage éminent

example: Irène a commencé à travailler pour cette société comme secrétaire. Maintenant elle est **grosse légume**!

translation: Irene started working for this company as a secretary. Now she's a **big wig**!

as spoken: Irène, elle a commencé à travailler pour cette société comme secrétaire. Maintenant c't'une **grosse légume**!

---

gros bonnet *m.* • (lit.): big bonnet.

grosse légume *f.* • (lit.): big vegetable.

huile *f.* • (lit.): oil.

singe *m.* the boss • (lit.): monkey.

BLABBERMOUTH (TO BE A)

bavard(e) (être)

example: Elle n'arrête pas de parler! Il faut dire qu'elle **a du bagout**!

translation: She just doesn't stop talking! You have to admit, she's a real **blabbermouth**!

as spoken: Elle arrête pas d'parler! Faut dire qu'elle **a du bagout**!

---

bagout (avoir du) *m.* to be talkative.
> **NOTE:** **bagouler** *v.* to talk a lot.

bavard(e) comme une pie (être) *exp.* • (lit.): to be talkative as a magpie.
> **NOTE:** **bavarder** *v.* to talk a lot.

gueulard(e) *n.* loud blabbermouth, one who uses his / her *gueule* a lot.
> **NOTE:** **gueule** *f.* derogatory for "mouth" • (lit.): mouth of an animal.

langue bien pendue (avoir la) *exp.* • (lit.): to have a well-hung tongue.
> **VARIATION:** **l'avoir bien pendue** *exp.* • **l'** referring to **la langue**.

langue dans sa poche (ne pas avoir la) *exp.* said of someone who is very talkative • (lit.): not to have one's tongue in one's pocket.

moulin à paroles *m.*
• (lit.): windmill of speech.

sacrée tapette (avoir une) *exp.* • (lit.): to have a sacred (one helluva) tongue.
> **ALSO:** **tapette** *f.* (derogatory) homosexual, fag.

vacciné(e) avec une aiguille de phono (être) *exp.* • (lit.): to be vaccinated with a phonograph needle.

verbe haut (avoir le) *m.*
• (lit.): to have the loud (or high) verb.

verbeux, euse *adj.* long-winded
• (lit.): to be "verby" or "verbose."

BLACK EYE

œil poché

example: Mais qu'est-ce qui t'est arrivé? Où as-tu eu cet **œil au beurre noir**?!

translation: What happened to you? Where did you get that **black eye**?!

as spoken: Mais qu'est-c'qui t'est arrivé? Où t'as eu c't'**œil au beurre noir**?!

---

coquard *m.* slang variant of: *coquelicot*.

coquelicot *m.* • (lit.): red poppy.

coquelique *m.* abbreviated form of: *coquelicot*.

œil au beurre noir *m.* • (lit.): eye of black butter.

pavoiser *v.* to go around with a black eye • (lit.): to be ornamented.

pocher un œil à quelqu'un *exp.* to give someone a black eye
• (lit.): to poach someone's eye.

BOTCH UP (TO)

ruiner

example: Georges a été mis à la porte. Chaque fois que le patron lui a donné du travail à faire, il l'a complètement **bousillé**!

translation: George was fired. Every time the boss gave him some work to do, he **bungled** it!

as spoken: Georges, il a été mis à la porte. Chaque fois que l'patron lui a donné du travail à faire, y l'a complètement **bousillé**!

---

amocher *v.* • (lit.): to make look bad or ugly.

NOTE: **moche** *adj.* ugly.

bousiller *v.* to botch up.

example: J'ai **bousillé** mon examen.

translation: I **botched** my exam.

as spoken: J'ai **bousillé** mon exam.

cochonner *v.* to do a task carelessly.

NOTE: **cochon** *m.* pig.

fusiller *v.* • (lit.): to shoot.

massacrer *v.* • (lit.): to massacre.

rater *v.* (very popular) to goof up.

savate *f.* bungler • (lit.): old worn out shoe.

savater *v.* to bungle.

savatier *m.* bungler • (lit.): cobbler.

torcher *v.* to do work quickly and carelessly • (lit.): to wipe.

torchonner *v.* a slang variant of: *torcher.*

travailler comme un sabot
exp. to work carelessly • (lit.): to work (nonstop) like a shoe.

NOTE: **sabot** *m.* shoe.

BREASTS

seins

example: Avec des **boîtes à lait** pareilles, Nancy devrait être mannequin!

translation: With **breasts** like hers, Nancy should be a model!

as spoken: Avec des **boîtes à lait** pareilles, Nancy, è d'vrait êt'mannequin!

---

amortisseurs *m.pl.* • (lit.): shock absorbers.

avant-scène *f.* • (lit.): the apron of the stage that protrudes past the proscenium.

blagues à tabac *f.pl.*
• (lit.): tobacco pouches.

boîtes à lait *f.pl.* • (lit.): milk bottles.

boîtes à lolo *f.pl.* • (lit.): milk bottles.

NOTE: **lolo** *m.* child's slang for "milk".

gros lolos *m.pl.* • (lit.): big milkers.

il y a du monde au balcon
exp. said of a woman with large breasts • (lit.): there are a lot of people on the balcony.

mandarines *f.pl.* tiny breasts
• (lit.): tangerines.

nénés *m.pl.* humorous slang for "breasts."

nichons *m.pl.* (extremely poplar) breasts.

œufs sur le plat *m.pl.* tiny breasts • (lit.): fried eggs on a plate.

> **VARIATION:** œufs au plat *m.pl.*

planche à pain *f.* said of a very flat chest • (lit.): bread board.

planche à repasser *f.* said of a very flat chest • (lit.): ironing board.

roberts *m.pl.*

rondins *m.pl.* • (lit.): log (of firewood).

roploplos *m.pl.*

tétasses *f.pl.* flabby breasts.

tétons *m.pl.* breasts.

> **NOTE:** This is where the Grand Tetons got their names, literally meaning, the "Big Tits."

tettes *f.pl.* nipples.

tripailles *f.pl.* flabby breasts • (lit.): intestines.

tripes *f.pl.* flabby breasts • (lit.): intestines.

BROKE (TO BE)

pauvre (être)

example: Henri a perdu tout son argent aux courses. Maintenant il est **dans la débine**.

translation: Henry lost all of his money at the races. Now he's **broke**.

as spoken: Henri, il a perdu tout son argent aux courses. Maintenant il est **dans la débine**.

argenté(e) comme une cuillière de bois (être) *exp.* • (lit.): to be silvered like a wooden spoon.

côte (être à la) *f.* • (lit.): to be on the shore (or "on the rocks").

court d'argent (être à) *exp.* • (lit.): to be short of money.

débine (être dans la) *f.* to be in a state of poverty.

décavé(e) (être) *adj.* to be financially ruined.

> **ALSO:** décaver quelqu'un *v.* to clean someone out.

déchard(e) *n.* one who is penniless.

dèche (être dans la) *exp.* to be in poverty, to be stone broke.

fauché(e) (être) *adj.* • (lit.): to be reaped (clean).

fleur (être) *adj.* • (lit.): to be flower.

misère (être dans la) *exp.* • (lit.): to be in misery.

mistoufle (être dans la) *exp.* to be in a state of poverty.

ne pas avoir un radis *exp.* not to have a red cent • (lit.): to be without a radish.

> **NOTE:** radis *m.* centime, cent.

ne pas avoir un rond *exp.* • (lit.): to be without a round.

> **NOTE:** rond *m.* centime, cent • (lit.): round thing.

purée (être dans la) *exp.* to be financially wiped out • (lit.): to be in the purée (or soup).

purotin *m.* sang variant of: *purée.*

sans un (être) *exp.* • (lit.): to be without one.

sec (être à) *adj.* • (lit.): to be dry (of money).

tomber dans la panade *exp.* to fall into poverty • (lit.): to fall into a bread, milk, and cheese soup.

vidé(e) (être) *adj.* • (lit.): to be emptied (of one's money).

CAR

voiture

example: Marcel a été dans une douzaine d'accidents d'auto cette année. Tu devrais voir sa **bagnole**!

translation: Marcel's been in a dozen car accidents this year. You should see his **car**!

as spoken: Marcel, il a été dans une douzaine d'accidents d'auto cette année. Tu d'vrais voir sa **bagnole**!

---

bagnole *f.* (extremely popular).

bahut *m.* old car, taxi.

caisse *f.* car in general • (lit.): case.

> example: **A fond la caisse**!
>
> translation: **Step on it**!
>
> as spoken: [no change]

chignole *f.* car in poor condition.

drôle de berlingot *m.* car in poor condition • (lit.): strange pimple or boil.

guimbarde *f.* old broken-down car.

tacot *m.* **1.** old broken-down car • **2.** taxi.

tas de boue *m.* old car • (lit.): pile of dirt.

teuf-teuf *m.* an old car • (lit.): an onomatopoeia for the sound of a car's noisy engine.

tinette *f.*

tire *f.* • (lit.): puller.

vieux clou *m.* old car in poor condition • (lit.): old nail.

CARE (NOT TO)

moquer (s'en)

example: Si tu veux inviter Gisèle à ta soirée, je **m'en balance**.

translation: If you want to invite Gisèle to your party, I **don't really care**.

as spoken: Si tu veux inviter Gisèle à ta soirée, j'**m'en balance**.

---

balancer (s'en) *v.* • (lit.): to throw it off.

> example: Je **m'en balance**!
>
> translation: I **don't give a hoot**!
>
> as spoken: J'**m'en balance**!

battre le coquillard (s'en) *exp.* • (lit.): to bat one's eye over it.

> **NOTE:** **coquillard** *m.* eye.

battre l'œil (s'en) *exp.* • (lit.): to bat one's eye over something.

contre-fiche (s'en) *v.*

> example: Je m'en fiche et **m'en contre-fiche**.

> translation: I **really couldn't care less about it**.

> as spoken: J'm'en fiche et **m'en contre-fiche**.

fiche (s'en) *v.* not to care at al about something.

fiche comme de sa première chausette (s'en) *exp.* not to care at all about something • (lit.): to care about something about as much as one's first sock.

fiche comme de sa première chemise (s'en) *exp.* not to care at all about something • (lit.): to care about something about as much as one's first shirt.

moquer (s'en) *v.* • (lit.): to mock something.

moquer du tiers comme du quart (se) *exp.* not to give a hoot about something • (lit.): to mock the third like the quarter.

tamponner le coquillard (s'en) *v.* • (lit.): to bad one's eye (of a fake tear).

> **NOTE:** **coquillard** *m.* eye.

CHILD

enfant

example: Il y a beaucoup de **mômes** dans mon immeuble.

translation: There are a lot of **children** in my apartment building.

as spoken: Y a beaucoup d'**mômes** dans mon immeuble.

criard *m.* baby • (lit.): yeller (from the verb *crier* meaning "to yell").

gamin(e) *n.* kid.

gavroche *m.* child of Paris.

gosse *n.* (extremely popular) kid.

lardon *m.* little kid, brat • (lit.): piece of larding bacon, lardon.

marmaille *f.* screaming little brats.

mioche *n.* kid.

môme *n.* kid.

morveux *m.* snot-nosed little boy.

> **NOTE:** This is from the feminine noun *morve* meaning "nasal mucus."

moujingue *n.* kid.

moutard(e) *n.* little kid.

petit salé *m.* newborn baby.

têtard *m.* • (lit.): tadpole.

titi *m.* street-wise child from Paris.

CIGARETTE

cigarette

example: Carole a toujours une **clope** dans la bouche.

translation: Carole always has a **cigarette** in her mouth.

as spoken: Carole, elle a toujours une **clope** dans la bouche.

---

bombarder *v.* to smoke • (lit.): to bombard (with cigarette smoke).

cibiche *f.* "cig."

clope *f.* (extremely popular).

griller une (en) *v.* • (lit.): to grill one (a cigarette).

mégot *m.* butt of a cigarette.

orphelin *m.* butt of a cigarette
• (lit.): orphan.

pipette *f.* • (lit.): a little pipe.

sèche *f.* • (lit.): a dry thing.

tige *f.* • (lit.): stem.

COMPLAIN (TO)
plaindre (se)

example: Antoine n'a jamais arrêter
de **rouspéter** pendant tout notre
voyage!

translation: Anthony never stopped
complaining during our entire trip!

as spoken: Antoine, il a jamais arrêter
d'**rouspéter** pendant tout not'voyage!

bougonner *v.* to grumble.

NOTE: bougon(ne) *n.*grumbler •
adj. grumpy.

marmonner *v.* • (lit.): to growl,
grumble.

râler *v.* to rattle (in one's throat).

NOTE: râleur, euse *n.*
bad-tempered person.

ronchonner *v.* to grumble.

rouscailler *v.* slang variant of:
rouspéter.

rouspéter *v.* • (lit.): to resist, protest.

CONCEITED (TO BE)
arrogant(e) (être)

example: Maintenant qu'elle est
devenue une grande vedette, elle **se
croit sortie de la cuisse de
Jupiter**.

translation: Now that she's become a
big star, she's **hot stuff**.

as spoken: Maintenant qu'elle est
dev'nue une grande vedette, è **s'croit
sortie d'la cuisse de Jupiter**.

afficher (s') *v.* to show off
• (lit.): to poster oneself.

crâneur, euse *n.* braggart,
show-off.

NOTE: crâner *v.*to show off.

croire (se) *v.* to be conceited
• (lit.): to think (highly) of oneself.

**croire sorti(e) de la cuisse
de Jupiter (se)** *exp.* to be very
conceited • (lit.): to believe to have
come out of Jupiter's thigh.

**donner des coups de pied
(ne pas se)** *exp.* to be very
conceited • (lit.): not to give oneself
any kicks (for inadequacy).

donner des gants (se) *exp.* to
brag, boast • (lit.): to give oneself
gloves.

faire du fla-fla *exp.* to show off.

faire le flambard *exp.* to show
off, to act like a conceited person.

faiseur *m.* conceited person
• (lit.): doer.

fanfaron *m.* braggart.

fanfaronner *v.* to brag.

frimeur, euse *n.* braggart, show-off.

m'as-tu-vu *m.* show-off • (lit.): one who constantly asks other people *m'as-tu-vu?* meaning "did you see me?"

plastronner *v.* • (lit.): to throw out one's chest, to swagger.

poseur *m.* conceited person.

CONFESS (TO)

avouer

example: Après trois heures d'interrogation, le suspect a **craché le morceau**.

translation: After three hours of interrogation, the suspect **fessed up**.

as spoken: Après trois heures d'interrogation, le suspect, il a **craché l'morceau**.

---

cracher *v.* • (lit.): to spit (the truth).

cracher le morceau *v.* • (lit.): to spit the piece (of information).

déballer *v.*

déballonner (se) *v.* • (lit.): to let the air out of the balloon.

déboutonner (se) *v.* to get something off one's chest • (lit.): to unbutton oneself.

goualer *v.* • (lit.): this is a slang term for "to sing."

manger le morceau *v.* • (lit.): to eat the piece (of information).

mettre à table (se) *v.* to confess • (lit.): to set oneself down at the table.

vider son sac *v.* to get something off one's chest • (lit.): to empty one's sack.

CRY (TO)

pleurer

example: En apprenant la mauvaise nouvelle, Pierre a commencé à **chialer**.

translation: Upon learning of the bad news, Pierre **cried his eyes out**.

as spoken: Après trois heures d'interrogation, le suspect, il a **craché l'morceau**.

---

brailler *v.* to bawl, to shout (of child. **ALSO: brailler une chanson** *exp.* to screech out a song.

chialer *v.* (extremely popular).

couiner *v.* • (lit.): to whimper, squeak or squeal.

ouvrir les écluses *exp.* • (lit.): to open the flood gates.

piailler *v.* • (lit.): to whimper (of children), to chirp (of small birds). **NOTE: enfant piailleur** *m.* cry-baby.

piauler *v.* • (lit.): to whimper (of children), to chirp (of small birds).

pleurer comme un veau *exp.* to cry heavily, to blubber • (lit.): to cry like a calf.

pleurer comme une madeleine *exp.* to cry heavily, to blubber.

verser des larmes de crocodile *exp.* • (lit.): to pour crocodile tears.

DARLING

chéri(e)

example: Je t'adore, mon **chou**!

translation: I love you, my **sweetheart**!

as spoken: J't'adore, mon **chou**!

---

chéri(e) coco *n.* sweetie-pie.

cocotte *f.* darling • **coco** *m.*

chou *m.* from *chou à la crème* meaning "cream puff."

chouchou(te) *n.* • (lit.): one's favorite or preferred person.

  example: C'est le **chouchou** du professeur.

  translation: He's the teacher's **pet**.

  as spoken: C'est l'**chouchou** du professeur.

loulou(te) *n.*

  example: Bonjour **loulou**!

  translation: Hello **sweetheart**!

  as spoken: [no change]

mon petit chou en sucre *exp.* • (lit.): my little sugary cream puff.

mon petit chou en susucre *exp.*

  NOTE: susucre *m.* baby talk for *sucre* meaning "sugar."

DIE (TO)

mourir

example: Tu as entendu les nouvelles? Notre professeur de géographie a **clapsé** hier soir!

translation: Did you hear the news? Our geography teacher **died** last night!

as spoken: T'as entendu les nouvelles? Not'prof de géo, il a **clapsé** hier soir!

---

avaler sa chique *exp.* • (lit.): to swallow one's quid (of tobacco).

avaler sa langue *exp.* • (lit.): to swallow one's tongue.

avaler son extrait de naissance *exp.* • (lit.): to swallow one's birth certificate.

calancer *v.* "to croak."

casser sa pipe *exp.* • (lit.): to break one's pipe.

clamser *v.* "to croak."

clapoter *v.* "to croak."

claquer *v.* "to croak" • (lit.): to slam shut.

déposer son bilan *exp.* • (lit.): to file one's petition (in bankruptcy).

dévisser son billard *exp.* • (lit.): to unscrew one's billiard.
  NOTE: billard *m.* head.

éteindre son gas *exp.* • (lit.): to turn off one's gas.

faire le grand saut *exp.* • (lit.): to make the big jump.

faire le grand voyage *exp.* • (lit.): to make the big trip.

faire un costume de bois (se)
exp. • (lit.): to make oneself a
costume of wood.

**habiller de quatre planches
(s')** exp. • (lit.): to dress oneself in
four boards.

lâcher la perle exp. • (lit.): to let
go of the pearl.

lâcher la rampe exp. • (lit.): to let
go of the ramp.

l'article de la mort (être à)
exp. to be at death's door.

les pieds devant (s'en aller)
exp. • (lit.): to go feet first.

**manger les pissenlits par la
racine** exp. • (lit.): to each
dandelions by the root.

passer l'arme à gauche exp.
• (lit.): to pass the firearm(s) to the left.

perdre le goût du pain exp.
• (lit.): to lose the taste of bread.

**pied dans la tombe (avoir
un)** exp. • (lit.): to have one foot in
the grave.

poser sa chique exp. • (lit.): to put
down one's quid (of tobacco).

cabot m.

> **NOTE:** This term is also used to
> mean "a ham actor."

chienchien m. term of endearment
for a dog, "doggy."

chiot m. puppy.

clébard m.

clebs m. (pronounced: *klèps*).

roquet m. dog that barks a lot,
ill-tempered dog.

toutou m. baby talk for "dog."

DOG

chien

example: Je n'ai pas dormi hier soir
parce que le **clébard** de la maison à
côté n'a pas arrêté d'aboyer toute la
nuit!

translation: I didn't sleep last night
because the **dog** next door didn't stop
barking the entire night!

as spoken: J'ai pas dormi hier soir
pasque l'**clébard** d'la maison à côté, il
a pas arrêté d'aboyer toute la nuit!

DRESS (TO)

habiller (s')

example: Va te **fringuer** tout de
suite! On risque d'être en retard pour
la soirée!

translation: Go **get dressed** right
away! We're going to be late for the
party!

as spoken: Va t'**fringuer** tout d'suite!
On risque d'êt'en r'tard pour la soirée!

---

accoutrer (s') v. to dress oneself
ridiculously.

affubler (s') v. to dress oneself
strangely and ridiculously.

attifer (s') v. to dress oneself
strangely and ridiculously.

débraillé(e) (être) adj. to be
dressed poorly, to have an messy
appearance.

dépenaillé(e) (être) adj. to be
dressed poorly, to have an messy
appearance.

endimancher (s') *v.* to dress well, in one's Sunday best.

> **NOTE:** This comes from the masculine noun *dimanche* meaning "Sunday."

fagoter (se) *v.* to dress without taste, to dress poorly.

fich(u) comme l'as de pique (être) *exp.* said of a poorly dressed individual • (lit.): to be put together like the ace of spades.

fringuer (se) *v.* to dress oneself.

> **NOTE:** **fringues** *f.pl.* clothes.

mal ficelé(e) (être) *adj.* to be poorly dressed • (lit.): to be badly strung together.

nipper (se) *v.* to dress oneself.

> **NOTE:** **nippes** *f.pl.* clothes.

saper (se) *v.* to dress oneself.

> **NOTE:** **sapes** *f.pl.* clothes.

DRINK (TO)

boire

example: Charles est toujours ivre. Il ne fait que **picoler**!

translation: Charles is always drunk. All he ever does is **drink**!

as spoken: Charles, il est toujours ivre. Y fait qu'**picoler**!

---

biberonner *v.* to tipple, to booze it up.

> **NOTE:** This comes from the masculine noun *biberon* meaning "feed-bottle."

boire en suisse *exp.* to drink alone • (lit.): to drink Swiss style.

boire à tire-larigot *exp.* to drink like a fish.

boire comme un sonneur *exp.* to drink a lot • (lit.): to drink like a bell-ringer.

boire comme un templier *exp.* to drink a lot • (lit.): to drink like a (Knight) Templar.

boire comme un tonneau *exp.* to drink a lot • (lit.): to drink like a barrel.

boire comme un trou *exp.* to drink a lot • (lit.): to drink like a hole.

boire comme une éponge *exp.* to drink a lot • (lit.): to drink like a sponge.

boire la goutte *exp.* to drink a little glass of an alcoholic beverage • (lit.): to drink the drop.

boire tout son soûl *exp.* to drink oneself under the table.

> **NOTE:** **soûl(e)** *adj.* drunk.

boire un pot *exp.* to have a drink • (lit.): to drink a pot.

boire un coup *exp.* to have a drink • (lit.): to drink a hit.

caresser la bouteille *exp.* to tipple • (lit.): to caress the bottle.

chopiner *v.* to tipple.

> **NOTE:** **chope** *f.* beer mug.

étouffer un (en) *v.* to have a drink • (lit.): to choke down one (a drink).

faire suisse *exp.* same as: *boire en suisse*.

gosier blindé (avoir le) *exp.* to have a throat that can handle the strongest liquors • (lit.): to have the numbed throat.

> **NOTE:** **gosier** *m.* throat.

humecter les amygdales (s')
exp. to wet one's whistle • (lit.): to moisten one's tonsils.

jeter un coup derrière le bouton de col (s'en) *exp.*
• (lit.): to throw one (a drink) behind the collar button.

jeter un derrière la cravate (s'en) *exp.* • (lit.): to throw one (a drink) behind the tie.

lamper *v.* to swig.

laper *v.* • (lit.): to lap up.

lever le coude *exp.* • (lit.): to lift the elbow (with a drink).

licher *v.*
NOTE: This slang synonym for "to drink" is often heard as: pourliche *m.* waiter's tip (from *pourboire*).

picoler *v.* to tipple.
NOTE: **pictance** *f.* booze.

pictonner *v.* same as: *picoler.*

pilier de cabaret *m.* habitual drinker, one who is always found in bars • (lit.): a cabaret pillar.

pinter (se) *v.* to drink a lot, to get drunk • (lit.): to drink by the pint.

pocharder (se) *v.* to drink a lot, to get drunk.

pomper *v.* • (lit.): to pump it down.

rincer le sifflet (se) *exp.*
• (lit.): to rinse one's throat.
NOTE: **sifflet** *m.*throat.

siffler un coup *exp.* • (lit.): to whistle (up) a hit.

siffler un godet *exp.* • (lit.): to whistle (up) a glass.
NOTE: **godet** *m.* glass.

siroter *v.* • (lit.): to sip.

DRUNK (TO BE)

ivre (être)

example: Si je bois juste deux sirotées de vin, je deviens **bourré**!

translation: If I drink just two sips of wine, I get **drunk**!

as spoken: Si j'bois juste deux sirotées d'vin, je d'viens **bourré**!

---

allumé(e) (être) *adj.* • (lit.): to be lit up.

beurré(e) (être) *adj.* • (lit.): to be buttered.

blindé(e) (être) *adj.* • (lit.): to be numbed.

bourré(e) (être) *adj.* • (lit.): to be stuffed (with booze).

brindezingue (être) *adj.*
• (lit.): to be loaded.

chargé(e) (être) *adj.* • (lit.): to be loaded.

cuité(e) (être) *adj.* • (lit.): to be baked.
SEE: **prendre une cuite**, *p. 228.*

dalle en pente (avoir la) *exp.*
• (lit.): to have the throat on a slant (in order to be able to drink constantly).

dans les vignes du Seigneur (être) *exp.* • (lit.): to be in the vines of the Lord.

ébreché(e) (être) *adj.* • (lit.): to be chipped.

éméché(e) (être) *adj.* to be slightly drunk, "buzzed."

émoustillé(e) (être) *adj.*
• (lit.): to be exhilarated.

empoivrer (s') *v.* to start to get drunk • (lit.): to pepper oneself.

> **SEE:** **poivrer (se)** • **poivre** • **poivrot**

ému(e) (être) *adj.* to be slightly drunk, to be "buzzed" • (lit.): to be moved.

en goguette (être) *adj.* to be slightly drunk, to be "buzzed."

en plein cirage (être) *adj.* to be bombed off one's rocker • (lit.): to be in a complete wax.

en ribote (être) *adj.* to be tipsy.

entre deux vins (être) *adj.* • (lit.): to be between two wines.

gai (être) *adj.* • (lit.): to be happy.

gris(e) (être) *adj.* to be "buzzed," to be on the verge of blacking out or becoming *noir(e)*.

> **SEE:** **noir(e) (être)**, *p. 227*.

gueule de bois (avoir la) *adj.* to have a hangover • (lit.): to have the mouth of wood.

> **NOTE:** **gueule** *f.* derogatory for "mouth" when applied to a person since the literal translation is "the mouth of an animal."

> **VARIATION:** **avoir la G.D.B.** *exp.* (pronounced: *jé-dé-bé*) an abbreviation of: *gueule de bois*.

lancé(e) (être) *adj.* • (lit.): to be thrown (into a drunken state).

mal aux cheveux (avoir) *adj.* to have a bad hangover • (lit.): to have a "hairache."

monté(e) (être) *adj.* • (lit.): to be lifted (to a drunken state).

mûr(e) (être) *adj.* • (lit.): to be ripe.

nez piqué (avoir le) *adj.* to have a red nose from drinking too much • (lit.): to have the nose that has been stung.

noir(e) (être) *adj.* to be bombed • (lit.): to be black (or ready to blackout).

noircir (se) *v.* to get bombed • (lit.): to become black (or in the blackout stage).

paf (être) *adj.* to be bombed.

parti(e) (être) *adj.* to be bombed • (lit.): to be gone.

piquer le nez (se) *exp.* to get bombed • (lit.): to get a reddened nose.

plein(e) (être) *adj.* to be bombed • (lit.): to be full (of booze).

plein(e) comme un boudin (être) *exp.* to be very drunk • (lit.): to be full as a blood sausage.

plein(e) comme un bourrique (être) *exp.* to be very drunk • (lit.): to be full as a donkey.

plein(e) comme une huître (être) *exp.* to be very drunk • (lit.): to be full as an oyster.

plein(e) comme un œuf (être) *exp.* to be very drunk • (lit.): to be full as an egg.

pochard(e) *n.* drunkard • (lit.): one who poaches.

poivre (être) *adj.* to be on the verge of getting drunk • (lit.): to be pepper(ed).

> **NOTE:** The steps of drunkenness (or to becoming *noir* or "drunk") are: after a few drink, one might be a little *poivre* (pepper), then *gris(e)*

(gray), and finally *noir(e)* (black or close to blacking out).

poivrer (se) *v.* to get drunk.
> **SEE:** **poivre**, *p. 227.*

poivrot *m.* drunkard.
> **SEE:** **poivre**, *p. 227.*

pompette (être) *adj.* to be slightly drunk.
> **NOTE:** This is from the verb **pomper** meaning "to drink" or literally meaning "to pump."

prendre une cuite *exp.* to get drunk • (lit.): to get baked.

raide (être) *adj.* to be bombed • (lit.): to be stiff.

rétamé(e) (être) *adj.* to be looped • (lit.): to be re-silvered.

rond(e) (être) *adj.* to be drunk • (lit.): to be round.

rond(e) comme une queue de pelle (être) *exp.* to be bombed off one's rocker • (lit.): to be round (drunk as a shovel handle).

salir le nez (se) *exp.* to get drunk • (lit.): to get one's nose dirty.

soiffard(e) *n.* one who is always thirsty for a drink.
> **NOTE:** This is from the masculine noun *soif* meaning "thirst."

soûl(e) (être) *adj.* (pronounced *soo / sool*) • (lit.): to be gorged.

soûl(e) comme trente-six-mille hommes (être) *exp.* to be dead drunk • (lit.): to be gorged (drunk) as 36,000 men.

soûl(e) comme une bourrique (être) *exp.* to be dead drunk • (lit.): to be gorged (drunk) as a donkey.

soûlard(e) *n.* drunkard.

soûlographie *f.* drunken state.

soûlot *m.* drunkard.

soûler (se) *v.* to get drunk • (lit.): to gorge oneself (with booze).
> **NOTE:** **soûler la gueule (se)** *exp.* to get roaring drunk • (lit.): to get one's mouth drunk • **gueule** *f.* derogatory for "mouth" when applied to a person since the literal translation is "the mouth of an animal."

sous la table (être) *exp.* to be dead drunk • (lit.): to be under the table.

teinté(e) (être) *adj.* to be "buzzed" • (lit.): to be tinted.

vent dans les voiles (avoir du) *exp.* to be slightly drunk • (lit.): to have wind in one's sails.

verre dans le nez (avoir un) *exp.* • (lit.): to have a glass in one's nose.

oreilles

example: Ce bébé a de grandes **esgourdes** et une petite tête!

translation: That baby has big **ears** and a little head!

as spoken: C'bébé, il a d'grandes **esgourdes** et une petite tête!

cliquettes *f.pl.*

écoutilles *f.pl.* "listeners."

> **NOTE:** This comes from the verb *écouter* meaning "to listen."

esgourdes *f.pl.*

> **NOTE:** **esgourder** *v.* to listen.

feuilles *f.pl.* • (lit.): leaves.

feuilles de chou *f.pl.* large ears • (lit.): cabbage leaves.

portugaises *f.pl.* • (lit.): Portuguese oysters.

voiles *f.pl.* large ears • (lit.): sails.

EASY

facile

example: Ne t'inquiète pas. Ce travail n'est pas du tout difficile. Au contraire! **C'est bête comme chou**!

translation: Don't worry. This work isn't hard at all. On the contrary! **It's a breeze**!

as spoken: T'inquiète pas. C'travail, il est pas du tout difficile. Au contraire! **C'est bête comme chou**!

---

aller comme sur des roulettes *exp.* to work out smoothly • (lit.): to go as if on wheels.

bête comme chou (c'est) *exp.* it's easy as pie • (lit.): it's silly as cabbage.

bonne franquette (à la) *exp.* simply, without fuss.

> example: Nous allons dîner **à la bonne franquette** ce soir.

translation: We're going to eat **without fuss** tonight.

as spoken: On va dîner **à la bonne franquette** c'soir.

ça passe comme une lettre à la poste *exp.* said of something that is easy to do • (lit.): it goes through (as easily) as a letter to the post office.

c'est pas sorcier *exp.* • (lit.): there is no wizardry in that.

c'est pas la mer à boire *exp.* (very popular) • (lit.): it's not like drinking the ocean.

couru d'avance (c'est) *exp.* it's as good as done • (lit.): it's already run.

dans le sac (c'est) *exp.* • (lit.): it's in the bag.

doigts dans le nez (les) *exp.* easily • (lit.): the fingers in the nose.

> example: Il peut le faire **les doigts dans le nez**.

translation: He can do it **as easy as pie**. • (lit.): the fingers in the nose.

as spoken: Y peut l'faire **les doigts dans l'nez**.

du beurre (c'est) *exp.* • (lit.): it's butter.

du billard (c'est) *exp.* said of something that goes along as smooth as silk (or more literally, that which rolls along a smoothly as a billiard ball).

du fromage (c'est) *exp.* • (lit.): it's cheese.

du velours (c'est comme) *exp.* • (lit.): it's velvet.

fastoche (être) *adj.* a slang variation of *facile* meaning "easy."

gâteau (c'est du) *exp.* • (lit.): it's cake.

les mains dans la poche *exp.* easily • (lit.): the hands in the pocket.

example: Tu pourras le faire **les mains dans la poche**.

translation: You'll be able to do it **with your eyes closed**.

as spoken: Tu pourras l'faire **les mains dans la poche**.

sans autre forme de procès *exp.* without further ceremony, without further ado • (lit.): without further process.

sans faire ni une ni deux *exp.* easily, without ceremony • (lit.): without doing either one nor two.

simple comme bonjour (c'est) *exp.* • (lit.): simple as good day.

sucre (c'est du) *exp.* • (lit.): it's sugar.

sur une jambe (se faire) *exp.* said of something easy to do • (lit.): to happen on one leg.

EAT (TO)

manger

example: J'ai **bouffé** chez Patricia ce soir. Sa mère est une excellente cuisinière!

translation: I **ate** at Patricia's house tonight. Her mother is an excellent cook!

as spoken: J'ai **bouffé** chez Patricia ce soir. Sa mère est une excellente cuisinière!

SEE: FOOD - *p. 239.*

---

bâfrer *v.* to eat a lot, to pig out.

becqueter *v.* • (lit.): (of birds) to peck at something.

bombance (faire) *v.* to have a blow-out of a meal, to pig out.

bon coup de fourchette (avoir un) *exp.* to have a hearty appetite • (lit.): to have a good touch" of the fork.

bouffer *v.* (extremely popular).
NOTE: **bouffer** literally means "to bolt down food" but is now commonly used to mean "to eat" in general.

bouffer à s'en faire crever la peau du ventre *exp.* to overeat • (lit.): to eat to the point of bursting the skin of the stomach.

boulotter *v.* to eat.
NOTE: **boulot(te)** *adj.* fat.

bourrer (se) *v.* • (lit.): to stuff oneself (with food).

boustifailler *v.* to eat or eat a lot.
NOTE: **boustifaille** *f.* food, grub.

briffer *v.* to eat.
NOTE: **briffe** *f.* food, grub.

caler les amygdales (se) *exp.* (pronounced: *amidale*) • (lit.): to steady one's tonsils (by eating).

caler les badigoinces (se) *exp.* • (lit.): to steady one's lips (by eat).
NOTE: **badigoinces** *f.pl.* slang for "lips."

caler les joues (se) *exp.* • (lit.): to steady one's cheeks (by eating).

caler l'estomac (se) *exp.* (pronounced: *estoma*) • (lit.): to steady one's stomach (by eating).

casser la croûte *exp.* to break bread • (lit.): to break crust.

casser la graine *exp.* to break bread • (lit.): to break grain.

coller plein la lampe (s'en) *exp.* to have a huge meal • (lit.): to stick lots of it (food) to the stomach.

> **NOTE: lampe** *f.* stomach • (lit.): lamp.

> **VARIATION: mettre plein la lampe (s'en)** *exp.*

croquer *v.* • (lit.): to crunch.

croûter *v.* to snack, to break bread or "crust."

> **NOTE:** This comes from the feminine noun *croûte* meaning "crust."

empiffrer (s') *v.* • (lit.): to cram, stuff (with food).

festin *m.* delicious meal of high elegance, feast.

festoyer *v.* to feast or to have a *festin*.

fourrer jusque là (s'en) *exp.* to eat to one's capacity • (lit.): to stuff oneself with it (food) up to there.

gaver (se) *v.* • (lit.): to stuff or force feed.

goberger (se) *v.* to feast.

godailler *v.* to gormandize, to feast.

goinfrer (se) *v.* to guzzle, to gorge.

> **NOTE: goinfre** *m.* one who overeats, "a porker."

grignoter *v.* to nibble at one's food.

gueuletonner *v.* to feast, to pig out.

> **NOTE: gueuleton** *m.* a huge meal.

manger sur le pouce *exp.* to grab a bite on the run • (lit.): to eat on the thumb.

mettre plein la panse (s'en) *exp.* • (lit.): to fill up the stomach with it (food).

> **NOTE: panse** *f.* stomach.

mettre une ventrée (s'en) *exp.* to eat a lot, to pig out.

> **NOTE: ventrée** *f.* belly full (from the masculine noun *ventre* meaning "belly").

picorer *v.* to pick at one's food • (lit.): (of birds) to scratch about for food.

pignocher *v.* • (lit.): to pick at one's food.

régaler (se) *v.* to enjoy greatly • (lit.): to feast, to have a treat.

ripaille (faire) *v.* to feast, to pig out.

ripailler *v.* to feast, to pig out.

ronger *v.* • (lit.): to nibble, gnaw.

taper la cloche (se) *exp.* to eat well • (lit.): to make one's bell ring (with joy from eating).

tortorer *v.* to eat.

> **NOTE: tortore** *f.* food, grub.

ENERGETIC (TO BE)

énergique (être)

example: Après avoir fait un somme pendant deux heures, je **pète le feu**!

translation: After napping for two hours, I'm **rarin' to go**!

as spoken: Après avoir fait un somme pendant deux heures, j'**pète le feu**!

---

allant (avoir de l') *exp.* to have plenty of get-up-and-go • (lit.): to have "go."

attaque (être d') *exp.* to have plenty of get-up-and-go • (lit.): to be (full) of attack.

bougeotte (avoir la) *exp.* to be fidgety • (lit.): to have the "budges."

> **NOTE:** This comes from the verb *bouger* meaning "to move or budge."

cracher le feu *exp.* to be very energetic • (lit.): to spit fire.

péter le feu *exp.* to be very energetic • (lit.): to fart fire.

dégourdi(e) (être) *adj.* to be wide awake • (lit.): to be revived or "un-numbed."

dégourdir (se) *v.* to become energetic • (lit.): to become revived or "un-numbed."

sang dans les veines (avoir du) *exp.* • (lit.): to have blood in the veins.

vif argent dans ses veines (avoir du) *exp.* • (lit.): to have quicksilver in one's veins.

EXAGGERATE (TO)

exagérer

example: Mais qu'est-ce que tu me racontes?! Tu **cherres dans les bégonias**, non?

translation: What are you talking about?! You're **exaggerating**, aren't you?

as spoken: Mais qu'est-c'que tu m'racontes?! Tu **cherres dans les bégonias**, non?

---

aller fort *v.* • (lit.): to go strongly.

aller mal *v.* • (lit.): to go badly.

allez! *exclam.* stop exaggerating! come off it!

> **NOTE:** Although *allez* is commonly used as the second person plural of the verb *aller*, meaning "to go," it may also be used in this context when speaking to only *one* person, formal or informal.

attiger *v.*

char *m.* exaggeration (heard as: *Arrête ton char!*; Stop exaggerating!)

> **NOTE:** This noun comes from the slang verb *charrier* meaning "to exaggerate."

charrier *v.* to get carried away in telling a story • (lit.): to cart, carry, transport.

cherrer *v.* to exaggerate.

cherrer dans les bégonias *exp.* • (lit.): to exaggerate in the begonias.

EYES

yeux

example: Nancy et David sont jumeaux, mais David a des **mirettes** brunes et Nancy en a des vertes!

translation: Nancy and David are twins, but David has brown **eyes** and Nancy has green ones!

as spoken: Nancy et David, y sont jumeaux, mais David, il a des **mirettes** brunes et Nancy, elle en a des vertes!

---

carreaux *m.pl.* • (lit.): small squares.

châsses *m.pl.* • (lit.): frame (of spectacles).

globes *m.pl.* globes.

lanternes *f.pl.* • (lit.): globes.

mirettes *f.pl.*

NOTE: **mirer** *v.* to see.

quinquet *m.pl.*

NOTE: This term is most often used with *ouvrir* (to open) and *fermer* (to close).

example: Je suis fatigué. Je crois qu'il est temps de **fermer les quinquets**.

translation: I'm tired. I think it's time to **close my eyes**.

as spoken: J'suis fatigué. J'crois qu'il est temps d'**fermer les quinquets**.

FACE

visage

example: Qui est cette dame-là? Je ne reconnais pas sa **tronche**.

translation: Who's that woman? I don't recognize her **face**.

as spoken: C'est qui c'te dame-là? J'reconnais pas sa **tronche**.

NOTE: Many of the slang synonyms for "face" can also be used to mean "head" as well. In fact, even the French word *tête* is commonly used to mean "head" or "face" • *Je ne reconnais pas sa tête;* I don't recognize his / her face.

---

balle *f.* face, head • (lit.): ball.

bille *f.* face, head • (lit.): small ball.

binette *f.* face, head • (lit.): hoe.

bobine *f.* face, head • (lit.): bobbin, spool, reel.

bouille *f.* face, head.

bouillotte *f.* face, head • (lit.): hot-water bottle.

boule *f.* face, head • (lit.): ball.

burette *f.* face, head • (lit.): oil-can.

fiole *f.* face, head • (lit.): phial, flask.

frimousse *f.* nice, roguish little face.

gaufre *f.* face, head • (lit.): waffle.

NOTE: **sucrer le gaufre (se)** *v.* to put on make-up • (lit.): to sugar the waffle.

gueule *f.* (derogatory) head, mouth, face • (lit.): mouth of an animal.

hure *f.* face, head • (lit.): head (of boar, pig).

margoulette *f.* "mug," "kisser."

poire *f.* face, head • (lit.): pear.

porte-pipe *m.* • (lit.): pipe-rack.

portrait *m.* face • (lit.): portrait.

trogne *f.* bloated face (of a drinker).

trombine *f.* funny face or head.

trompette *f.* face, head
• (lit.): trumpet.

tronche *f.* face, head • (lit.): log.

FALL (TO)

tomber

example: J'ai failli **me casser la gueule** en descendant l'escalier!

translation: I almost **broke my neck** coming down the stairs!

as spoken: J'ai failli **m'casser la gueule** en descendant l'escalier!

---

casser son verre de montre
exp. • (lit.): to break the face of one's watch.

chuter *v.* to fall hard • (lit.): to chute.

étaler (s') *v.* • (lit.): to display oneself, to spread, stretch, sprawl oneself out (in an armchair, etc.).

fiche la gueule par terre (se)
exp. to hit one's face on the ground.
NOTE: **gueule** *f.* derogatory for "mouth" or "face" since its literal translation is the "mouth of an animal."

plaquer par terre (se) *exp.*
• (lit.): to flatten oneself out on the ground.

ramasser une bûche *exp.*
• (lit.): to pick up a log.

ramasser une pelle *exp.*
• (lit.): to pick up a shovel.

viander (se) *v.* • (lit.): to spread out one's "meat" (in a fall), to "meet" oneself (the English equivalent may be "to skin oneself").
NOTE: This is from the feminine noun *viande* meaning "meat."

FAST (TO)

jeûner

example: J'ai trop mangé hier soir. Donc, demain je vais **me serrer la ceinture**.

translation: I ate too much last night. So tomorrow I'm **going on a fast**.

as spoken: J'ai trop mangé hier soir. Donc, demain j'vais **m'serrer la ceinture**.
SEE: **EAT (TO)** *p. 230.*

---

ballon (faire) *m.* • (lit.): to do the balloon.
NOTE: **ballon** *m.* stomach
• (lit.): balloon.

becqueter / bouffer des briques *exp.* • (lit.): to eat bricks.
NOTE: **becqueter / bouffer** *v.* (extremely popular verbs) to eat.

becqueter / bouffer des clarinettes *exp.* • (lit.): to eat tools.
NOTE: **clarinettes** *f.pl.* tools in general.

brosser le ventre (se) *exp.*
- (lit.): to brush one's stomach.

manger avec les chevaux de bois . • (lit.): to eat with the wooden horses.

serrer la ceinture (se) *exp.*
- (lit.): to tighten the belt.

FED UP (TO BE)

assez (en avoir)

example: J'**en ai marre de** mon patron! Un de ces jours, je vais finir par donner ma démission!

translation: I'm **fed up with** my boss. One of these days, I'm going to end up giving my notice!

as spoken: J'**en ai marre d'**mon patron! Un d'ces jours, j'vais finir par donner ma démission!

---

basta (en avoir) *exp.* • (lit.): to have had enough.

example: J'**en ai basta**!

translation: I'**ve had it**!

as spoken: [no change]

NOTE: **basta** *adv.* (borrowed from Italian) enough.

ALSO: **C'est basta!** or **Basta!** *exclam.* That's enough! Enough!

classe (en avoir) *exp.*

example: J'**en ai classe**!

translation: I'**ve had it**!

as spoken: [no change]

ALSO: **C'est classe!** *exclam.* That's enough!

donné (en avoir) *exp.* (very popular).

VARIATION: **donné (avoir)** *exp.*

example: J'ai **donné** aujourd'hui!

translation: I'm **fed up** today!

as spoken: [no change]

marre (en avoir) *exp.* (extremely popular).

ALSO: **C'est marre!** *exclam.* That's enough!

par-dessus la tête (en avoir) *exp.* • (lit.): to have had it about the head!

plein le dos (en avoir) *exp.* to have had a backful.

plein les bottes (en avoir) *exp.* • (lit.): to have had a bootful.

ras le bol (en avoir) *exp.*
- (lit.): to have had it to the rim of the bowl.

sa claque (en avoir) *exp.*

soupé (en avoir) *exp.* • (lit.): to have eaten some for dinner, "to have taken in all one can."

FEEL BLAH (TO)

sentir dans un état de faiblesse (se)

example: Je **ne suis pas dans mon assiette** ce matin. J'espère que je ne deviens pas malade.

translation: I **feel out of it** this morning. I hope I'm not getting sick.

as spoken: J'**suis pas dans mon assiette** c'matin. J'espère que j'deviens pas malade.

---

dans son assiette (ne pas être) *exp.* • (lit.): not to be in one's plate.

dans son train (ne pas être) *exp.* • (lit.): to be out of pace.

flagada (être) *adj.* to feel "blah."

raplapla (se sentir) *adj.* to feel "blah."

tout chose (se sentir) *adj.* to feel "out of it."

vaseux (se sentir) *adj.* • (lit.): to feel muddy.

FEEL

pieds

example: J'ai mal aux **arpions**. Je pense que j'ai trop marché aujourd'hui.

translation: My **feet** hurt. I think I walked too much today.

as spoken: J'ai mal aux **arpions**. J'pense que j'ai trop marché aujourd'hui.

---

argasses *f.pl.*

arpions *m.pl.*
> **NOTE:** **arpionner** *v.* to walk, to "hoof it."

artous *m.pl.*

bateaux *m.pl.* large feet • (lit.): boats.

nougats *m.pl.* • (lit.): nuggets.

panards *m.pl.*

patins *m.pl.* • (lit.): skates.

paturons *m.pl.* • (lit.): pastern (of horse).

pinceaux *m.pl.* • (lit.): paint brush.

pingots *m.pl.* abbreviated form of *pingouins* meaning "penguins."

radis *m.pl.* toes • (lit.): radishes.

raquettes *f.pl.* • (lit.): rackets.

ripatons *m.pl.*
> **NOTE:** **ripatonner** *v.* to talk, to "hoof it."

FIGHT (TO)

battre (se)

example: Je ne veux pas aller dîner chez mes cousins. Ils ne font que **se bagarrer** tout le temps.

translation: I don't want to have dinner at my cousins' house. They do nothing but **fight** all the time.

as spoken: Je veux pas aller dîner chez mes cousins. Y font que **s'bagarrer** tout l'temps.

---

accrocher avec quelqu'un (s') *v.* • (lit.): to hook oneself with someone (in a fight).

avoir des mots avec quelqu'un *exp.* • (lit.): to have words with someone.

bagarrer (se) *v.* to fight, to scuffle, to brawl.
> **NOTE:** **bagarre** *f.* fight, scuffle, brawl.

baroud *m.* (pronounced: *baroude*) originally military slang for "fight."

battre à plate(s) couture(s) *exp.* to beat someone to a pulp • (lit.): to beat to a flat fashion.

battre quelqu'un comme plâtre *exp.* to beat someone to a pulp • (lit.): to beat someone into plaster.

bigorner (se) *v.* to fight.

NOTE: **bigorne** *f.* battle.

bisbille avec quelqu'un (être en) *exp.* to be in a dumb little quarrel with someone.

NOTE: **bisbille** *f.* bickering.

casser la gueule à quelqu'un *exp.* to punch someone's lights out • (lit.): to break someone's face.

NOTE: **gueule** *f.* derogatory for "mouth" since its literal translation is "the mouth of an animal."

chamailler (se) *v.* to fight loudly over stupid little things, to bicker, to squabble.

chercher à quelqu'un des poux dans la tête *exp.* to look for a fight, to nitpick • (lit.): to look for lice in someone's head.

chercher chicane à quelqu'un *exp.* to look for a fight.

NOTE: **chicane** *f.* quibbling, quarreling.

chercher la petite bête *exp.* to be overcritical, to nitpick • (lit.): to look for the little beast.

chercher noise à quelqu'un *exp.* to look for a fight.

NOTE: **noise** *f.* quibbling, quarreling.

chercher quelqu'un *exp.* to provoke someone, to look for a fight • (lit.): to look for someone.

chercher querelle à quelqu'un *exp.* to look for a fight • (lit.): to look for a quarrel with someone.

chicaner *v.* to fight.

NOTE: **chicane** *f.* quibbling, quarreling.

colleter (se) *v.* to grapple, scuffle with someone.

coltiner (se) *v.* to fight.

example: Je me suis **coltiné** avec un mec dans le métro.

translation: I **had it out** with a guy in the subway.

as spoken: Je m'suis **coltiné** avec un mec dans l'métro.

ALSO: **coltiner (se)** *v.* to do, to carry out.

example: Je ne peux pas **me coltiner** seul tout ce travail.

translation: I can't **carry out** all this work by myself.

as spoken: J'peux pas **m'coltiner** seul tout c'travail.

corrida *f.* free-for-all fight.

coup de chien *m.* free-for-all fight • (lit.): dog fight.

échauffourrée *f.* free-for-all fight, scuffle.

NOTE: This comes from the verb *chauffer* meaning "to heat up."

fiche sur la gueule (se) *exp.* to beat each other up • (lit.): to throw each other on the mouth.

NOTE -1: **fiche** *v.* to throw, to do.

NOTE -2: **gueule** *f.* derogatory for "mouth" since its literal translation is "the mouth of an animal."

grabuge *m.* big fight, squabbling.

example: Il y aura du **grabuge**!

translation: There's going to be a **fight**!

as spoken: Y aura du **grabuge**!

manger le nez (se) *exp.* to fight
• (lit.): to each other's nose.

NOTE -1: This humorous expression describes two people yelling at each other so closely that they look as if they are eating each other's noses.

NOTE -2: This expression can be used with any synonym for *manger*.

SEE: **EAT (TO)** *p. 230.*

mettre quelqu'un en capilotade *exp.* to knock the stuffing out of someone.

NOTE: **capilotade** *f.* jelly.

peigner (se) *v.* humorous for "to fight • (lit.): to comb each other's hair.

example: Il **se peignent** comme d'habitude.

translation: They're **going at it** as usual.

as spoken: Y **s'peignent** comme d'habitude.

piler *v.* to beat • (lit.): to pound, crush.

example: Notre équipe s'est fait **piler**!

translation: Our team got **creamed**!

as spoken: Notre équipe, è s'est fait **piler**!

rêver que plaies et bosses (ne) *exp.* said of a person who is always ready for a fight • (lit.): to dream only of sores and bruises.

rififi *m.* free-for-all fight, scuffle.

tabasser *v.* to beat up.

ALSO: **passer quelqu'un à tabac** *exp.* to beat someone up • (lit.): to beat someone as one would beat tobacco leaves.

triquer *v.* to beat up with a stick.

NOTE: This comes from the feminine noun *trique* meaning "a big club."

FIRE SOMEONE (TO)

mettre quelqu'un à la porte

example: Le patron vient de **m'envoyer balader**!

translation: The boss just **fired me**!

as spoken: Le patron, y vient d'**m'envoyer balader**!

---

aller à la pêche *exp.* to be jobless
• (lit.): to go fishing.

bain (envoyer au) *m.* • (lit.): to send to the bath.

balancer *v.* to throw, chuck
• (lit.): to balance.

balanstiquer *v.* slang variant of: *balancer.*

baller (envoyer) *v.* • (lit.): to send someone rolling like a ball.

débarquer *v.* • (lit.): to discharge.

déboulonner *v.* to take away someone's job or *boulot.*

NOTE: **boulot** *m.* job.

dégommer *v.* • (lit.): to ungum or unstick someone (from his / her job).

flanquer quelqu'un à la porte *exp.* • (lit.): to throw at the door.

> **NOTE:** **flanquer** *v.* to throw, to chuck.

pelotes (envoyer aux) *exp.* • (lit.): to send someone rolling like a ball.

> **NOTE:** **pelote** *f.* ball (used in the game of *pelotes*).

sacquer quelqu'un *v.* • (lit.): to sack someone.

venir aux coups (en) *exp.* • (lit.): to come to blows over something.

venir aux mains (en) *exp.* • (lit.): to come to hands (or fisticuffs) over something.

vider quelqu'un *v.* • (lit.): to empty someone.

virer quelqu'un *v.* • (lit.): to turn someone around (in the opposite direction of their work place).

FLATTER (TO)

flatter

example: Chaque fois que Gisèle veut se faire aumenter, elle **passe les mains dans les cheveux** du patron.

translation: Every time Gisele wants to get a raise, she **kisses up to** the boss.

as spoken: Chaque fois qu'Gisèle, è veut s'faire aumenter, è **passe les mains dans les ch'veux** du patron.

caresser dans le sens du poil *exp.* to butter someone up • (lit.): to caress someone in the direction of his / her hair.

musicien *m.* flatterer, softsoap artist • (lit.): musician.

passer de la pommade à quelqu'un *exp.* to flatter someone, to butter someone up • (lit.): to give ointment to someone.

passer la main dans les cheveux *exp.* • (lit.): to give someone the hand in the air.

FOOD

nourriture

example: Tu as vu la **bouffe** que Suzanne a préparé pour le dîner?

translation: Did you see the **food** Suzanne made for dinner?

as spoken: T'as vu la **bouffe** que Suzanne a préparé pour l'dîner?

> **SEE:** **EAT (TO)** *p. 230.*

---

bectance *f.* "grub."

> **NOTE:** **becqueter** *v.* to eat, to chow down • (lit.): (of birds) to peck.

bouffe *f.* "grub."

bouffer *v.* to eat, to chow down.

bouffetance *f.* slang variant of: *bouffe.*

boustifaille *f.* slang variant of: *bouffe.*

> **NOTE:** **boustifailler** *v.* to eat, to chow down.

briffe *f.* "grub."

> **NOTE:** **briffer** *v.* to eat, to chow down.

croûte *f.* • (lit.): crust.

> **NOTE:** **croûter** *v.* to eat, to break bread (or crust in this case).

> **ALSO:** **casser la croûte** *exp.* to break bread.

frichti *m.* "grub."

fricot *m.* "grub."

mangeaille *f.* "eats."

> **NOTE:** This comes from the verb *manger* meaning "to eat."

ragougnasse *f.* bad food.

> **NOTE:** This comes from the masculine noun *ragoût* meaning "stew."

tambouille *f.* bad food.

> **NOTE:** Originally this was used only as military slang.

tortore *f.* food in general.

> **NOTE:** **tortorer** *v.* to eat.

FUNNY

amusant

example: Ce comédien est très **marrant**!

translation: That comedian is very **funny**!

as spoken: Ce comédien, il est très **marrant**!

SEE: **LAUGH (TO)** *p. 259.*

---

bidonnant(e) *adj.* that which causes the *bidon* to move with laughter.

> **NOTE -1:** **bidon** *m.* stomach, belly.

> **NOTE -2:** **bidonner (se)** *v.* to belly laugh.

boyautant(e) *adj.* that which causes the *boyaux* to move with laughter, a real gut-splitter.

> **NOTE -1:** **boyaux** *m.pl.* guts.

> **NOTE -2:** **boyauter (se)** *v.* to laugh.

désopilant(e) *adj.* screamingly funny.

> **NOTE:** **désopiler (se)** *v.* to shake with laughter.

gondolant(e) *adj.* excruciatingly funny.

> **NOTE:** **gondoler (se)** *v.* to shake with laughter • (lit.): to warp, to buckle up (with laughter).

marrant(e) *adj.* (extremely popular) very funny, strange.

> **NOTE -1:** This is used in the same way as the English word "funny." Its definition is twofold, meaning "that which makes one laugh" and "that which is odd or strange."

> **NOTE -2:** **marrer (se)** *v.* to laugh hard.

poilant(e) *adj.* very funny.

> **NOTE -1:** This could be loosely translated as "that which causes one's hair (*poil*) to shake with laughter."

> **NOTE -2:** **poiler (se)** *v.* to laugh hard.

pouffant(e) *adj.* extremely funny.

> **NOTE -1:** This comes from the verb *pouffer* meaning "to puff up."

> **NOTE -2:** **pouffer (se)** *v.* to laugh hard.

rigolard(e) *adj.* happy, light-hearted, funny.

> **NOTE:** **rigoler** *v.* to laugh.

rigolboche *adj.* a slang variant of: *rigolard(e)*.

rigolo(te) *adj.* a slang variant of **rigolard(e)**.

roulant(e) *adj.* extremely funny.

> **NOTE:** A loose literal translation of this adjective might be "that which causes one to roll forward *(rouler)* from laughter."

> **NOTE: rouler (se)** *v.* to laugh hard.

tirebouchonnant(e) *adj.* extremely funny.

> **NOTE -1:** A loose literal translation of this might be "that which causes one to rise up and down like a corkscrew *(un tire-bouchon)* as one takes in air repeatedly to laugh."

> **NOTE -2: tirebouchonner (se)** *v.* to laugh hard.

tordant(e) (être) *adj.* excruciatingly funny • (lit.): to be twisting (said of something that is so funny it causes one to twist with laughter).

bavardage

example: Ce bébe est adorable mais je ne comprends pas sa **jactance**.

translation: This baby is adorable but I don't understand his **gibberish**.

as spoken: C'bébe, il est adorable mais j'comprends pas sa **jactance**.

baragouin *m.*

> **NOTE: baragouiner** *v.* to jabber.

bla-bla-bla *m.* constant jabber.

cancan *m.*

> **NOTE -1:** This is usually seen as *colporter des cancans sur quelqu'un* meaning "to spread rumors about someone."

> **NOTE -2: cancanier, ière** *n.* one who spreads rumors or gossip, a gossip.

causette *f.* little chat • *faire la causette avec quelqu'un;* to have a little chat with someone.

> **NOTE: causer** *v.* to chat.

charabia *m.* jargon, gibberish.

et patati et patata *exp.* yackety-yack.

> **NOTE:** This is an onomatopoeia for the sound one makes when jabbering on and on.

example: **Et patati, et pata**! Ils n'arrêtent jamais de parler!

translation: **Yackety-yack**! They never stop talking!

as spoken: **Et patati, et pata**! Y z'arrêtent jamais d'parler!

jacasserie *f.*

> **NOTE: jacasser** *v.* to talk gibberish.

papotage *m.* idle talk, chatter.

example: Il passe son temps en **papotages**.

translation: He spends his time **gabbing**.

as spoken: Y passe son temps en **papotages**.

> **NOTE: papoter** *v.* to talk gibberish.

parlote f. little chat • *faire la parlote avec un voisin;* to have a little chat with a neighbor.

NOTE: same as: *causette.*

potin m. piece of gossip / **potins** *m.pl.* gossip.

NOTE: faire des potins sur quelqu'un *exp.* to tell little rumors about someone.

racontars *m.pl.* rumors.

NOTE: This is from the verb *raconter* meaning "to tell, to recount."

ragot m. same as: *potin.*

verbiage m. nothing but talk, gibberish, hogwash.

example: Tu vas écouter ce **verbiage**?

translation: You're going to listen to that **bunk**?

as spoken: Tu vas écouter c'**verbiage**?

GIFTED FOR (TO BE)

avoir le don pour

example: Paul est musician excellent. Il faut dire qu'il a **la bosse du** piano.

translation: Paul is an excellent musician. You have to admit that he has a **knack for** piano.

as spoken: Paul, il est musicien excellent. Faut dire qu'il a **la bosse du** piano.

---

bosse de quelque chose (avoir la) *exp.* • (lit.): to have the bump for something.

example: Grégoire **a la bosse** du piano.

translation: Greg **has a knack** for piano.

as spoken: Grégoire, il **a la bosse** du piano.

NOTE: This comes from phrenology: the study of the conformation of the skull based on the belief that it is indicative of mental and physical abilities.

chic pour quelque chose (avoir le) *exp.* • (lit.): to have the skill (or knack) for something.

truc pour quelque chose (avoir le) *exp.* • (lit.): to have the "thing" for something.

GIRL / WOMAN

fille / femme

example: Elle est belle, cette **nana**. Je me demande si elle est mannequin.

translation: That **girl** is beautiful. I wonder if she's a model.

as spoken: Elle est belle, c'te **nana**. Je m'demande si elle est mannequin.

NOTE: Many of the following synonyms for "girl" are derogatory. Pay special attention to their explanations to get a good feeling for their weight and connotation.

---

beau brin de fille m. good-looking girl • (lit.): nice little bit of girl.

beau châssis m. well-built girl • (lit.): nice chassis.

bécasse f. 1. girl • 2. a gossip.

bergère *f.* • (lit.): shepherdess.

bêtasse *f.* dumb girl.

> **NOTE:** **bête** *adj.* dumb, stupid.

bien balancée *adj.* said of a girl with a good figure • (lit.): well-tossed.

bien faite de sa personne *exp.* said of a good-looking girl • (lit.): well-made of her person.

bien fichue *adj.* said of a girl with a good body • (lit.): well-made.

> **NOTE:** Oddly enough, *fiche* is a verb (although it does not have a traditional ending) and is conjugated as a regular "er" verb: *je fiche, tu fiches, il / elle fiche, nous fichons, vous fichez, ils fichent.* However, its past participle is that of a regular "re" verb: *fichu(e).*

bien roulée *adj.* said of a girl with a good body • (lit.): well-rolled (together).

bonne femme *f.* (extremely popular) woman in general • (lit.): good woman.

boude *m.* a shorted version of *boudin,* meaning "blood sausage," used to describe a fat woman.

boudin *m.* heavy and unattractive woman • (lit.): blood sausage.

bougresse *f.* (old-fashioned yet used ironically) country woman.

carrossée (être bien) to have a beautiful body.

> **SEE:** **carrosserie**, *(next entry).*

carrosserie *f.* body (used as: *Quelle carrosserie!;* What a beautiful body!) • (lit.): body of a car.

cateau *f.* girl of easy morals, loose woman or girl.

catin *f.* same as: *cateau.*

cato *f.* same as: *cateau.*

chipie *f.* a shrew, often used in reference to an ill-tempered little girl.

coureuse *f.* girl of loose morals who gets around • (lit.): runner.

créature *f.* • (lit.): creature.

dévoreuse *f.* girl who is thirsty for love, who needs to devour as much love as she can.

> **NOTE:** **dévorer** *v.* to devour.

dondon *f.* fat woman or girl.

donzelle *f.* a pretentious, showy girl.

dragon *m.* shrew • (lit.): dragon.

fatma *f.* (from Arabic) commonly used to mean "wife" as well.

fatmuche *f.* a slang variation of: *fatma.*

> **SEE:** **fatma**, *(previous entry).*

femelle *f.* "broad" • (lit.): female.

femme à passions *f.* loose woman or girl • (lit.): woman of passion(s).

fendue *f.* (very derogatory) • (lit.): slit.

frangine *f.* • (lit.): sister.

> **NOTE:** This is a popular slang term for "sister" or "girl."

garce *f.* bitch.

génisse *f.*

gigolette *f.* girl of easy morals, loose girl.

> **NOTE:** This is the feminine form of: *gigolo.*

gonzesse *f.* (extremely popular) woman or girl, "chick."

gourgandine *f.* girl of easy morals, loose girl.

grande bringue *f.* tall and lanky woman • (lit.): big piece or bit.

grande perche *f.* tall and lanky woman • (lit.): big pole.

greluche *f.* "chick," pretentious girl.

grenouille *f.* girl of easy morals, loose girl • (lit.): frog.

grimbiche *f.* young girl.

harpie *f.* shrew.

laidasse *f.* ugly woman.

lamfé *f.* woman in general.

> **NOTE:** This is a *largonji* transformation of the feminine noun *femme* meaning "woman."
>
> **SEE:** *STREET FRENCH 2, Largonji -* p. 216.

lièvre *m.* • (lit.): hare.

mémé *f.* grandma.

ménesse *f.* woman, "broad."

meuf *f.* (very popular).

> **NOTE:** This is a *verlan* transformation of the feminine noun *femme* meaning "woman."
>
> **SEE:** *STREET FRENCH 2, Verlan -* p. 187.

moukère *f.* (from Arabic).

nana *f.* (extremely popular) "chick."

nénesse *f.*

nénette *f.*

paillasse *f.* • (lit.): straw mattress.

paillasson *m.* • (lit.): door mat.

peau (de vache) *f.* bitch • (lit.): (cow) skin.

> **NOTE:** This can also be used as a disparaging insult for a man.

pépée *f.* • (lit.): doll.

> **NOTE:** This is child's language for *poupée* meaning "doll."

pétasse *f.* (derogatory).

pouffiasse *f.* (derogatory).

poule *f.* "chick," girlfriend • (lit.): hen.

poulette *f.* • (lit.): a young hen.

pouliche *f.* young girl • (lit.): filly.

poupée *f.* • (lit.): doll.

rombière *f.* a fat woman.

saucisson *m.* "blimp," heavy woman • (lit.): sausage.

sauteuse *f.* girl of loose morals.

> **NOTE: sauter** *v.* to jump sexually • (lit.): to jump.

souris *f.* • (lit.): mouse.

typesse *f.* girl.

> **NOTE: type** *m.* guy.

vache *f.* • (lit.): cow.

GIVE (TO)
donner

example: C'est le mien, ça! **File**-moi ça, tout de suite!

translation: That's mine! **Give** that to me right now!

as spoken: C'est l'mien, ça! **File**-ça moi, tout d'suite.

---

abouler *v.* • **1**. to bring • **2**. to give, to hand over.

example (1): **Aboule** ça ici!

translation: **Bring** that here!

as spoken: [no change]

example (2): **Aboule** ton argent!

translation: **Hand over** your money!

as spoken: [no change]

fendre (se) *v.* to give with much pain • (lit.): to split, crack, cut.

example: Michel **s'est fendu** de mille francs.

translation: Michel **reluctantly parted** with a thousand francs.

as spoken: Michel, y **s'est fendu** d'mille francs.

filer *v.* to give, to hand over.

flanquer *v.* • (lit.): to throw, chuck.

refiler *v.* to give someone something that is no longer wanted.

example (1): Son ami m'a **refilé** un faux billet!

translation: His friend **passed off** a fake bill on me!

as spoken: Son ami, y m'a **r'filé** un faux billet!

example (2): Nicholas m'a **refilé** sa vieille chemise.

translation: Nicholas **handed me down** his old shirt.

as spoken: Nicholas, y m'a **r'filé** sa vieille ch'mise.

GOOF UP (TO)

faire une faute

example: Je lui ai donné la simple tâche d'ajouter quelques chiffres, mais il a tout **bousillé**!

translation: I have him the simple task of adding a few numbers, but he totally **blew it**!

as spoken: J'lui ai donné la simple tâche d'ajouter quèque chiffres, mais il a tout **bousillé**!

---

boulette (faire une) *exp.* to make a blunder.

faire quelque chose à la noix de coco *exp.* to bungle something, to goof up • (lit.): to do something like a coconut.

fiche dedans (se) *v.* to make a mistake • (lit.): to throw oneself inside.

NOTE: fiche *v.* (a variation of *ficher*) • **1.** to give • **2.** to put • **3.** to do.

gaffe (faire une) *exp.* to make a big mistake.

NOTE: faire gaffe *exp.* to be careful.

example: **Fais gaffe**! C'est chaud, ça!

translation: **Be careful**! That's hot!

as spoken: [no change]

gourer (se) *v.* to make a mistake.

pas de clerc (faire un) *exp.* (pronounced: *clair*) to make a blunder • (lit.): to make a clerk's step.

planter (se) *v.* to fail, to botch up.

example: Je **me suis planté** à l'examen.

translation: I **failed** the test.

as spoken: Je **m'suis planté** à l'exam.

rater *v.* • **1.** to goof up, to fail • **2.** to miss.

example (1): J'ai **raté** mon examen.

translation: I **blew** the test.

as spoken: J'ai **raté** mon exam.

example (2): J'ai **raté** mon bus.

translation: I **missed** my bus.

as spoken: [no change]

viander (se) *adj.* to fail, to botch up.

example: Je **me suis viandé** à l'examen.

translation: I **blew** the test.

as spoken: Je **m'suis viandé** à l'exam.

ALSO: **viander (se)** *v.* to fall • (lit.): to spread one's meat (on the ground during a fall).

GUY

individu

example: Tu connais ce **mec**? Je ne l'ai jamais vu avant!

translation: Do you know that **guy**? I've never seen him before!

as spoken: Tu connais c'**mec**? J'l'ai jamais vu avant!

---

bonhomme *m.* (extremely popular) guy.

bonne pâte *f.* "a good egg," a person with a good personality • (lit.): good dough.

NOTE: **pâte molle** *f.* a person with no personality, a boring person.

bougre *m.* (pejorative) • (lit.): country man.

chic type *m.* same as: *bonne pâte.*

client *m.* • (lit.): client.

coco *m.*

frangin *m.*

NOTE -1: This is a popular slang term for "brother" or "man."

NOTE -2: **frangine** *f.* sister.

gars *m.* (very popular) guy, "dude."

gugusse *m.* idiot.

gus *m.* (very popular).

guss(e) *m.*

Jules *m.* guy, boyfriend, "dude."

NOTE: **Julie** *f.* woman / girl, "chick."

Julot *m.* guy, "dude."

NOTE: This is a slang variation of: *Jules.*

loulou *m.*

loustic *m.*

mec *m.* (one of the most popular slang words for "guy").

mecqueton *m.* (also spelled *mecton*).

NOTE: This is a slang variation of: *mec.*

numéro *m.* • (lit.): number.

oiseau *m.* • (lit.): bird.

paroissien *m.* • (lit.): Parishioner.

piaf *m.* a small man • (lit.): Parisian sparrow.

pierrot *m.*

pistolet *m.* • (lit.): pistol.

tartempion *m.* also used to mean "so-and-so" or "what's-his-name."

type *m.* (very popular) guy, "dude."

zèbre *m.* guy, "dude."

ALSO: drôle de zèbre *m.* weirdo.

zig *m.* (also spelled *zigue*) guy, "dude."

zigomar(d) *m.*
NOTE: This is a slang variation of: *zig.*

zigoteau *m.*
NOTE: This is a slang variation of: *zig.*

zigoto *m.*
NOTE: This is a slang variation of: *zig.*

zouave *m.* • (lit.): a type of soldier (known for being very tough) in the Napoleonic army.

HANDS

mains

example: Tu peux me donner un coup de **pince**?

translation: Can you lend me a **hand**?

as spoken: Tu peux m'donner un coup d'**pince**?

---

cuillières *f.pl.* • (lit.): spoons.

louches *f.pl.* • (lit.): soup-ladles.

patoches *f.pl.* slang variant of: *pattes.*

pattes *f.pl.* • (lit.): paws.

pinces *f.pl.* • (lit.): pinchers.

pognes *f.pl.*
NOTE: This noun is commonly used in the expression *passer la pogne* meaning "to shake hands and make up."

example: Après leur dispute, ils ont **passé la pogne**.

translation: After their fight, **they made up**.

as spoken: Après leur dispute, y z'ont **passé la pogne**.

HEAD

tête

example: Cette musique est trop forte! Ça me donne **mal au caillou**!

translation: That music is too loud! It's giving me a **headache**!

as spoken: C'te musique, elle est trop forte! Ça m'donne **mal au caillou**!

NOTE: Many of the slang synonyms for "head" can also be used to mean "face" as well. In fact, even the French word *tête* is used to mean "head" or "face." • *Je ne reconnais pas sa tête;* I don't recognize his / her face.

---

balle *f.* head, face • (lit.): ball.

bille *f.* head, face • (lit.): small ball.

bobèche *f.* head, face • (lit.): socket (of candle stick).

bobéchon *m.* same as: *bobèche.*

bobine *f.* head, face • (lit.): bobbin.

bougie *f.* • (lit.): candle.

bouille *f.* head, face.

bouillotte *f.* head, face
  • (lit.): hot-water bottle.

boule *f.* head, face • (lit.): ball.

boussole *f.* • (lit.): compass.

bulbe *m.* • (lit.): bulb.

burette *f.* head, face • (lit.): oil-can.

cabèche *f.*

caboche *f.*

cafetière *f.* • (lit.): coffeepot.

caillou *m.* • (lit.): pebble.

carafe *f.* • (lit.): carafe.

carafon *m.* • (lit.): small carafe.

cassis *m.* (pronounced: *kassiss*)
  • (lit.): black currant.

cerise *f.* • (lit.): cherry.

chou *m.* • (lit.): cabbage.

ciboulot *m.*

cigare *m.* • (lit.): cigar.

citron *m.* • (lit.): lemon.

coco *m.*

dôme *m.* • (lit.): dome.

gaufre *f.* head, face • (lit.): waffle.
  NOTE: sucrer la gaufre (se)
  exp. to put on makeup • (lit.): to sugar the waffle.

gueule *f.* derogatory for head, mouth, or face • (lit.): mouth of an animal.

lampe *f.* • (lit.): lamp.

patate *f.* • (lit.): potato.

plafond *m.* • (lit.): ceiling.

poire *f.* • (lit.): pear.

pomme *f.* • (lit.): apple.

portrait *m.* head, face
  • (lit.): portrait.

timbre *m.* • (lit.): bell, gong (of clock).

tirelire *f.* • (lit.): piggy-bank.

tranche *f.* • (lit.): slice.

trompette *f.* head, face
  • (lit.): trumpet.

tronche *f.* head, face • (lit.): log.

HIT / HIT (TO)

coup / frapper

example: Quand je l'ai insulté, il m'est **rentré dans le lard**!

translation: When I insulted him, he **hit me**!

as spoken: Quand j'l'ai insulté, y m'est **rentré dans l'lard**!

---

beigne *f.* a blow to the face
  • (lit.): doughnut.

bourrade *f.* a blow, a thrust that one gives with the fist or elbow • *une bourrade amicale;* a friendly hit (on the shoulder).

calotte *f.* a hit • (lit.): skull cap, calotte.

calotter *v.* to hit (someone) on the head.

châtaigne *f.* a blow, a hit
  • (lit.): chestnut.

gifle *f.* a slap to the face • *flanquer une gifle à quelqu'un;* to slap someone in the face.
  NOTE: flanquer *v.* to throw.

gifler *v.* to slap in the face.

giroflée à cinq feuilles *f.* a slap in the face with a wide opened hand • (lit.): slap with five leaves.

gnon *m.* (pronounced as one syllable: *nion*) a blow, a punch, a dent in the car.

marron *m.* a blow, a punch • (lit.): chestnut.

mornifle *f.* a blow, a punch.

pain *m.* a blow, a punch • (lit.): bread.

example: Il lui a collé un **pain**.

translation: He **punched** him **out**.

as spoken: Y lui a collé un **pain**.

NOTE: coller *v.* to give, to throw • (lit.): to stick.

pêche *f.* a blow, a punch • (lit.): peach.

prune *f.* a blow, a punch • (lit.): plum.

NOTE: The term *"prune"* falls into the category of *"faux amis"* ("false friends") referring to the many words which resemble English words but have different definitions. For example: *prune* = plum; *pruneau* = prune.

ramponneau *m.* a hit, a punch • *recevoir un ramponneau;* to get hit.

rentrer dans la gueule à quelqu'un *exp.* to hit someone in the mouth • (lit.): to reenter in someone's mouth.

NOTE: gueule *f.* derogatory for "head" or "mouth" since its literal translation is "the mouth of an animal."

rentrer dans le chou à quelqu'un *exp.* to attack someone verbally • (lit.): to reenter in someone's head.

NOTE: chou *m.* head • (lit.): cabbage.

rentrer dans le lard à quelqu'un *exp.* to attack someone verbally • (lit.): to reenter in someone's lard.

rentrer dans le portrait à quelqu'un *exp.* to hit someone in the face or head • (lit.): to reenter in someone's face.

NOTE: portrait *m.* face, head • (lit.): portrait.

sifflet *m.* a hit, a blow • (lit.): a whistle.

soufflet *m.* a hit, a punch • (lit.): bellows, blowing machine.

souffleter *v.* to box someone's ears.

HOUSE

maison

example: Avec l'argent que j'ai gagné au loto, je vais acheter une grande **baraque**!

translation: With the money I won in the lottery, I'm going to buy a big **house**!

as spoken: Avec l'argent qu'j'ai gagné au loto, j'vais ach'ter une grande **baraque**!

---

baraque *f.* (extremely popular) • (lit.): barracks.

bicoque *f.* • (lit.): house with a mediocre appearance, little house, shanty.

cabane *f.* • (lit.): hut, shanty.

cagna *f.*

cahute *f.* • (lit.): hut, shanty.

case *f.* • (lit.): small dwelling, hut, cabin • *une case africaine;* a (primitive) African hut.

crèche *f.* dwelling • (lit.): manger, crib.
NOTE: **crécher** *v.* to live.

gourbi *m.* • (lit.): hut, shack.

guitoune *f.* • (lit.): military dug-out, foxhole, tent.

hutte *f.* • (lit.): hut.

kasbah *f.* (from Arabic).

turne *f.* dirty and uncomfortable house or bedroom.
NOTE -1: This term comes from university slang meaning "bedroom" or "study room."
NOTE -2: **co-turne** *m.* roommate.

HOW'S IT GOING?

ça va?

example: Salut Marcel! **Ça boume**?

translation: Hi Marcel! **How's it going**?

as spoken: [no change]

NOTE: The following are synonyms for *Ça va?* meaning "How's it going?" and may all be constructed the same way: *Ça biche?* • *Ça boulotte?* • *Ça carbure?* • *Ça colle?* • *Ça gaze?* • *etc.*

---

bicher *v.* to go very well.
example (1): Ça **biche**?
translation: How's **it going**?
as spoken: [no change]
example (2): Ça **biche** entre eux.
translation: They're **hitting it off very well**.
as spoken: Ça **biche** entr'eux.

boulotter *v.* to go very well.

example: Ça **boulotte**?

translation: How's **it going**?

as spoken: [no change]

ALSO: **boulotter** *v.* to eat a lot.
SEE: **EAT (TO)** *p. 230.*

boumer *v.* to go very well • (lit.): to be booming.

carburer *v.* to go very well • (lit.): said of a carburetor that is working well.

coller *v.* to go very well • (lit.): to stick.

gazer *v.* to go very well • (lit.): to go full steam ahead.

gazouiller *v.* a slang variant of: *gazer.*

marcher *v.* to go very well • (lit.): to walk, to work well.

ronfler *v.* to go very well, to be running at a nice hum • (lit.): to snore.

rouler *v.* to go very well • (lit.): to roll (along).

roulotter *v.* a slang variant of: *rouler.*

rupiner *v.* • (lit.): to do well (at an examination, to succeed.

qu'est-ce qu'il y a de nouveau? *exp.* • (lit.): what's new?

quoi de neuf? *exp.* • (lit.): what's new?

tourner *v.* to go very well • (lit.): to turn (without any unforeseen stops).

HUNGRY (TO BE)

faim (avoir)

example: J'ai **les crocs**. Je vais prendre un casse-croûte.

translation: I'm **hungry**. I'm gonna get a snack.

as spoken: J'ai **les crocs**. J'vais prendr'un casse-croûte.

---

claquer du bec *exp.* to be very hungry • (lit.): to smack one's lips in hunger.

NOTE: **bec** *m.* mouth • (lit.): beak of a bird.

crever de faim *exp.* • (lit.): to die of hunger.

NOTE: **crever** *v.* to die.

crocs (avoir les) *exp.* • (lit.): to have the canine teeth (that are ready to bite down on food).

dalle (avoir la) *exp.* • (lit.): to have the throat (that is ready to received food).

NOTE: **dalle** *f.* throat.

ALSO: **rincer la dalle (se)** *exp.* to drink • (lit.): to rinse one's throat.

dent (avoir la) *exp.* to be very hungry • (lit.): to have the tooth (that is ready to bite down on food).

dent creuse (avoir une) *exp.* to be very hungry • (lit.): to have a hollow tooth.

fringale (avoir la) *exp.*

l'estomac creux (avoir) *exp.* to be very hungry • (lit.): to have a hollow stomach.

NOTE: The masculine noun *estomac* (meaning "stomach") is pronounced: *estoma*.

l'estomac dans les talons (avoir) *exp.* to be terribly hungry • (lit.): to have the stomach in the heels.

petit creux (avoir un) *exp.* to be a little hungry • (lit.): to have a little hollow (spot).

IDIOT

idiot

example: Quelle **jobard**! J'ai complètement oublié où j'ai placé mes clés!

translation: What an **idiot**! I completely forgot where I put my keys!

as spoken: [no change]

---

abruti *m.* idiot.

NOTE: **abrutir** *v.* to make stupid, to drive crazy.

andouille *f.* nerd • (lit.): sausage.

animal *m.* • (lit.): animal.

araignée dans le plafond (avoir une) *exp.* to have bats in the belfry • (lit.): to have a spider in the ceiling.

NOTE: **plafond** *m.* head • (lit.): ceiling.

ballot *m.* • (lit.): bundle.

baluchard *m.*

barjot *m.* crazy.

> **NOTE:** This is a verlan transformation of *jobard* meaning "crazy."

> **SEE:** *STREET FRENCH 2, A Closer Look II: The Language of "Verlan"* - p. 192.

battre la breloque *exp.* to be off one's rocker, to function badly • (lit.): to beat the drum.

bécasse *f.* stupid woman or girl, "Dumb Dora."

bêta *m.* silly or stupid person.

> **NOTE:** This is from the adjective *bête* meaning "stupid."

bêtasse *f.* stupid woman or girl, "Dumb Dora."

> **NOTE:** This is from the adjective *bête* meaning "stupid."

bête à bouffer du foin (être) *exp.* • (lit.): to be stupid enough to eat hay.

bête comme ses pieds (être) *exp.* • (lit.): to be stupid as one's feet.

bourrique *f.* jackass, stubborn individual • (lit.): donkey.

branquignolle *adj.* a little crazy, touched in the head.

braque *m.* harebrained individual • (lit.): hound.

buse *m.* extremely stupid person • (lit.): buzzard.

> **SEE:** **triple buse**, p. 255.

case en moins (avoir une) *exp.* • (lit.): to be missing one division of the brain.

cave *m.* gullible person, sucker.

chonosof *m.*

cinglé(e) (être) *adj.* • (lit.): to be cracked.

comprenette dure (avoir la) *exp.* to be dense, thick skulled.

> **NOTE:** This is from the verb *comprendre* meaning "to understand."

corniaud *m. & adj.* • (lit.): crossbred dog.

> example: Ce qu'il peut être **corniaud**, celui-là!

> translation: Can he ever be a **jerk**!

> as spoken: C'qu'y peut êt' **corniaud**, çui-là!

cornichon *m.* • (lit.): pickle.

couche (en avoir une) *exp.* to be stupid • (lit.): to have a coat (of paint, etc.) on it (the brain).

> **VARIATION:** **tenir une couche (en)** *exp.*

cruche *f.* a real idiot • (lit.): pitcher.

cruchon *m.* a real idiot • (lit.): small pitcher.

détraqué(e) (être) *adj.* • (lit.): to be out of whack (said of health, mental state, machinery, etc.).

dinde *f.* • **1.** stupid woman or girl, "Dumb Dora" • **2.** derogatory for "homosexual," "queer" • (lit.): turkey.

dingo *m. & adj.* idiot, crazy, cracked.

écervelé(e) (être) • **1.** *n.* scatterbrain • **2.** *adj.* scatterbrained • (lit.): to be "unbrained."

tenir une dose (en) *exp.* to be hopelessly dumb • (lit.): to hold a dose of it (stupidity).

tenir une pochetée (en) *exp.* to be hopelessly dumb • (lit.): to hold a pocketful of it (stupidity).

enflé *m.* fat-head • (lit.): swollen.

étourdi(e) (être) *adj.* to be scatterbrained.

évaporé(e) (être) • **1**. *n.* irresponsible person, scatterbrain • **2**. *adj.* irresponsible, flighty, scatterbrained • (lit.): to be evaporated.

fada *adj.* crazy, cracked.

fêlé(e) (être) *adj.* • (lit.): to be cracked.

fêlure (avoir une) *exp.* • (lit.): to have a crack.

follette *adj.* crazy (used only for woman).

foldingue *adj.* crazy, nuts.

fou-fou / fofolle *adj.* a little crazy, eccentric.
> **NOTE:** This comes from the adjective *fou / folle* meaning "crazy."

ganache *f.* complete idiot, person with no intelligence or talent, a real "zero" • (lit.): a creamy filling for truffles typically made of chocolate and cream.

givré(e) (être) *adj.* • (lit.): to be frosted over.

gobeur *m.* gullible person, sucker.
> **NOTE:** gober *v.* to eat, to gobble up.

> **ALSO:** gobe-tout *m.* one who believes everything he / she hears, sucker.

godichard(e) *adj.* awkward and clumsy.

godiche *n. & adj.* same as: *godichard(e)*.

gogo *m.* a personal easily fooled, a sucker.

gourde *f.* idiot • (lit.): gourde.

grain (avoir un) *m.* to be nuts, to be touched in the head • (lit.): to have a grain (in the brain).

huître *f.* silly person, dope • (lit.): oyster.

hurluberlu *m.* scatterbrain.

job *m.* abbreviated form of: *jobard*.

jobard • **1**. *n.* idiot, sucker • **2**. *adj.* stupid.

louf *adj.*
> **NOTE:** This is largonji for the adjective *fou* meaning "crazy."

> **SEE:** *STREET FRENCH 2, A Closer Look II: The Language of "Largonji"* - p. 216.

louftingue *adj.*
> **NOTE:** This is largonji for the adjective *fou* meaning "crazy."

lourdeau *m.* • **1**. *n.* idiot • **2**. *adj.* thick-headed, slow.
> **NOTE:** This is from the adjective *lourd(e)* meaning "heavy."

maboul(e) *adj.* crazy, mad.

manquer une case *exp.* • (lit.): to be missing a division in the brain.
> **SEE:** case en moins (avoir une), p. 252.

marteau • **1**. *n.* idiot • **2**. crazy, cracked • (lit.): hammer.

moule *f.* dumbbell, fat-head • (lit.): mussel.

plomb dans la cervelle (ne pas avoir de) *exp.* said of an idiot, to be without any gray matter • (lit.): not to have any lead in the brain.

inventé la poudre (ne pas avoir) *exp.* said of an idiot
• (lit.): not to have invented powder.

inventé le fil à couper le beurre (ne pas avoir) *exp.* said of an idiot • (lit.): not to have invented the wire to cut butter.

nouille *f.* nerd • (lit.): noodle.

onduler de la toiture *exp.* humorous for "to have a screw loose" • (lit.): to have a rood that is buckling.

pante *m.* gullible man, a sucker.

perdre la boule *exp.* to lose one's mind • (lit.): to lose the ball.

perdre la boussole *exp.* to lose one's mind • (lit.): to lose the compass.

perdre le nord *exp.* to lose one's mind • (lit.): to lose the north (point on the compass).

phénomène *m.* strange person, freak of nature • (lit.): phenomenon.

pigeon *m.* gullible person, sucker • (lit.): pigeon.

piqué(e) (être) *adj.* cracked, touched in the head • (lit.): to be stung.

pocheté(e) *n.* idiot.

recevoir un coup de bambou *exp.* to become crazy • (lit.): to receive a blow of bamboo.

saucisse *f.* idiot, nerd • (lit.): sausage.

schnock *m.* imbecile, jerk.
VARIATION: duchenock *m.*

sinoque (être) *adj.* crazy, cracked.
VARIATION: cinoque *adj.*

siphoné(e) (être) *adj.* to be crazy • (lit.): to be siphoned (of all intelligence).

sonné(e) (être) *adj.* to be cracked, to be a "ding-a-ling" • (lit.): to be rung.

sot(te) à vingt-quatre carats *n.* • (lit.): a twenty-four-carat idiot.

souche *f.* silly person, dumbbell • (lit.): stump (of a tree).

tapé(e) (être) *adj.* • (lit.): touched (in the head).

tête de linotte *f.* scatterbrain • (lit.): head of feathers.

tête dure (avoir la) *exp.* to be thick-skulled, dense • (lit.): to have a hard head.

timbré(e) (être) *adj.* to be crazy, cracked • (lit.): to be rung.

timbre fêlé *m.* crackpot, idiot • (lit.): cracked bell.

toqué(e) (être) *adj.* to be crazy, cracked.

tordu(e) (être) *adj.* to be crazy, cracked • (lit.): to be twisted.

tourte *f.* stupid person • (lit.): tart.

tranche (en avoir une) *exp.* • (lit.): to have a slice of it (craziness).

travailler de la chéchia *exp.* to be crazy • (lit.): to work from the hat.
NOTE: chéchia *f.* military cap.

travailler du chapeau *exp.* to be crazy • (lit.): to work from the hat.

travailler du chou *exp.* to be crazy • (lit.): to work from the cabbage.

NOTE: chou *m.* head
• (lit.): cabbage.

triple buse *m.* an extremely stupid person • (lit.): triple idiot.
NOTE: buse *m.* • (lit.): buzzard.

JAIL

prison

example: Le voleur a été arrêté et mis en **taule**.

translation: The thief was arrested and put in **prison**.

as spoken: Le voleur, il a été arrêté et mis en **taule**.

---

ballon *m.* slammer • (lit.): balloon.
NOTE: ballonner *v.* to throw in jail.

bloc *m.* slammer.

boître *f.* • (lit.): box.

cabane *f.* • (lit.): hut.

cachot *m.* prison cell • (lit.): dark dungeon.

cellule *f.* • (lit.): cell.

frigo *m.* "deep freeze," "cooler" • (lit.): an abbreviation of *réfrigérateur* meaning "refrigerator."

gnouf *m.*

jettard *m.* slammer.

> **NOTE:** This comes from the verb *jeter* meaning "to throw (away)."

ombre *m.* • (lit.): shadow • *être à l'ombre;* to be in jail.

placard *m.* • (lit.): wall cupboard.

séchoir *m.* • (lit.): dryer.

taule *m.*

> **NOTE: taulier** *m.* prisoner.

trou *m.* • (lit.): hole.

violon *m.* violin.

JAM (TO BE IN A)

être dans une situation inextricable

example: Quel **pastis**! Mes parents ont décidé de rentrer de leurs vacances cet après-midi. Le problème est que j'ai invité une centaine de mes amis pour faire la fête chez eux ce soir!

translation: What a **mess**! My parents decided to come home from their vacation this afternoon. The problem is that I invited about a hundred of my friends to party at their house tonight!

as spoken: Quel **pastis**! Mes parents, y z'ont décidé d'rentrer d'leurs vacances c't'après'm. Le problème, c'est qu'j'ai invité une centaine de mes amis pour faire la fête chez eux c'soir!

SEE: OUT OF A FIX (TO GET), *p. 275.*

beaux draps (être dans de)
exp. • (lit.): to be in pretty sheets.

bouscaille (être dans la) *exp.*
• (lit.): to be in the mud.

embrouillamini *m.* an extremely complicated and confused mess.

marmelade (être dans la) *exp.*
• (lit.): to be in marmalade.

mauvais pas (être dans un)
exp. • (lit.): to be in a bad step.

mélasse (être dans la) *exp.*
• (lit.): to be in molasses.

me voilà frais *exp.* "Boy, am I in a mess!" • (lit.): here I am fresh.

me voilà propre *exp.* "Boy, am I in a mess!" • (lit.): here I am clean.

mouscaille (être dans la) *exp.*
• (lit.): to be in mud.

pagaille (être dans la) *exp.*
(extremely popular).

pastis (être dans le) *m.*
(pronounced: *pastisse*) • (lit.): to be in an alcoholic drink made with anisette.

pétrin (être dans le) *exp.*
• (lit.): to be in the kneading trough.

JUNK

marchandise de mauvaise qualité

example: Cette nouvelle machine à laver ne marche pas! Quelle **pacotille**.

translation: This new washing machine doesn't work! What a piece of **junk**!

as spoken: C'te nouvelle machine à laver, è marche pas! Quelle **pacotille**!

camelote *f.* junk.

NOTE: The feminine noun *camelote* can also be used to mean: **1.** junk; or **2.** merchandise in general.

example (1): C'est de la **camelote**, ça!

translation: That's **junk**!

as spoken: C'est d'la **cam'lote**, ça!

example (2): C'est de la bonne **camelote**.

translation: That's a really nice **piece of goods**.

as spoken: C'est d'la bonne **cam'lote**.

fichaise *f.* something worthless, junk.

NOTE: This is from the slang verb *fiche* (yes, this is a verb even though it does not have a typical ending) meaning "to do" or "to make" whose past tense, *fichu(e),* is used to mean "ruined" or "done for."

gomme (à la) *adj.* • *un truc à la gomme;* a worthless piece of junk • (lit.): sticky.

manque (à la) *adj.* • *un truc à la manque;* a worthless piece of junk • (lit.): missing.

noix (à la) *adj.* • *un truc à la noix;* a worthless piece of junk • (lit.): nutty.

pacotille *f.* junk • *des bijoux de pacotille;* junk jewelry.

peau d'hareng *f.* • (lit.): herring skin.

peau de saucisson *f.*
• (lit.): sausage skin.

rossignol *m.* • (lit.): nightingale.

roupe de singe *f.* • (lit.): monkey mucus.

roupie de sansonnet *f.*
• (lit.): starling mucus.

toc *m.* fake.

example: Ta montre Cartier est **toc**.

translation: You're Cartier watch is a **fake**.

as spoken: Elle est **toc**, ta montre Cartier.

tocard *m.* fake.

valoir chipette (ne pas) *exp.* said of something worthless, not to be worth a penny.

valoir pipette (ne pas) *exp.* said of something worthless, not to be worth a penny.

valoir que dalle (ne) *exp.*
• (lit.): to be worth nothing.

NOTE: **que dalle** *adv.* nothing.

example: Je ne comprends **que dalle**!

translation: I don't understand **a thing**!

as spoken: J'comprends **que dalle**!

valoir tripette (ne pas) *exp.* said of something worthless, not to be worth a penny.

valoir un coup (ne pas) *exp.* said of something worthless, not to be worth a penny.

valoir une roupie (ne pas) *exp.* said of something worthless, not to be worth a penny • (lit.): not to be worth a rupee.

tuer

example: Mon petit frère a ruiné mon collier! Je vais le **foutre en l'air**!

translation: My little brother ruined my necklace! I'm going **to kill** him!

as spoken: Mon p'tit frère, il a ruiné mon collier! J'vais l'**foutr'en l'air**!

---

assommer *v.* • (lit.): to knock someone senseless.

avoir la peau de quelqu'un *exp.* to have someone's hide • (lit.): to have someone's skin.

bousiller *v.* • (lit.): to break.

example: Arrête ou je te **bousille**!

translation: Stop it or I'll **knock your block off**!

as spoken: Arrête ou j'te **bousille**!

crever *v.* • **1.** to die • **2.** to kill.

example (1): Toute la population a **crevé** de faim.

translation: The entire popular **died** of hunger.

as spoken: Toute la population, elle a **crevé** d'faim.

example (2): Où est-il?! Je vais le **crever**!

translation: Where is he?! I'm gonna **kill** him!

as spoken: Où ce'qu'il est?! J'vais l'**crever**!

débarrasser de quelqu'un (se) *exp.* to knock someone off • (lit.): to get rid of someone.

descendre quelqu'un *exp.* to waste someone • (lit.): to down someone.

estourbir *v.* to kill, to do in.

fiche quelqu'un en l'air *exp.* to blow someone away, to waste someone • (lit.): to send or throw into the air.

liquider quelqu'un *v.* • (lit.): to liquidate someone.

passer le goût du pain à quelqu'un (faire) *exp.* • (lit.): to make someone lose the taste of bread (as well as all other senses).

rectifier quelqu'un *v.* to fix someone but good • (lit.): to rectify someone.

refroidir quelqu'un *v.* "to put someone on ice" • (lit.): to chill someone.

> **NOTE:** **refroidi** *m.* cadavre.

sauter le caisson (se faire) *exp.* to kill oneself, to blow out one's brains • (lit.): to blow-up one's locker.

> **NOTE -1:** **sauter (faire)** *exp.* to blow up • (lit.): to make jump.
>
> example: Les soldats ont **fait sauter** le pont.
>
> translation: The soldiers **blew up** the bridge.
>
> as spoken: Les soldats, y z'ont **fait sauter** l'pont.
>
> **NOTE -2:** **caisson** *m.* head • (lit.): locker.

suriner quelqu'un *v.* to kill someone with a knife, to stab someone to death.

> **NOTE:** **surin** *m.* knife.

zigouiller quelqu'un *v.* to rub someone out.

KISS (TO)

embrasser

example: Avant de quitter la maison, mon père donne toujours un **bisou** à ma mère.

translation: Before leaving the house, my father always gives my mother a **kiss**.

as spoken: Avant d'quitter la maison, mon père, y donne toujours un **bisou** à ma mère.

---

bécot *m.* a kiss • (lit.): a peck.

> **NOTE:** This is from the masculine noun *bec* meaning "the mouth" or literally "the beak of a bird").
>
> **SEE:** **bécoter (se)** *v.*

bécoter (se) *v.* to kiss, to neck.

bise *f.* a kiss.

> **SEE:** **biser** *v.*

biser *v.* to kiss.

bisou *m.* a little kiss.

fricassée de museaux *f.* a whole mess of kisses and hugs • (lit.): a snout or muzzle fricassee.

papouille *f.* hug, embrace, caress.

KIT AND CABOODLE

le tout

example: Après la tornade, ils ont pris **tout le barda** et se sont installés à New York.

translation: After the tornado, they took their **whole kit and caboodle** and moved to New York.

as spoken: Après la tornade, y z'ont pris **tout l'barda** et se sont installés à New York.

---

baraque (toute la) *f.* • (lit.): the whole house.

> **NOTE:** **baraque** *f.* house • (lit.): barracks.

barda (tout le) *m.*

> **NOTE:** This is military slang for "pack" or "kit."

bastringue (tout le) *m.* the whole kit and caboodle.

bataclan (tout le) *m.*
• (lit.): belongings, paraphernalia.

bazar (tout le) *m.* • (lit.): bazaar, emporium.

boutique (toute la) *f.* • (lit.): the whole boutique.

fourbi (tout le) *m.*
• (lit.): soldier's kit or equipment.

saint-frusquin (tout le) *m.* all the worldly goods of a person.

> **NOTE:** **frusques** *f.pl.* clothes.

smala (toute la) *f.* (from Arabic) • (lit.): the whole family.

tremblement (tout le) *m.*
• (lit.): all the trembling.

LAUGH (TO)

rire

example: Je me suis **marré** pendant tout le film! Que c'était comique!

translation: I **laughed like crazy** during the entire film! Was it ever funny!

as spoken: Je m'suis **marré** pendant tout l'film! Que c'était comique!

SEE: **FUNNY** *p. 240.*

---

bidonner (se) *v.* to laugh hard, to belly laugh • (lit.): to shake one's belly (with laughter.

> **NOTE:** **bidon** *m.* belly.

boyauter (se) *v.* to laugh hard, to laugh till it hurts • (lit.): to shake one's guts (with laughter).

> **NOTE:** **boyaux** *m.pl.* guts.

désopiler (se) *v.* • (lit.): to shake or roar with laughter.

dilater la rate (se) *exp.* to laugh hard • (lit.): to swell up or dilate one's spleen (from laughter).

esclaffer (s') *v.* to laugh loudly, to burst out in loud laughter.

fendre la pipe (se) *exp.* to split one's sides laughing • (lit.): to spit one's mouth (from laughing).

> **NOTE:** **pipe** *f.* mouth • (lit.): pipe.

gondoler (se) *v.* to shake with laughter • (lit.): to warp, to buckle up (with laughter).

marrer (se) *v.* (extremely popular) to laugh.

mourir de rire *exp.* • (lit.): to die laughing.

poiler (se) *v.* to laugh loudly.

> **NOTE:** This could be loosely translated as "that which causes one's hair (*poil*) to shake with laughter."

pouffer *v.* to burst out laughing • (lit.): to puff up (with laughter).

rigolade (ne pas être de la) *exp.* to be no laughing matter.
SEE: **rigoler**.

rigoler *v.* to laugh.

rouler (se) *v.* to laugh hard • (lit.): to roll (with laughter).

tirebouchonner (se) *v.* to laugh hard and continuously.

> **NOTE:** A loose literal translation of this might be "to rise up and down like a corkscrew (*un tire-bouchon*) as one takes in air repeatedly in order to laugh."

tordre (se) *v.* to split one's sides with laughter • (lit.): to twist oneself (from laughter).

tordre comme un bossu (se) *exp.* to split one's sides with laughter • (lit.): to twist oneself (from laughter) like a hunchback.

> **NOTE:** This expression comes from the visual comparison of someone curling up with laughter and a hunchback with a severely curved back.

tordre comme une baleine (se) *exp.* to split one's sides with laughter • (lit.): to twist oneself (from laughter) like a whale.

> **NOTE:** This expression comes from the comparison of the explosive sound made by someone bursting out with laughter and the sound of a whale spouting air through its blow hole.

LAZY

paresseux

example: Il ne fait rien que regarder la télévision toute la journée. Il ne fait pas de doute que c'est un **flemmard**.

translation: He doesn't do anything but watch TV all day. There's no question that he's a **lazy bum**.

as spoken: Y fait rien que regarder la télé toute la journée. Y fait pas d'doute que c't'un **flemmard**.

---

casser (ne rien se) *exp.* said of a very lazy person, not to lift a finger • (lit.): not to break any part of oneself.

cossard(e) • 1. *n.* lazy person • 2. *adj.* lazy.

example (1): C'est un **cossard**, lui.

translation: He's a **lazy bum**.

as spoken: C't'un **cossard**, lui.

example (2): Il est très **cossard**.

translation: He's very **lazy**.

as spoken: [no change]

cosse (avoir la) *f.* to be lazy • (lit.): to have laziness.

côtes en long (avoir les) *exp.* said of a lazy person • (lit.): to have long ribs.

coup (ne pas en fiche un) *exp.*
to do nothing, to be idle • (lit.): not
to do a stroke (of work).

NOTE: **fiche** *v.* to do, to make.

datte (ne pas en fiche une)
exp. to do nothing, to be lazy
• (lit.): not to be a date.

NOTE: **datte** *f.* nothing • (lit.): date.

enfiler des perles *exp.* said of
someone who just loafs around
• (lit.): to string pearls.

envers (les avoir à l') *exp.* said
of a very lazy person • (lit.): to have
them (hands) inside out,
upside-down (and is therefore
unable to do any physical labor).

fainéant(e) • 1. *n.* lazy person
• 2. *adj.* lazy.

faire le lézard *exp.* to do nothing
but lie in the sun, to laze • (lit.): to
act like the lizard.

feignant(e) • 1. *n.* lazy person
• 2. *adj.* lazy.

feignasser *v.* to laze around and do
nothing.

flemmard(e) • 1. *n.* lazy person
• 2. *adj.* lazy.

flemmarder *v.* to be lazy, to laze
around.

flemme *f.* extreme laziness • *avoir la
flemme;* to be lazy.

SEE: **tirer sa flemme**, *p. 261.*

palmées (les avoir) *exp.* said of a
very lazy person • (lit.): to have
them (hands) webbed (and is
therefore unable to do any physical
labor).

peigner la girafe *exp.* to do
nothing • (lit.): to comb the giraffe.

poignet (ne pas se fouler le)
exp. said of a very lazy person
• (lit.): not to sprain one's wrist.

poil dans la main (avoir un)
exp. said of someone who is very
lazy • (lit.): to have a hair in the
hand.

rame (ne pas en fiche une)
exp. to do nothing, to be lazy
• (lit.): not to do an oar's worth of
work (referring to a ship full of
slaves who rowed all day long).

rate (ne pas se fouler la) *exp.*
said of a very lazy person • (lit.): not
to sprain one's spleen.

rester en tas *exp.* to do nothing,
not to move • (lit.): to stay in a heap.

retourne (les avoir à la) *exp.*
said of a very lazy person • (lit.): to
have them (hands) inside out (and
is therefore unable to do any
physical labor).

**secousse (ne pas en fiche
une)** *exp.* to do nothing, to be very
lazy • (lit.): not to do any movement
at all.

NOTE: Since the feminine noun
secousse comes from the verb
secouer, meaning "to shake" or "to
jerk," this expression might be
loosely translated as "to do nothing
that would cause any movement
whatsoever."

tirer sa flemme *exp.* to laze
around and do nothing • (lit.): to
pull one's laziness (around).

tourner les pouces (se) *exp.*
• (lit.): to twirl one's thumbs.

traînasser *v.* to loaf around.

traîner la savate *exp.* to loaf
• (lit.): to drag around one's slipper.

traîner ses patins *exp.* to loaf
  • (lit.): to drag around one's feet.

  NOTE: patins *m.pl.* feet
  • (lit.): skates.

user le soleil *exp.* to do nothing
  but lie around under the sun
  • (lit.): to use up the sun.

**venu(e) au monde un
  dimanche (être)** *exp.* said of a
  person who is born lazy • (lit.): to
  have come to the world on a
  Sunday.

LEAVE (TO)

partir

example: Le film va commencer d'ici
quinze minutes! Il faut **se calter** tout
de suite!

translation: The film is going to start in
fifteen minutes! We have **to leave**
right away!

as spoken: Le film, y va commencer
d'ici quinze minutes! Faut **s'calter**
tout d'suite!

NOTE: All following imperative forms
= *Beat it! Scram!*

adja (se faire l') *exp.* to leave
  quickly.

  IMPERATIVE:
  (formal): *Faites-vous l'adja!*
  (informal): *Fais-toi l'adja!*

arracher (s') *v.* • (lit.): to tear out,
  to pull oneself out.

  IMPERATIVE:
  (formal): *Arrachez-vous!*
  (informal): *Arrache-toi!*

barrer (se) *v.* • to get the heck out
  • (lit.): to cross out oneself, to strike
  out oneself.

  IMPERATIVE:
  (formal): *Barrez-vous!*
  (informal): *Barre-toi!*

briser (se la) *v.* to leave quickly, to
  leave in a breeze (from the feminine
  noun *brise* meaning "breeze").

calter (se) *v.* to leave quickly, to
  run away.

  IMPERATIVE:
  (formal): *Caltez!*
  (informal): *Calte!*

carapater (se) *v.* to leave quickly,
  to run away.

  IMPERATIVE:
  (formal): *Carapatez-vous!*
  (informal): *Carapate-toi!*

cavaler (se) *v.* to run away (Note:
  être en cavale; to be on the lam, to
  be running away from the police).

débarrasser le plancher *exp.*
  to leave quickly • (lit.): to get rid of
  the floor.

  IMPERATIVE:
  (formal): *Débarrassez le plancher!*
  (informal): *Débarrasse le plancher!*

débiner (se) *v.* to leave quickly.

décamper *v.* to clear out fast
  • (lit.): to pull up camp.

  IMPERATIVE:
  (formal): *Décampez!*
  (informal): *Décampe!*

décaniller *v.* to clear out fast.

IMPERATIVE:
(formal): *Décanillez-vous!*
(informal): *Décanille-toi!*

défiler (se) *v.* to clear out at the critical moment.

example: Je comptais sur lui, mais il **s'est défilé**!

translation: I was counting on him, but he **left when I needed him most**!

as spoken: J'comptais sur lui, mais y **s'est défilé**!

déguiser en courant d'air (se) *exp.* to leave without being seen, to vanish into thin air • (lit.): to disguise oneself in a breeze.

example: Quelle soirée horrible! On **se dérobe**?

translation: What a horrible party? Shall we **make a quiet getaway**?

as spoken: Quelle soirée horrible! On **s'dérobe**?

démurger (se) *v.* to clear out.

dérober (se) *v.* to slip away without being seen.

donner de l'air (se) *exp.* to slip away without being seen • (lit.): to give oneself to the air.

éclipser (s') *v.* to disappear, vanish • (lit.): to eclipse oneself.

IMPERATIVE:
(formal): *Eclipsez-vous!*
(informal): *Eclipse-toi!*

esbigner (s') *v.* to leave.

IMPERATIVE:
(formal): *Esbignez-vous!*
(informal): *Esbignes-toi!*

faire son baluchon *exp.* to pack up and leave • (lit.): to fix up one's bundle (of belongings).

IMPERATIVE:
(formal): *Faites votre baluchon!*
(informal): *Fais ton baluchon!*

filer à l'anglaise *exp.* to "hit the road," to take French leave • (lit.): to spin off English style.

filer *v.* to "split" • (lit.): to spin (off).

IMPERATIVE:
(formal): *Filez!*
(informal): *File!*

foncer dans le brouillard *exp.* to leave "full steam ahead" • (lit.): to charge into the fog.

IMPERATIVE:
(formal): *Foncez dans le brouillard!*
(informal): *Fonce dans le brouillard!*

gagner le large *exp.* to leave • (lit.): to gain width.

IMPERATIVE:
(formal): *Gagnez le large!*
(informal): *Gagne le large!*

jouer des compas *exp.* to run away • (lit.): to play the legs.

IMPERATIVE:
(formal): *Jouez des compas!*
(informal): *Joue des compas!*

NOTE: **compas** *m.pl.* legs • (lit.): compass (needles).

jouer des flûtes *exp.* same as: *jouer des compas.*

IMPERATIVE:
(formal): *Jouez des flûtes!*
(informal): *Joue des flûtes!*

NOTE: **flûtes** *f.pl.* legs • (lit.): flutes.

jouer des gambettes *exp.* same as: jouer des compas.

> IMPERATIVE:

(formal): *Jouez des gambettes!*
(informal): *Joue des gambettes!*

> NOTE: **gambettes** *f.pl.* legs
> • (lit.): red-shanks.

jouer des guibolles *exp.* same as: *jouer des compas.*

> IMPERATIVE:

(formal): *Jouez des guibolles!*
(informal): *Joue des guibolles!*

> NOTE: **guibolles** *f.pl.* legs.

jouer des quilles *exp.* same as: *jouer des compas.*

> IMPERATIVE:

(formal): *Jouez des quilles!*
(informal): *Joue des quilles!*

> NOTE: **quilles** *f.pl.* (bowling) pins.

jouer rip *exp.* to leave quickly, to disappear.

laisser une queue *exp.* to leave without paying the bill • (lit.): to leave a tail.

lever l'ancre *exp.* to leave
• (lit.): to lift anchor.

malle (faire la) *exp.* to jilt, to leave without warning • (lit.): to pack up one's trunk.

mettre (les) *exp.* to scram • (lit.): to set them (the sails) up.

> IMPERATIVE:

(formal): *Mettez-les!*
(informal): *Mets-les!*

> NOTE: les refers to *les voiles* (sails) •
See: **mettre les voiles**, *p. 264.*

mettre les bâtons *exp.* to leave quickly, to run • (lit.): to put the clubs (to work).

> IMPERATIVE:

(formal): *Mettez les bâton!*
(informal): *Mets les bâtons!*

> NOTE: **bâtons** *m.pl.* legs
> • (lit.): clubs.

mettre les bouts de bois *exp.* to leave quickly • (lit.): to put the ends of wood (to work).

> IMPERATIVE:

(formal): *Mettez les bouts de boi!*
(informal): *Mets les bouts de bois!*

> NOTE: **bouts de bois** *m.pl.* legs
> • (lit.): ends of wood.

mettre les bouts *exp.* to leave quickly • (lit.): to put the ends (to work).

> IMPERATIVE:

(formal): *Mettez les bout!*
(informal): *Mets les bouts!*

> NOTE: **bouts** *m.pl.* legs
> • (lit.): ends.

mettre les cannes *exp.* to leave quickly • (lit.): to put the canes (to work).

> IMPERATIVE:

(formal): *Mettez les cannes!*
(informal): *Mets les cannes!*

> NOTE: **cannes** *f.pl.* legs
> • (lit.): canes.

mettre les voiles *exp.* to leave, to pull up anchor • (lit.): to set sail.

> IMPERATIVE:

(formal): *Mettez les voiles!*
(informal): *Mets les voiles!*

paire (se faire la) *exp.* to run away, to disappear • (lit.): to get the pair (of legs) working.

IMPERATIVE:

(formal): *Faites-vous la paire!*
(informal): *Fais-toi la paire!*

planter un drapeau *v.* to leave without paying the bill (in a restaurant, hotel, etc.) • (lit.): to drive a flag into the ground.

plaquer *v.* to jilt (someone).

VARIATION: **plaquouser** *v.*

plier bagages *exp.* to pick up and leave • (lit.): to fold baggage.

IMPERATIVE:

(formal): *Pliez bagages!*
(informal): *Plie bagages!*

prendre la tangente *exp.* to leave quickly without being seen • (lit.): to take the tangent.

IMPERATIVE:

(formal): *Prenez la tangente!*
(informal): *Prends la tangente!*

prendre le large *exp.* to leave • (lit.): to take width.

IMPERATIVE:

(formal): *Prenez le large!*
(informal): *Prends le large!*

prendre ses cliques et ses claques *exp.* to leave with one's entire kit and caboodle • (lit.): to take one's belongings (and leave).

IMPERATIVE:

(formal): *Prenez vos cliques et vos claques!*
(informal): *Prends tes cliques et tes claques!*

sauver (se) *v.* to run away and escape from danger, to leave in a hurry • (lit.): to save oneself.

IMPERATIVE:

(formal): *Sauvez-vous!*
(informal): *Sauve-toi!*

tailler (se) *v.* to dash off • (lit.): to trim oneself.

IMPERATIVE:

(formal): *Taillez-vous!*
(informal): *Taille-toi!*

tirailleur marocain (se) *v.* humorous for "to leave."

NOTE: **tirailleur marocain** (Moroccan gunman) is a humorous transformation of *se tirer* ("to leave").

example: On se **tirailleur marocain**?

translation: Shall we **hit the road**?

as spoken: On s'**tirailleur marocain**?

tirer (se) *v.* to dash off • (lit.): to pull oneself (away).

IMPERATIVE:

(formal): *Tirez-vous!*
(informal): *Tire-toi!*

tirer les pincettes (se) *v.* to leave quickly • (lit.): to pull away one's legs.

IMPERATIVE:

(formal): *Tirez-vous les pincettes!*
(informal): *Tire-toi les pincettes!*

NOTE: **pincettes** *f.pl.* legs • (lit.): tweezers.

trisser (se) *v.* to go away, to leave.

IMPERATIVE:

(formal): *Trissez-vous!*
(informal): *Trisse-toi!*

trotter (se) *v.* to leave • (lit.): to trot off.

| IMPERATIVE: |
(formal): *Trottez-vous!*
(informal): *Trotte-toi!*

trousser baggage *exp.* to leave • (lit.): to tuck up one's baggage.

| IMPERATIVE: |
(formal): *Troussez baggage!*
(informal): *Trousse baggage!*

virer (se) *v.* to scram • (lit.): to veer oneself off.

| IMPERATIVE: |
(formal): *Virez-vous!*
(informal): *Vire-toi!*

LEGS

jambes

example: Elle a des **guibolles** super musclées. Elle doit être danseuse.

translation: She has extremely muscular **legs**. She must be a dancer.

as spoken: Elle a des **guibolles** super musclées. È doit êt'danseuse.

---

allumettes *f.pl.* thin legs • (lit.): matches.

bâtons *m.pl.* • (lit.): clubs.

cannes *f.pl.* • (lit.): canes.

colonnes *f.pl.* strong legs • (lit.): columns, pillars.

crayons *m.pl.* thin legs • (lit.): pencils.

échalas *m.pl.* thin legs • (lit.): vine-props.

échasses *f.pl.* thin legs • (lit.): stilts.

flûtes *f.pl.* thin legs • (lit.): flutes.

gambettes *f.pl.* • (lit.): red shanks.

gigots *m.pl.* thighs • (lit.): legs of lamb.

guibolles *f.pl.* legs.

pattes *f.pl.* legs, hands • (lit.): paws.

poteaux *m.pl.* strong legs • (lit.): posts.

quilles *f.pl.* • (lit.): (bowling) pins.

LOOK (TO)

regarder

example: Ce mec n'arrête pas de te **bigler** Tu le connais?

translation: That guy doesn't stop **looking** at you. Do you know him?

as spoken: C'mec, il arrête pas d'te **bigler** Tu l'connais?

---

avoir quelqu'un à l'œil *exp.* to observe someone, to have an eye on someone • (lit.): to have someone in the eye.

bigler *v.* to look.

châsser *v.* to look, to eye.

NOTE: **châsses** *f.pl.* eyes • (lit.): glasses frame.

chauffer *v.* to look • (lit.): to heat (up).

faire des yeux de merlan frit *exp.* to gaze ecstatically at someone with wide-open eyes • (lit.): to make eyes like a fried whiting (fish).

guigner *v.* to eye someone or something.

example: Il **guigne** ton jeu.

translation: He's **eyeing** your hand (of cards).

as spoken: Y **guigne** ton jeu.

loucher *v.* to look • (lit.): to squint, to look cross-eyed.

mater *v.* (very popular) to look • (lit.): to master something or someone.

mirer *v.* to look, to eye.
NOTE: mirettes *f.pl.* eyes.

mordre *v.* to look, to get a load of something or someone • (lit.): to bite.

reluquer *v.* to look at something or someone at the corner of one's eye with interest and curiosity.

rincer l'œil (se) *exp.* to look at something or someone with particular pleasure • (lit.): to rinse the eye (with something nice).

viser *v.* to look • (lit.): to aim, to take sight on.

zieuter *v.* to look.
NOTE: This comes from the masculine plural noun *yeux* meaning "eyes": *les z'yeux = z'yeux-ter = zieuter*.

LOVE (TO)
aimer / plaire

example: J'ai décidé de demander à Sophie de m'épouser. Après tout, je suis **mordu d'**elle!

translation: I've decided to ask Sophie to marry me. After all, I'm **crazy about** her!

as spoken: J'ai décidé de d'mander à Sophie d'm'épouser. Après tout, j'suis **mordu d'**elle!

NOTE: Note that although many of the following expressions are constructed similarly, there is an inconsistency. In

some expressions, *de* follows the adjective: *coiffé(e) de • entiché(e) de • fou / folle de • mordu(e) de • raffoler de*, whereas in others, *pour* follows the adjective: *chipé(e) pour • pépin pour • en pincer pour • toquade pour* and one expression takes *par*: *emballé(e) par*.

avoir quelqu'un dans la peau *exp.* to have a mad crush on someone • (lit.): to have someone in the skin.

chanter à *v.* to please • (lit.): to sing to (someone).

example: Ça me **chante** d'aller au théâtre.

translation: I **love** going to the theater.

as spoken: Ça m'**chante** d'aller au théâtre.

chipé(e) pour quelqu'un (être) *exp.* to have a mad crush on someone • (lit.): to be stolen for someone.
NOTE: chiper *v.* to steal.

coiffé(e) de quelqu'un (être) *exp.* to have a mad crush on someone • (lit.): to be coiffed with someone.

emballé(e) par quelqu'un (être) *exp.* to be infatuated with someone • (lit.): to be wrapped up by someone.

entiché(e) de quelqu'un (être) *adj.* to be infatuated with someone.
VARIATION: enticher de quelqu'un (s') *exp.*

fou / folle de quelqu'un (être) *exp.* • (lit.): to be mad about someone.

**mordu(e) de quelqu'un
(être)** *exp.* to have a mad crush
on someone • (lit.): to be bitten by
someone • *être mordu du golf;* to be
hooked on golf. • *les mordus du
tennis;* fans of tennis.

morgan de quelqu'un (être)
exp. to be in love with someone.

NOTE: This expression comes from
a popular song by a famous French
singer named *Renaud.*

**pépin pour quelqu'un
(avoir le)** *exp.* to be the apple of
one's eye • (lit.): to have the pippin
for someone.

pincer pour quelqu'un (en)
exp. • (lit.): to pinch it for someone.

raffoler de quelqu'un *exp.* to
be crazy about someone or
something • (lit.): to go crazy over
someone.

example: Je **raffole du** chocolat!

translation: I'm **nuts over**
chocolate!

as spoken: J'**raffole du** chocolat!

**tenir à quelqu'un comme à
la prunelle de ses yeux** *exp.*
• (lit.): to care for someone like the
apple (pupil) of one's eyes.

**toquade pour quelqu'un
(avoir une)** *exp.* to have a little
crush on someone.

LUCKY (TO BE)

chance (avoir de la)

example: Anne vient de gagner le
loto? Elle a **du pot**, celle-là!

translation: Anne just won the lotto?
She's really **lucky!**

as spoken: Anne, è vient d'gagner
l'loto? Elle a **du pot**, celle-là!

SEE: BAD LUCK (HAVE TO),
p. 212.

---

bidard *m.* happy or lucky individual.

bien loti(e) (être) *adj.* • (lit.): to
be well allotted.

bol (avoir du) *m.* • (lit.): to have
bowl.

example: Quel **bol!**

translation: What **luck!**

as spoken: [no change]

chançard(e) *n.* lucky individual.

embellie *f.* unexpected good
fortune, godsend.

né(e) coiffé(e) (être) *adj.* to be
born under a lucky star • (lit.): to be
born coiffed.

pot (avoir du) *exp.* • (lit.): to have
some from the pot.

veinard(e) *n.* lucky individual.

veine (avoir de la) *exp.* to have
luck • *un coup de veine;* a stroke of
luck.

veine de coco (avoir une) *exp.*
to have great or remarkable luck.

veine de pendu (avoir une)
exp. to have great or remarkable
luck.

verni(e) (être) *adj.* to always be
lucky • (lit.): to be varnished (with
luck).

MEAN (TO BE)

méchant(e) (être)

example: Je n'aime pas mon professeur de biologie. Il est **méchant comme une teigne**.

translation: I don't like my biology teacher. He's **really mean**.

as spoken: J'aime pas mon prof de bio. Il est **méchant comme une teigne**.

---

bas(se) (être) *adj.* to be low and despicable • (lit.): to be low.

mauvaise(e) comme la gale (être) *exp.* • (lit.): to be as bad as scabies.

méchant(e) comme une teigne (être) *exp.* • (lit.): to be mean as a moth.

mauvais crin (être de) *exp.* to be ill-tempered • (lit.): to be of bad horsehair.

mauvais poil (être de) *exp.* to be ill-tempered, to be in a bad mood • (lit.): to be of bad hair.

mal vissé(é) (être) *adj.* to be ill-tempered, to be in a bad mood • (lit.): to be badly screwed together.

MONEY

argent

example: Je n'ai pas assez de **fric** pour acheter cette robe.

translation: I don't have enough **money** to buy that dress.

as spoken: J'ai pas assez d'**fric** pour ach'ter c'te robe.

SEE: **RICH (TO BE)**, *p. 279*.

---

balle *f.* (extremely popular) one franc.

example: Cette robe m'a coûté 500 **balles**.

translation: This dress cost me 500 **francs** (approximately 100 US dollars).

as spoken: Cette robe, è m'a coûté 500 **balles**.

NOTE: This is an extremely popular way of saying "one franc." However, when used by street beggers, *balle* is used to mean "centime" as heard in this common plea for money: *Vous avez cent balles?*; Do you have a franc (you could give me)?

beurre *m.* money in general • (lit.): butter.

blé *m.* money in general • (lit.): wheat.

bougie *f.* 5-franc piece • (lit.): candle.

braise *f.* money in general • (lit.): live charcoal.

brique *f.* ten thousand francs • (lit.): brick.

cigue *m.* 20-franc gold piece.

fafiot *m.* banknote, paper.

ferraille *f.* change • (lit.): scrap iron.

fric m. (extremely popular) money in general.

galetouse f. money in general.

galette f. money in general • (lit.): a type of cake.

grand format m. a 1,000-franc bill • (lit.): big format.

grisbi m. money in general.

grisbinette f. a 100-franc coin.

gros papa m. a 1,000-franc bill • (lit.): big daddy.

livre f. 100 francs • (lit.): a pound.

misérable m. a 500-franc bill (from the work of Victor Hugo).

mitraille f. small coins • (lit.): hail of bullets.

oseille f. money in general • (lit.): sorrel.

pelot m. a 5-centime coin.

pépètes f.pl. money in general.

pesètes f.pl. money in general.

pèze m. money in general.

picaillons m.pl. small coins.

pognon m. (very popular) money in general.

poussières f.pl. small supplementary amount of francs that is added to a basic amount • (lit.): dusts.

example: Ce livre coûte vingt balles et des **poussières**.

translation: This book costs twenty francs and **some change**.

as spoken: Ce livre, y coûte vingt balles et des **poussières**.

NOTE: The French use decimal points where Americans use commas, and commas where

Americans use decimal points! For example: *Il y avait 1.000 personnes à la soirée!*; There were 1,000 people at the party! • *Ça coûte £2,50*; That costs $2.50.

radis m. one centime • (lit.): radish.

raide m. a 1,000-franc bill • (lit.): stiff.

ronds m.pl. (popular) • **1.** coins • **2.** money in general • (lit.): rounds.

sigue f. a 20-franc coin.

sous m.pl. (extremely popular).

thunard m. an old 5-franc coin.

thune • **1.** f. an old 5-franc coin • **2.** f.pl. money in general.

thunette f. a old 5-franc coin.

ticket m. a 1,000-franc bill.

MOUTH

bouche

example: Maurice fume trop. Il a toujours une cigarette dans la **gueule**.

translation: Maurice smokes too much. He always has a cigarette in his **mouth**.

as spoken: Maurice, y fume trop. Il a toujours une cigarette dans la **gueule**.

bavarde f. • (lit.): the "blabberer."
NOTE: This comes from the verb *bavarder* meaning "to blabber," "to chatter," "to chat."

bec m. • (lit.): beak of bird.

boîte f. • (lit.): box.

égout m. • (lit.): sewer, drain.

évier m. • (lit.): sink.

fente *f.* • (lit.): crack, crevice, slit.

gargoulette *f.* • (lit.): the gargler.

> **NOTE:** This comes from the verb *se gargariser* meaning "to gargle."

gargue *f.* same as: *gargoulette*.

gobeuse *f.* • (lit.): the gobbler.

> **NOTE:** This comes from the verb *gober* meaning "to gulp down (food)."

goulot *m.* gullet, mouth • (lit.): neck (of bottle).

gueule *f.* derogatory for "mouth" or "face" since its literal translation is "the mouth of an animal."

margoulette *f.*

respirante *f.* • (lit.): the respirator.

example: Je ne peux pas supporter Béatrice. Je vais l'inviter à dîner chez moi **quand les poules auront des dents**.

translation: I can't stand Beatrice. I'll invite her to my house **when hell freezes over**.

as spoken: J'peux pas supporter Béatrice. J'vais l'inviter à dîner chez moi **quand les poules auront des dents**.

à pâques ou à la trinité *exp.* very late, never • (lit.): at Easter or at Trinity.

jusqu'à la Saint-Glinglin *exp.* never, • (lit.): when hell freezes over.

la semaine des quatre jeudis *exp.* • (lit.): the week of four Thursdays.

quand les poules auront des dents *exp.* • (lit.): when chicken have teeth.

example: Je ne peux pas dormir. Les voisins font un de ces **boucans**!

translation: I can't sleep. The neighbors are making a real **racket**!

as spoken: J'peux pas dormir. Les voisins, y font un d'ces **boucans**!

> **NOTE:** **un(e) de ces** *exp.* one heck of a.

baraouf *m.* (pronounced: *baroufe*) loud noise.

> **ALSO:** **barouf du diable** *m.* devil of a noise.

boucan *m.* loud noise.

bousin *m.* • *faire du bousin;* to make a lot of noise.

chahut *m.* rowdiness, noise.

chahuter *v.* to be rowdy and loud (said of students who are partying).

chambard *m.* loud noise.

charivari *m.* loud noise.

foin *m.* loud noise • (lit.): hay.

hourvari *m.* loud noise.

potin *m.* loud noise.

raffut *m.* loud noise.

tam-tam *m.* loud noise.

tapage *m.* loud noise.

tintouin *m.* loud and tiring noise.

ALSO: **tintouin** *m.* a large worry.
SEE: **WORRY (TO)**, *p. 297*.

tumulte *m.* tumult.

vacarme *m.* loud noise.

NONSENSE

baliverne

example: Mais qu'est-ce que tu racontes? C'est du **boniment**!

translation: What are you talking about? That's **nonsense**!

as spoken: Mais qu'est-c'que tu racontes? C'est du **boniment**!

---

baratin *m.* a bunch of B.S.

NOTE: **baratiner** *v.* to B.S. someone.

bobard *m.* • *les bobards de la presse;* exaggerations of the press.

boniment *m.*.

example: Quel **boniment**!

translation: What **baloney**!

as spoken: [no change]

chansons que tout ça! *exp.* this exclamation is used to signify "baloney."

NOTE: This comes from the verb *chanter* meaning "to sing." However, in colloquial French it takes on the meaning of "to talk nonsense":

example: Mais qu'est-ce que tu me **chantes**-là?.

translation: What are you **handing** me?

as spoken: Mais qu'est-c'que tu m'**chantes**-là?.

postiche *f.* sales talk.

raconter des salades *exp.* to talk nonsense.

sornettes *f.pl.* baloney.

example: Il m'a raconté des **sornettes**.

translation: He told me **all sorts of baloney**.

as spoken: Y m'a raconté des **sornettes**.

taratata! *exclam.* this exclamation is used to signify disbelief in something that is being told.

tu veux rire! *exp.* this expressions is used to signify disbelief, "you've got to be kidding" • (lit.): you want to laugh.

NOSE

nez

example: Jimmy Durante était connu pour son grand **blair**.

translation: Jimmy Durante was known for his big **shnozola**.

as spoken: Jimmy Durante, il était connu pour son grand **blair**.

baigneur *m.* • (lit.): bather.

betterave *f.* nose that is red as a beet • (lit.): beet.

blair *m.* "schnoz."

> **NOTE:** **blairer** *v.* to smell, to tolerate • used in the negative (as seen in the following).
>
> example: Je ne peux pas le **blairer**!
>
> translation: I can't **stand** him (so much that even the mere smell of him would be too much to bear).
>
> as spoken: J'peux pas l'**blairer**!

blaireau *m.* slang variant of: *blair.*

éteignoir *m.* • (lit.): candle extinguisher.

patate *f.* big fat nose • (lit.): potato.

pif *m.* "schnoz."

> **NOTE:** **piffrer** *v.* to smell, to tolerate • used in the negative (same as: *blairer*).

piffard *m.* slang variant of: *pif.*

radar *m.* radar.

tarin *m.* big "schnoz."

tube *m.* • (lit.): tube.

NOTHING

rien

example: Tu sais ce qu'il m'a donné pour mon anniversaire? **Que dalle**!

translation: You know what he gave me for my birthday? **Zip**!

as spoken: Tu sais c'qu'y m'a donné pour mon anniversaire? **Que dalle**!

balpeau *m.* verlan for: **peau de ball** • (lit.): skin of a ball.

> **SEE:** *STREET FRENCH 2, A Closer Look II: The Language of "Verlan"* - p. 192.

clous (des) *m.pl.* nothing, "zip" • (lit.): nails.

> example: Tu ne vas pas croire combien d'argent il me reste dans mon compte de banque. **Des clous**!
>
> translation: You're not going to believe how money I have left in my bank account. **Zip**!
>
> as spoken: Tu vas pas croire combien d'argent y m'reste dans mon compte de banque. **Des clous**!

dattes (des) *f.pl.* nothing, "zip" • (lit.): dates.

nèfles (des) *m.pl.* nothing, "zip" • (lit.): medlar (fruit).

nib *m.* nothing, "zip."

nib de nib *m.* nothing at all, "zip!"

niente *m.* (borrowed from Italian).

nix *m.* • (lit.): nix.

peau (la) *f.* • (lit.): skin.

peau de balle *f.* • (lit.): skin of ball.

pour la gloire *exp.* • (lit.): just for the glory of it.

> example: Je ne passe pas huit heures par jour au bureau juste **pour la goire**!
>
> translation: I don't spend eight hours a day at work just **for my health**!
>
> as spoken: J'passe pas huit heures par jour au bureau juste **pour la goire**!

pour des pruneaux *exp.* "for peanuts" • (lit.): for prunes.

pour des prunes *exp.* "for peanuts" • (lit.): for plums.

NOTE: As seen in the literal translation, *prunes* means "plums" not "prunes" as one would think. In the category of fruit, there are a few *faux amis* to be aware of:
pruneaux = prunes;
prune = plumes;
raisin = grape;
raisin sec = raisin.

que dalle *exp.* nothing, "zip."

que fifre *exp.* nothing, "zip."

que lape *exp.* nothing, "zip."

que pouic *exp.* nothing, "zip."

que't *exp.* nothing, "zip."

que t'chi *exp.* nothing, "zip."

radis (des) *m.pl.* • (lit.): radishes.

tringle (la) *f.* nothing, "zip."

vent (du) *m.* • (lit.): wind.

OLD PERSON

vieux / vieille

example: Tu as rencontré le nouveau voisin? Il est très méchant et doit avoir 90 ans. Quel **vieux birbe**!

translation: Have you met the new neighbor? He's really mean and must be 90 years old. What an **old fart**!

as spoken: T'as rencontré l'nouveau voisin? Il est très méchant et doit avoir 90 ans. Quel **vieux birbe**!

---

baderne (vieille) *f.* old biddy.

barbe (vieille) *f.* • (lit.): old beard.

birbe (vieux) *m.* old codger.

bonze (vieux) *m.* old codger.

gaga (vieux) *m.* old codger.

gâteux (vieux) *m.* old codger • (lit.): old spoiler (or "one who is spoiled due to age").

individu vieux jeu *m.* person with old ideas, old-fashioned • (lit.): old-game person (person who plays by the old rules).

marcheur (vieux) *m.* • (lit.): old walker.

mémère *f.* crotchety middle-aged woman.

noix (vieille) *f.* • (lit.): old nut.

peau (vieille) *f.* • (lit.): old skin.

perruque (vieille) *f.* • (lit.): old wig.

ramolli(e) (être) *adj.* • (lit.): to be soft.

ramollo (vieux) *m.* • (lit.): old soft person.

toupie (vieille) *f.* old unpleasant woman • (lit.): old top.

viocard *m.* old codger.

vioc *m.* / **vioque** *f.* old codger.

NOTE: **vioquir** *v.* to get old.

OUT OF A FIX (TO GET)

débrouiller (se)

example: Mon loyer est dû demain et je n'ai pas d'argent. Je ne sais pas comment je vais pouvoir **me dépatouiller**.

translation: My rent is due tomorrow and I don't have any money. I don't know how I'm going to be able **to get out of this fix**.

as spoken: Mon loyer, il est dû d'main et j'ai pas d'argent. J'sais pas comment j'vais pouvoir **m'dépatouiller**.

SEE: **JAM (TO BE IN A)**, *p. 255.*

---

démerder (se) *v.* (vulgar and extremely popular) • (lit.): to get out of shit.

> **NOTE:** This verb comes from the feminine noun *merde* meaning "shit" and should therefore be used with discretion.

démouscailler (se) *v.* • (lit.): to get oneself out of the mud.

> **NOTE:** **mouscaille** *f.* mud.

dépanner (se) *v.* • (lit.): to repair something that was broken down (or *en panne*).

dépatouiller (se) *v.* • (lit.): to get one's feet out of a mess.

> **NOTE:** **patttes** *f.pl.* feet
> • (lit.): paws.

PANTS

pantalon

example: J'ai gagné trop de poids. Je ne peux plus porter mon **falzar**!

translation: I gained too much weight. I can't wear my **pants** anymore!

as spoken: J'ai gagné trop d'poids. J'peux pu porter mon **falzar**!

> **NOTE:** Since "pants" is plural in English, many Americans assume that the same holds true in French. This is not the case! In French, a pair of "pants" is singular: <u>un</u> *pantalon*.

---

bénard *m.*

culbutant *m.*

> **NOTE:** This is from the verb *culbuter* meaning "somersault."

culbute *m.* • (lit.): somersault.

falzar *m.*

fendart *m.*

froc *m.* frock, grown.

futal *m.*

grimpant *m.* climber.

> **NOTE:** This is from *grimper* meaning "to climb."

pantalzar *m.* a combination of *falzar* and *pantalon*.

PARENTS

parents

example: Mes **vieux** et mes frères vont venir dîner chez moi pour Noël.

translation: My **folks** and my brothers are coming to have dinner at my house for Christmas.

as spoken: Mes **vieux** et mes frères, y vont v'nir dîner chez moi pour Noël.

---

ancêtres *m.pl.* parents
  • (lit.): ancestors.

dab *m.* father.

dabesse *f.* mother.

dabs *m.pl.* parents.

dabuche *f.* mother.

daron *m.* father.

daronne *f.* mother.

doche *f.* mother.

matère *f.* mother.

maternelle *f.* mother
  • (lit.): maternal.

matouze *f.* mother.

pater *m.* father (pronounced: *patère*).

paternel *m.* father • (lit.): paternal.

patouze *m.* father.

patron *m.* father • (lit.): (male) boss.

patronne *f.* mother • (lit.): (female) boss.

vieille *f.* mother • (lit.): old woman.

vieux *m.* father • (lit.): old man.

PARTY (TO)

fête (faire la)

example: Pour mon anniversaire, je veux **faire la bringue**!

translation: For my birthday, I want **to paint the town red**!

as spoken: Pour mon anniversaire, j'veux **faire la bringue**!

---

bambocher *v.* to party.

  NOTE: **bambocheur, euse** *n.* party animal.

casser les vitres *v.* • (lit.): to break windowpanes.

bombe (faire la) *exp.*

boum (faire la) *exp.* (used in reference to an party of adolescents).

bringue (faire la) *exp.*

faridon (faire la) *exp.*

foire (faire la) *exp.* • (lit.): to do the fair.

grande nouba (faire la) *exp.*

noce (faire la) . to do the (wedding) celebration.

ribouledingue (faire la) *exp.*

  SEE: **ribouledinguer** *v.*

partir en bombe *exp.* to go out and party.

partir en ribouledingue *v.* to go out and party.

ribouledinguer *v.* to go out and party.

QUICKLY

vite

example: Nous devons partir **à tire d'aile**! Voilà notre autobus!

translation: We have to leave **quickly**! That's our bus!

as spoken: On doit partir **à tire d'aile**! V'là not' bus!

à fond la caisse *exclam*. Step on it! (said of a car) • (lit.): all the way the case.

> **NOTE:** **caisse** *f*. car • (lit.): case.

à la six-quat'-deux *adv*. quickly, in a slapdash manner
• (lit.): six-four- two style.

à tire d'aile *adv*. flying away swiftly
• (lit.): to the pull of the wings.

à toute pompe *adv*. "pumped out"
• (lit.): to the complete pump.

à toutes jambes *adv*. all out fast
• (lit.): to the complete legs.

activez! *exclam*. hurry!
• (lit.): activate!

allez, ouste! *exclam*. hurry!

au triple galop *adv*. • (lit.): to the triple gallop.

courir comme un dératé *exp*. to run like a maniac • (lit.): to run like a spleenless person.

courir ventre à terre *exp*. to run like the wind • (lit.): to run with the stomach close to the ground.

dare-dare *adv*.

donner à plein tubes *exp*. to hurry, full steam ahead, full power
• (lit.): to give full tubes.

donner plein gaz *exp*. to hurry
• (lit.): to give full gas.

en cinq sec(s) *adv*. • (lit.): in five seconds.

en deux temps, trois mouvements *adv*. • (lit.): in half time and three movements.

en moins de deux *adv*. • (lit.): in less than two (shakes).

en quatrième vitesse *adv*.
• (lit.): in fourth gear.

et que ça saute *exp*. and make it snappy • (lit.): and let it jump.

foncer *v*. to hurry • (lit.): to forge ahead.

gazer *v*. to hurry • (lit.): to gas up.

gigoter *v*. to hurry • (lit.): to shake a leg.

> **NOTE:** **gigot** *m*. leg • (lit.): leg of lamb.

> **ALSO:** **gigoter** *v*. to dance.

grouiller (se) *v*. to hurry, "to haul," to look alive • (lit.): to swarm, to be alive with.

example: **Grouille-toi**! Tu vas être en retard!

translation: **Move it**! You're going to be late!

as spoken: **Grouille-toi**! Tu vas êtr'en r'tard!

illico (presto) *adv*. (borrowed from Italian) quickly.

le temps de dire ouf *adv.* in no time at all • (lit.): the time to say "ouf."

magner (se) *v.* to hurry, to move it • (lit.): to manipulate or direct oneself.

magner le derche (se) *exp.* to "move one's buns" • (lit.): to manipulate or direct one's "derrière."

> **NOTE -1:** **derche** *m.* slang for "derrière."

> **NOTE -2:** Any slang synonym for "buttocks" can be used in this expression. SEE: POSTERIOR, *p. 316.*

> **VARIATION:** **magner le derrière (se)**.

quatre à quatre *adv.* • (lit.): four at a time.

> **NOTE:** Used in *monter l'escalier quatre à quatre;* to take the stairs four at a time.

rapido *adv.* (borrowed from Spanish) quickly.

secouer (se) *v.* to hurry • (lit.): to shake oneself.

averse / pleuvoir

example: Regarde toute cette pluie. Quelle **saucée**!

translation: Look at this rain. What a **downpour**!

as spoken: Regarde toute c'te pluie. Quelle **saucée**!

bouillon *m.* downpour • (lit.): bouillon (broth).

dégringoler *v.* to fall hard.

> example: Regarde comme ça **dégringole**!

> translation: Look at it **come down**!

> as spoken: [no change]

flotter *v.* to rain • (lit.): to float.

> **NOTE:** **flotte** *f.* water, rain.

lancequiner *v.* • **1**. to rain • **2**. to urinate.

> **NOTE:** **lancequine** or **lance** *f.* rain • (lit.): slang for "urine."

pleuvasser *v.* to drizzle.

pleuvoir des cordes *exp.* to downpour • (lit.): to rain cords.

pleuvoir à sceaux *exp.* • (lit.): to rain buckets.

pleuvoir à verse *exp.* to pour.

pleuvoir des hallebardes *exp.* • (lit.): rain spears.

rincée *f.* downpour • (lit.): rinsing.

> **ALSO:** **rincée** *f.* scolding.

saucée *f.* downpour.

> **NOTE:** **saucée** *f.* scolding.

tomber des cordes *exp.* to pour down • (lit.): to drop cords.

vaser *v.* to rain.

> **NOTE:** **vase** *f.* mud, sludge.

verser *v.* • (lit.): to pour.

RECONCILE (TO)

réconcilier

example: Henri et Laurent se sont disputés la semaine dernière mais je pense qu'ils vont **passer l'éponge** bientôt.

translation: Henri and Laurent had a fight last week but I think they'll **patch things up** soon.

as spoken: Henri et Laurent, y s'sont disputés la s'maine dernière mais j'pense qu'y vont **passer l'éponge** bientôt.

---

passer la pogne *exp.* • (lit.): to pass the hand (of friendship).

> **NOTE:** **pogne** *f.* hand.

passer l'éponge *exp.* to make up and not speak about it anymore • (lit.): to pass the sponge (that "soaks up" our differences).

rabibocher (se) *v.* • (lit.): to patch up.

> example: Ils **se sont rabibochés**.
>
> translation: They **patched up everything** (between themselves).
>
> as spoken: Y **s'sont rabibochés**.

rafistoler (se) *v.* • (lit.): to patch up • same as: *rabibocher*.

RICH (TO BE)

riche (être)

example: Tu as vu sa maison? C'est plutôt un château! Il doit être **cousu d'or**!

translation: Did you see his house? It's more like a castle! He must **have money to burn**!

as spoken: T'as vu sa maison? C'est plutôt un château! Y doit êt' **cousu d'or**!

SEE: MONEY, p. 269.

---

bourré(e) (être) *adj.* • (lit.): to be stuffed (with money or alcohol, depending on the context).

calé(e) (être) *adj.* to be financially set • (lit.): to be wedged or set (for life).

cousu(e) d'or (être) *exp.* to be made of money • (lit.): to be sewn up of gold.

faire son beurre *exp.* to make a lot of money.

> **NOTE:** **beurre** *m.* money • (lit.): butter.

flot (être à) *adj.* to be financially stable • (lit.): to be afloat.

galeteux, euse (être) *adj.* to have lots of *galetouse*.

> **NOTE:** **galetouse** *f.* money.

galettard(e) *n.* one who has lots of *galetouse* meaning "money."

galetouse *f.* money.

gousset bien garni (avoir le) *exp.* • (lit.): to have one's pocket well garnished.

> **NOTE:** **gousset** *m.* small pocket on a vest or pants.

paré(e) (être) *adj.* • (lit.): to be adorned, bedecked.

plein(e) aux as (être) *adj.* to be born rich • (lit.): to have all the aces.

plein les profondes (en avoir)
exp. to be very rich • (lit.): to have lots of it (money) in the pockets.

NOTE: **profondes** *f.pl.* pockets (from the adjective *profond* meaning "deep").

reins solides (avoir les) *m.pl.*
to be financially set • (lit.): to have a solid (lower) back or "to be sturdy."

rempli(e) (être) *adj.* to be rich
• (lit.): to be filled up (with money).

remplir (se) *v.* to get rich • (lit.): to fill oneself (with money).

remuer l'argent à la pelle *exp.*
to have money to burn • (lit.): to stir money with a shovel.

richard(e) *n.* one who is rich.

riche comme Crésus (être)
exp. to be very rich • (lit.): to be rich like Crœsus.

NOTE: **Crésus** *m.* a very rich man.

rupin(e) *adj.*

example: C'est un quartier **rupin**.

translation: It's a **rich** neighborhood.

as spoken: C't'un quartier **rupin**.

vivre sur un grand pied *exp.*
to live high on the hog • (lit.): to live on a big foot.

■ RUMMAGE (TO) ■

chercher en bouleversant tout

example: Je n'aime pas qu'on **fouine** dans mes affaires!

translation: I don't like people **rummaging** through my stuff!

as spoken: J'aime pas qu'on **fouine** dans mes affaires!

chambarder *v.* to turn everything topsy-turvy.

example: Les cambrioleurs ont tout **chambardé** dans la baraque.

translation: The burglars **turned everything upside-down** in the house.

as spoken: Les cambrioleurs, y z'ont tout **chambardé** dans la baraque.

NOTE -1: **chambard** *m.* upheaval.

NOTE -2: **baraque** *f.* house
• (lit.): barracks.

chambouler *v.* • **1.** to rummage by turning everything upside-down • **2.** to devestate (someone).

example: Les mauvaises nouvelles m'ont **chamboulé**.

translation: The bad news **overwhelmed me over**.

as spoken: Les mauvaises nouvelles, è m'ont **chamboulé**.

farfouiller *v.* to rummage without taking any care.

example: Qu'est-ce que tu cherches?! Arrête de **farfouiller** dans mes tiroirs!

translation: What are you looking for?! Stop **rummaging around** in my drawers!

as spoken: Tu cherches quoi?! Arrête de **farfouiller** dans mes tiroirs!

fouiller *v.* to rummage for something • (lit.): to frisk.

example: Quel **fouillis**!

translation: What a **mess**!

as spoken: [no change]

NOTE: **fouillis** *m.* jumbled mess.

fouiner *v.* to rummage, to nose or ferret about.

example: Ma mère n'aime pas qu'on **fouine** dans ses affaires.

translation: My mother doesn't like it when people **nose around** in her belongings.

as spoken: Ma mère, elle aime pas qu'on **fouine** dans ses affaires.

fourgonner *v.* to poke around turning everything upside-down.

fourrager *v.* to rummage.

example: J'ai **fourragé** dans des tas de papiers pour trouver cette facture!

translation: I **rummaged around** in piles of papers to find this bill!

as spoken: J'ai **fourragé** dans des tas d'papiers pour trouver c'te facture!

fureter *v.* to nose or pry about • (lit.): to ferret (about).

trifouiller *v.* • **1.** to rummage, to turn everything upside-down • **2.** to fiddle (with something).

example: Ne **trifouille** pas avec ça!

translation: Don't **fiddle** with that!

as spoken: **Trifouille** pas avec ça!

RUNT

chétif

example: Maurice a l'air d'un petit **mecton** mais il est très fort!

translation: Maurice may look like a little **runt** but he's very strong!

as spoken: Maurice, il a l'air d'un p'tit **mecton** mais il est très fort!

---

demi-portion *m. / f.* half-pint
• (lit.): half-portion.

gringalet *m.* shrimp (of a man or boy), puny little fellow.

example: Ce **gringalet** ne me fait pas peur!

translation: This **little runt** doesn't scare me!

as spoken: Ce **gringalet**, y m'fait pas peur!

mecton *m.* little guy.

NOTE: **mec** *m.* guy, man, "dude."

petit bout d'homme *m.* • (lit.): a little end of a man.

rabougri(e) (être) *adj.* • (lit.): to be stunted (in growth), to shrivel up.

ratatiné(e) (être) *adj.* • (lit.): to be shrunken and deformed.

ALSO: **ratatiner** *v.* to clobber.

example: Reviens tout de suite ou je te **ratatine**!

translation: Come back right now or I'll **clobber** you!

as spoken: Reviens tout d'suite ou j'te **ratatine**!

SAD (TO BE)

triste (être)

example: J'ai le **cafard** parce que mon meilleur ami est parti pour la France pour deux mois.

translation: I'm **depressed** because my best friend left for France for two months.

as spoken: J'ai l'**cafard** pasque mon meilleur ami, il est parti pour la France pour deux mois.

---

bourdon (avoir le) *m.* to be down in the dumps • (lit.): to have the bumblebee.

broyer du noir *exp.* to be depressed • (lit.): to crush or smash the black.

cafard (avoir le) *m.* (extremely popular) to be depressed • (lit.): to have the cockroach.

dans son assiette (ne pas être) *exp.* to feel blah, out of sorts • (lit.): not to be in one's plate.

figure d'enterrement (avoir une) *f.* to look depressed, to have a sad face • (lit.): to have a burial face.

malheureux, euse comme les pierres (être) *exp.* to be very sad and alone • (lit.): to be as sad as the rocks.

mine d'enterrement (avoir une) *exp.* same as: *figure d'enterrement (avoir une)*.

ronger le cœur (se) *exp.* to cause oneself great anguish • (lit.): to gnaw at one's heart.

spleen (avoir le) *exp.* to be very depressed.

> **NOTE:** **spleen** *m.* lowness of spirits.

tête d'enterrement (avoir une) *exp.* same as: *figure d'enterrement (avoir une)*.

> **NOTE:** Many of the slang synonyms for "face" can also be used to mean "head" as well. In fact, even the French word *tête* is used to mean "head" or "face."

example: Je ne reconnais pas sa **tête**.

translation: I don't recognize his / her **face**.

as spoken: J'reconnais pas sa **tête**.

SHOES

chaussures

example: Je viens d'acheter une nouvelle robe et des **pompes** pour la grande fête ce soir!

translation: I just bought a new dress and some **shoes** for the big party tonight!

as spoken: J'viens d'ach'ter une nouvelle robe et des **pompes** pour la grande fête c'soir!

bateaux *m.pl.* big shoes or feet
- (lit.): boats.

boîtes à violon *f.pl.* • (lit.): violin cases.

croquenots *m.pl.*

godasses *f.pl.* (very popular).

godillots *m.pl.*

grolles *f.pl.*

pompes *f.pl.* (very popular).

targettes *f.pl.*

tartines *f.pl.*

tatanes *f.pl.*

SHUT UP (TO)

taire (se)

example: **Ta gueule**! Tu commences à m'énerver avec tes questions stupides!

translation: **Shut up**! You're starting to bug me with your stupid questions!

as spoken: [no change]

---

bouche cousue (faire) *exp.* to close one's mouth • (lit.): to make the sewn up mouth.

bouchon (y mettre un) *exp.*
- (lit.): to put a cork in it.

boucler (la) *v.* to shut up • (lit.): to buckle it (*la bouche* meaning "the mouth").

example: **La boucle**! Tu m'énerves!

translation: **Shut up**! You're bugging me!

as spoken: [no change]

boucler son égout *exp.* to shut one's mouth • (lit.): to buckle one's sewer or drain.

NOTE: **égout** *m.* mouth
- (lit.): sewer, drain.

cadenas (y mettre un) *exp.* to put a padlock on it.

fermer *v.* to shut up • (lit.): to close.

ferme ça! *exp.* shut up! • (lit.): close it!

fermer sa gueule *exp.* to shut one's mouth • (lit.): to close one's mouth.

NOTE: **gueule** *f.* derogatory for "mouth" when applied to a person since its literal translation is the "mouth of an animal."

fermer son bec *exp.* to shut one's mouth • (lit.): to close one's beak.

NOTE: **bec** *m.* mouth • (lit.): beak of a bird.

fermer son micro *exp.* to shut one's mouth • (lit.): to close one's microphone.

NOTE: **micro** *m.* mouth
- (lit.): microphone.

fermer (la) *v.* to shut it (*la bouche* meaning "mouth").

example: **La ferme**! Tu n'arrête jamais de palabrer!

translation: **Shut up**! You never stop blabbing!

as spoken: **La ferme**! T'arrête jamais d'palabrer!

la barbe! *interj.* shut up! • (lit.): the beard!

rideau! *interj.* shut up! put a sock in it! • (lit.): curtain.

sourdine (y mettre une) *exp.*
- (lit.): to put a mute on it.

ta bouche, bébé, t'auras des frites *exp.* an abusive remark made at someone who is talking too much • (lit.): your mouth, baby, you're gonna have fainting spells (from all the oxygen you're losing).

> **NOTE:** **tomber dans les frites** *exp.* to faint • (lit.): to fall in the (French) fries.

ta gueule! *interj.* (extremely popular) shut up! • (lit.): your mouth.

> **NOTE:** **gueule** *f.* derogatory for "mouth" when applied to a person since its literal translation is the "mouth of an animal."

tenir sa langue *exp.* • (lit.): to hold one's tongue.

tirer la fermeture éclair *exp.* to close one's mouth • (lit.): to pull up one's zipper.

<hr/>

SLEEP (TO)

dormir

<u>example:</u> Je suis très fatigué. J'ai envie de **faire une ronflette**.

<u>translation:</u> I'm really tired. I feel like **taking a nap**.

<u>as spoken:</u> J'suis très fatigué. J'ai envie d'**faire une ronflette**.

> **SEE:** **BED (TO GO TO)**, *p. 214.*

<hr/>

coucher à la belle étoile *exp.* to sleep outside • (lit.): to sleep by the pretty star.

découcher *v.* to sleep somewhere other than one's house.

dormir à poings fermés *exp.* to sleep soundly • (lit.): to sleep close-fisted.

dormir comme une souche *exp.* to sleep like a log • (lit.): to sleep like a stump.

écraser (en) *v.* to sleep, "to crash" • (lit.): to crush some.

> **NOTE:** This expression was probably created due to the "crushing" sound that one makes when snoring.

faire dodo *exp.* to go "night-night."

> **NOTE:** This is child's language yet used commonly in jest by adults.

faire la grasse matinée *exp.* to sleep in • (lit.): to make the fat morning.

faire le tour du cadran *exp.* to sleep in • (lit.): to make the (circular) tour of the face of the clock.

faire une ronflette *exp.* to take a nap, to take a snooze.

> **NOTE:** **ronfler** *v.* to sleep • (lit.): to snore.

pioncer *v.* to sleep, to snooze.

romance (piquer une) *exp.* to take a nap.

> **NOTE:** **piquer** *v.* to take or steal.

ronflaguer *v.* to snore, to snooze.

ronfler *v.* to sleep, to snooze • (lit.): to snore.

roupiller *v.* to sleep, to snooze.

roupillon (piquer un) *exp.* same as: *piquer une romance.*

sieste *f.* (from the Spanish term *siesta*) a little nap.

SNAG

obstacle caché

example: Je veux bien aller te
chercher à l'aéroport ce soir, mais
voici le **chiendent**... ma voiture est
tombée en panne ce matin.

translation: I'd like to pick you up at
the airport tonight but here's the
hitch... my car broke down this
morning.

as spoken: J'veux bien aller t'chercher
à l'aéroport c'soir, mais voici
l'**chiendent**... ma voiture, elle est
tombée en panne c'matin.

---

accroc m. the snag, hitch • (lit.): hook.

chiendent m. the snag, hitch
• (lit.): couch grass.

hic m.

pépin m. • (lit.): pip (of apple), seed.

**rembourré(e) avec des
noyaux de pêches (être)**
exp. said of something difficult to do
• (lit.): to be stuffed with peach pits.

SPEAK (TO)

parler

example: Jeanette a **babillé** pendant
toute une heure de son dispute avec
Henri.

translation: Jeanette **babbled on
and on** for an entire hour about her
fight with Henry.

as spoken: Jeanette, elle a **babillé**
pendant toute une heure d'son dispute
avec Henri.

SEE: NONSENSE, p. 272.

---

avoir voix au chapitre exp. to
  have one's say • (lit.): to have voice
  to the chapter.

babiller v. to chatter on about
  nothing • (lit.): to babble (of brook).

bafouiller v. to talk nonsense,
  to speak incoherently.
  NOTE: bafouille f. a letter.

baliverner v. to talk nonsense,
  to B.S.
  NOTE: balivernes m.pl.
  nonsense.

baragouiner v. to talk gibberish, to
  jabber.
  NOTE: baragouineur, euse n.
  one who talks about nothing.

bavasser v. to talk about nothing.
  NOTE: This is a slang variant of the
  verb *baver* literally meaning "to
  dribble" or "to drool."

bredouiller v. to speak quickly and
  indistinctly.

  example: Sandra m'a **bredouillé**
  une excuse.

  translation: Sandra **jabbered out**
  an excuse to me.

  as spoken: Sandra, è m'a
  bredouillé une excuse.

cancaner v. to gossip.
  **ALSO: colporter des cancans
  sur quelqu'un** exp. to spread
  rumors about someone.

débiter *v.* to reel off a long story.

example: Chaque fois que Marc me voit, il me **débite** une longue harangue.

translation: Every time Marc sees me, he **reels off** a long and boring story.

as spoken: Chaque fois que Marc, y m'voit, y m'**débite** une longue harangue.

NOTE: **harangue** *f.* a long and endless story, harangue.

SEE: **haranguer**, p. 286.

débloquer *v.* to talk nonsense.

déjanter *v.* (*extremely popular*) to talk nonsense.

déménager *v.* to talk nonsense • (lit.): to move out (in this case, from one's senses).

dérailler *v.* to talk nonsense • (lit.): to derail.

dévider *v.* to talk nonstop • (lit.): to unwind, reel off (thread, etc.).

divaguer *v.* to talk nonsense.

fariboler *v.* to talk nonsense.

NOTE: **faribole** *f.* nonsense.

haranguer *v.* to reel off a long and boring speech • (lit.): to harangue.

joboter *v.* to chatter, to jabber.

jacasser *v.* to chatter, to jabber.

jacter *v.* to speak, to jabber.

NOTE: **jactance** *f.* talking, speech.

example: Mais qu'est-ce qu'il a dit? Je ne comprends pas sa **jactance**.

translation: What did he say? I don't understand his **gibberish**.

as spoken: Mais qu'est-c'qu'il a dit? J'comprends pas sa **jactance**.

jaspiner *v.* to chatter, so speak.

palabrer *v.* to talk nonsense • (lit.): to palaver.

papoter *v.* to talk a lot about insignificant things, to blabber.

parler à bâtons rompus *exp.* to talk by fits and starts • (lit.): to talk with broken clubs.

parler à tort et à travers *exp.* to talk without knowledge of one's subject • (lit.): to speak randomly.

parler affaires *exp.* • (lit.): to talk business.

parler dans le vide *exp.* to talk without being listened to • (lit.): to speak in a vacuum.

parler de la pluie et du beau temps *exp.* to chat • (lit.): to talk about the rain and nice weather.

parler en l'air *exp.* to talk idly • (lit.): to talk in the air.

piquer un laïus *exp.* to make a long-winded speech.

prêcher à un sourd *exp.* to talk without being listened to • (lit.): to preach to a deaf person.

ragoter *v.* to gossip.

NOTE: **ragots** *m.pl.* piece of gossip.

raisonner comme un sabot *exp.* to talk nonsense • (lit.): to reason like a shoe.

raisonner comme un tambour mouillé *exp.* to talk nonsense • (lit.): to reason like a wet drum.

raisonner comme une pantoufle *exp.* to talk nonsense • (lit.): to reason like a slipper.

tailler une bavette *exp.* to chat • (lit.): to trim a bib.

tenir le crachoir *exp.* to have the floor (in a discussion).

> **NOTE:** This is from the verb *cracher* meaning "to spit."

travailler du pick-up *exp.* to talk a lot, to talk like a broken record • (lit.): to work on the record player.

user sa salive *exp.* to waste one's breath • (lit.): to use one's saliva.

STINK (TO)

puer

example: Ça **shlingue** dans cette poissonnerie!

translation: It **stinks** in this fish market!

as spoken: Ça **shlingue** dans c'te poissonn'rie!

---

cocoter *v.*

> **VARIATION:** **cocotter** *v.*

cogner *v.* • (lit.): to hit.

coincer *v.* • (lit.): to stick.

corner *v.*

emboucaner *v.*

fouetter *v.* • (lit.): to whip.

repousser *v.* • (lit.): to repel.

schemecter *v.*

schlingoter *v.* a slang variant of: *schlinguer* (see next entry).

schlinguer *v.*

schlipoter *v.*

taper . to tap, strike, hit.

STOMACH

ventre

example: Si tu n'arrêtes pas de manger tous ces desserts, tu vas finir par avoir mal au **bide**!

translation: If you don't stop eating all those desserts, you're going to end up with a **belly** ache!

as spoken: Si t'arrêtes pas d'manger tous ces desserts, tu vas finir par avoir mal au **bide**!

---

bedaine *f.* paunch, round belly.

bedon *m.* paunch, round belly.

bide *m.* belly.

bidon *m.* belly • (lit.): can, drum (for oil).

bocal *m.* • (lit.): goldfish bowl.

buffet *m.* • (lit.): buffet.

burlingue *m.*

estome *m.* an abbreviated form of: *estomac* meaning "stomach."

globe *m.* • (lit.): globe, sphere.

panse *f.* belly.

tiroir *m.* • (lit.): drawer.

STORY

histoire

STROLL (TO)

promener (se)

example: Quelle histoire marrante! C'est une **bien bonne**, celle-là!

translation: What a funny story! That's a **good one**!

as spoken: Quelle histoire marrante! C't'une **bien bonne**, celle-là!

---

example: Si on **se baladait** le long de la Seine après le dîner?

translation: Suppose we **stroll** along the Seine after dinner?

as spoken: Si on **s'baladait** le long d'la Seine après l'dîner?

---

bien bonne (une) *f.* a good and interesting story, a "good one."

des vertes et des pas mûres *exp.* risqué or raw and dirty stories • (lit.): green and not ripe.

> **NOTE:** **la langue verte** *f.* slang.

galéjade *f.* far-fetched story.

> **NOTE:** **galéjer** *v.* to tell far-fetched stories.

histoire à dormir debout *f.* a long and boring story • (lit.): a story that makes one sleep standing up.

histoire abracadabrante *f.* cock-and-bull story.

histoire de bonnes femmes *f.* old wive's tale.

histoire marseillaise *f.* far-fetched story • (lit.): a Marseillaise story.

rengaine *f.* repetitious story.

> example: C'est toujours la même **rengaine**!
>
> translation: It's always the **same ol' story**!
>
> as spoken: [no change]

badauder *v.* to walk slowly and sightsee, to rubberneck.

> **NOTE:** **badaud(e)** *n.* rubber-necker.

baguenauder *v.* to stroll with no destination, to stroll.

> **ALSO:** **baguenaude (être en)** *exp.* to be on a stroll.

balader (se) *v.* (extremely popular) to stroll, to wander, to saunter.

> **NOTE:** **baladeur, euse** *n.*
> • **1.** wanderer • **2.** this is also the name given to a portable radio with a headset (also commonly called *un Walkman*).

déambuler *v.* to stroll about, to wander.

flânocher *v.* a slang variation of the verb *flâner* meaning "to stroll."

vadrouiller *v.* to stroll with no destination.

> **ALSO:** **vadrouille (être en)** *exp.*

virée (être en) *exp.* to be on a quick little jaunt.

STUBBORN PERSON

personne têtue

example: Quelle **tête de cochon**! Il pense qu'il a toujours raison!

translation: What a **pig-headed person**! Il pense qu'il a toujours raison!

as spoken: Quelle **tête de cochon**! Y pense qu'il a toujours raison!

---

tête de cochon f. • (lit.): pig-head.

tête de lard f. • (lit.): fat-head.

tête de mule f. • (lit.): mule-head.

tête de pioche f. • (lit.): pickax-head.

STUPEFIED (TO BE)

stupéfait(e) (être)

example: Quand le patron m'a donné une promotion, j'**en restais comme deux ronds de flan**!

translation: When the boss gave me the promotion, I was **floored**!

as spoken: Quand l'patron, y m'a donné une promotion, j'**en restais comme deux ronds d'flan**!

---

aplati(e) (être) adj. to be floored • (lit.): to be flattened.

assis(e) (en être) adj. to be floored • (lit.): to be seated.

boucher un coin (en) exp. to be flabbergasted.

boucher une surface (en) exp. to be flabbergasted.

deux ronds de flan (en être comme) exp. to be flabbergasted • (lit.): to be like two rounds of flan (or custard) about something.

deux ronds de frites (en être comme) exp. to be flabbergasted • (lit.): to be like two rounds of fries about something.

épater v. to flabbergast, to bowl over.

époustouflé(e) (être) adj. to be flabbergasted.

estomaquer v. to flabbergast, to take one's breath away • (lit.): to affect one's *estomach* (pronounced: *estoma*) meaning "stomach."

rester baba (en) exp. to be so stunned with amazement or surprise that the sound "bah-bah" is all that can be uttered.

rester comme une tomate (en) exp. to be flabbergasted • (lit.): to stay there like a tomato (and be red with shock) about something.

rester comme une tourte (en) exp. to be flabbergasted • (lit.): to stay there like an idiot about something.

NOTE: **tourte** f. idiot • (lit.): (fruit) tart.

sidérer v. to flabbergast.

tomber de haut exp. to fall over with surprise • (lit.): to fall from a height.

tomber des nues exp. to fall over with surprise • (lit.): to fall from the high clouds.

NOTE: **nues** f.pl. an old term for "clouds."

tomber sur le cul exp. • (lit.): to fall on one's ass (due to surprise).

TELEPHONE

téléphone

example: J'ai passé une heure au **bigophone** avec ma sœur qui habite à l'étranger. Ça va coûter cher, ce coup de fil!

translation: I spend an hour on the **phone** with my sister who lives overseas. That phone call is going to be expensive!

as spoken: J'ai passé une heure au **bigophone** avec ma sœur qui habite à l'étranger. Ça va coûter cher, c'coup d'fil!

---

bigophone *m.*

NOTE: **bigophoner** *v.* to telephone (someone).

cornichon *m.* • (lit.): pickle (since it resembles the shape of the receiver).

phonard *m.*

téléphon *m.*

THIN

mince

example: Mange quelque chose! Tu es **maigre comme un clou**!

translation: Eat something! You're **thin as a rail**!

as spoken: Mange quèque chose! T'es **maigre comme un clou**!

asperge *f.* a very thin person
• (lit.): an asparagus.

maigre comme un clou (être) *exp.* to be terribly thin • (lit.): to be as thin as a nail.

maigre comme une lame de rasoir (être) *exp.* to be terribly thin • (lit.): to be as thin as a razor blade.

maigrichon(ne) (être) *adj.* to be a little thin.

maigriot(te) (être) *adj.* to be a little thin.

manche à balai *m.* a very thin person • (lit.): a broomstick.

n'avoir que la peau sur les os *exp.* to be nothing but skin and bones • (lit.): to have nothing but skin on the bones.

sac d'os *m.* a very thin person • (lit.): sack of bones.

sec comme un coup de trique (être) *exp.* to be very thin • (lit.): to be as dry as a hit from a heavy stick.

THIRSTY (TO BE)

soif (avoir)

example: J'**ai le gosier sec**, moi. Veut-tu aller boire un pot quelque part?

translation: I'm **thirsty**. Do you want to go get something to drink somewhere?

as spoken: J'**ai l'gosier sec**, moi. Tu veux aller boire un pot, quèque part?

gosier sec (avoir le) *exp.*
  • (lit.): to have a dry throat.
  NOTE: **gosier** *m.* throat.

pépie (avoir la) *exp.* to be very
  thirsty.
  NOTE: **la pépie** *f.* • (lit.): a disease
  of the tongue of fowl.

sécher (la) *v.* • (lit.): to have it (the
  throat) dry.

THRASHING

volée de coups

example: Quand Marc a menti à sa
mère, elle lui a donné une vraie
dégelée!

translation: When Mark lied to his
mother, she gave him a **thrashing**!

as spoken: Quand Marc, il a menti à sa
mère, è lui a donné une vraie **dég'lée**!
SEE -1: **BAWL SOMEONE OUT
(TO)**, *p. 213.*
SEE -2: **FIGHT (TO)**, *p. 236.*
NOTE: The verbs *filer* (slang for "to
give") and *recevoir* ("to receive") are
commonly used with synonym for
"thrashing." For example: *filer une
peignée;* to give a thrashing (to someone) • *recevoir une correction;* to get
a thrashing.

carder le cuir à quelqu'un
  exp. to tan someone's hide • (lit.): to
  card leather.

correction *f.* • (lit.): correction.

danse *f.* • (lit.): dance.

dégelée *f.* • (lit.): defrosting, thawing
  out.

dérouillée *f.* • (lit.): "derusting."

distribution *f.* • (lit.): distribution.

floppée *f.* • (lit.): a large quantity
  (in this case) of hits.

fricassée *f.* • (lit.): a fricassee.

frottée *f.* • (lit.): a rubbing.

moucher *v.* to give someone a
  thrashing • (lit.): to wipe.
  NOTE: **moucher (se faire)** *v.* to
  get oneself severely reprimanded.

passer à tabac *exp.* to give
  someone a thrashing • (lit.): to
  make (someone) into tobacco.
  NOTE: **passage à tabac** *m.*
  thrashing.
  SEE: **tabasser**, *p. 238.*

pâtée *f.* • (lit.): mash, mush.

peignée *f.* • (lit.): a combing.

raclée *f.* • (lit.): scraping.

ramasser *v.* to give a thrashing
  • (lit.): to collect.
  NOTE: **ramassée** *f.* a thrashing.

ratatouille *f.* • (lit.): stew.

rincée *f.* • (lit.): a rinsing out.

rosser *v.* to thrash someone.
  NOTE: **rossée** *f.* thrashing.

schlague *f.* military slang for
  "flogging."

sonner les cloches (faire) *exp.*
  to get severely reprimanded
  • (lit.): to make the bells ring.

tannée *f.* • (lit.): a tanning.

tanner le cuir *exp.* to tan one's
  hid • (lit.): to tan leather.

tatouille *f.* a thrashing.

tortignole *f.* a thrashing.

tournée *f.* • (lit.): a round (of drinks,
  etc.).

trempe *f.* • (lit.): a soaking.

trifouillée *f.* • (lit.): a "rummaging."

triquée *f.* a thrashing, beating.

> **NOTE:** This comes from the feminine noun *trique* meaning "a heavy stick."

TIRED (TO BE)

fatigué(e) (être)

example: Je me suis levé à 5h du matin. Je vais aller me coucher. J'**ai un coup de pompe**.

translation: I got up at 5:00 in the morning. I'm going to bed. I'm **pooped**.

as spoken: Je m'suis levé à 5h du mat'. J'vais aller m'coucher. J'**ai un coup d'pompe**.

---

ciboulot qui se coince (avoir le) *exp.* to be very tired • (lit.): to have the head that is jamming.

battre de l'aile *exp.* to be exhausted • (lit.): (of a wounded bird) to flutter, to beat the wing.

canuler *v.* to tire or wear someone out.

> example: Il me **canule** avec ses histoires!

> translation: He's **wearing me out** with his stories!

> as spoken: Y m'**canule** avec ses histoires!

claqué(e) (être) *adj.* to be "wiped out."

coltar (être dans le) *exp.* to be in a fog after waking up in the morning.

coup de barre (avoir un) *exp.* to be suddenly exhausted • (lit.): to have a sudden bar or rod (that is weighing one down).

THROAT

gorge

example: Je crois que je suis malade. J'ai très mal à la **gargoulette**.

translation: I think I'm sick. My **throat** really hurts.

as spoken: J'crois qu'sh'ui malade. J'ai très mal à la **gargoulette**.

---

avaloir *m.* • (lit.): swallower.

> **NOTE:** This comes from the verb *avaler* meaning "to swallow."

col *m.* • (lit.): collar.

colback *m.* • (lit.): collar.

gargane *f.* • (lit.): the "gargler."

> **NOTE:** This comes from the verb *se gargariser* meaning "to gargle."

gargoulette *f.* same as: *gargane*.

gosier *m.* • (lit.): gullet.

goulot *m.* • (lit.): the neck of a bottle.

sifflet *m.* • (lit.): (a) whistle.

tube *m.* • (lit.): tube.

coup de pompe (avoir un)
exp. to be suddenly exhausted
• (lit.): to have a sudden
pumped-out-of-energy feeling.

crevé(e) (être) *adj.* to be
dead-tired • (lit.): to be dead.
NOTE: **crever** *v.* to die.

éreinté(e) (être) *adj.* to be
exhausted, to be "wiped out"
• (lit.): to be sprained.

éreinter *v.* to tire out • (lit.): to
sprain.

flagada (être) *adj.* to be pooped.

flapi(e) (être) *adj.* to be
exhausted.

**guibolles en accordéon
(avoir les)** *exp.* to be exhausted,
to be hardly able to stand due to
fatigue • (lit.): to have legs like an
accordion.

lessivé(e) (être) *adj.* to be
drained of all one's energy, to be
"wiped out" • (lit.): to be washed
(out).

moulu(e) (être) *adj.* to be
exhausted • (lit.): to be powdered.

nettoyé(e) (être) *adj.* to be
drained of all one's energy, to be
exhausted • (lit.): to be cleaned (of
all one's energy).

pompé(e) (être) *adj.* to be
pooped • (lit.): to be pumped (of all
one's energy).

pomper quelqu'un *v.* to tire
someone out • (lit.): to pump
someone (of all his energy).

**ramasser à la petite cuillère
(être à)** *exp.* to be completely
exhausted • (lit.): to be picked up
with a little spoon.

raplapla (être) *adj.* to feel blah.

rincé(e) (être) *adj.* to be "wiped
out" • (lit.): to be rinsed (of all one's
energy).

rompu(e) (être) *adj.* to be "wiped
out" • (lit.): to be broken.

sentir à plat (se) *exp.* to feel blah
• (lit.): to feel flattened out.

sur les genoux (être) *exp.* to be
"wiped out" • (lit.): to be on one's
knees.

sur les rotules (être) *adj.* to be
"wiped out" • (lit.): to be on one's
kneecaps.

vanné(e) (être) *adj.* to be "wiped
out" • (lit.): to be fanned, winnowed.

vanner quelqu'un *v.* to wear
someone out • (lit.): to fan or
winnow someone.

**yeux en capote de fiacre
(avoir les)** *exp.* to have tired
and swollen eyes • (lit.): to have
eyes like the bonnet of a
horse-drawn carriage.

**yeux qui se coincent (avoir
les)** *exp.* to be exhausted, to be
unable to see straight due to
excessive fatigue • (lit.): to have
eyes that are jamming or "crossing."

UGLY

laid(e)

example: Tu as vu le mari de Béatrice?
Il **a une gueule à caler les roues
de corbillard**!

translation: Did you see Beatrice's husband? He's **butt-ugly**!

as spoken: T'as vu l'mari d'Béatrice? **Il a une gueule à caler les roues d'corbillard**!

---

gueule à caler les roues de corbillard (avoir une) *exp.* said of a very ugly person • (lit.): to have a face that could stop the wheels of a hearse.

> **NOTE -1:** **gueule** *f.* derogatory for "face" or "mouth" since its literal translation is the "mouth of an animal."

> **NOTE -2:** Any synonym for "face" could be used in place of *gueule* in this expression.

> **SEE:** **FACE**, *p. 233*.

gueule d'empeigne *f.* ugly face • (lit.): a face that looks like the upper part of a shoe.

laidasse *f.* ugly woman.

> **NOTE:** This comes from the adjective *laid(e)* meaning "ugly."

mochard(e) • **1**. *n.* an ugly person • **2**. *adj.* ugly.

example (1): Quel **mochard**!

translation: What an **ugly person**!

as spoken: [no change]

example (2): Il est **mochard**!

translation: He's **ugly**!

as spoken: [no change]

moche *adj.* (extremely popular) ugly.

mochetée *f.* ugly woman.

remède contre l'amour *m.* humorous for "ugly" • (lit.): remedy for love.

tête à coucher dehors avec un billet de logement dans sa poche (avoir une) *exp.* said of a very ugly person • (lit.): to have a face that should be made to sleep outside even with a billeting order in his / her pocket.

> **NOTE -1:** The feminine noun *tête*, literally meaning "head," is commonly used in spoken French to mean "face" as well.

> **NOTE -2:** Any slang synonyms for "head" or "face" could replace *tête* in this expression.

> **SEE:** **FACE**, *p. 233* and **HEAD**, *p. 247*.

toc *adj.* ugly.

tocard(n) *n. & adj.* same as: *mochard(e)*.

tocasse *adj.* slang variant of: *toc*.

tocasson *adj.* slang variant of: *toc*.

UMBRELLA

parapluie

example: Il commence à pleuvoir. Va chercher ton **pébroc**.

translation: It's starting to rain. Go get your **umbrella**.

as spoken: Y commence à pleuvoir. Va chercher ton **pébroc**.

---

chamberlain *m.*

paralance *m.*

> **NOTE:** **lance** *f.* rain.

pébroc m. (very popular).

pépin m.

riflard m. • (lit.): plastering trowel.

UP TO DATE (TO BE)

courant (être au)

example: David et Laurent se sont disputés à la soirée? Qu'est-ce qui s'est passé? Je ne suis pas **à la page**!

translation: David and Laurent had a fight at the party? What happened? I'm not **up-to-speed**!

as spoken: David et Laurent, y s'sont disputés à la soirée? Qu'est-c'qui s'est passé? J'suis pas **à la page**!

à la coule (être) *exp.* • (lit.): to be in the flow.

à la hauteur (être) *exp.* to be up on what's going on • (lit.): to be at the height.

à la page (être) *exp.* to be with it • (lit.): to be at the page.

au parfum (être) *exp.* to be informed • (lit.): to be in the perfume.

dans la note (être) *exp.* to be with it • (lit.): to be in the note.

dans le mouvement (être) *exp.* to be with it • (lit.): to be in the movement.

dans le train (être) *exp.* to be with it, in the swing of things • (lit.): to be in the movement or pace.

dans le vent (être) *exp.* • (lit.): to be in the wind.

UPPER SOCIETY

haute société

example: Christine sort avec Norbert? Mais c'est un marchand, lui, tandis qu'elle, elle est **aristo**!

translation: Christine is going out with Norbert? But he's a shopkeeper, whereas she is a **member of the elite**.

as spoken: Christine, è sort avec Norbert? Mais c't'un marchant, lui tandis qu'elle, è fait partie d'**l'aristo**!

---

aristo (l') m. a member of the "aristocracy."

aristoche (l') m. a slang variant of: *aristo (l')*.

gratin (le) m. the "upper crust" of society.

> **NOTE:** **au grain** m. that which is cooked with bread crumbs and cheese.

Tout Paris (le) m. the upper society of Paris.

WIFE

épouse

example: Je te présent ma **légitime**. Nous sommes mariés depuis vingt ans.

translation: I'd like you to meet my **better half**. We've been married for twenty years.

as spoken: J'te présent ma **légitime**. On est marié depuis vingt ans.

---

bérgère (ma) *f.* • (lit.): my shepherdess.

bourgeoise *f.*

cinquante-pour-cent (mon) *m.* • (lit.): my fifty percent.

gouvernement (mon) *m.* • (lit.): my government.

légitime (ma) *f.* • (lit.): legitimate.

moitié (ma) *f.* my better half • (lit.): my half.

panthère (ma) *f.* • (lit.): panther.

régulière (ma) *f.* • (lit.): regular one.

WORK (TO)

travailler

example: Mon père commence à **bosser** à 7h du matin et termine à 3h de l'après-midi.

translation: My father starts **work** at 7:00 in the morning and finishes at 3:00 in the afternoon.

as spoken: Ma père, y commence à **bosser** à 7h du mat' et termine à 3h d'l'après-m'.

---

bosser *v.* (extremely popular) to work.
  NOTE: bosseur, euse *n.* worker.

boulonner *v.* to work.

NOTE: boulot *m.* (extremely popular) work.

bricoler *v.* to do small jobs, to tinker.
  NOTE: bricoleur *m.* handyman.

bûcher *v.* to work hard, to study hard.
  NOTE: bûcheur, euse *n.* one who works or studies hard.

chiader *v.* to work, to prepare for an examination.

décarcasser (se) *v.* to work one's butt off • (lit.): to "decarcass" oneself.

démancher (se) *v.* to work hard, to bend over backwards • (lit.): to disjoint oneself.

gratter *v.* to do a lot of paper work • (lit.): to scratch.

job *m.* job.

labeur *m.* hard work • (lit.): labor, toil.

marner *v.* to work hard.
  NOTE: marne *m.* work.

masser *v.* to work • (lit.): to massage.
  NOTE: masseur, euse *n.* worker.

suer sang et eau *exp.* to work extremely hard • (lit.): to sweat blood and water.

travailler pour des prunes *exp.* to work for "peanuts" • (lit.): to work for plums.

travailler pour des pruneaux *exp.* to work for "peanuts" • (lit.): to work for prunes.

travailler pour la peau *exp.* to work for nothing • (lit.): to work for skin (meaning a handshake).

trimer *v.* to work terribly hard, to drudge, to toil.

turbiner *v.* to work hard, to toil.

NOTE -1: **turbin** *m.* work, grind.

NOTE -2: **turbineur, euse** *n.* worker.

WORRY (TO)

inquiéter (s')

example: Ma mère est **aux cent coups** parce que mon père est en retard de deux heures!

translation: My mother is **worrying herself to death** because my father is two hours late!

as spoken: Ma mère, elle est **aux cent coups** pasque mon père, il est en r'tard de deux heures!

---

biler (se) *v.* to worry, to get all worked up and upset • (lit.): to make oneself bilious.

bileux, euse • 1. *n.* one who worries a lot, a "worrywart" • 2. *adj.* worried.

example (1): C'est un **bileux**.

translation: He's a **worrywart**.

as spoken: C't'un **bileux**.

example (2): Il est **bileux**.

translation: He's **worried**.

as spoken: [no change]

cent coups (être aux) *exp.* to be extremely worried • (lit.): to be at one hundred blows.

chiffonner *v.* to worry, to make feel uneasy • (lit.): to crumple (a piece of paper, etc.).

faire de la bile (se) *exp.* to worry, to get all worked up and upset • (lit.): to make oneself bilious.

faire du mauvais sang (se) *exp.* to get all worked up and upset • (lit.): to make oneself bad blood.

frapper (se) *v.* to worry greatly • (lit.): to hit oneself.

frapper le biscuit (se) *v.* to worry greatly • (lit.): to hit oneself in the biscuit (meaning "head").

mettre martel en tête (se) *exp.* to worry • (lit.): to put a hammer in the head.

NOTE -1: This expression conjures up an image of a person who is so worked up over something that he can hear his own pulse banging like a hammer in his head.

NOTE -2: **martel** *m.* old term for "hammer" – the current term for hammer is the masculine noun *marteau*.

tintouin *m.* worry, trouble, grief.

turlupiner *v.* to plague with worry.

STREET FRENCH THESAURUS

Part 5

*(Obscenities, Vulgarities, Insults,
Bodily Functions & Sounds,
Sexual Slang, Offensive Language, etc.)*

ANUS

anus

boîte à pâté *f.* • (lit.): pâté box.

cul *m.* • (lit.): ass.

> **NOTE:** The term *cul* is also used to means "buttocks."

entrée de service *f.* • (lit.): service entrance.

fion *m.* • (lit.): the finish (of an article).

luc *m.*

> **NOTE:** This is *verlan* for *cul* meaning "ass" — *SEE: Street French 2, Verlan, p. 187.*

œil de bronze *m.* • (lit.): bronze eye.

œillet *m.* *(extremely popular)* • (lit.): carnation.

pastille *f.* *(popular)* • (lit.): lozenge.

pot d'échappement *m.* • (lit.): exhaust pipe.

> **NOTE:** This can also be shorten to: *pot.*

petit *m.* • (lit.): the little (area).

rondelle *f.* *(popular)* • (lit.): washer.

rosette *f.* *(popular)* • (lit.): that which is pink.

trou de balle *m.* • (lit.): gunshot hole.

trou du cul *m.* • (lit.): asshole.

troufignard *m.*

> **NOTE:** A slang variation of: *troufion.*

troufignon *m.*

> **NOTE:** A slang variation of: *troufion.*

troufion *m.* • (lit.): asshole (since *fion* means "anus" in French slang).

turbine à chocolat *f.* • (lit.): chocolate turbine.

tuyau à gaz *m.* • (lit.): gas pipe.

BAD BREATH (TO HAVE)

mauvaise haleine (avoir une)

plomber du goulot *exp.* • (lit.): to fall like lead from the bottleneck.

puer du bec *exp.* • (lit.): to stink from the mouth.

> **NOTE:** **bec** *m.* mouth • (lit.): beak of a bird.

puer de la gueule *exp.* • (lit.): to stink from the mouth.

> **NOTE:** **gueule** *f.* derogatory for the "mouth" of a human being • (lit.): mouth of an animal.

repousser du goulot *exp.* • (lit.): to repel from the bottleneck.

> **NOTE:** **goulot** *m.* neck • (lit.): bottleneck.

taper du saladier *exp.* • (lit.): to knock from the salad bowl.

> **NOTE:** **saladier** *m.* head • (lit.): salad bowl.

tuer les mouches à quinze pas

pas *exp.* • (lit.): to kill flies fifteen feet away.

BATHROOM

cabinet

NOTE: In France, the bathtub and toilet are often in two separate rooms. Therefore, the *salle de bain* (literally: "bathroom") refers to the room containing only the bathtub, and the *cabinet* refers to the room where the toilet is located.

---

cabzingue *m.* (short for *cabinet*).

chiards *m.pl.* the shithouse.
   NOTE: This comes from the verb *chier* meaning "to shit."

chiottes *f.pl. (extremely popular)* the shithouse.
   NOTE: This comes from the verb *chier* meaning "to shit."

lieux *m.pl.* • (lit.): the places.

ouatères *m.pl. (from British-English)* a shorten version of *water-closet* meaning "bathroom."

petit coin *m. (child language)* • (lit.): the little corner.

pipi-room *m. (Americanism).*

téléphone *m.*
   NOTE: This comes from the fact that many public outhouses on the street are shaped like telephone booths.

vécé *m. (extremely popular).*

NOTE: This is a twice-shortened version of the masculine noun *water-closet* meaning "bathroom." *Water-closet* is commonly shortened to *W.C.* and further shortened to *V.C.* (pronounced: *vécé*).

BREASTS

seins

amortisseurs *m.pl.* • (lit.): shock absorbers.

ananas *m.pl.* • (lit.): pineapples.

avant-postes *m.pl.* • (lit.): outposts.

avant-scènes *f.pl.* • (lit.): apron (of stage).

avantages *m.pl.* • (lit.): advantage.

balcon *m.* • (lit.): balcony.

ballons *m.pl.* large breasts • (lit.): balloons.

boîtes à lait *f.pl.* • (lit.): milk cans.

devanture *f.* • (lit.): front (of building, etc.).

flotteurs *m.pl.* • (lit.): floaters.

globes *m.pl.* • (lit.): globes, spheres.

il y a du beau monde *exp.* said of a woman with large breasts • (lit.): there are a lot of people there.

il y a du monde au balcon *exp.* said of a woman with large breasts • (lit.): there are people on the balcony.

il y a de quoi s'amuser *exp.* said of a woman with large breasts • (lit.): there's a lot to have fun with.

lolos *m.pl.* • (lit.): little milkers.
   NOTE: **lolo** *m.* child's language for "milk."

mamelles *f.pl.* large breasts
• (lit.): *(anatomy)* mammae.

mappemonde *f.* • (lit.): map of the world showing two hemispheres.

melons *m.pl.* large breasts
• (lit.): melons.

miches *f.pl.* • (lit.): loaves of bread.

nénés *f.pl.*

nibards *m.pl.*

nichons *m.pl. (very popular).*

oranges *f.pl.* • (lit.): oranges.

pare-chocs *m.pl.* • (lit.): bumpers.

pelotes *f.pl.* • (lit.): balls (of wool, string, etc.).

roberts *m.pl.*

tétés *m.pl.*
   NOTE: This comes from the verb *téter* meaning "to suck (a mother's breast)."

tétons *m.pl.* tits.
   NOTE: As with the previous entry, this comes from the verb *téter* meaning "to suck (a mother's breast)."

BROTHEL

maison de prostitution

baisodrome *m.*
• (lit.): "fuckodrome."
   NOTE: This comes from the verb *baiser* meaning "to fuck."

boxon *m.*
   NOTE: This comes from the masculine noun *box* meaning "cubicle (in a dormitory)."

casbah *f.*

   NOTE: From Arabic meaning "the Arab city" or "the house."

chabanais *m.*

clandé *m.* • (lit.): clandestine.

claque *m.* • (lit.): opera hat.
   NOTE: Also spelled: *clac.*

foutoir *m.* • **1.** brothel • **2.** a big dirty mess • (lit.): "fuckodrome."
   NOTE: This comes from the verb *foutre* meaning "to fuck."

maison d'abattage *f.* high-volume house • (lit.): house of slaughter (referring to a business where the pace is fast and mechanical).

maison de passe *f.* an official word for "brothel" • (lit.): house of transaction.

pinarium *m.*
   NOTE: This comes from the feminine noun *pine* meaning "penis."

tringlodrome *m.*
   NOTE: This comes from the feminine noun *tringle* which literally means "rod" but has taken the slang connotation of "penis, dick."

volière *f.* • (lit.): henhouse (since *poule*, literally meaning "hen," is used in French slang to mean "prostitute").

BURP (TO)

roter

renvoi (faire un) *exp.*
   NOTE: This comes from the verb *renvoyer* meaning "to send back" or in this case "to send back up."

rot (faire un) *exp.* • (lit.): to make a burp.

CLITORIS

clitoris

berlingot *m.* • (lit.): a type of candy made out of burnt sugar.

bouton d'amour *m.* • (lit.): love button.

bouton de rose *m.* • (lit.): rose button.

clicli *m.* a slang abbreviation of: *clitoris.*

cliquette *f.* a slang abbreviation of: *clitoris.*

clito *m.* *(extremely popular)* a slang abbreviation of: *clitoris.*

cliton *m.* a slang abbreviation of: *clitoris.*

framboise *f.* • (lit.): raspberry.

grain de café *m.* • (lit.): coffee bean.

noisette *f.* • (lit.): hazelnut.

praline *f.* • (lit.): praline.

CONDOM

préservatif

NOTE: A common *faux ami* is the masculine noun *préservatif* mistakenly used by native English speakers to mean "preserves." Remember: "condom" = **préservatif** *m.* "preserves" = **confiture** *f.*

capote *f.* *(very popular)*
• (lit.): bonnet.
SYNONYM: **capote anglaise**
• (lit.): English bonnet.

chapeau *m.* • (lit.): hat.

imper(méable) à Popol *m.*
• (lit.): Popol's raincoat.
NOTE -1: **Popol** *m.* penis.
NOTE -2: Also spelled: *Popaul.*

scaphandre de poche *m.*
• (lit.): pocket-size diving suit.

DEFECATE (TO)

déféquer

affaires (faire ses) *exp.* • (lit.): to do one's business.

aller où le Roi va à pied *exp.*
• (lit.): to go where the king goes by foot.

caca (faire) *exp.* • (lit.): to make caca.

chier *v.* • (lit.): to shit.

couler un bronze *exp.* • (lit.): to flow out a bronze (thing).

débloquer *v.* • (lit.): to free, to unblock.

déboucher son orchestre *exp.*
• (lit.): to uncork one's orchestra (of farting sounds).

débourrer sa pipe *exp.* • (lit.): to remove the tobacco from one's pipe.
> **NOTE:** This expression may also be shorted simply to: *débourrer*.

grande commission (faire sa) *exp.* • (lit.): to do one's big job.
> **SEE: faire sa petite commission**, *p. 322.*

grands besoins (faire ses) *exp.*
• (lit.): to do one's big needs.

gros (faire son) *exp.* • (lit.): to do one's fat (job).

mouler un bronze *exp.* • (lit.): to mold a bronze (thing).

planter une borne *exp.* • (lit.): to plant a milestone.

poser sa pêche *exp.* • (lit.): to deposit one's peach.

poser un colombin *exp.* • (lit.): to deposit pigeon manure.

poser un rondin *exp.* • (lit.): to set down a log.

poser une prune *exp.* • (lit.): to set down a plum.

poser une sentinelle *exp.*
• (lit.): to set down a sentinel.

pousser le bouchon *exp.*
• (lit.): to push the cork.

DIARRHEA

diarhée

chiasse (avoir la) *f.*
• (lit.): to have the shits.
> **NOTE:** This comes from the verb *chier* meaning "to shit."

courante (avoir la) *f.* • (lit.): to have the runs.

foirade (avoir la) *f.*

> **NOTE:** This comes from the crude verb *foirer* meaning "to have diarrhea."
> **VARIATION: foire (avoir la)** *f.*
• (lit.): to have diarrhea.

EJACULATE (TO) / ORGASM

éjaculer / orgasme

balancer *v.* • (lit.): to sway and rock.

balancer la sauce *exp.* • (lit.): to throw the sauce.

balancer la / sa purée *exp.*
• (lit.): to throw the / one's purée.

cracher son venin *exp.* • (lit.): to spit one's venom.

décharger *v.* • (lit.): to discharge.

dégorger *v.* • (lit.): to vomit.

égoutter son cyclope *exp.*
• (lit.): to drain one's cyclops.
> **NOTE:** The masculine noun *cyclope* is a popular synonym for "penis" or "one-eyed monster."

envoyer en l'air (s') *exp.*
• (lit.): to throw oneself into the air.

envoyer sa came / la purée / la sauce / la semoule *exp.*
• (lit.): to send out one's junk / purée / sauce / cream of wheat.
> **NOTE: came** *f.* • **1.** sperm • **2.** junk (in general) • **3.** personal belongings, one's "stuff" • **4.** cocaine.

faire une carte *exp.* to have a wet dream • (lit.): to make a map.

jeter sa purée / son venin *exp.*
• (lit.): to throw one's purée / one's venom.

jouir *v. (very popular)* • (lit.): to enjoy.

juter *v. (very popular)* • (lit.): to give off juice.

lâcher sa came / une giclée / son jus / sa purée / la semoule / son venin *exp.*
• (lit.): to release one's cum / a squirt / juice / purée/ cream of wheat / venom.

mettre les doigts de pieds en éventail *exp.* • (lit.): to spread one's toes apart.
NOTE: This expression also means "to relax."

pleurer le cyclope (faire) *exp.*
• (lit.): to make the cyclops cry.
NOTE: The masculine noun *cyclope* is a popular synonym for "penis" or "one-eyed monster."

prendre son panard / son pied *exp. (extremely popular)*
• (lit.): to take one's foot / one's foot.

tirer une giclée *exp.* • (lit.): to pull a squirt.

vider les burettes (se) *exp.*
• (lit.): to empty one's testicles.
NOTE: **burettes** *f.pl.* testicles, balls • (lit.): oilcans.

voir les anges *exp.* • (lit.): to see angels.

ERECTION (TO HAVE AN)

érection (avoir une)

air (l'avoir en l') *exp.* • (lit.): to have it in the air.

arquer *v.* • (lit.): to bend.

balle dans le canon (avoir une) *exp.* • (lit.): to have a bullet in the cannon.

bandaison (avoir une) *f.*
• (lit.): to have a boner.
SEE: **bander**, *(next entry)*.

bander *v. (extremely popular)* to be erect • (lit.): to tighten or stretch.

bandocher *m.* to get a semi-hardon.
NOTE: This is a slang variation of: *bander.*

bâton (avoir le) *m.* • (lit.): to have the club.

canne (avoir la) *exp.* • (lit.): to have the cane.

dure (l'avoir) *exp.* • (lit.): to have it hard.

garde-à-vous (être au) *exp.*
• (lit.): (military) to be at attention.

gaule (avoir la) *f. (popular)*
• (lit.): to have the pole.

gourdin (avoir le) *m.* • (lit.): to have the club or bludgeon.

manche (avoir le) *m.* • (lit.): to have the sleeve.

marquer midi *exp.* • (lit.): to be hitting straight up at noon.

os (avoir l') *m.* • (lit.): to have the bone.

porte-manteau dans le pantalon (avoir un) *exp.*
• (lit.): to have a coat rack in the pants.

raide (l'avoir) *exp.* • (lit.): to have it stiff.

tendre pour *exp.* • (lit.): to tighten for (someone).

tringle (avoir la) *f.* (popular) • (lit.): to have the rod.

trique (avoir la) *f.* (popular) • (lit.): to have the heavy stick.
> **SEE:** **triqué (être)**, *(next entry)*.

triqué (être) *adj.* • (lit.): to be "sticked."
> **SEE:** **trique (avoir la)**, *(previous entry)*.

péter

déchirer la toile *exp.* • (lit.): to rip the linen.

détacher une pastille *exp.*
• (lit.): to detach a lozenge.
> **SEE:** **pastille**, *p. 131*.

flouser *v.*

flousse *m.* fart.

fusante *f.* • (lit.): that which bursts out (like *une fusée* meaning "a rocket").

fuser *v.* • (lit.): to burst out.
> **NOTE:** **fusée** *f.* rocket.

lâcher les gaz *exp.* • (lit.): to release gases.

lâcher un(e) (en) *exp.* • (lit.): to let one go.

lâcher une louise *exp.* • (lit.): to release a louise.
> **SEE:** **louise**, *p. 112*.

lâcher une perle *exp.* • (lit.): to release a pearl.
> **SEE:** **perle**, *p. 134*.

lâcher une perlouse *exp.*
variation of: *lâcher une perle*.

louise *f.* fart.

pastille *f.* fart • (lit.): lozenge.
> **SEE:** **détacher une pastille**, *p. 65*.

perle *f.* fart • (lit.): pearl.

perlouse *f.* slang variation of: *perle*.

pet mouillé (faire un) *exp.* to wet fart • (lit.): [same].

vesse *f.* silent fart, S.B.D. (silent but deadly).

vesser *v.* to fart silently.

fellation (faire une)

croquer (se faire) *exp.* • (lit.): to get oneself eaten or munched.

manger *v.* • (lit.): to eat.

pipe (faire une) *exp.* (extremely popular) • (lit.): to do a pipe.

pomper *v.* (very popular) • (lit.): to pump.

pompette *f.* blow job.
> **NOTE:** This is from the verb *pomper* meaning "to pump."

pompier (faire un) *exp.*
• (lit.): to do (like) a fireman and pump (water).

pomplard (faire un) *exp.*
• (lit.): to do (like) a fireman.

NOTE -1: This is a variation of: *faire un pompier.*

NOTE -2: The masculine noun *pomplard* is a slang synonym for *pompier* meaning "fireman."

souffler dans la canne *exp.*
• (lit.): to blow in the cane.

souffler dans le mirliton *exp.*
• (lit.): to blow in the toy flute.

sucer *v.* (*very popular*) • (lit.): to suck.

tailler une pipe *exp.* • (lit.): (*very popular*) • (lit.): to trim a pipe.

tailler une plume *exp.* • (lit.): to trim a pen.

FORNICATE (TO)

forniquer

aiguiller *v.* to "dick" someone
• (lit.): to give the needle.

NOTE: **aiguille** *f.* penis, dick • (lit.): needle.

amener le petit au cirque *exp.*
• (lit.): to take the little one to the circus.

asperger le persil *exp.* • (lit.): to sprinkle water on the parsley.

NOTE -1: **asperge** *f.* penis • (lit.): asparagus.

NOTE -2: **persil** *m.* vagina, pubic hair • (lit.): parsley.

baiser *v.* • (lit.): to fuck.

NOTE: There is an *enormous* difference between *baiser* the verb and *baiser* the noun. As a noun, *baiser* simply means a "kiss." For example: *Il m'a fait un baiser en rentrant;* He gave me a kiss upon coming home. Mistakenly and dangerously, many Americans use *baiser* as a verb assuming that it means "to kiss" when it actually means "to fuck." Therefore, *Il m'a baisé en rentrant* would be translated as "He fucked me upon coming home."

baisouiller *v.* a slang variation of: *baiser.*

besogner *v.* • (lit.): to work hard.

biter *v.* to "dick" someone.

NOTE: **bite** *f.* penis, dick.

bourre (aller à la) *exp.* • (lit.): to screw.

NOTE: **bourre** *f.* lay, screw • *Carole, c'est une bonne bourre!;* Carole is a good lay.

bourrer *v.* (*popular*) • (lit.): to stuff.

bourriquer *v.* to screw like a donkey.

NOTE: **bourrique** *f.* donkey, she-ass.

caramboler *v.* • (lit.): to push and shove.

caser *v.* • (lit.): to put or stow (something) away.

ALSO: **casé(e) (être)** *adj.* to be married.

casser la canne *exp.* • (lit.): to break the cane.

NOTE: **canne** *f.* penis, dick • (lit.): cane.

chevaucher *v.* • (lit.): to ride horseback.

cogner quelqu'un (se) *v.* • (lit.): to hit (one's body against) someone.

coucher avec *exp. (very popular)* • (lit.): to sleep with.

cracher dans le bénitier *exp.* • (lit.): to spit in the holy water basin.
> **NOTE: bénitier** *m.* vagina • (lit.): holy water basin.

défoncer *v.* • (lit.): to break open (a box, etc.).

dérouiller *v.* • (lit.): to rub the rust off (something).

dérouiller à sec *exp.* to dry fuck • (lit.): to rub the rust off (something dry).

dérouiller son petit frère *exp.* • (lit.): to rub the rust off one's little brother.
> **NOTE: petit frère** *m.* penis, dick • (lit.): little brother.

dérouiller Totor *exp.* • (lit.): to rub the rust off Totor.
> **NOTE: Totor** *m.* penis, dick.

enfiler (s') *v.* • (lit.): to thread oneself.

enfoncer (se l') *v.* • (lit.): to drive it in.

enjamber *v.* • (lit.): to put in one's "third leg."
> **NOTE:** This comes from the feminine noun *troisième jambe* meaning "third leg" or "penis, dick."

envoyer en l'air (s') *exp.* *(extremely popular)* • (lit.): to send oneself into the air.

faire (le) *exp.* • (lit.): to do it.

faire ça *exp.* • (lit.): to do it.

faire la bête à deux dos *exp.* • (lit.): to make like the beast with two backs (said of two people who are fused together during sex).

faire quelqu'un (se) *v. (very popular)* • (lit.): to do someone.

faire un carton *exp.* • (lit.): to do some target practice.

faire une partie d'écarté *exp.*
> **NOTE:** This is a pun based on the expression *faire une partie de cartes* meaning "to play a hand of cards." However, in this expression, the noun *cartes* has been replaced with the adjective *écarté* meaning "spread apart" as with one's legs during sex.

faire une partie de jambes en l'air *exp.* • (lit.): to play a game of "legs in the air."

faire une partie de balayette *exp.* • (lit.): to "play a hand of" small broom.
> **NOTE: balayette** *f.* penis, dick • (lit.): small broom.

farcir quelqu'un (se) *v.* • **1.** to fornicate • **2.** to put up with someone (ex: *Je ne peux pas supporter mon nouveau voisin, mais il faut **se le farcir**!*; I can't stand my new neighbor but I have to put up with him! • (lit.): to stuff oneself with someone.

filer un coup d'arbalète *exp.* • (lit.): to give (someone) a shot with the crossbow.
> **NOTE: arbalète** *f.* penis, dick • (lit.): crossbow.

filer un coup de sabre *exp.* • (lit.): to give (someone) a shot with the saber.
> **NOTE: sabre** *m.* penis, dick • (lit.): saber.

filer un coup de brosse *exp.*
- (lit.): to give (someone) a shot of the brush.

fourailler *v.* • (lit.): to stuff.

> **NOTE:** This is a variation of the verb *fourrer* meaning "to stuff."

fourrer *v.* • (lit.): to stuff.

limer *v.* • (lit.): to polish.

mettre (le) *exp.* • (lit.): to put it (in).

mouiller le goupillon *exp.*
- (lit.): to wet one's sprinkler.

> **NOTE:** **goupillon** *m.* penis, dick
- (lit.): sprinkler (for holy water).

niquer *v.* *(from Arabic)* • (lit.): to fuck.

payer un petit coup (s'en) *exp.*
- (lit.): to treat oneself to a little bit.

piner *v.* • (lit.): to "dick" (someone).

> **NOTE:** This comes from the feminine noun *pine* meaning "penis, dick."

planter *v.* • (lit.): to plant.

pousser sa pointe *exp.* • (lit.): to push (in) one's point.

> **NOTE:** **pointe** *f.* penis, dick
- (lit.): point.

queuter *v.* • (lit.): to "dick" (someone).

> **NOTE:** This comes from the feminine noun *queue* which literally means "tail" but has taken the slang connotation of "penis, dick" particularly in Belgium.

ramoner *v.* *(humorous)* • (lit.): to sweep (a chimney).

> **NOTE:** **cheminée** *f.* vagina
- (lit.): chimney.

sauter *v.* *(very popular)* • (lit.): to jump (one's bones).

taper (se) *v.* *(very popular)* • (lit.): to treat oneself.

torpiller *v.* • (lit.): to torpedo (someone).

tremper son baigneur *exp.*
- (lit.): to dip one's bather.

> **NOTE:** **baigneur** *m.* penis, "dick"
- (lit.): bather.

tremper son biscuit *exp.*
- (lit.): to dip one's biscuit.

tringler *v.* *(very popular)* • (lit.): to "dick" (someone).

> **NOTE:** This comes from the feminine noun *tringle* which literally means "rod" but has taken the slang connotation of "penis, dick."

verger *v.* • (lit.): to "dick" (someone).

> **NOTE:** This comes from the feminine noun *verge* which literally means "rod, wand, cane," but has taken the slang connotation of "penis, dick."

voir la feuille à l'envers *exp.*
to have sex under a tree • (lit.): to see the leaf (or leaves) from underneath.

castapiane *f.*

chaude-lance *f.* • (lit.): hot urine.

NOTE -1: **lance** *f.* • **1.** water • **2.** urine.

NOTE -2: **lancequiner** *v.* • **1.** to rain • **2.** to urinate.

chaude-pince *f.* • (lit.): hot claw.

chaude-pisse *f.* *(very popular)* • (lit.): hot piss.

    NOTE: **pisser** *v.* to urinate, to piss.

coulante *f.* • (lit.): dripper (since gonorrhea causes the penis to drip).

HUSTLE (TO)

prostituer (se)

arpenter le bitume *exp.* • (lit.): to survey the asphalt.

asperges (aller aux) *exp.* to go to (find) some penis • (lit.): to go to the asparagus.

    NOTE: **asperge** *f.* penis • (lit.): asparagus.

bitume (faire le) *m.* • (lit.): to do the asphalt.

business (faire le) *m.* • (lit.): to do the business.

chasser le mâle *exp.* • (lit.): to hunt the male (species).

défendre (se) *v.* to make a living • (lit.): to defend oneself.

dérouiller *v.* to get the first client of the day • (lit.): to take the rust off (something).

cents pas (faire les) *exp.* to pace • (lit.): to do the one hundred steps.

draguer *v.* • (lit.): to cruise (someone).

emballer *v.* • (lit.): to excite (someone).

grue (faire la) *f.* • (lit.): to do like a crane (since cranes are known for standing on one foot much like a prostitute who waits for a client while leaning back against the wall of a building, one foot on the ground with the other against the wall).

levage (faire un) *m.* • (lit.): to make a pickup.

lever un client *exp.* • (lit.): to pick up a client.

macadam (faire le) *exp.* *(very popular)* • (lit.): to do the macadam or sidewalk.

pavé (faire le) *m.* • (lit.): to do the pavement.

quart (faire le) *m.* • (lit.): to keep watch.

tapin (faire le) *exp.* *(very popular)* to do the street.

    NOTE: **tapineuse** *f.* hooker, prostitute.

tapiner *v.*

    SEE: **tapin (faire le)**, *(previous entry).*

tas (faire le) *m.* • (lit.): to do (a lot of) work.

    NOTE: **tas** *m.* work • (lit.): heap, stack.

trottoir (faire le) *exp.* *(very popular)* • (lit.): to do the sidewalk.

turbin (faire le) *exp.* • (lit.): to do hard work

NOTE: turbin *m.* work, grind.

turbiner *v.*

   SEE: turbin (faire le), *(previous entry)*.

turf (aller au) *exp.* • (lit.): to go to the turf.

   SEE: turf (faire le), *(next entry)*.

turf (faire le) *exp.* • (lit.): to do the turf.

turfer *v.*

   SEE: turf (faire le), *(previous entry)*.

MASTURBATE (TO) [men]

masturber (se) [hommes]

NOTE: Some of these terms may be used in reference to a woman as well, while others may only be used in reference to a man.

   SEE: MASTURBATE (TO), [women], *p. 312.*

achever à la manivelle (s')

exp. • (lit.): to reach completion with the hand crank.

agacer le sous-préfet *exp.*

• (lit.): to annoy the subprefect.

agiter le poireau (s') *exp.*

• (lit.): to agitate the leek.

   NOTE: poireau *m.* penis, "dick" • (lit.): leek.

astiquer (s') *v.* • (lit.): to polish oneself.

astiquer la baguette (s') *exp.*

• (lit.): to polish one's baguette.

   NOTE: baguette *f.* penis, "dick" • (lit.): baguette, long rounded loaf of bread.

branler (se) *v. (very popular)*

• (lit.): to shake oneself.

   NOTE: branlette *f.* masturbation.

chatouiller le poireau (se)

exp. • (lit.): to tickle one's leek.

   NOTE: poireau *m.* penis, "dick" • (lit.): leek.

cinq contre un (faire) *exp.*

• (lit.): to do five against one.

douce (se faire une) *exp.*

• (lit.): to do oneself a sweet thing.

écrémer (se faire) *exp.* • (lit.): to make oneself cream.

épouser la veuve Poignet *exp.*

• (lit.): to marry the Widow Wrist.

étrangler Popaul *exp.* • (lit.): to strangle Popaul.

   NOTE -1: Also spelled: *Popol.*

   NOTE -2: Popaul / Popol *m.* penis, "dick."

glouglouter le poireau (se faire) *exp.* • (lit.): to make one's leek gurgle.

   NOTE: poireau *m.* penis, "dick" • (lit.): leek.

gonfler son andouille *exp.*

• (lit.): to swell one's sausage.

mettre la main à la pâte *exp.*

(used in the culinary world) to get in there with one's hands • (lit.): to put the hand to the dough.

mousser le créateur (se faire) *exp.* • (lit.): to make one's creator foam.

palucher (se) *v.* • (lit.): to give oneself a hand job.

> **NOTE:** **paluche** *f.* hand.

pogne (se faire une) *exp.* • (lit.): to give oneself a hand job.

> **NOTE:** **pogne** *f.* fist, hand.

pogner (se) *v.* • (lit.): to have oneself a hand job.

> **NOTE:** **pogne** *f.* fist, hand.

reluire (se faire) *exp.* • (lit.): to make oneself glisten.

sauter la cervelle à Charles-le-Chauve (faire) *exp.* • (lit.): to blow out the brains of Charles-the-Bald.

secouer le bonhomme (se) *exp.* • (lit.): to shake one's good-natured man.

soulager (se) *v.* **1.** to masturbate • **2.** to go to the bathroom • (lit.): to relieve oneself.

taper sur l'os (se) *exp.* • (lit.): to tap on one's bone.

taper sur la colonne (se) *exp.* • (lit.): to tap on one's column.

> **NOTE:** **colonne** *f.* penis, "dick" • (lit.): column.

taper une queue (se) *exp.* • (lit.): to treat oneself to a "dick" (since *queue*, literally meaning "tail," is used as a slang term for "penis").

taper une (s'en) *exp.* • (lit.): to treat oneself to one.

toucher (se) *v.* • (lit.): to touch oneself.

> **NOTE:** This applies to both male and female and is often used as a

polite way to report that a child has started masturbating.

touche (se faire une) *exp.* • (lit.): to give oneself a touch.

tripoter (se) *v.* • (lit.): to play with oneself.

> **NOTE:** This verb is used the same as *se toucher* but is more familiar.

venir aux mains (en) *exp.* • (lit.): to come to hands.

> **NOTE:** The expression *en venir aux mains* is commonly used to mean "to come to blows." However, since it literally means "to come to hands," it may be used humorously to suggest masturbation.

visiter la veuve et les cinq orphelines *exp.* • (lit.): to visit the widow and five orphans.

MASTURBATE [women]

masburber (se) [les femmes]

> **NOTE:** Some of these terms may be used in reference to a man as well, while others may only be used in reference to a woman.

> **SEE:** MASTURBATE (TO) **[men]**, *p. 311.*

---

astiquer le bouton (s') *exp.* • (lit.): to polish one's button.

> **NOTE:** **bouton** *m.* clitoris • (lit.): button.

compter les poils (se) *exp.* • (lit.): to count one's (pubic) hairs.

jouer de la mandoline *exp.* • (lit.): to play the mandolin.

NOTE: This is based on a famous painting depicting a naked woman playing the mandolin which covers her genitalia.

secouer son grain de café *exp.*
• (lit.): to shake one's coffee bean.

soulager (se) *v.* • (lit.): to comfort oneself.

toucher (se) *v.* • (lit.): to touch oneself.

MASTURBATION/ HANDJOB

masturbation / poigne

branlée *f.* • (lit.): shaking.
NOTE: **branler (se)** *v.* to masturbate • (lit.): to shake oneself.

branlette *f.* (*popular*) • (lit.): shaking.
NOTE: **branler (se)** *v.* to masturbate • (lit.): to shake oneself.

branlette maison *f.*
• (lit.): shaking of the house.
NOTE -1: **branler (se)** *v.* to masturbate • (lit.): to shake oneself.
NOTE -2: This construction, where *maison* is used as an adjective, is commonly seen in restaurants referring to the "house" specialty such as *pâté maison*.

branlure *f.* • (lit.): shaking.
NOTE: **branler (se)** *v.* to masturbate • (lit.): to shake oneself.

paluche *f.* hand job • (lit.): slang for "hand."

pignole *f.*

pogne *f.* hand job • (lit.): slang for "fist."

secouette *f.* • (lit.): shaking.

NOTE: **secouer (se)** *v.* to masturbate • (lit.): to shake oneself.

veuve Poignet *m.* • (lit.): Widow Wrist.

MENSTRUATE (TO)

règles (avoir ses)

affaires (avoir ses) *f.pl.* • (lit.): to have one's business.

anglais (avoir ses) *m.pl.*
• (lit.): to have one's English.

argagnasses (avoir ses) *f.pl.*

cardinales (avoir ses) *f.pl.*
• (lit.): to have one's cardinals.

coquelicots (avoir ses) *m.pl.*
• (lit.): to have one's red poppies.

drapeau-rouge (avoir son) *m.*
• (lit.): to have one's red flag.
SEE: **pavoiser**, *p. 313.*

époques (avoir ses) *exp.*
• (lit.): to have one's epoch or era.

histoires (avoir ses) *exp.*
• (lit.): to have one's stories.

marquer *v.* • (lit.): to mark.

ours (avoir ses) *m.pl.* • (lit.): to have one's bears.

pavoiser *v.* • (lit.): to deck (house, etc.) with flags, in this case, red flags.
SEE: **drapeau-rouge (avoir son)**, *p. 67.*

ramiaous (avoir ses) *m.pl.*

recevoir sa famille *exp.* • (lit.): to receive one's family.

recevoir ses cousins *exp.*
• (lit.): to receive one's cousins.

repeindre sa grille en rouge
exp. • (lit.): to repaint one's grill red.

rue barrée (avoir sa) *f.*
- (lit.): to have one's street closed •
Rue barrée; No thoroughfare.

sauce-tomate (avoir sa) *f.*
- (lit.): to have one's tomato sauce.

tomates (avoir ses) *f.pl.* • (lit.): to have one's tomatoes.

trucs (avoir ses) *m.pl.* • (lit.): to have one's things.

visite (avoir de la) *f.* • (lit.): to have visitors.

andouille à col roulé *f.*
- (lit.): sausage with a rolled-down collar.

anguille de calecif *f.*
- (lit.): underwear eel.
NOTE: **calecif** *m.* a slang transformation of *caleçon* meaning "underwear."

asperge *f.* • (lit.): asparagus.

baigneur *m.* • (lit.): bather

baïonnette *f.* • (lit.): bayonet.

baisette *f.* • (lit.): little fucker.
NOTE: This comes from the slang verb *baiser* meaning "to fuck."

balayette *f.* • (lit.): small broom.

baveuse *f.* • (lit.): drooler.

bazar *m.* penis and testicles
- (lit.): bazaar.

béquille *f.* • (lit.): crutch.

berloque *f.* • (lit.): charm, trinket.

bijoux de famille *m.pl.* penis and testicles • (lit.): family jewels.

bite *f. (very popular)* • (lit.): bitt, bollard (on a ship).

boudin blanc *m.* • (lit.): white sausage.

bout *m.* • (lit.): end.

braquemard *m.* • (lit.): the pointer.
NOTE: This comes from the verb *braquer* meaning "to point a gun (at something or someone)."
VARIATION: **braquemart** *m.*

canne *f.* • (lit.): cane.

carabine *f.* • (lit.): rifle.

Charles-le-Chauve *m.*
- (lit.): Charles the Bald.

chose *f.* • (lit.): thing.

cigare à moustache *m.*
- (lit.): cigar with a moustache.

clarinette *f.* • (lit.): clarinet.

colonne *f.* • (lit.): column.

cornemuse *f.* • (lit.): bagpipe.

cyclope *m.* the "one-eyed monster"
- (lit.): cyclops.

dard *m.* • (lit.): prick.

dardillon *m.* • (lit.): small prick.

défonceuse *f.* • (lit.): penetrator.

doigt du milieu *m.* • (lit.): middle finger.

flageolet *m.* • (lit.): flageolet (which is a type of flute).

flûte *f.* • (lit.): flute.

frétillante *f.* • (lit.): wagger.

> **NOTE:** This comes from the verb *frétiller* meaning "to wag."

frétillard *m.* • (lit.): wagger

> **NOTE:** This comes from the verb *frétiller* meaning "to wag."

gaule *f.* penis or erection
• (lit.): (long, thin) pole, stick.

gland *m.* • (lit.): acorn.

> **NOTE:** This comes from the masculine noun *gland* meaning "acorn," and is used to refer to the head of the penis due to its shape.

goupillon *m.* • (lit.): sprinkler (for holy water).

gourde à poils *f.* • (lit.): gourd with hairs.

gourdin *m.* • (lit.): club, bludgeon.

instrument *m.* • (lit.): instrument.

jambe du milieu *f.* • (lit.): middle leg.

macaroni *m.* • (lit.): macaroni.

machin *m.* • (lit.): thing.

mandrin *m.* • (lit.): bandit, ruffian.

marchandise *f.* penis and testicles
• (lit.): merchandise.

marsouin *m.* • (lit.): porpoise.

monté (être bien) *adj.* to be well hung • (lit.): to be well mounted.

morceau *m.* • (lit.): morsel, piece.

nœud *m.* • (lit.): knot.

os à moelle *m.* • (lit.): marrow bone.

outil *m.* • (lit.): tool.

paquet *m.* penis and testicles
• (lit.): package.

petit frère *m.* • (lit.): little brother.

pine *f.* (*extremely popular*).

pointe *f.* • (lit.): point.

poireau *m.* • (lit.): leek.

Popaul *m.*

> **VARIATION:** **Popol** *m.*

quéquette *f.* (*child language*).

queue *f.* • (lit.): tail.

quille *f.* • (lit.): (bowling) pin.

quiquette *f.*

quiqui *m.* (*child language*).

sabre *m.* • (lit.): saber.

tracassin *m.* • (lit.): worrier (since the penis has a tendency to get wet when excited, like a person's forehead when worried).

tringle *f.* • (lit.): rod.

trique *f.* • (lit.): heavy stick.

troisième jambe *f.* • (lit.): third leg.

verge *f.* (*medical term*) • (lit.): rod, wand, cane.

zeb *m.*

zizi *m.* (*child language*).

zob *m.* (*extremely popular*).

zobi *m.*

PIMP

souteneur

> **NOTE:** Many of the following slang synonyms for "pimp" are, oddly enough, types of fish.

barbeau *m.*

brochet *m.* • (lit.): pike.

hareng *m.* • (lit.): herring.

Jules *m.* (*very popular*) • **1**. pimp • **2**. boyfriend • (lit.): Jules (a man's first name).

Julot *m.* diminutive of: *Jules.*

mac *m.* (*very popular*) abbreviation of: *macquereau.*

maquereau *m.* (*very popular*) • (lit.): mackerel.

marchand de barbaque *m.* pimp, white slaver • (lit.): meat seller.
> **NOTE:** **barbaque** *f.* (low quality) meat.

marchand de bidoche *m.* pimp, white slaver • (lit.): meat seller.
> **NOTE:** **bidoche** *f.* (low quality) meat.

marchand de viande *m.* pimp, white slaver • (lit.): meat seller.

marle *m.* an abbreviation of: *marlou.*

marlou *m.*

merlan *m.* • (lit.): whiting.

proxémac *m.*
> **NOTE:** This is a slang transformation of the masculine noun *proxénète* meaning "white slaver."

proxo *m.* an abbreviation of: *proxénète.*

POSTERIOR

postérieur

arrière-boutique *m.* • (lit.): back-shop.

arrière-train *m.* • (lit.): caboose.

baba *m.* • (lit.): from baba-au-rhum (due to its round shape, like one's buttocks).

ballon *m.* • (lit.): **1**. balloon • **2**. rubber ball.

bottom *m.* (*Americanism*).

brioches *f.pl.* • (lit.): brioches (breads).

cadran solaire *m.* • (lit.): sundial.

croupe *f.* • (lit.): rump.

croupion *m.* (*also spelled: "croupillon"*) • (lit.): rump (of bird).

cul *m.* (*very popular*) • (lit.): ass.

demi-lunes *f.pl.* • (lit.): half moons.

der *m.* • (lit.): abbreviation of *derrière* meaning "backside."

derche *m.*
> **NOTE:** This is a slang variation of *derrière* meaning "backside."

derge *m.*
> **NOTE:** This is a slang variation of *derrière* meaning "backside."

derrière *m.* • (lit.): behind.

deux frangines *f.pl.* • (lit.): two sisters.

faubourg *m.* • (lit.): suburb, outlying part (of town).

fessier *m.* • (lit.): buttock (academic term).
> **NOTE:** This comes from the feminine noun *fesse* meaning the "cheek of the buttock."

fiacre *m.* • (lit.): cab.

fion *m.* (*extremely popular*) • (lit.): end or finish (of an article).

luc *m.* (*extremely popular*) • (lit.): a *verlan* transformation of *cul* meaning "ass."

lune *f.* • (lit.): moon.

médaillon *m.* • (lit.): medallion.

meules *f.pl.* **1.** posterior • **2.** breasts • (lit.): stacks, piles (of hay, etc.).
> **NOTE:** The difference between definitions **1.** and **2.** simply depends on the context.

pains au lait *m.pl.* • (lit.): white breads.

panier à crottes *m.* • (lit.): turd basket.

pétard *m.* • (lit.): farter (from the verb *péter* meaning "to fart").

pont arrière *m.* • (lit.): rear axle.

popotin *m.* *(extremely popular)* • (lit.): [no literal translation].

postère *m.* an abbreviation of *postérieur* meaning "posterior, buttocks."

postérieur *m.* • (lit.): posterior.

pot *m.* • (lit.): pot.

pot à crottes *m.* • (lit.): turd pot.

train *m.* • (lit.): train.
> **ALSO:** **arrière-train** *m.* • (lit.): caboose.

PREGNANT

enceinte

arrondir (s') *v.* • (lit.): to make oneself round.

arrondir le devant (se faire) *exp.* • (lit.): to get one's front end rounded.

arrondir le globe (se faire) *exp.* • (lit.): to get one's globe rounded.

attraper le ballon *exp.* • (lit.): to catch the balloon (in one's stomach).

avalé le pépin (avoir) *exp.* • (lit.): to have swallowed the seed.

ballon (avoir le) *exp.* • (lit.): to have the balloon (in one's stomach).

butte (avoir sa) *exp.* • (lit.): to have one's little hill.

cloque (être en) *exp.* *(very popular)* to be knocked up • (lit.): to be in a big blister.
> **NOTE -1:** **mettre en cloque** *exp.* to knock up.
> **NOTE -2:** **encloquer** *v.* to knock up.

engrossée (être) *adj.* *(pejorative)* to be knocked up • (lit.): to be fattened up (used for animals).
> **NOTE:** **engrosser** *v.* to knock up.

gondoler de la devanture *exp.* • (lit.): to warp from the display window.

moufflet dans le tiroir (avoir un) *exp.* • (lit.): to have a kid in the drawer.

petit polichinelle dans le tiroir (avoir un) *exp.* • (lit.): to have a little joker in the drawer.
> **NOTE:** A *polichinelle* is the little clown figure often seen in a group of marionettes.

tombée sur un clou rouillé (être) *exp.* • (lit.): to have fallen on a rusty nail (and therefore swollen).

travailler pour Marianne *exp.*
> **NOTE:** *Marianne* is the female incarnation of France and the revolution. Therefore, if you are having a baby, you are said to be producing a new citizen for Marianne and the Republic.

PROSTITUTE

prostituée

amazone *f.* • (lit.): high-class prostitute.

bisenesseuse *f.* • (lit.): business woman, working girl.

bourrin *m.* prostitute, loose woman • (lit.): horse or nag.

dossière *f.* • (lit.): a woman who lies on her back often.
> **NOTE:** This comes from the masculine noun *dos* meaning "back."

essoreuse *f.* a prostitute who squeezes her clients dry of all their money • (lit.): spin dryer.

fille de joie *f.* • (lit.): girl of joy (or who spreads joy).

fille *f.* • (lit.): girl.

gagneuse *f.* • (lit.): girl who earns money.

grue *f.* • (lit.): a crane (since cranes are known for standing on one foot much like a prostitute who waits for a client while leaning back against the wall of a building; one foot on the ground with the other against the wall).

horizontale *f.* • (lit.): a horizontal (because of the position she frequently assumes).
> **ALSO:** **grande horizontale** *f.* a very high-class prostitute.

marcheuse *f.* a girl who walks the streets • (lit.): walker.

pétroleuse *f.* • (lit.): a woman who heats up a man (since *pétrole*, meaning "petroleum").

pouffiasse *f.* low-class prostitute • (lit.): *(derogatory)* woman.

poule *f.* girl • (lit.): hen.

pouliche *f.* young girl • (lit.): filly.

putain *f.* *(very popular)* whore.

pute *f.* an abbreviation of: *putain*.

racoleuse *f.* • (lit.): woman who recruits or solicits men.

sauterelle *f.* • (lit.): grasshopper.
> **NOTE:** This is actually a play on words since the verb *sauter* (literally meaning "to jump") has the slang meaning of "to jump sexually."

tapin *f.*
> **NOTE:** **faire le tapin** *exp.* to prostitute oneself.

tapineuse *f.*

traînée *f.* slut • (lit.): one who loiters (on the sidewalk, etc.).
> **NOTE:** This comes from the verb *traîner* meaning "to dawdle, to loiter."

travailleuse *f.* • (lit.): working girl.

PUBLIC URINAL

urinoir

ardoises *f.pl.* • (lit.): slates.

lavabe *m.*
> **NOTE:** This is short for *lavabo* meaning "sink."

lav *m.*
> **NOTE:** This is short for *lavabo* meaning "sink."

pissoir *m.*
> **NOTE:** This comes from the verb *pisser* meaning "to piss."

pissotière *f.*
> **NOTE -1:** This comes from the verb *pisser* meaning "to piss."

NOTE -2: Although the *pissotières* no longer exist (due to their odor), the term is still used in jest.

SODOMIZE (TO)

sodomiser

casser le pot *exp.* • (lit.): to break the pot.
> **NOTE:** **pot** *m.* buttocks • (lit.): pot.

défoncer la pastille *exp.*
• (lit.): to smash through the lozenge.
> **NOTE:** **pastille** *f.* anus
• (lit.): lozenge.

emmancher *v.*

empaffer *v.*

empaler *v.* • (lit.): to impale.

empapaouter *v.*

empétarder *v.* • (lit.): to receive something through the back.
> **NOTE:** This is an "antonym" of the verb *pétarader* meaning "to backfire."

enculer *v.*
> **NOTE -1:** This comes from the masculine noun *cul* meaning "ass."
> **NOTE -2:** This verb originally meant "to sodomize" and is now mainly used to mean "to fornicate."

enfoirer *v.* • (lit.): to "enter something into one's anus."
> **NOTE:** This is an "antonym" of the verb *foirer* meaning "to have diarrhea."

englander *v.* • (lit.): to insert the acorn (which looks like the head of a penis).
> **NOTE:** This comes from the masculine noun *gland* meaning "acorn" and is used to refer to the head of the penis due to its shape.

entuber *v.* • (lit.): to put one's "tube" into something.

jouer au bilboquet ensemble *exp.*
> **NOTE:** *Bilboquet* is a child's game in which the player holds a long wooden peg which has a string attached to it. At the end of the string is a ball with a hole. The object is to swing the ball up then down onto the peg using only one hand.

péter la rondelle *exp.* • (lit.): to explode the ring.
> **NOTE:** **rondelle** *f.* anus
• (lit.): ring, small round disc.

troncher *v.* • **1**. to sodomize • **2**. to fornicate.
> **NOTE:** This comes from the feminine noun *tronche* meaning "log."

SPERM

sperme

blanc *m.* • (lit.): white (stuff).

came *f.* • (lit.): cum.
> **NOTE:** **came** *f.* • **1**. sperm • **2**. junk (in general) • **3**. personal belongings, one's "stuff" • **4**. cocaine.

foutre *m.* (*very popular*).

NOTE: This is from the verb *foutre* meaning "to fuck."

jus de corps *m.* • (lit.): body juice.

jus de cyclope *m.* • (lit.): cyclops juice.

> **NOTE:** **cyclope** *m.* penis, "one-eyed bandit" • (lit.): cyclops.

purée *f.* • (lit.): purée.

sauce *f.* • (lit.): sauce.

semoule *f.* • (lit.): cream of wheat.

venin *m.* • (lit.): venom.

jus *m.* • (lit.): juice.

SPIT (TO)

cracher

glaviot *m.* spit wad, loogie.

glavioter *v.* to hawk a loogie.

gluau *m.* spit wad, loogie.

graillon *m.* spit wad, loogie.

graillonner *v.* to cough up phlegm.

huître *f.* spit wad, loogie • (lit.): oyster.

molard *m.* spit wad, loogie.

molarder *v.* to spit, to hawk a loogie.

postillon *m.* spit, spittle.

> **NOTE:** **postillonner** *v.* to spit while one speaks.

STINK (TO)

puer

boucaner *v.* • (lit.): to cure or smoke-dry meat.

cocoter *v.*

fouetter *v.* • (lit.): to whip.

puer *v.* • (lit.): to stink.

refouler *v.* • (lit.): to push back.

rougnotter *v.*

schlingotter *v.*

schlinguer *v.*

sentir le fauve *exp.* • (lit.): to smell like wild animal.

taper *v.* • (lit.): to hit.

SYPHILIS

syphillis

schtouille *f.* (also spelled: *chtouille*).

syph *f.* an abbreviation for: *syphilis*.

syphlotte *f.* a slang variation for: *syphilis*.

vérole *f.* • (lit.): the old-fashioned word for "pox."

TESTICLES

testicules

balloches *f.pl.* • (lit.): balls.

bibelots *m.pl.* • (lit.): trinkets.

bijoux de famille *m.pl.* • (lit.): family jewels.

billes *f.pl.* • (lit.): (small) balls.

bonbons *m.pl.* • (lit.): goodies.

breloques *f.pl.* • (lit.): charms, trinkets.

burettes *f.pl.* • (lit.): oilcans.

burnes *f.pl. (extremely popular).*

couilles *f.pl. (very popular).*

couillons *m.pl.*

> **NOTE:** This is a masculine variation of the feminine plural noun *couilles.*

croquignoles *f.pl.* • (lit.): biscuits.

joyeuses *f.pl.* • (lit.): the joyful ones, the ones that cause great joy.

noisettes *f.pl.* • (lit.): hazelnuts.

noix *f.pl.* • (lit.): nuts.

olives *f.pl.* • (lit.): olives.

pendeloques *f.pl.*
> • (lit.): **1.** pendants • **2.** jewels (of drop earring).

pendentifs *m.pl.*
> • (lit.): pendentives, "hangers."

petits oignons *m.pl.* • (lit.): little onions.

précieuses *f.pl.* • (lit.): precious ones.

rognons *m.pl.* • (lit.): kidneys.

rouleaux *m.pl.* • (lit.): rollers.

roustons *m.pl. (extremely popular).*

valseuses *f.pl.* • (lit.): waltzers.

TURD

étron

borne *f.* • (lit.): milestone.

boudin *m.* • (lit.): blood sausage.

bouse *f.* • *bouse de vache;* cow patty.

bronze *m.* • (lit.): a bronze (one).

caca *m.* • (lit.): caca.

colombin *m.* • (lit.): pigeon manure.

merde *f.* • (lit.): shit.

orphelin *m.* • (lit.): orphan.

pêche *f.* • (lit.): peach.

prune *f.* • (lit.): plum.

rondin *m.* • (lit.): log.

URINATE (TO)

uriner

arroser les marguerites *exp.*
> • (lit.): to water the daisies.

égoutter (se l') *exp.* • (lit.): to drain it.

égoutter Popol *exp.* • (lit.): to drain Popol.

> **NOTE -1:** **Popol** *m.* penis, dick.
> **NOTE -2:** Also spelled: *Popaul.*

égoutter sa sardine *exp.*
> • (lit.): to drain one's sardine.

égoutter son colosse *exp.*
> • (lit.): to drain one's giant.

égoutter son cyclope *exp.*
> • (lit.): to drain one's cyclops.

faire pipi *exp.* • (lit.): to go pee-pee.

faire pleurer le costaud *exp.*
> • (lit.): to make the hefty one cry.

faire pleurer le petit Jésus *exp.* • (lit.): to make little Jesus cry.

faire sa goutte *exp.* • (lit.): to do one's drop.

faire sa petite commission
exp. • (lit.): to go do one's little job.

SEE: **grande commission (faire sa)**, *p. 98.*

faire une vidange (se) *exp.*
• (lit.): to do an emptying of oneself.

glisser un fil *exp.* • (lit.): to slip (out) a thread (of urine).

jeter de la lance *exp.* • (lit.): to throw out urine.

NOTE: **lance** *f.* • **1.** urine • **2.** water.

SEE: **lancequiner**, *p. 110.*

lâcher l'écluse *exp.* • (lit.): to release the floodgate.

lâcher les vannes *exp.* • (lit.): to release the floodgates.

lâcher un fil *exp.* • (lit.): to release a thread (of urine).

lancequiner *v.* **1.** to urinate • **2.** to rain.

SEE: **jeter de la lance**, *p. 106.*

mouiller le mur *exp.* • (lit.): to wet the wall.

mouiller une ardoise *exp.*
• (lit.): to wet a slate.

ouvrir les écluses *exp.* • (lit.): to open the floodgates.

pisser *v.* • (lit.): to piss.

pisser son coup *exp.* • (lit.): to piss one's shot.

tenir l'âne par la queue *exp.*
• (lit.): to hold the donkey by the tail.

vagin

baisoir *m.* • (lit.): a place where one has sex such as the bedroom, brothel, etc.

NOTE: This comes from the slang verb *baiser* meaning "to fuck."

barbu *m.* • (lit.): the bearded one.

baveux *m.* • (lit.): drooler.

bénitier *m.* • (lit.): (holy water) basin.

boîte à ouvrage *f.* • (lit.): work box.

bonbonnière *f.* • (lit.): sweetmeat box.

bonnet à poils *m.* • (lit.): hair bonnet.

bréviaire d'amour *m.*
• (lit.): breviary of love.

chagatte *f.* • (lit.): cat, "pussy."

NOTE: This is a javanais transformation of the feminine word *chatte* meaning "cat" or "pussy." Javanais is a formula occasionally applied to slang words where the letters "ag" or "av" are added between syllables. Therefore *chat* becomes *chagatte*.

chat *m.* • (lit.): cat, "pussy."

chatte *f.* (*extremely popular*)
• (lit.): cat, "pussy."

cheminée *f.* • (lit.): chimney.

cicatrice *f.* • (lit.): scar.

con *m.* • (lit.): cunt.

crevasse *f.* • (lit.): crevice.

étau *m.* • (lit.): vise.

fente *f.* • (lit.): crack, crevice, split.

figue *f.* • (lit.): fig.

greffier *m.* • (lit.): cat, scratcher, "pussy."
> **NOTE:** This comes from the verb *griffer* meaning "to scratch."

grippette *f.* • (lit.): pouncer.
> **NOTE:** This comes from the verb *gripper* meaning "to seize, pounce upon."

mille-feuilles *m.pl.*
• (lit.): Napoleon pastry.

mimi *m.* • (lit.): kitty, "pussy."

minou *m.* • (lit.): kitty, "pussy."

motte *f.* • (lit); mound.

moule *f. (extremely popular)*
• (lit.): mussel.

panier *m.* • (lit.): basket.

panier d'amour *m.* • (lit.): love basket.

pince *f.* • (lit.): holder, gripper.

portail *m.* • (lit.): portal.

tire-lire *f.* • (lit.): piggy bank.

trou *m.* • (lit.): hole.

VOMIT (TO)

vomir

aller au renard *exp.* • (lit.): to go to the fox.

dégobiller *v. (very popular).*
> **NOTE:** This comes from the verb *gober* meaning "to gobble down (food, etc.)."

dégueuler *v. (extremely popular).*
> **NOTE:** This comes from the feminine noun *gueule* meaning "mouth."

évacuer le couloir *exp.* • (lit.): to evacuate the hall.

gerber *v.* • (lit.): to sheave (corn, etc.).

rendre son quatre heures *exp.*
• (lit.): to give back one's cookies and milk (that which one eats at *quatre heures* meaning "four o'clock").

rendre *v. (a polite form of "vomir")*
• (lit.): to give back.

ORDER FORM ON BACK

Prices subject to change

SPANISH	BOOK	CASSETTE
STREET SPANISH 1	$15.95	$12.50
The Best of Spanish Slang		
STREET SPANISH 2	$15.95	$12.50
The Best of Spanish Idioms (available '98)		
STREET SPANISH 3	$15.95	$12.50
The Best of Naughty Spanish (available '98)		
STREET SPANISH SLANG DICTIONARY	$16.95	
(available '98)		

FRENCH	BOOK	CASSETTE
STREET FRENCH 1	$15.95	$12.50
The Best of French Slang		
STREET FRENCH 2	$15.95	$12.50
The Best of French Idioms		
STREET FRENCH 3	$15.95	$12.50
The Best of Naughty French		
STREET FRENCH SLANG DICTIONARY & THESAURUS	$16.95	

AMERICAN-ENGLISH	BOOK	CASSETTE
STREET TALK 1	$16.95	$12.50
How to Speak & Understand American Slang		
STREET TALK 2	$16.95	$12.50
Slang Used in Popular American TV Shows		
STREET TALK 3	$18.95	$12.50
The Best of American Idioms		
BIZ TALK 1	$16.95	$12.50
American Business Slang & Jargon		
BIZ TALK 2	$16.95	$12.50
More American Business Slang & Jargon		
BLEEP!	$14.95	$12.50
A Guide to Popular American Obscenities		

GERMAN	BOOK	CASSETTE
STREET GERMAN 1	$16.95	$12.50
The Best of German Idioms		

Caslon Books

P.O. Box 519 • Fulton, CA 95439 • USA

TOLL FREE Telephone/FAX (US/Canada):
1-888-4-ESLBOOKS (1-888-437-2665)

International orders Telephone/FAX line:
707-546-8878

ORDER FORM

Name _____

(School/Company) _____

Street Address _____

City _____ State/Province _____ Postal Code _____

Country _____ Phone _____

Quantity	Title	Book or Cassette?	Price Each	Total Price

Total for Merchandise	
Sales Tax (California Residents Only)	
Shipping (See Below)	
ORDER TOTAL	

METHOD OF PAYMENT (check one)

☐ Check or Money Order   ☐ VISA   ☐ Master Card   ☐ American Express   ☐ Discover
(Money orders and personal checks must be in U.S. funds and drawn on a U.S. bank.)

Credit Card Number: Card Expires:

| | | | | | | | | | | | | | | | | | | | | |

Signature *(important!)* ➜

SHIPPING

Domestic Orders: SURFACE MAIL (delivery time 5-7 days).
Add $4 shipping/handling for the first item · $1 for each additional item.
RUSH SERVICE available at extra charge.

International Orders: OVERSEAS SURFACE (delivery time 6-8 weeks).
Add $5 shipping/handling for the first item · $2 for each additional item.
OVERSEAS AIRMAIL available at extra charge.